Treatments for Anger in Specific Populations

Treatments for Anger in Specific Populations

Theory, Application, and Outcome

EDITED BY

EPHREM FERNANDEZ

OXFORD
UNIVERSITY PRESS

OXFORD
UNIVERSITY PRESS

Oxford University Press is a department of the University of Oxford.
It furthers the University's objective of excellence in research, scholarship,
and education by publishing worldwide.

Oxford New York
Auckland Cape Town Dar es Salaam Hong Kong Karachi
Kuala Lumpur Madrid Melbourne Mexico City Nairobi
New Delhi Shanghai Taipei Toronto

With offices in
Argentina Austria Brazil Chile Czech Republic France Greece
Guatemala Hungary Italy Japan Poland Portugal Singapore
South Korea Switzerland Thailand Turkey Ukraine Vietnam

Published in the United States of America by
Oxford University Press
198 Madison Avenue, New York, NY 10016

Library of Congress Cataloging-in-Publication Data
Treatments for anger in specific populations : theory, application, and
outcome/edited by Ephrem Fernandez.
pages cm
Includes bibliographical references and index.
ISBN 978-0-19-991466-1 (pbk.)
1. Anger—Treatment. 2. Anger—Psychological aspects. 3. Life change events—Psychological
aspects. 4. Psychology, Pathological. I. Fernandez, Ephrem, editor of compilation.
RC569.5.A53T74 2013
36219689—dc23
2013006564

9 8 7 6 5 4 3 2
Printed in the United States of America
on acid-free paper

This book is dedicated to Raphael, Rebecca, Greté C, Pravin, and Sara

CONTENTS

PREFACE

Anger has been viewed as a motivating force to be harnessed as well as the most destructive of all emotions and the bane of human relations. This book acknowledges the functional significance of anger but focuses on anger that is dysfunctional. Such anger is particularly manifest in certain clinical populations and it crosses the boundaries of gender, age, and ethnicity. Therefore, anger treatments can be examined in the context of the population of interest, and that is how the chapters in this volume are organized.

My foray into the field of anger began 18 years ago with a publication on the relationship between anger and pain. I was struck by the unmistakable quality that is anger, by its ubiquity and its adverse repercussions, and yet equally struck by its lack of representation in psychiatric nosology. At that time, significant inroads had already been made into the field of anger treatment, and I am pleased that many of the pioneers then have contributed to the present volume. Further, I am encouraged by the emergence of new experts, many of whom have also become a part of this project.

The collective efforts of 29 authors went into making the 14 chapters of this volume. Each chapter underwent peer review not only by me but also by another expert from the contributing team. The journey has been an adventure in intellectual exchange, planning, organization, and creative problem solving—appropriately punctuated by moments of banter and healthy digression.

The end result is original in presenting anger treatments population by population and then extracting what is common across treatments and what is uniquely tailored to particular groups of clients. The product is also intended to be clinically useful by virtue of describing the "how to" of anger regulation techniques and illustrating them with reference to case studies. We have been decidedly evidence-based in this book but without ignoring the new wave of ideas for enhancement of this enterprise. Therefore, a framework is also put in place to allow for further innovation and integration of anger treatments.

I thank my assistants, Nikki Prins, Alex Fields, and Salvador Macias for checking citations against references, indexing, and attention to format. Over the years, numerous students have worked in my Sensation & Emotion Lab at Southern Methodist University and University of Texas at San Antonio; they deserve credit for having interviewed thousands of people in a variety of field settings from public libraries and college campuses to parole centers and jails, and for having administered psychometric tests of anger. Drs. Richard Beck, Stephen Scott, and Valerie Herd Parker bravely joined me in facilitating anger management groups. The participants who volunteered are appreciated not just for their numerical responses to many questions but also for their candid disclosures, which have helped advance knowledge. Findings from our research program have been and continue to be presented at conferences and published in scholarly outlets, in addition to receiving mention in this volume.

In the course of writing and editing, I have consulted both academics and clinicians in the health sciences. On occasion, I have turned to scholars in other disciplines including cultural anthropology, linguistics, and philosophy. Much more remains to be done to make this a cross-disciplinary endeavor, and this book is a move in that direction.

At Oxford University Press, Sarah Harrington, as senior editor, provided valuable guidance in the preparation of the book proposal and the utilization of feedback from expert reviewers. Andrea Zekus, in her role as assistant editor, provided important logistical and organizational help during the production phase of the book. Thanks also to Reny Edwin Joseph at Newgen Knowledge Works in India and Danielle Michaely for copyediting and page proofing and to various professionals involved in the marketing and distribution of this book.

To all who have contributed to this book in one way or another, may our collaboration not stop here. To those who read this book, your own responses and ideas are most welcome. To my trusted friends, dear siblings, and beloved parents, many thanks, as always.

ABOUT THE EDITOR

Ephrem Fernandez is Professor of Psychology at the University of Texas at San Antonio, previously on the faculty at SMU and visiting scholar at the University of California Berkeley. He has published more than 70 scientific articles, book chapters, and books. He has delivered more than 100 scholarly presentations (including workshops) at international venues/events, for example, the Swiss Center for Affective Sciences; the Australian National University; the University of Wisconsin, Madison; the University of Amsterdam; the First Asian Conference in Psychology, Singapore; and the meeting of the Society for the Exploration of Psychotherapy Integration, Santiago, Chile. His teaching, research, and clinical specializations are in affect science (with a focus on anger), the psychosomatics of pain and illness, and integrative therapies.

CONTRIBUTORS

Caroline L. Boxmeyer, PhD
The University of Alabama
Center for the Prevention of Youth Behavior Problems

Catherine Bradshaw, PhD
Johns Hopkins Bloomberg School of Public Health

Amanda Carson-Wong, MA
Rutgers University

Claude Chemtob, PhD
Langone Medical Center
New York University

Andrew Day, DClinPsy
Forensic Psychology Centre
Deakin University, Australia

Jerry L. Deffenbacher, PhD
Department of Psychology
Colorado State University

Casey Dillon, BA
Center for the Prevention of Youth Behavior Problems
The University of Alabama

Ephrem Fernandez, PhD
Department of Psychology
University of Texas at San Antonio

David Forbes, PhD
Australian Centre for Posttraumatic Mental Health
Department of Psychiatry
University of Melbourne, Australia

A. Antonio González-Prendes, PhD
School of Social Work
Wayne State University

Julie A. Hubbard, PhD
Department of Psychology
University of Delaware

Andrew Jahoda, PhD
Department of Psychological Medicine
University of Glasgow, UK

Meghann Kelly, BA
Center for the Prevention of Youth Behavior Problems
The University of Alabama

Peter Larkin, PhD
Department of Psychological Medicine
University of Glasgow, UK

John E. Lochman, PhD, ABPP
The University of Alabama
Center for the Prevention of Youth Behavior Problems

Kathleen Malley-Morrison, EdD
Department of Psychology
Boston University

Tony McHugh, MA
Austin Health, Australia

Raymond W. Novaco, PhD
Department of Psychology & Social Behavior
University of California, Irvine

Sandra C. Paivio, PhD
Department of Psychology
University of Windsor, Canada

Antonio Pascual-Leone, PhD
Department of Psychology
University of Windsor, Canada

Nicole P. Powell, PhD, MPH
The University of Alabama
Center for the Prevention of Youth Behavior Problems

Patrick M. Reilly, PhD
University of California, San Francisco
San Francisco Department of Veterans Affairs Medical Center

Shireen L. Rizvi, PhD
School of Applied & Professional Psychology
Rutgers University

Michael S. Shopshire, PhD
Department of Psychiatry
University of California, San Francisco

Lauren M. Steffel, PsyM
Rutgers University

Lauren E. Swift, MA
University of Delaware

James Vess, PhD
Deakin University, Australia

Richard Whittington, PhD
Institute of Psychology, Health & Society
University of Liverpool, UK

Paul Willner DSc, CPsychol
Department of Psychology
Swansea University, UK

1

Anger Dysfunction and Its Treatment

EPHREM FERNANDEZ

ANECDOTES OF ANGER

Narratives about anger are scattered throughout literature, history, mythology, current affairs, celebrity news, and gossip columns. Over the years, a rich repository of anger stories has also accrued to my research team in response to our questions about anger in the clinical milieu, in educational settings, and in the community at large. Here are some vignettes drawn from this collection. Brief as these are, they illustrate the variety of eliciting conditions of anger while also highlighting certain themes that will form the basis for our definition of anger.

A friend becomes an irreconcilable enemy after a suspected betrayal. An employee, aggrieved by the unreasonable demands on the job, sues the employer. A child, begrudging parental abandonment a long time ago, rebuffs the parents' efforts to restore contact. Annoyed by automated prerecorded calls from telemarketers, a customer repeatedly swears and slams down the phone. An individual reproaches a sibling for the latter's seeming callousness and ingratitude. Frustrated by neighborhood apathy, a resident vandalizes a street sign. A young adult spreads malicious rumors following rejection by a romantic partner. A spectator instantly punches another when pushed and shoved at a public event. Resenting a decline in intimacy, a married couple punish each other by pursuing objectionable liaisons. A client takes issue with bureaucracy, subjecting it to public ridicule on the Internet. "Fed up and let down" by teammates, an athlete contemplates defecting to the rival team. A citizen takes to the streets to launch a public demonstration against social injustice.

ANGER DEFINITION

Reflecting on the aforementioned vignettes, it is safe to begin with the assumption that anger is intrinsically unpleasant or what psychologists refer to as a negatively valenced feeling. In taxonomies of affect, whether they are hierarchical models (e.g., Ortony, Clore, & Collins, 1988), circumplex models (e.g., Russell, Lewicka, & Niit, 1989), or categorical models (e.g., Izard, 1991), anger occupies a position in the negative sector where it shares company with fear, sadness, shame, guilt, and so forth. Anger is neither relished by the experiencer nor welcomed by the recipient, though this does not exclude the prospect of some favorable consequences of anger. Examining how anger has been depicted in the humanities, Potegal and Novaco (2010) find that in religion, mythology, and classical literature, there is overwhelming disapproval of anger and much admonition of its "baleful" influences.

What differentiates anger from other unpleasant feelings like fear and sadness are its cognitive and motivational components. From a cognitive-motivational perspective, all emotion comprises a cognitive appraisal and an action tendency (Frijda, 2004; Lazarus, 2000; Scherer, 2012). With respect to anger, this entails an appraisal or interpretation of wrongdoing and a tendency or motivation to counter or redress that wrongdoing (Fernandez & Wasan, 2010). The appraisal is, of course, a subjective one that is open to individual differences (Tong et al., 2009). The ensuing tendency is typically within the range from active retaliation to passive resistance.

Points of Emphasis

Various facets of the concept of anger have received different degrees of emphasis. Several scholars (e.g., Hutcherson & Gross, 2011) refer to anger as a moral emotion that arises when behavior is deemed to have fallen below a standard of what is right or proper. There may be blame for anything from profound moral transgression to mere neglect or ineptitude. Ordinarily, the blame is leveled at others, and therefore anger is also viewed as a socially constructed emotion (Averill, 1983; Schieman, 2010) or a relational emotion (Laughlin & Warner, 2005; Hall, 2009), though it is certainly permissible to blame oneself. Accordingly, clinicians dating back to Freud have spoken of the conflictual nature of anger between persons while also recognizing the intrapersonal dynamics when the self becomes the object of blame (e.g., Knafo & Moscovitz, 2006; Zinner, 2009). Anger is also viewed as an "approach emotion," unlike fear, which motivates avoidance (Carver & Harmon-Jones, 2009). This corresponds to the fight–flight response systems, though anger may sometimes result in neither approach nor avoidance but resistance (as pointed out later). Angry as one may be, the means for countering a wrongdoing or "righting a wrong" so to speak may be covert and indirect (Buss & Durkee, 1957; Fernandez, 2008). Whether covert or overt, direct or indirect, anger generally promotes some level of engagement with the opponent. Another point of much emphasis in anger research has been on autonomic events which have been further linked to distinct facial expressions (Ekman, Levenson, & Friesen, 1983). In a critical review of the physiological correlates of anger, Stemmler (2010) notes that there are hundreds of studies, many of which are riddled with inconsistencies of methodology and findings. From meta-analytic synthesis of this body of research, he adduces evidence for a somatovisceral response, specifically, alpha-adrenergic activity (to enable muscle exertion), blood pressure increases, and electroencephalographic arousal. However, he cautions that only in a subset of recordable variables is there strong physiological correlation with anger and even then, there is much physiological overlap between anger and other affective qualities, particularly fear.

Forms of Anger

Any single language is bound to have gaps and redundancies, and so, at best, the vernacular offers only an approximation of the phenomena it attempts to represent. In the science of affect, a particular feeling may be differentiated in terms of state versus trait (Spielberger, 1999). In other words, like anxiety, anger can be situation specific or it can be part of an individual's disposition. This dichotomy, while well entrenched within clinical psychology, leaves mood lost in the mix. Clearly, mood is not transfixed in the present, nor does it endure for years. Hence, the dichotomy may be better expanded into a trichotomy comprising emotion, mood, and affective temperament, which are characterized by notable differences in intensity, duration, and frequency.

As explained in Fernandez (2008), as an emotion, anger is episodic or phasic, having a discrete onset and offset. Its intensity can vary from annoyance or irritation to rage or fury. As mood, anger is tonic, or relatively prolonged in duration. The angry mood is generally less intense than the angry emotion, though it can vary from irritability to irascibility. As temperament, anger is recurrent, having a frequency that suggests anger proneness. This disposition is often referred to as hostility (e.g., Buss & Durkee, 1957; Ramírez, & Andreu, 2006).

A hostile individual is not just momentarily angry or just in an angry mood, but one whose anger is recurrent and pervasive. This trichotomy of anger as emotion, mood, and temperament is congruent with other affective disturbance. For example, depression can take the form of major depression, which is relatively high in intensity and brief in duration; dysthymia, which is mild but prolonged; and depressive personality disorder, which is characterized by an enduring and pervasive pattern (American Psychiatric Association, 2000).

Anger, Aggression, and Violence

The terms *anger*, *aggression*, and *violence* are often used interchangeably in view of the frequent co-occurrence of these phenomena. However, as demonstrated in the classic paper by Averill (1983), one can be angry and not aggressive, and aggressive and not angry. One can even go so far as to be violent without a trace of anger. For example, pyromania and vandalism are often driven by thrill seeking, and armed robbery and assault may be motivated primarily by sheer greed.

Clearly, anger, aggression, and violence are not synonymous, and so, where do their boundaries lie? Anger, as elucidated earlier, is a feeling connected to perceived wrongdoing and a tendency to counter or redress that wrongdoing. Aggression, as construed within social psychology, is actual behavior (physical or verbal) that is intended to hurt. Violence is behavior that intentionally brings about actual physical injury or material damage. As shown in Figure 1.1, (physical) aggression intersects with anger, while violence is a subtype of this aggression. As illustrated in the case study by Day and Vess (this volume), in one and the same person, violence can co-occur with anger and at other times occur without anger.

Even though the English language represents only one frame of reference here, it does offer a sketch of the boundaries for naturally occurring phenomena like anger.

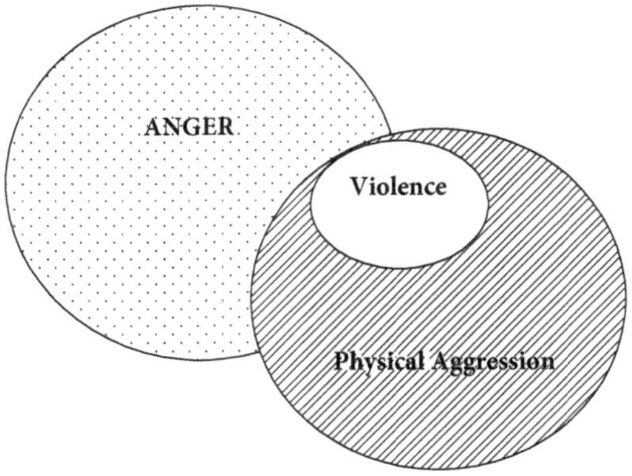

Figure 1.1 Boundaries of anger, (physical) aggression, and violence.

Similar delineations can be found in other languages. For example, in Latin, *īra,* or "anger," is distinguished from *incursiō*, or "aggression," which is further differentiated from *vīs*, or "violence." In Sanskrit, *krodhaḥ* refers to "anger," *atikramaḥ* to "aggression," and *hiḥsram* to "violence." Of course, many other nuances of anger are apparent across classical and modern languages, but the resounding emphasis on boundaries for anger, aggression, and violence suggest that there are meaningful and useful distinctions to be made among these phenomena.

In research, several studies represent anger in terms of behavior that is aggressive. Others use violence as a sort of proxy-dependent measure for anger problems. This is because it is easier to quantify observable behavior than it is to measure feelings that are, strictly speaking, private experiences. Where underlying feelings and intentions can be inferred, a clearer distinction is sometimes made between aggression that is anger driven and aggression that is not (as in the chapters by Hubbard & Swift, Lochman et al., this volume).

ADVERSE EFFECTS OF ANGER

It is the destructive potential of anger that has pushed it to the forefront of the mass media while also putting it on the assessment and treatment agenda across mental health settings. However, it should be recognized that even in the absence of aggression and violence, anger can incur or inflict many untoward effects.

Interpersonal Conflict

In close relationships, anger often leads to antagonistic and controlling behaviors that are less conducive to harmony (Lemay, Overall, & Clark, 2012). In lab-simulated business negotiations, the expression of anger by one party is often met with retaliation or else concession, though the latter tends to be accompanied by covert anger (Wang, Northcraft, & Van Kleef, 2012). In the workplace, anger reduces productivity (Domagalski & Steelman, 2007) and can potentiate serious conflict (Dupree & Barling, 2006). In adolescents, anger seems to be a significant predictor of not only physical aggression but also verbal and indirect aggression (Fives, Kong, Fuller, &

DiGiuseppe, 2011). Most germane to present purposes is the disruptive effect of anger on the very therapeutic alliance required to treat it (e.g., Shopshire & Reilly, this volume; Rizvi, Steffel, & Carson-Wong, this volume).

Impaired Judgment

Anger increases the likelihood of risk taking (Lerner & Keltner, 2001; Deffenbacher, this volume), possibly because of the boost it gives to confidence or performance efficacy (Litvak, Lerner, Tiedens, & Shonk, 2010) and especially when the situation calls for logical-conceptual analysis instead of intuitive feeling-based judgments (Baumann & DeSteno, 2012). Thus, risk taking during driving increases under conditions of induced anger (Abdu, Shinar, & Meiran, 2012; Deffenbacher, this volume). Anger induced in undergraduate students reduces their performance on mental arithmetic tasks (Kazén, Kuenne, Frankenberg, & Quirin, 2012).

Physical Health Risks

By far the most serious health risk from maladaptive anger relates to cardiovascular function. In a longitudinal study, Everson, Goldberg, Kaplan, Julkunen, and Salonen (1998) discovered a link between anger and hypertension in more than 500 Finnish men. The observed effect was stated in the following terms: between baseline and 4-year follow-up, a 1-point increase in either anger-out or anger-in was associated with a 12% increased risk for hypertension. This effect held up despite statistical adjustments for other behaviors such as smoking, alcohol intake, physical activity, and body mass index or even after adjustments for baseline resting blood pressure and parental history of hypertension.

In a recent study of more than 6,000 subjects, Ohira et al. (2012) found that arteriosclerosis was significantly associated with trait anger. Specifically, the thickness of the walls of the carotid arteries was associated with trait anger but not trait anxiety or depressiveness. This effect applied to both males and females and across four different ethnic subsamples (Euroamericans, African Americans, Hispanics, and Chinese).

Further support for the link between various aspects of anger and types of cardiovascular disease comes from population-based studies, community surveys, and experimental investigations, spanning the medical as well as social sciences. Many of these are now summarized in extensive reviews (e.g., Everson-Rose & Lewis, 2005; Low, Thurston, & Matthews, 2010; Williams, 2010). There is now interest in a widening spectrum of physical health problems also linked to anger (Fernandez & Kerns, 2008; Iyer, Korin, Higginbotham, & Davidson, 2010).

ANGER DYSFUNCTION

The term *anger disorder* is often used interchangeably with *anger dysfunction*, *anger dysregulation*, and *maladaptive anger*. These carry no suggestion of organic pathology but instead hinge on how the individual functions (e.g., Pascual-Leone &

Paivio, this volume; Forbes, McHugh, & Chemtob, this volume). Indeed, anger can be functional by virtue of mobilizing the individual to action (e.g., Kubo, Okanoya, & Kawai, 2012) and because of its communicative value (e.g., Wilkowski, 2012). In short, anger, "like any emotion, is part of a repertoire for handling various adaptational demands" (Fernandez, 2010, p. 499).

Diagnostic and Statistical Manual of Mental Disorders

Dysfunctional or maladaptive anger is that which significantly disrupts day-to-day functioning so that adaptation is compromised. For almost two decades since the publication of the *Diagnostic and Statistical Manual of Mental Disorders*, fourth edition (DSM-IV; American Psychiatric Association, 1994), an even wider net has been cast by defining a mental disorder as a clinically significant psychological syndrome associated with present distress or disability "or with a significantly increased risk of suffering death, pain, disability, or an important loss of freedom" (p. xxi). So, barring impairment, a marked increase in *risk* of impairment would evince a DSM mental disorder. In other words, anger that significantly threatens family stability, employment, health, legal rights, or basic human rights would quite likely amount to a disorder. This reference to "risk" factor appears to have been dropped from the proposed DSM-V definition of mental disorder due to be released in 2013 (American Psychiatric Association, 2012). Still, with distress or disability regarded as associated characteristics, any anger that bothers or impairs the person concerned (and is not approved within a sociocultural context) would satisfy the key criteria for a mental disorder.

Surprisingly, there is only one anger disorder in the whole DSM—intermittent explosive disorder (IED). It is grouped not with other affective disorders like anxiety and depression but with impulse control diagnoses (e.g., trichotillomania, pyromania, and pathological gambling). An IED diagnosis indicates that the person in question has recurrent bouts of uncontrolled anger culminating in physical aggression that is highly disproportionate to the provocation. IED has a 12-month prevalence rate of about 4% in the community per the National Comorbidity Survey Replication study of households in the United States (Kessler, Coccaro, & Maurizio, 2007).

No other anger-specific diagnoses exist in DSM. In the rest of the manual, anger does appear as a symptom in other psychiatric syndromes such as borderline personality disorder and oppositional defiant disorder. Passive aggressive personality disorder used to be an axis II disorder in DSM-III but now appears in the appendix as a disorder in need of further investigation.

A Stimulus-Response Perspective

Another basis for determining problem anger is to pit the response against the stimulus. Where there is anger, there is perceived wrongdoing, and by weighing the latter, one can gauge whether the former is proportionate or appropriate. As can be recalled, one of the key criteria for IED is aggression that is grossly out of proportion to the provocation. Put in the context of behaviorism, a response that far outweighs the stimulus is likely to be an overreaction. By the same token, it is possible to underreact to provocation, as when the response falls far short of the stimulus. As in behavior theory, a disorder can take the form of an excess or deficit in one and the same behavior. Excessive or deficient responses to provocation lie at the roots of explosive anger and repressive anger, respectively, both of which are maladaptive (Fernandez, 2008). Of course, the lines between what is excessive and deficient are not arbitrary but drawn in relation to norms for the individual's particular reference group (e.g., González-Prendes, this volume). In keeping with this perspective, the various controlling factors of the behavior can be represented in a functional analysis (e.g., Haynes, 1998; Willner, Jahoda, & Larkin, this volume).

Parameters of Anger

It would be an oversimplification to measure anger as a whole, because an individual may be dysfunctional in only a circumscribed aspect of anger, and individual differences abound as to which aspect of anger turns out dysfunctional. This raises the question of what aspects of anger are worth differentiating. Based on some of our studies on the self-monitoring of anger (Beck & Fernandez, 1998; Fernandez & Beck, 2001), it became apparent that anger could actually be viewed as an activity analogous to a signal on a screen. In this way, anger could be measured in terms of five key parameters that are also applicable to other emotions (Fernandez, Vargas, & Garza, 2010; Fernandez & Sriram, in press). These parameters of anger activity are frequency (how often one gets angry), duration (how long the anger lasts), intensity (how strong the anger is), latency (how quick to anger), and threshold (how sensitive to provocation).

Of these parameters, frequency and intensity have been used as units of measure in several studies of anger. Duration, an important feature in affective chronometry (Davidson, 1998), has been recently investigated in the temporal dynamics of anger (Potegal, 2010). However, the remaining parameters have been minimally studied, and only recently have norms been generated for all five parameters of anger (Fernandez et al., 2010). Additionally, distinct profiles of dysfunctional anger have been identified based on patterns of elevations and dips across these five parameters (Garza, Fernandez, & Vargas, 2011).

Standardized Tests of Anger

Approximately 20 different psychometric tests of anger have been published in the psychological literature. Not all of them measure the same constructs, and not all have been used to the same degree. What follows is a brief description of four tests that are particularly pertinent to the question of how to measure anger and its change during treatment.

Buss-Durkee Hostility Inventory (BDHI; Buss & Durkee, 1957*).* This is evidently the first psychometric test developed to assess constructs related to anger. It has two main factors: neurotic aspects of hostility and behavioral expression of hostility. The first factor relates to two subscales: resentment and suspicion. The second factor relates to five subscales: assault, indirect hostility, verbal hostility, negativism, and irritability. In addition, one subscale is devoted to the assessment of guilt.

Though the factor structure of the BDHI has not been replicated consistently, its potential to assess indirect aspects of hostility has been put to use in many studies. Thus, it has become the basis for much treatment outcome data that continues to be cited or synthesized within meta-analytic reviews.

Novaco Scales. Another pioneering development in anger assessment was the Anger Inventory, which appeared in 1975 and underwent revisions leading up to the current Novaco Anger Scale and Provocation Inventory (NASPI; Novaco, 2003). The NASPI contains 25 scenarios that are potentially anger provoking. In addition, there are 60 items for assessing cognitive, behavioral, and arousal-related aspects of anger, as well as anger-regulatory efforts. Data from various versions of the Novaco scales are reported in several anger treatment outcome studies, especially in the last quarter of the 20th century.

State-Trait Anger Expression Inventory-2 (STAXI-2; Spielberger, 1999*).* In this century, the STAXI-2 has emerged as the most widely used instrument for assessing anger. Its differentiation between state and trait anger has been particularly welcome in clinical psychology where the state–trait distinction has long been applied to the anxiety disorders. Furthermore, the STAXI-2 taps into the expression and control of anger, with two of its subscales (anger-in vs. anger-out) receiving much attention in treatment outcome studies.

Anger Disorders Scale (ADS; DiGiuseppe & Tafrate, 2004*).* A recent attempt at constructing a clinically relevant instrument for assessing anger is the ADS. It contains a total of 18 subscales divided into five domains. Specifically, the Provocations domain comprises (a) scope of anger provocations and (b) hurt/social rejection; the Arousal domain comprises (a) physiological, (b) duration, and (c) episode length; the Cognitions domain comprises (a) suspicion, (b) resentment, (c) rumination, and (d) impulsivity; the Motives domain comprises (a) tension reduction, (b) coercion, and (c) revenge; the Behaviors domain comprises (a) anger-in, (b) physical aggression, (c) verbal expression, (d) indirect aggression, (e) passive aggression, and (f) relational aggression. Subscale scores can be plotted as coordinates on a graph. Given the 18 subscales, the number of possible profiles where just half of the subscales are elevated is close to 50,000. Accordingly, a Short Form with three subscales (expression, anger-in, and vengeance) is available.

Expression Styles of Anger

Much mileage has been gained from the distinction between anger-in versus anger-out as found in the STAXI-2 and the distinction between direct versus indirect anger as in the BDHI. However, these dichotomies are, in effect, blending locus of anger with direction of anger. We have chosen to disentangle and reincorporate these as two separate dimensions within the six bipolar dimensions of the new Anger Expressions Scale (AES; Fernandez, 2008). In the AES, Direction refers to a continuum from reflection to deflection of anger, Locus refers to the continuum from internalization to externalization of anger, Reaction refers to resistance at one end and retaliation at the other, Modality is physical at one end and verbal at the other, Impulsivity extends from controlled to uncontrolled anger, and Objective ranges from expressing anger in a way that is punitive to one that is restorative.

TREATMENT OF MALADAPTIVE ANGER

It is the ideal in clinical psychology, as in medicine, that diagnosis is the precursor of treatment. In the case of anger, this ideal is yet to be realized, primarily because of the earlier-mentioned limitations of the DSM where only one diagnostic category pertains specifically to dysfunctional anger. This is now viewed as a glaring omission (e.g., Kassinove & Tafrate, 2006) and an unacceptable anachronism (Anand & Malhi, 2009).

Nevertheless, as briefly described earlier, a variety of standardized assessment instruments are available for the purpose of obtaining dependent measures of anger. Unfortunately, there is little agreement on the prime aspects of anger to be measured, with each test mapping quite different features of the same landscape of anger. The typical course of action is to use a whole array of dependent measures to take a "broad sweep" in the hope of picking up some aspect of anger that is dysfunctional. Therefore, at this time, treatment outcome is hardly geared toward any particular anger construct or subscale; instead, it is operationalized in terms of multiple subscores corresponding to multiple subscales from a particular test of preference. This makes the general goal of relating anger treatments to anger diagnoses or dependent measures an elusive one.

A more effective way of organizing the literature on anger treatments is by specific populations. This is helped by the fact that many studies have focused on homogenous subject samples to minimize error variance. Where heterogeneous samples have been used, certain client variables have been analyzed as covariates. This has produced a critical mass of studies on anger treatments within particular populations. Some of these are clinical populations with comorbid anger problems; others are populations that differ along sociodemographic lines.

For the purposes of this book, grouping the anger treatments according to specific populations is not only a convenient way to organize the literature but also a meaningful way to contextualize the treatment of anger. The main clinical populations around which a sufficient number of anger treatment studies have accumulated are inmates or detainees in forensic settings, substance-dependent patients, people with intellectual disabilities, patients with psychoses, patients with post-traumatic stress disorder, individuals suffering complex trauma of abuse, clients with borderline personality disorder, and angry drivers. In addition to the clinical populations, anger treatment along sociodemographic lines will also be reviewed. Specifically, this includes treatment of anger in children, in adolescents, by gender, and by cultural background.

It will be noticed that the treatment of anger in certain populations has been dominated by particular theoretical orientations. For others, the treatment approach may be more generic. Each population is briefly described, and this is accompanied by the relevant theory of anger treatment and an outline of treatment procedures; anger treatment is further illustrated with reference to case studies. Finally, the efficacy of these treatments for anger is evaluated and followed by closing comments for future consideration.

The chapter by Deffenbacher is timely in its scholarly analysis of what is popularly termed "road rage." As pointed out, angry drivers are clearly in distress but also endanger the well-being of others. Fortunately, they are treatable by established cognitive-behavioral techniques. The chapter by Pascual-Leone and Paivio tackles the sensitive problem of anger arising from the complex trauma of repeated abuse as a child. Here, there is a special need for emotion-focused therapy. In a subsequent chapter by Forbes, McHugh, and Chemtob, a case is made for treating anger in posttraumatic stress disorder in military personnel. Cognitive and affective change are attempted and achieved within the framework of re-exposure to traumatic cues. The chapter by Shopshire and Reilly focuses on a subset of clients who have anger comorbid with substance use disorders. The authors' own treatment program for anger in this population has been adopted by the Department of Health and Human Services; it is fundamentally cognitive-behavioral with special attention to the ways in which anger and substance abuse influence each other. In the next chapter, Willner, Jahoda, and Larkin take up the need for anger management in intellectually disabled individuals whose anger-related difficulties often compound their already stigmatized status. Cognitive-behavioral therapy is the platform upon which anger regulation skills are delivered, but the authors go much further in dealing with the many barriers to engagement in this population. Another clinical population often underserved consists of those with psychoses. Novaco and Whittington trace the history of anger in conjunction with madness and touch on the possibility that aggressiveness can be secondary to fear in delusional and paranoid patients. They show how anger-related problems can be treated cognitive-behaviorally and with due consideration of the frustrations of the hospital environment and the compounding psychiatric symptoms of the patient. Not psychotic but often portrayed as prone to outbursts of anger is the person with borderline personality disorder. Rizvi, Steffel, and Carson-Wong provide a schema for analyzing such anger in the context of personal relationships as well as therapeutic interactions. Dialectical behavior therapy is presented as the treatment of choice here. The next chapter by Day and Vess turns to the vast literature on anger in forensic settings. The authors outline ways to incorporate newer approaches like mindfulness and acceptance into the standard cognitive-behavioral programs for reducing anger and the risk of aggression/violence. The problems presented by court-mandated anger management are also broached. Turning our attention to children and adolescents, Lochman, Powell, Boxmeyer, Kelly, Dillon, and Bradshaw articulate a social-cognitive view of anger. This forms the basis for their Coping Power curriculum, which is designed for students in schools while also being alert to the influences of parents and peers. Hubbard and Swift direct their focus to anger and reactive aggression in young children, pointing out the trajectory of social problems that can arise in this group. They present several programs for equipping children with skills to handle anger and accompanying problems of aggression. Room for innovation in this area is identified. Fernandez and Malley-Morrison examine how anger treatment might take gender into account. This is hinged on answers to two questions: (a) Are there gender differences in anger in the first place? and (b) Are there gender differences in psychotherapy? The findings support a gender-inclusive approach to anger treatment that is also attuned to differences in how males and females seek out and respond to psychotherapy. In the same vein, González-Prendes builds the argument for a culture-sensitive treatment of anger based on observations of important differences in anger display rules. Important lessons for anger management are taken from existing multicultural approaches to psychotherapy. Studies of anger treatment in different ethnic groups are reported and the potential of multicomponent treatments is raised.

At the end of these 13 chapters, a final chapter is provided as a synthesis of the main conclusions emerging from the foregoing. An attempt is made to identify what is common across anger treatments for the different populations. Complementing this is the attempt to uncover what is unique about the different treatments for anger in different populations. This is done with two main goals in mind: (a) to establish some basic overarching guidelines for the treatment for anger and (b) where possible, to enable anger treatments to be tailored to the specific needs of particular groups of individuals. In this way, the overall efficacy of anger treatment may be improved. Methodologically, too, benefits may accrue from reduced sampling error within treatment outcome studies in this field.

ACKNOWLEDGMENTS

Dr. Todd B. Krause of the Linguistics Research Center at the University of Texas at Austin reviewed and refined the translations of anger and related concepts into other languages, including Sanskrit and Latin.

REFERENCES

Abdu, R., Shinar, D., & Meiran, N. (2012). Situational (state) anger and driving. *Transportation Research Part F: Traffic Psychology and Behaviour, 15*(5), 575–580.

American Psychiatric Association. (1994). *Diagnostic and statistical manual of mental disorders* (4th ed.). Washington, DC: American Psychiatric Publishing.

American Psychiatric Association. (2000). *Diagnostic and statistical manual of mental disorders* (4th ed., text rev.). Washington, DC: American Psychiatric Publishing.

American Psychiatric Association. (2012). DSM-5 development. Retrieved October 20, 2012, from http://www.dsm5.org/proposedrevisions/pages/proposedrevision.aspx?rid=465

Anand, S., & Malhi, G. S. (2009). Why DSM-V needs to address anger. *Journal of Clinical Psychiatry, 70*(10), 1478–1480.

Averill, J. R. (1983). Studies on anger and aggression: Implications for theories of emotion. *American Psychologist, 38*, 1145–1160.

Baumann, J., & DeSteno, D. (2012). Context explains divergent effects of anger on risk taking. *Emotion, 12*, 1196–1199.

Beck, R., & Fernandez, E. (1998). Cognitive-behavioral self-regulation of the frequency, duration, and intensity of anger. *Journal of Psychopathology and Behavioral Assessment, 20*, 217–229.

Buss, A. H., & Durkee, A. (1957). An inventory for assessing different kinds of hostility. *Journal of Consulting Psychology, 21*, 343–349.

Carver, C. S., & Harmon-Jones, E. (2009). Anger is an approach-related affect: Evidence and implications. *Psychological Bulletin, 135*, 183–204.

Davidson, R. J. (1998). Affective style and affective disorders: Perspectives from affective neuroscience. *Cognition and Emotion, 12*, 307–330.

DiGiuseppe, R., & Tafrate, R. C. (2004). *Anger Disorders Scale: Manual.* Toronto, Ontario, Canada: Multi Health Systems.

Domagalski, T. A., & Steelman, L. A. (2007). The impact of gender and organizational status on workplace anger expression. *Management Communication Quarterly, 20*, 297–315.

Dupré, K. E., & Barling, J. (2006). Predicting and preventing supervisory workplace aggression. *Journal of Occupational Health Psychology, 11*, 13–26.

Ekman, P., Levenson, R. W., & Friesen, W. V. (1983). Autonomic nervous system activity distinguishes among emotions. *Science, 221*, 1208–1210.

Everson, S. A., Goldberg, D. E., Kaplan, G. A., Julkunen, J., & Salonen, J. T. (1998). Anger expression and incident hypertension. *Psychosomatic Medicine, 60*, 730–735.

Everson-Rose, S., & Lewis, T. T. (2005). Psychosocial factors and cardiovascular diseases. *Annual Review of Public Health, 26*, 469–500.

Fernandez, E. (2008). The angry personality: A representation on six dimensions of anger expression. In G. J. Boyle, D. Matthews, & D. Saklofske (Eds.), *International handbook of personality theory and testing: Vol. 2: Personality measurement and assessment* (pp. 402–419). London, England: Sage Publications.

Fernandez, E. (2010). Toward an integrative psychotherapy for maladaptive anger. In M. Potegal, G. Stemmler, & C. Spielberger (Eds.), *The international handbook of anger: Constituent and concomitant biological, psychological, and social processes* (pp. 499–514). New York, NY: Springer Science+Business Media.

Fernandez, E., & Beck, R. (2001). Cognitive-behavioral self-intervention versus self-monitoring of anger: Effects on anger frequency, duration, and intensity. *Behavioural and Cognitive Psychotherapy, 29*, 345–356.

Fernandez, E., & Kerns, R. D. (2008). Anxiety, depression, and anger: The core of negative affect in medical populations. In G. J. Boyle, D. Matthews, & D. Saklofske (Eds.), *International handbook of personality theory and testing: Vol. 2: Personality measurement and assessment* (pp. 659–676). London, England: Sage Publications.

Fernandez, E., & Sriram, N. (in press). Psychometric instruments for assessing anger and hostility. In G. J. Boyle & D. Saklofske (Eds.), *Measures of personality and social psychology constructs*. Academic Press.

Fernandez, E., Vargas, R., & Garza, C. (2010). Five parameters for mapping the angry person: Results from a community sample. Association for Psychological Science 22nd Annual Convention, Boston, MA.

Fernandez, E., & Wasan, A. (2010). The anger of pain sufferers: Attributions to agents and appraisals of wrongdoing. In M. Potegal, G. Stemmler, & C. Spielberger (Eds.), *The international handbook of anger: Constituent and concomitant biological, psychological, and social processes* (pp. 449–464). New York, NY: Springer.

Fives, C., Kong, G., Fuller, J. R., & DiGiuseppe, R. (2011). Anger, aggression, and irrational beliefs in adolescents. *Cognitive Therapy & Research, 35*, 199–208.

Frijda, N. H. (2004). Emotions and action. In A. S. R. Manstead, N. H. Frijda, & A. Fischer (Eds.), *Feelings and emotions: The Amsterdam symposium* (pp. 158–173). New York, NY: Cambridge University Press.

Garza, C., Fernandez, E., & Vargas, R. (2011). *The five parameters of anger: A configural analysis*. Association for Psychological Science 23rd Annual Convention, Washington, DC., May 2011.

Hall, S. P. (2009). *Anger, rage, and relationship: An empathic approach to anger management*. London, England: Routledge.

Haynes, S. N. (1998). The assessment–treatment relationship and functional analysis in behavior therapy. *European Journal of Psychological Assessment, 14*(1), 26–35.

Hutcherson, C. A., & Gross, J. J. (2011). The moral emotions: A social-functionalist account of anger, disgust, and contempt. *Journal of Personality and Social Psychology, 100*(4), 719–737.

Iyer, P., Korin, M. R., Higginbotham, L., & Davidson, K. W. (2010). Anger, anger expression, and health. In P. Iyer, M. Korin, M. Rom, L. Higginbotham, & K. W. Davidson (Eds.), *Handbook of health psychology and behavioral medicine* (pp. 120–132). New York, NY: Guilford Press.

Izard, C. E. (1991). *The psychology of emotions.* New York, NY: Plenum Press.

Kassinove, H., & Tafrate, R. C. (2006). Anger-related disorders: basic issues, models, and diagnostic considerations. In H. Kassinove & R. C. Tafrate (Eds.), *Anger-related disorders: A practitioner's guide to comparative treatments.* New York: Springer Publishing.

Kazén, M., Kuenne, T., Frankenberg, H., & Quirin, M. (2012). Inverse relation between cortisol and anger and their relation to performance and explicit memory. *Biological Psychology, 91,* 28–35.

Kessler, R., Coccaro, E., & Maurizio, F. (2007). The prevalence and correlates of DSM-IV intermittent explosive disorders. *Directions in Psychiatry, 27,* 221–229.

Knafo, D., & Moscovitz, S. (2006). Psychoanalytic treatment of anger and aggression. In E. L. Feindler (Ed.), *Anger related disorders: A practitioner's guide to comparative treatments* (pp. 97–114). New York, NY: Springer Publishing.

Kubo, K., Okanoya, K., & Kawai, N. (2012). Apology isn't good enough: An apology suppresses an approach motivation but not the physiological and psychological anger. *PLoS ONE, 7,* 1–5.

Laughlin, M. J., & Warner, K. (2005). A relational approach to anger: A case study. *Journal of Systemic Therapies, 24,* 75–89.

Lazarus, R. S. (2000). Cognitive-motivational-relational theory of emotion. In Y. L. Hanin (Ed.), *Emotions in sport* (pp. 39–63). Champaign, IL: Human Kinetics.

Lemay, E. P., Overall, N. C., & Clark, M. S. (2012). Experiences and interpersonal consequences of hurt feelings and anger. *Journal of Personality and Social Psychology, 103,* 982–1006.

Lerner, J. S., & Keltner, D. (2001). Fear, anger, and risk. *Journal of Personality and Social Psychology, 81,* 146–159.

Litvak, P. M., Lerner, J. S., Tiedens, L. Z., & Shonk, K. (2010). Fuel in the fire: How anger impacts judgment and decision-making. In M. Potegal, G. Stemmler, & C. Spielberger (Eds.), *The international handbook of anger: Constituent and concomitant biological, psychological, and social processes* (pp. 287–310). New York, NY: Springer Science+Business Media.

Low, C. A., Thurston, R. C., & Matthews, K. A. (2010). Psychosocial factors in the development of heart disease in women: Current research and future directions. *Psychosomatic Medicine, 72,* 842–854.

Novaco, R. W. (2003). *The Novaco Anger Scale and Provocation Inventory: Manual.* Los Angeles, CA: Western Psychological Services.

Ohira, T., Roux, A. V. D., Polak, J. F., Homma, S., Iso, H., & Wasserman, B. A. (2012). Associations of anger, anxiety, and depressive symptoms with carotid arterial wall thickness: The multi-ethnic study of atherosclerosis. *Psychosomatic Medicine, 74,* 517–525.

Ortony, A., Clore, G., & Collins, A. (1988). *The cognitive structure of emotions.* New York, NY: Cambridge University Press.

Potegal, M. (2010). The temporal dynamics of anger: Phenomena, processes, and perplexities. In M. Potegal, G. Stemmler, & C. Spielberger (Eds.), *The international handbook of anger: Constituent and concomitant biological, psychological, and social processes* (pp. 385–401). New York, NY: Springer Science+Business Media.

Potegal, M., & Novaco, R. W. (2010). A brief history of anger. In M. Potegal, G. Stemmler, & C. Spielberger (Eds.), *The international handbook of anger: Constituent and concomitant biological, psychological, and social processes* (pp. 9–24). New York, NY: Springer Science+Business Media.

Ramírez, J. M., & Andreu, J. M. (2006). Aggression, and some related psychological constructs (anger, hostility, and impulsivity): Some comments from a research project. *Neuroscience and Biobehavioral Reviews, 30*, 276–291.

Russell, J. A., Lewicka, M., & Niit, T. (1989). A cross-cultural study of a circumplex model of affect. *Journal of Personality and Social Psychology, 57*, 848–856.

Scherer, K. R. (2012). Neuroscience findings are consistent with appraisal theories of emotion; but does the brain "respect" constructionism? *Behavioral and Brain Sciences, 35*, 163–164.

Schieman, S. (2010). The sociological study of anger: Basic social patterns and contexts. In M. Potegal, G. Stemmler, & C. Spielberger (Eds.), *The international handbook of anger: Constituent and concomitant biological, psychological, and social processes* (pp. 329–347). New York, NY: Springer Science+Business Media.

Spielberger, C. D. (1999). *Professional manual for the State-Trait Anger Expression Inventory-2 (STAXI-2)*. Odessa, FL: Psychological Assessment Resources.

Stemmler, G. (2010). Somatovisceral activation during anger. In M. Potegal, G. Stemmler, & C. Spielberger (Eds.), *The international handbook of anger: Constituent and concomitant biological, psychological, and social processes* (pp. 103–121). New York, NY: Springer Science+Business Media.

Tong, E. M. W., Bishop, G. D., Enkelmann, H. C., Why, Y. P., Diong, S. M., Khader, M., & Ang, J. (2009). Appraisal underpinnings of affective chronometry: The role of appraisals in emotion habituation. *Journal of Personality, 77*, 1103–1136.

Wang, L., Northcraft, G. B., & Van Kleef, G. A. (2012). Beyond negotiated outcomes: The hidden costs of anger expression in dyadic negotiation. *Organizational Behavior and Human Decision Processes, 119*, 54–63.

Wilkowski, B. M. (2012). Responding to social signals for response inhibition: A psychological process underlying trait anger. *Social Psychological and Personality Science, 3*, 72–79.

Williams, J. E. (2010). Anger/hostility and cardiovascular disease. In M. Potegal, G. Stemmler, & C. Spielberger (Eds.), *The international handbook of anger: Constituent and concomitant biological, psychological, and social processes* (pp. 435–447). New York, NY: Springer Science+Business Media.

Zinner, J. (2009). Psychodynamic couples therapy: An object relations approach. In J. Zinner (Ed.), *Textbook of psychotherapeutic treatments* (pp. 581–601). Arlington, VA: American Psychiatric Publishing.

2

Cognitive-Behavioral Therapy for Angry Drivers

JERRY L. DEFFENBACHER

Nearly all drivers have firsthand experience with anger on the road. They have encountered erratic, enraged drivers or know otherwise reasonable people who change when they get behind the wheel, turning into furious, swearing, gesturing, menacing people. This anger can escalate and lead to vitriolic verbal exchanges, physical assaults, use of the vehicle as a weapon, crashes, and even death. Such anger is a significant problem for the angry driver and for those who ride or share the road with him or her.

Currently, there are no adequate mental health diagnoses that capture the dysfunctional, impairing responses of the angry driver. Some road rage incidents (i.e., angry, aggressive encounters involving physical or vehicular assault) fit criteria for intermittent explosive disorder, and aggressive drivers disproportionately experience substance abuse disorders, cluster B personality disorders, and attention-deficit/hyperactivity disorder (Malta, Blanchard, & Freidenberg, 2005). However, many other people have a history of experiencing intense anger in response to frustrating and provocative driving situations but do not meet criteria for any defined mental health disorder. As such, dysfunctional anger while driving is best conceptualized as a syndrome (Averill, 1982; Kassinove & Tafrate, 2006) consisting of emotional experience (e.g., feelings of fury and rage), physiological arousal (e.g., elevated heart rate and blood pressure, tense shoulders, upset stomach), cognitive processing (e.g., malicious attributions, obscene ascriptions, self-centered demands, catastrophic interpretations, thoughts and images of revenge and retaliation), and associated behavior (e.g., verbal, physical, or vehicular aggression; speeding and reckless driving; impulsive hitting or kicking of the vehicle). Anger while driving may lead to significant personal distress (e.g., feeling out of control, feeling guilty or depressed about one's anger) and/or negative consequences to the individual or others (e.g., injury to self or others, legal difficulties, job loss, impaired relationships, property damage). Highly angry drivers suffer and are worthy of our clinical attention, even if our current diagnostic systems do not accurately encompass their experiences and difficulties.

This chapter addresses interventions for angry drivers. Conceptually, interventions target different aspects of the trigger–cognitive–emotional–physiological–behavioral–outcome/consequence sequence such that anger is reduced and negative behaviors and consequences are lowered or eliminated. First, relevant characteristics and experiences of angry drivers will be described in relation to relaxation intervention, cognitive intervention, and behavioral intervention. Then, common steps or stages of each therapeutic approach will be described. When interventions have been described, the current status of outcome research for angry drivers will be reviewed. The chapter will conclude with a case study that employed several of these interventions.

RELAXATION INTERVENTIONS

High-anger drivers (upper quartile on driving anger) experience heightened emotional and physiological arousal (Deffenbacher, 2009). For example, compared to low-anger drivers (lower quartile on driving anger), high-anger drivers report greater anger in response to commonly occurring situations (e.g., rush-hour traffic), traffic obstructions, impediments, and discourteous behavior of other drivers and pedestrians, as well as in frustrating driving simulations (e.g., being stuck in heavy traffic or unable to pass a slow driver) and visualized driving-related provocations (e.g., being stuck behind an inattentive driver in a left-hand turn lane and having a parking spot stolen) (Deffenbacher, 2009). They report more intense anger in day-to-day driving than low-anger drivers ($M = 58$ vs. 27 on 0 to 100 anger rating) (Deffenbacher, 2009). Moreover, on the same scale, high-anger drivers indicated that 40 was the level at which anger started to become problematic, which means on average their most intense daily anger experience was at the problem level. They are also angered more frequently. High-anger drivers were angered an average of 2.43 times a day versus 0.90 for low-anger drivers, or 2.7 times more often (729 vs. 270 per 300 driving days per year) (Deffenbacher, 2009). This arousal appears triggered by more driving-related situations. When given a large number of potential frustrations/provocations on the road, high-anger drivers reported 3.4 times more events that elicited "much" or "very much" anger (Deffenbacher, 2009).

Relaxation interventions target this elevated emotional and physiological arousal. The logic is that if the angry driver is skilled and efficacious in employing relaxation coping skills (RCS), then he or she can initiate relaxation upon the onset of anger, become calmer, and apply skills and approaches that are associated with a less aroused state. This calming down alleviates the arousal component of anger. Additionally, with repeated application of relaxation skills, clients may also lower their baseline level of arousal.

Relaxation interventions vary somewhat in design but generally include a set of overlapping, emergent elements. Early in therapy, the therapist identifies (e.g., from client descriptions, questionnaires, self-monitoring of anger reactions while driving) elevated emotional physiological arousal as a key part of the client's anger experience. If the client concurs, a relaxation rationale is introduced (i.e., if the client could relax and calm down when becoming angry, then he or she could lower anger and handle the situation with better judgment). The rationale is linked to the general tasks of therapy: (a) developing a relaxation response, (b) developing brief relaxation coping skills with which he or she can quickly initiate relaxation, (c) increasing the client's awareness of and sensitivity to the internal emotional and physiological cues of anger arousal so that he or she can initiate relaxation when the cues begin to appear, (d) rehearsing relaxation coping skills for anger reduction within and between sessions so the client is proficient and confident he or she can employ relaxation coping skills behind the wheel, and (e) developing strategies to maintain use of relaxation coping skills after termination of therapy.

Increasing awareness of the internal cues of anger arousal and developing a relaxation response generally take place concurrently. Clients self-monitor anger arousal, paying particular attention to emotional and physiological sensations of anger arousal. Clients might be asked to visualize a recent anger event and then pay attention to the physical/emotional experience of anger arousal. They are also asked to pay attention to areas of tension and areas that are most difficult to relax during relaxation training, because these often are areas of arousal as well. They are asked to pay particular attention to the earliest and strongest cues of anger arousal, as these are the cues, along with situational triggers, they will use to initiate relaxation coping skills.

Although a relaxation response can be developed through a variety of methods (e.g., biofeedback), the muscle tension-release procedures of progressive relaxation are commonly used and more flexible in group interventions. The therapist demonstrates and then trains clients in progressive relaxation, which clients practice daily at home. Typically within 2 to 3 weeks, the tension-release exercise is dropped, and clients achieve relaxation by simply focusing on the muscle area and letting it become more relaxed.

When a basic relaxation response has been learned by the client, it is associated with briefer relaxation coping skills, which can be employed in a few seconds to a minute or so for rapid arousal reduction. Five of the most commonly used relaxation coping skills are (a) relaxation without tension (i.e., focusing on and releasing muscle tension in a specific area such as the stomach or shoulders); (b) breathing-cued relaxation (i.e., relaxing more with each of three to five deep breaths); (c) cue-controlled relaxation (i.e., relaxing to the repetition of some word such as "relax" or a phrase like "calm control"); (d) relaxation imagery (i.e., visualization of a specific, personal relaxation experience); and (e) unobtrusive tension release of a key muscle area (e.g., tensing and releasing the stomach or shrugging the shoulders three times). These coping skills are added to relaxation practice both within and between sessions.

Clients are now ready for rehearsal of relaxation coping skills for anger reduction. Although coping skill training could be done in vivo, anger imagery is most often employed, because it is easier to control in a graded fashion and can be used more efficiently in a group.

Clients visualize specific, personal driving-related frustrations (e.g., a time in heavy traffic) and provocations (e.g., another driver making an obscene gesture or yelling at the client). Clients visualize the situation, pay attention to anger arousal for 30 to 60 seconds, and then initiate relaxation coping skills to actively manage and reduce anger. The therapist does three things to facilitate clients smoothly moving toward self-control of anger. First, the anger-arousing capacity of the scenes starts at mild to moderate levels (30 to 50 on 0 to 100 anger scale) and is increased across sessions as clients demonstrate greater success in anger reduction. In the last sessions, clients visualize intense anger scenes (70 to 90 level) ending with their "worst case" scenarios. Second, two scenes are often employed and alternated. This provides for greater application across types of angering situations. Third, the therapist provides greater control and assistance in the retrieval of relaxation application in early sessions and fades this assistance as the client demonstrates success in reducing arousal. For example, in the initial rehearsal sessions, the therapist turns on the scene, instructs the client to experience the arousal and signal when feeling anger, continues to instruct the client to experience anger for the next 60 seconds, clears the scene from visualization, and then instructs the client in one or more of the relaxation coping skills. The next step parallels the aforementioned procedures, but instead of the therapist coaching the relaxation coping skill after scene termination, the client is instructed to relax away the anger by his or her best relaxation method and signal when relaxed. The last step approximates full client self-control. The therapist instructs the client to visualize the scene and signal when angry by raising a finger and keeping it up, then after paying attention to anger arousal to stay in the scene and actively relax away anger, signaling by lowering his or her finger when anger is reduced. The therapist then clears the scene and prepares the client for the visualization of the alternate scene.

In vivo application of relaxation coping skills is added to homework; the client applies relaxation whenever he or she becomes angry while driving and records the experience. Exposure to specific triggers may be contracted (e.g., client agrees to travel a busy freeway at rush hour, to try to find a parking spot in a busy mall parking lot on a weekend, or to drive a twisting, slow mountain road where there is likely to be a good chance of slow driving). The client monitors arousal and applies relaxation in these contracted situations. At the next session, the therapist and client review homework and make adaptations in coping skill application as needed.

As clients become proficient in anger reduction in the highest anger scenes in session and demonstrate in vivo success while driving, the focus shifts to two other tasks. First, because high-anger drivers also tend to report more anger in general, possible applications to other sources of anger and distress are explored. Appropriate scenes and rehearsal are employed to address other issues identified by the client. Second, attention focuses on maintenance and relapse prevention strategies (e.g., planned booster sessions, for example, at 1 and 3 months after termination, continued coping skills application with records sent to the therapist, 15-minute phone reviews, coping skill review by the client at scheduled intervals, once-a-week coping skill review with another member of a driving anger group). These activities are designed to keep the client attending to and applying relaxation coping skills for anger management over time.

COGNITIVE INTERVENTIONS

Anger while driving develops, in part, as a function of the ways the driver codes, construes, and appraises situations on the road. Anger-engendering cognitions include things like making hostile appraisals of wrongdoing and attributions of blame (e.g., "He did that on purpose."); catastrophizing (e.g., "I can't stand this."); coding other drivers in highly inflammatory, derogatory ways (e.g., "Asshole!" "Idiot."); anger- and aggression-supportive beliefs and expectancies (e.g., "People like that ought to be run over."); rigid demands (e.g., "Slow drivers should get the hell out of the way."); thoughts and images of revenge (e.g., "Nobody can do that to me and get away with it. I'll cut him off and see how he likes it."), and the like.

High-anger drivers engage in more accusatory, aggressive thinking (Deffenbacher, Richards, Filetti, & Lynch, 2005). For example, they report engaging in more (a) judgmental and disbelieving thoughts (i.e., mild to moderate derogation of other drivers, statements and questions suggesting that they cannot believe other drivers drive the way they do, and statements that others should not be able to drive); (b) pejorative labeling/verbally aggressive thoughts (i.e., very negative, derogative, often obscene judgments and labels and thoughts about engaging in verbally aggressive behavior such as wanting to tell the person off); (c) revengeful/retaliatory thoughts (i.e., thinking about getting back at others, showing them they cannot treat him or her the way they have, and engaging in behaviors necessary to extract revenge and retaliation); and (d) physically aggressive thoughts (i.e., thinking about harming others and about behaviors necessary to do so such as hitting or punching them). High-anger drivers also tend to engage in less positive coping thinking (i.e., thinking about how to handle the situation in adaptive ways). These cognitive patterns also appear more highly correlated with certain forms of anger expression. For example, pejorative labeling/verbally aggressive thinking correlates higher with verbally aggressive anger expression, revengeful/retaliatory thinking more with using the vehicle to express anger, coping self-instruction more with adaptive/constructive anger expression, and revengeful/retaliatory and physically aggressive thinking more with personal physical anger expression.

Cognitive therapy focuses on identifying and altering these anger-engendering cognitive biases and processes. The theoretical rationale is that as the person can appraise and process situations in less rigid, demanding, inflammatory, offensive ways and respond with calmer, more realistic, task-oriented cognitions, then anger will be reduced and other cognitive and behavioral skills will be more readily accessed and employed.

Cognitive approaches generally involve several overlapping therapeutic tasks. One involves increasing the client's awareness of his or her cognitive processes and how they influence anger arousal. This might be done by having clients review specific instances of anger while driving and clarify the thoughts, images, beliefs, and attitudes involved. Alternatively, the client might visualize a recent, highly angering event and then describe and clarify cognitive processes. Such in-session activities are likely to be accompanied by self-monitoring of triggers, emotional and behavioral reactions, with an emphasis on identifying both anger-enhancing and anger-quieting cognitions. Even as cognitive processes are clarified, the client may not make the connection between types of cognitions and anger arousal. Because cognitive processes are often on automatic processing, clients may not be aware of how thinking in certain ways increases or decreases anger. Having clients notice contrasts in the emotions and thought processes is generally needed for them to understand the connection between cognitions and angry emotion and behavioral responding. Once this linkage is established, a cognitive rationale is introduced (i.e., if clients can identify and replace anger-enhancing cognitions with anger-lowering ones, they will have a set of cognitive skills with which to lower anger and access other coping skills).

Anger-related cognitions are not accepted at face value, but are explored along dimensions such as their validity (i.e., are they true?), applicability (i.e., do they fit the situation?), functionality (i.e., are they getting the person the outcomes he or she wants?), breadth (i.e., are they applied too broadly?), and safety (i.e., do they lead the person to engage in aggressive or risky behavior that does or could lead to adverse consequences?). As errors or problems with various cognitive processes are identified during dialogue, therapist and client work to generate believable alternatives with which to counter and replace the habitual information processing.

These anger-reducing cognitions are then strengthened through practice. Training procedures for cognitive coping skills (CCS) can follow procedures described for RCS, except that cognitive responses are rehearsed rather than relaxation (see later for examples). As with RCS, therapist assistance in retrieval of the specific cognitions identified for rehearsal is high initially and faded to very general prompts such as "listen and replace those 'shoulds' and 'oughts' with your preferences" or "turn to the revenge and retaliation thoughts and counteract those" as the client demonstrates skill and efficacy in cognitive restructuring. Additionally, the anger-arousing capacity of scenes is increased. Cognitive change is strengthened through in vivo application while driving occurs and, in some cases, in contracted experiences such as purposefully exposing one's self to an area with traffic obstructions and detours, all the while confronting, challenging, and changing anger-related cognitions. As success is demonstrated, then attention shifts to maintenance and relapse prevention, much as with RCS, except the focus is on consolidating and maintaining cognitive change.

Some cognitive themes and anger-lowering alternative cognitions are described to follow to demonstrate the kind of cognitive content that is addressed and rehearsed in cognitive interventions for angry drivers. Not all are relevant to every angry driver, but these are some of the themes that have emerged from cognitive interventions with angry drivers.

Redirection of attention. Diverting attention from angering situations reduces the salience of anger triggers and disrupts sustained cognitive attention to anger triggers and angry rumination. Cognitive change helps the person to consciously shift attention to other things (e.g., "No use getting all angry about this. Let me think about the upcoming meeting and how I want to handle it.").

Letting go and ignoring. This strategy has the angry driver self-instruct him- or herself to cognitively distance from the situation (e.g., "Unhook. If I don't, we'll have two stupid drivers—him and me." "Stuff happens. It's not worth getting all worked up about. Just let it go and focus on safe driving.").

Acceptance, tolerance, and realistic expectations. Many angry drivers think they should never encounter difficulties when they drive. Yet, these difficulties continue to happen. Cognitive restructuring helps the angry driver not like, but accept and tolerate inevitable negative events (e.g., "This happens to everyone now and then. So just get in line and take your turn." "Looks like I am stuck in traffic. I don't like it, but it happens to the best of us. Basically, I have two choices. I can be stuck and mad as hell because I insist that it should not happen to me, or I can be stuck and fairly calm, accepting that it just happens this way sometimes. Either way, I am stuck, but the choice of how angry I get is mine.").

Being less demanding. Many angry drivers act as if they are a road czar who gets to tell the rest of the world how to drive. They elevate their desires for driving into a variety of rules for how others and events "should" or "ought" to be and then become very angry when others violate these conditions. Cognitive change involves helping them have and accept their personal standards but keep them at the level of personal preferences rather than lifting them to the level of commandments (e.g., "I don't always do what others want, so why should he?" "He has a right to be wrong and boy is he exercising his rights. I don't like it, but nobody appointed me God to tell others how to drive. I will take care of my driving and let someone else worry about the rest." "I wished slow drivers moved over. But there are discourteous, inattentive drivers out there. Being all pissed because he doesn't live up to my standards just makes me mad and doesn't change his driving a bit. He doesn't have to live according to my rules, even if I think they are best.").

Perspective taking/decatastrophizing. When negative events happen, many angry drivers label them in highly negative ways (e.g., horrible, awful, terrible, can't stand it) and then respond accordingly. They are reacting not to how negative things are, but to how negative they think they are. Cognitive intervention focuses on helping them evaluate the validity of the coding by asking, "How bad is it really?" As clients explore the high negativity of appraisals, they replace them with realistically negative evaluations (e.g., disappointing, unfortunate, frustrating, a hassle, etc.) and prepare to cope with that level of negativity (e.g., "It's not the end of the world. It's just a traffic jam. So chill out." "This is horrible and terrible! Wait a minute. How bad is it? Does it stack up with terrorism, war, or famine? Of course not. Get real. It's just frustrating. Nothing more, nothing less. So just cope with it.").

No revenge, no retaliation. Angry drivers, like many angry individuals, engage in blame. When bad, illegal, unsafe, discourteous things happen, they appoint themselves judge, jury, and executioner and seek to get back at and punish the offender. Cognitive intervention helps the person accept and deal with negative events but disconnect from punishment (e.g., "I am not going to stoop to his level." "It's not my job to 'show them.' My job is focusing on being a calm, safe driver. That's a big enough job for me. I am going to do my job and let the police do theirs." "If he did that to piss me off, he is sure going to be disappointed. I am going to stay calm and back away from him. I win by not getting caught up in the craziness.").

Forgiving. Many angry drivers think that poor behavior and conditions are purposeful; however, most are not. Poor behavior by others generally results from human error, natural human characteristics, and uncontrollable events. Cognitive change focuses on assisting angry clients to see things in this way and forgiving the errors (e.g., "Wow, that was unsafe! Don't get tangled up in it. But you know, I've done stuff like that too. We all make mistakes. Cut him a little slack." "This happens to everyone. Treat him with a little kindness, like I'd hope he would do for me if I did something dumb. It's not like I've never made a mistake on the road.").

Considering alternatives. Many angry drivers quickly jump to angry, hostile conclusions (hostile attributional bias). They think others are trying to frustrate and anger them, others are trying to take advantage of them, others are in an aggressive competition of wills, and so forth. They tend not to entertain less hostile possibilities (e.g., person was inattentive, made a mistake, had equipment malfunction, is inexperienced, or is unfamiliar with the geography, or rush hour is not a conspiracy to frustrate him or her but just a large number of people trying to get to or from work at the same time). Cognitive change involves getting the person to consider less antagonistic alternatives (e.g., "Where's my evidence that he did that on purpose? Maybe he didn't know any better. Maybe he is a lousy driver. Maybe he missed the sign. Maybe, maybe, maybe. Maybe I'll just focus on my driving." "I think it is inconsiderate to travel that speed in the fast lane. But maybe he thinks the speed limit is 65. Maybe he is having car trouble. Maybe he is just not paying close attention. Whatever. Do I think I can safely pass him on the right? If not, lag back and don't become part of the problem.").

Taking a silly, humorous perspective. Many angry drivers look at and label things in ways that engender anger. However, if these same notions are looked at through the lens of silly humor, they often become funny, and anger is defused. For example, if a driver refers to another driver as a "dumb ass," he or she responds to the cognitive meaning of this label. However, if the person concretely defined and pictured his or her terms, he or she might visualize a retarded donkey or the cheeks of the buttocks with a dunce's hat on it. The event suddenly takes on a very different emotional tone. Cognitive interventions help angry drivers come up with alternative, amusing attributions. For example, instead of reacting with fury and aggression in response to someone giving him or her the finger, the person might think that the other person is signaling that he or she thinks the person is "number 1," that the person has a bad case of digital confusion and meant to give a "thumbs up," or that the person is signaling the number of friends he or she has. For example, instead of reacting with indignation when exposed to a driver who rapidly cuts in and out of traffic, the person might think that the other driver has a bad case of diarrhea and is trying to hurry to an exit. Not everything on the road is a laughing matter, but some angry thinking is. Where relevant, the goal is for clients to look for humorous, nonangry ways to view things; have a chuckle; and reduce anger.

Taking control. Angry drivers often feel out of control. They can recapture a sense of control by thinking in ways that give them self-control. Increasing such cognitions is often empowering and steadying (e.g., "Bottom line, I am in control here. Before I do anything really stupid, I will pull over and call a friend to come get me." "Look, professional athletic teams take time-outs all the time. It is one of those times where I need to take a time-out and get my act together before driving on." "I can't seem to change things. So, just back off and figure a way to calm down. I can do that.").

Thinking about safe, nonaggressive driving. Angry drivers can lower anger by attending to and self-instructing about being a safe, courteous driver. Cognitive intervention focuses on increasing self-dialogue that guides the person toward driving safely and courteously (e.g., "Heads up. Let the anger go, and focus on being a good, safe driver. Pay attention to brake lights ahead and be ready to slow down." "That guy may be dangerous. Back away slowly. No sudden moves or gestures that may make him madder. Stay cool and take it slow and easy." "Move over and let him by. If he's in a hurry to have an accident, don't let me get in his way. I'm going to focus on being a safe driver.").

BEHAVIORAL INTERVENTIONS

Behavioral repertoires can influence dysfunctional anger via at least two different paths. First, if one is not skilled and efficacious in a situation, then he or she may react with elevated anger and frustration. For example, if a parent did not have adequate child management skills, then he or she might react angrily and perhaps aggressively when confronted with child misbehavior. Applied to driving, if a person was not skilled in driving in heavy traffic or high-speed traffic or in dealing with erratic or discourteous behavior of other drivers, then he or she might respond with anger and perhaps aggressive or other dysfunctional behavior when confronting these situations. Second, individuals may have learned dysfunctional ways of expressing their anger. For example, high-anger drivers report more verbal (e.g., yelling or cursing at another driver), physical (e.g., giving the finger to or shaking a fist at another driver, engaging in a physical altercation), and vehicular (e.g., tailgating, flashing lights at, or cutting off an offending driver) anger expression (Deffenbacher, 2009). In surveys, diaries, visualized provocations, or driving simulations, high-anger drivers report more verbal and physical aggressive urges and behaviors. For example, driving diaries showed that high-anger drivers engaged in just over two (M = 2.03) aggressive behaviors per day while driving versus approximately one half (M = 0.54) for low-anger drivers, or 3.8 times more aggression than low-anger drivers (609 vs. 162 aggressive behaviors per 300 driving days per year) (Deffenbacher, 2009). Compared to low-anger drivers, high-anger drivers swore at or called other drivers names 3.0 times more often and, when angry, flashed their lights, honked their horn, tailgated, and cut other drivers off 3.0, 3.1, 3.8, and 8.0 times more often, respectively (Deffenbacher, 2009). They also hit and damaged their car 2.5 times more often and were 10 to 11 times more likely to injure themselves doing so (Deffenbacher, Huff, Lynch, Oetting, & Salvatore, 2000). Additionally, high-anger drivers were less likely to express their anger in adaptive and constructive ways (e.g., engaging in calming and distracting behaviors such as turning on the radio or focusing on safe driving and distancing from problem drivers). In summary, high-anger drivers appear to behave in more aggressive, revengeful, and intimidating ways when angered behind the wheel.

Behavioral interventions target these behavioral excesses and deficits. The rationale is that as the person learns and deploys more effective emotional expression skills, cycles of anger and aggression escalation are broken, and the person feels less angry and engages in safer, less problem-prone behavior behind the wheel. Many behavioral anger reduction interventions have targeted patterns of negative interpersonal anger expression and replaced them with positive, conflict and anger management skills such as basic listening, assertion, and respectful feedback and negotiation skills (e.g., Deffenbacher, Thwaites, Wallace, & Oetting, 1994; Moon & Eisler, 1983). These interventions, however, do not map well onto the reduction of driving anger. Many driving-related provocations are interpersonal in nature (e.g., being "cut off" or someone driving too slowly), but the capacity for quality interpersonal communication is generally greatly reduced because of the interpersonal distance and communication barriers caused by enclosure in two moving vehicles. Other effective anger expression skills are needed.

The following, somewhat overlapping classes of anger-reducing behaviors were identified by participants in behavioral coping skills (BCS) interventions for driving anger: (a) *calming, distracting behavior* (i.e., behavior that directs attention away from angering events and/or is calming such as turning on the radio, playing music, or humming a song); (2) *focusing on safe driving* (i.e., behaviors such as backing away from a frustrating driver, purposefully driving 3 to 5 mph slower than the speed limit for the next 5 minutes, moving to a slower lane of traffic, or purposefully letting other drivers into one's lane); (3) *disengaging/time-out* (i.e., distancing from or removing anger triggers by things such as pulling the car off the road, backing away from provocation, changing lanes, altering one's route, not making eye contact with an offending driver, slowing down to let others pass); (4) *avoiding sources of anger* (i.e., purposefully avoiding anger triggers such as leaving extra time to get somewhere, taking a route that avoids congestion or construction, commuting earlier or later to avoid traffic jams, not riding with someone who makes the person tense or angry, or taking a bus or carpooling to avoid anger at parking); (5) *problem solving* (i.e., coming up with and implementing solutions such as calling and telling others that one will be late, not riding with or giving a ride to someone who is habitually late); and (6) *aggression-incompatible behavior* (i.e., engaging in behavior that interrupts or prevents aggressive responding such as keeping one's hands at the 10 and 2 o'clock positions to prevent giving the finger or other gestures or placing one's tongue gently against the roof of the mouth and holding it there to prevent yelling at an offending driver).

Therapy format for BCS is similar to RCS and CCS, except that the focus is on the identification and strengthening of behavioral skills such as those outlined previously. As with CCS, therapy often relies on Socratic questions (e.g., "What's another way of handling that?", "How do your less angry friends deal with that kind of situation?", "When you handle the situation without much anger, what do you do instead of yelling at and flipping the person off?", "Can you think of a way that you might avoid that situation altogether?") and behavioral experiments (e.g., asking 10 people how they handle a certain situation on the road) to identify effective ways of handling frustrating/provocative situations and expressing anger while driving. Once calmer, less aggressive behaviors are identified, then they are rehearsed. Rehearsal might also be conducted in vivo. For example, a driver who became angered in heavy, congested traffic might ride with his or her therapist, who coaches behaviors identified. Rehearsal with imagery is more flexible, because it is often difficult to control or arrange provocative events (e.g., someone cutting the person off or stealing a parking spot for which he or she had been waiting). The training format for RCS and CCS can be adapted. That is, clients visualize angering situations, experience anger arousal, and then visualize themselves engaging in the behaviors identified. Over sessions, the degree of therapist assistance in prompting the behaviors is reduced and the anger-arousing capacity of scenes is increased. Behavior transfer is strengthened by the client applying the different behaviors any time he or she encounters a frustrating or provocative situation. Contracted experiences are often used as well. For example, the client agrees to travel a certain stretch of road at rush hour to deal with slow, congested traffic or is purposefully late (usually to an event that is not highly important so as to minimize negative consequences) and employs behaviors identified for coping with being late or in a hurry. Behavioral application in vivo is recorded and discussed with the therapist at the next session. Behaviors are honed and modified as needed, rehearsed again in session, and then applied again in vivo. Over time, clients develop a repertoire of calm, effective ways of handling angering events and of expressing anger in less aggressive, dysfunctional ways. Procedures for enhancing maintenance and preventing relapse are adapted to behavioral skill maintenance.

MULTICOMPONENT INTERVENTIONS

Anger reductions can combine the focus and procedures of two or more of the cognitive, relaxation, and behavioral interventions described earlier. For example, cognitive and relaxation, cognitive and behavioral, and all three components have been successfully integrated for driving anger reduction (see next section).

DRIVING ANGER REDUCTION OUTCOME RESEARCH

An early study (Rimm, DeGroot, Boord, Heiman, & Dillow, 1971) employed desensitization. This study was seriously flawed methodologically. Pre–post intensity ratings on scenes from the hierarchy served as the single outcome measure. Because clients were exposed to these items and had signaled absence of anger repeatedly, this measure was highly sensitive to demand characteristics, and there were no other measures upon which to assess effects.

Table 2.1 summarizes subsequent outcome research with angry, aggressive drivers. This table shows substantial empirical support for relaxation (six studies), cognitive (two studies), behavioral (two studies), combination cognitive and relaxation (three studies), and combination cognitive and behavioral (one study) interventions. Interventions were effective with court-referred and self-referred community members, as well as angry college students. Positive findings were found on emotional, cognitive, and behavioral-expressive measures, as well as measures of aggression and risky behavior. Treatment effect sizes are generally moderate to large. Treatment effects have been maintained at short- and long-term follow-ups and have generalized to general anger and outward, negative anger expression.

Table 2.1 Treatment Outcome Research with Angry, Aggressive Drivers

Study	Sample	Findings
Galovski, Blanchard, Malta, and Freidenberg (2003)	Self- and court-referred aggressive drivers	RCS-like intervention < C on driving anger and physiological arousal in response to personal driving vignettes
Deffenbacher et al. (2000)	High-anger college students	*(RCS = CRCS) < C on overall driving anger and 3 measures of driving anger *RCS < (CRCS = C) on 3 measures of driving anger *RCS < C, CRCS ns RCS and C on 1 measure of driving Anger *CRCS < C, RCS ns CRCS and C on frequency of driving anger and risky driving *RCS = CRCS = C on 1 measure of driving anger, aggressive behavior, and general anger
Deffenbacher, Filetti, Lynch, Dahlen, and Oetting (2002)	High-anger college students	*(RCS = CRCS) on 3 measures of driving anger, frequency of driving anger, and general anger *CRCS < C, RCS ns CRCS and C on aggressive anger expression and risky driving *(RCS = CRCS) > C on adaptive/constructive driving anger expression *RCS = CRCS on 1 measure of driving anger and aggressive behavior

(*continued*)

Table 2.1 (Continued)

Study	Sample	Findings
Richards, Deffenbacher, Filetti, Lynch, and Kogan (2001)	High-anger college students	*(RCS = CRCS) < C on 5 measures of driving anger, aggressive driving anger expression, 2 measures of aggressive behavior, and general anger *(RCS = CRCS) > C on adaptive/constructive driving anger expression *RCS < C, CRCS ns RCS and C on 2 measures of risky driving *RCS = CRCS = C on frequency of driving anger
	Year follow-up	*(RCS = CRCS) < C on 3 measures of driving anger, aggressive driving anger expression, aggressive behavior *(RCS = CRCS) > C on adaptive/constructive driving anger expression *CRCS < C, RCS ns CRCS and C on general anger *RCS = CRCS = C on risky driving
Kogan, Richards, and Deffenbacher (2001)	High-anger college students	*(RCS = CBCS) < C on 4 measures of driving anger, frequency of driving anger, 4 measures of hostile thinking, aggressive driving anger expression, aggressive behavior, and general anger *(RCS = CBCS) > C on adaptive/constructive driving anger expression *RCS = CBCS = C on coping thinking and risky driving
Deffenbacher, Richards, and Kogan (2002)	Year follow-up of Kogan et al. (2001)	*(RCS = CBCS) < C on 3 measures of driving anger, 4 measures of hostile thinking, aggressive driving anger expression, aggressive behavior, general anger, and outward general anger expression *CBCS > C, RCS ns CBCS and C on adaptive/constructive driving anger expression *RCS < C, CBCS ns RCS and C on risky driving *RCS = CBCS = C on coping thinking
Deffenbacher & Alcázar-Olán (2011)	High-anger college students	*BCS < C on 3 measures of driving anger, 4 measures of hostile thinking, aggressive driving anger expression, aggressive behavior, risky driving, general anger, and outward general anger expression *BCS > C on coping thinking, adaptive/constructive driving anger expression, and general anger control

(*continued*)

Study	Sample	Findings
	Year follow-up	*BCS < C on 3 measures of driving anger, aggressive driving anger expression, aggressive behavior, risky driving, general anger, and outward general anger expression *BCS > C on coping thinking and adaptive/constructive driving anger expression *BCS = C on 4 measures of hostile thinking and general anger control
Deffenbacher (2012)	High-anger college students	*CCS < C on 3 measures of driving anger, 4 measures of hostile thinking, aggressive driving anger expression, aggressive behavior, risky driving, general anger, and outward general anger expression *CCS > C on coping thinking and adaptive/constructive driving anger expression
	Year follow-up	*CCS < C on 3 measures of driving anger, 4 measures of hostile thinking, aggressive driving anger expression, aggressive behavior, risky driving, general anger, and outward general anger expression *CCS > C on coping thinking and adaptive/constructive driving anger expression
Deffenbacher and Richards (2012)	High-anger college students	*(RCS = CCS = BCS) < C on 4 measures of driving anger, frequency of driving anger, 4 measures of hostile thinking, aggressive driving anger expression, 2 measures of aggressive behavior, 2 measures of risky driving, general anger, and outward general anger expression *(RCS = CCS = BCS) > C on coping thinking, adaptive/constructive driving anger expression, and general anger control
	Year follow-up	*(RCS = CCS = BCS) < C on 3 measures of driving anger, 4 measures of hostile thinking, aggressive driving anger expression, aggressive behavior, risky driving, general anger, and outward general anger expression *(RCS = CCS = BCS) > C on coping thinking and adaptive/constructive driving anger expression *(RCS = CCS) > C, BCS ns RCS, CCS, and C on general anger control

Note: RCS = relaxation coping skills; CCS = cognitive coping skills; BCS = behavioral coping skills; CRCS = cognitive–relaxation coping skills; CBCS = cognitive–behavioral coping skills; C = control; ns = not significantly different from; > or < signs = significant between-group differences in a positive direction (e.g., less driving anger or aggressive behavior and more adaptive/constructive driving anger expression).

Moreover, combinations of effective interventions (e.g., cognitive–relaxation or cognitive–behavioral) do not interact synergistically and lead to greater effects. Although some between-treatment differences were reported, these have not been replicated or been consistent and the bulk of comparisons between interventions are not significant. This suggests a rough equivalence of interventions, at least in the relatively short-term (6- to 10-session), small group interventions employed to date. That is, there is no gold standard from which to select a best practice for angry, aggressive drivers. In summary, there is promising evidence for cognitive, behavioral, and relaxation interventions and combinations of these components for assisting angry drivers. Practitioners can use this building empirical literature to select effective interventions that map onto the presenting characteristics of a client's driving anger (e.g., cognitive intervention for hostile, aggressive thinking; behavioral interventions for dysfunctional anger expression and aggressive and risky behaviors; and relaxation interventions for heightened emotional, physiological arousal).

Case Study of Driving Anger Reduction

The client was a 27-year-old, single, white, college-educated male. He lived in a large metropolitan area, commuted to work about 30 to 35 minutes morning and evening, drove frequently as part of his work in sales and marketing for a high-tech company, and averaged 400 miles per week. He was self-referred and motivated as he reported four reasons for seeking therapy. First, if he received another traffic citation, he would lose his license, which was necessary for work and his lifestyle. He also reported that police officers had warned him about being verbally abusive, and he was worried about further legal problems. Second, his fiancé was afraid to ride with him and very embarrassed by his behavior. He did not think that she would terminate the relationship because of his driving anger, but it led to arguments and put a strain on their relationship. Third, he felt out of control and embarrassed by his anger and aggressive driving and felt that he was lucky that his anger had not caused a wreck or a severe physical altercation or irreparably damaged relationships. A minor fourth reason was that friends and coworkers made fun of him because of his anger and antics behind the wheel.

He described himself generally as an angry, impatient perfectionist who becomes angry when people are late, do not do their jobs, refuse to cooperate and be part of a team, or belittle or make fun of him. He stated that driving was the "worst anger" and that he had always been an angry driver. He described himself as being very frequently angry when driving, which was supported by his driving log where he reported being angry five to six times per day and where frequency and duration of anger sometimes became confused, because he reported being angry from the start to the end of a trip. He reported high emotional (i.e., angry, furious, livid, mad as hell) and physiological (i.e., clenched jaws and fists; tension in the neck, shoulders, and back sometimes to the point of pain and headaches; hot and sweaty) arousal. Driving-related cognitions were marked by inflammatory labeling (i.e., many derogatory, inventively obscene labels for other drivers), absolutistic thinking (i.e., large number of "shoulds" for driving conditions and behavior of others), catastrophizing (i.e., how terrible and awful things were on the road, especially regarding conditions that impeded his progress and interfered with reaching his destination on time), overgeneralization (i.e., application of broad labels for conditions and people and use of "always" and "never" to describe conditions), and highly personalized explanations of other people's behavior (i.e., people were purposely doing things to frustrate, anger, or slow him down and otherwise make his life miserable). He reported many aggressive (e.g., yelling at and cursing of other drivers, shaking head and fists at other drivers, making obscene gestures, flashing lights, tailgating, loud horn honking, racing his engine when behind someone at a stop light or sign, yelling at other drivers in parking lots), dysfunctional (e.g., hands clenched around the wheel to the point of pain and cramping, kicking or punching the car), and risky (e.g., rapidly cutting in and out of traffic, speeding, passing on the shoulder on the freeway) behaviors.

Self-reports were consistent with responses to driving anger questionnaires. He scored at the 91st percentile on the Driving Anger Scale (Deffenbacher, Oetting, & Lynch, 1994), reporting greatest anger in response to slow drivers, discourteous drivers, traffic obstructions, and presence of the police. On the Driver's Angry Thoughts Questionnaire (Deffenbacher, Petrilli, Lynch, Oetting, & Swaim, 2003), he showed significant elevations on all four forms of hostile/aggressive thinking and an average level of coping self-instruction. On the Driving Anger Expression Inventory (Deffenbacher, Lynch, Oetting, & Swaim, 2002), he reported a high level of aggressive anger expression overall and scored high on scales of verbal, personal physical, and vehicular aggressive anger expression.

Assessment consisted of a 2-hour intake, completion of psychometric instruments, and a driving diary over a 2-week period. Therapy combined relaxation, cognitive, and behavioral approaches and consisted of seven 2-hour sessions every other week, because of the distance to the therapist's office. The client e-mailed homework to the therapist each week, which was reviewed in a 10- to 15-minute phone call in the week between sessions.

Therapy began with a behavioral and relaxation focus. Behavioral elements were aimed at rapid reduction of aggressive and risky behavior, whereas RCS was included because the client wanted to reduce the high level of emotional and physiological arousal and because relaxation interventions appear to lower resistance to cognitive elements. The first portion of the session identified less angry/aggressive ways of handling situations when he had become angry during the past week. Socratic questions and behavioral data collection (e.g., interviewing 10 friends and coworkers about what they do to handle situations in which they were going to be late for an important meeting; they were stuck in slow, heavy traffic; another driver gave them the finger or made a gesture; etc.) identified several anger-lowering behaviors: (a) distraction (e.g., listening to music); (b) calling ahead to let people know he would be late; (c) leaving earlier with a time buffer to reduce the pressure of being in a hurry; (d) distancing (e.g., slowing down and moving over a lane when angry); (e) safe driving (e.g., self-instructing and then executing things such as paying extra attention to events ahead on the road); (f) placing his tongue gently against the roof of his mouth to disrupt verbally aggressive responding (he reported giggling every time he tried to yell or curse at someone while doing this); and (g) keeping his hands at the 10 and 2 o'clock positions or laying his hand on the seat and making a "peace" sign to interfere with angry gestures. Behaviors were demonstrated and practiced within the session (e.g., placing the tongue against the roof of the mouth and yelling curses at another driver, role playing a phone conversation in which he called his administrative assistant and explained he would be late). He wrote these behaviors down in detail and reviewed them before driving, practiced them in every relevant occasion, and, in some cases, contracted to engage specific situations with an increased probability of needing them (e.g., traveling through the middle of town at rush hour). Application was recorded and reviewed in the next session. The second half of the first three sessions was devoted to relaxation training and initial relaxation coping skill rehearsal.

In reviewing homework at the beginning of the third session, the therapist noted that the client had encountered markedly slowed traffic and discourteous behavior but had not been highly angry. When asked why there was not much anger, the client said that he just "gave up" thinking something like, "It is just one of those days when the world is populated with idiots. I can't change them. To hell with it." He turned on the radio low and thought about the upcoming meeting (behaviors worked on in therapy). The therapist reinforced behavioral efforts, paraphrased his thoughts and feelings, and asked him what he usually thought and felt in this kind of situation. The client indicated that he would have been very angry and outlined a number of inflammatory, overgeneralized, demanding, and catastrophe thoughts. The therapist noted the contrast of feelings when the situation remained and asked the client why he thought there was a difference. The client indicated that the difference was due to how he looked at the situation. A cognitive rationale was introduced and linked to the rationale for changing behaviors. For each driving anger scene, anger-engendering thoughts were identified along with alternative anger-lowering cognitions. These were added to relaxation in the coping skills rehearsal (i.e., client visualized the scene, became angry, and then rehearsed both relaxation and cognitive coping skills). Cognitive change was added to homework such that the client employed relaxation, cognitive, and behavioral skills and recorded those in his log. He also contracted to enter specific situations where he would apply cognitive, relaxation, and behavioral skills in those situations. One of these, being purposefully late to a meeting with his assistant, led him to be angry with the therapist. He thought the therapist was telling him that he should not care about other people and being late. The therapist took this as an opportunity to immediately explore the thoughts and assumptions he was making about the therapist and to consider other alternative reasons that the therapist might have had. This led to a range of different possibilities and a lowering of his anger, but more importantly it fostered his insight that he had been "mind reading" other people's motives all the time without checking out assumptions or entertaining other possibilities.

In the fourth session, the client reported using relaxation to deal with other sources of anger and distress. This was encouraged along with a clarification of how cognitive and behavioral strategies could be adapted to other sources of anger. Application to other sources of anger and distress was added to homework and explored briefly in coming sessions.

After seven sessions, the client reported the same anger frequency, but much less intense anger, aggression, and risky behavior while driving. Regarding anger frequency, the client indicated that he still became irritated at a 20 to 30 intensity level on a 0 to 100 intensity scale (hence the frequency being the same), but that anger was less intense and did not last long. Responses to questionnaires were consistent with self-report and diary data. He dropped to the 45th percentile on the Driving Anger Scale total and was at or near the mean on cognitive and anger expression measures.

Therapeutic focus shifted to maintenance and relapse prevention and generalization to other sources of anger including the following: (a) The client made a detailed list of the most effective cognitive, relaxation, and behavioral coping skills and a list of the most angering situations. He agreed to review at least two situations per week; to develop a list of appropriate cognitive, relaxation, and behavioral skills for that situation; and to visualize and rehearse these at least five times. (b) The client continued to apply skills and record them in his log, which was e-mailed to the therapist, who reviewed them and sent back comments. (c) Four "booster" sessions were scheduled at 1-month intervals. The first portion of the session was devoted to a review and honing of coping skill application to driving anger, whereas the remainder of the session was devoted to identifying nondriving situations and adapting and rehearsing skills for these situations. The fourth booster session was canceled, because the client and therapist agreed it was not needed. Therapy was successfully terminated with an understanding that the client could contact the therapist if anger became an issue again, behind the wheel or elsewhere.

CONCLUSION

Angry drivers experience significant distress and negative consequences to themselves and others. Research suggests that cognitive, relaxation, and behavioral coping skills and their combination lower anger, aggression, risky, and other dysfunctional behavior in angry drivers. Although there is no gold standard treatment, it is suggested that clinicians employ this budding literature to work collaboratively with clients and adapt interventions to the presenting characteristics of the client's anger behind the wheel.

REFERENCES

Averill, J. R. (1982). *Anger and aggression: An essay on emotion*. New York, NY: Spring/Verlag.

Deffenbacher, J. L. (2009). Angry drivers: Characteristics and clinical interventions. *Mexican Journal of Psychology, 26*, 5–16.

Deffenbacher, J. L. (2012). *Cognitive therapy with angry drivers*. Department of Psychology, Colorado State University, Fort Collins, Colorado. Manuscript in preparation.

Deffenbacher, J. L., & Alcázar-Olán, R. J. (2011, August). *A behavioral approach to reducing driving anger*. Paper presented at the 119th Annual Convention of the American Psychological Association, Washington, DC.

Deffenbacher, J. L., Filetti, L. B., Lynch, R. S., Dahlen, E. R., & Oetting, E. R. (2002). Cognitive-behavioral treatment of high anger drivers. *Behaviour Research and Therapy, 40*, 895–910.

Deffenbacher, J. L., Huff, M. E., Lynch, R. S., Oetting, E. R., & Salvatore, N. F. (2000). Characteristics and treatment of high anger drivers. *Journal of Counseling Psychology, 47*, 5–17.

Deffenbacher, J. L., Lynch, R. S., Oetting, E. R., & Swaim, R. C. (2002). The Driving Anger Expression Inventory: A measure of how people express their anger on the road. *Behaviour Research and Therapy, 40*, 717–737.

Deffenbacher, J. L., Oetting, E. R., & Lynch, R. S. (1994). Development of a driving anger scale. *Psychological Reports, 74*, 83–91.

Deffenbacher, J. L., Petrilli, R. T., Lynch, R. S., Oetting, E. R., & Swaim, R. C. (2003). The Driver's Angry Thoughts Questionnaire: A measure of angry cognitions when driving. *Cognitive Therapy and Research, 27*, 383–402.

Deffenbacher, J. L., & Richards, T. L. (2012). *Cognitive, behavioral, and relaxation interventions for driving anger reduction.* Department of Psychology, Colorado State University, Fort Collins, Colorado. Manuscript in preparation.

Deffenbacher, J. L., Richards, T. L., Filetti, L. B., & Lynch, R. S. (2005). Angry drivers: A test of State-Trait theory. *Violence and Victims, 20*, 455–469.

Deffenbacher, J. L., Richards, T., & Kogan, L. (2002, August). *Long-term effects of relaxation and cognitive therapies for driving anger.* Paper presented at the 110th Annual Convention of the American Psychological Association, Chicago, IL.

Deffenbacher, J. L., Thwaites, G. A., Wallace, T. L., & Oetting, E. R. (1994). Social skills and cognitive-relaxation approaches to general anger reduction. *Journal of Counseling Psychology, 41*, 386–396.

Galovski, T. E., Blanchard, E. G., Malta, L. S., & Freidenberg, B. M. (2003). The psychophysiology of aggressive drivers: Comparison to non-aggressive drivers and pre- to post-treatment change following a cognitive-behavioural treatment. *Behaviour Research and Therapy, 41*, 1055–1067.

Kassinove, H., & Tafrate, R. C. (2006). Anger-related disorders: Basic issues, models and diagnostic considerations. In E. L. Feindler (Ed.), *Anger-related disorders* (pp. 1–27). New York, NY: Springer.

Kogan, L. R., Richards, T. L., & Deffenbacher, J. L. (2001, August). *Effects of relaxation and cognitive therapy for driving anger reduction.* Paper presented at the 109th Annual Convention of the American Psychological Association, San Francisco, CA.

Malta, L. S., Blanchard, E. B., & Freidenberg, B. M. (2005). Psychiatric and behavioral problems in aggressive drivers. *Behaviour Research and Therapy, 43*, 1467–1484.

Moon, J. R., & Eisler, R. M. (1983). Anger control: An experimental comparison of three behavioral treatments. *Behavior Therapy, 14*, 493–505.

Richards, T. L., Deffenbacher, J. L., Filetti, L. B., Lynch, R. S., & Kogan, L. (2001, August). *Short- and long-term effects of interventions for driving anger reduction.* Paper presented at the 109th Annual Convention of the American Psychological Association, San Francisco, CA.

Rimm, D. C., DeGroot, J. C., Boord, P., Heiman, J., & Dillow, P. V. (1971). Systematic desensitization of an anger response. *Behaviour Research and Therapy, 9*, 273–280.

3

Emotion-Focused Therapy for Anger in Complex Trauma

ANTONIO PASCUAL-LEONE AND SANDRA C. PAIVIO ■

This chapter will describe emotion-focused therapy applied to anger-related problems that stem from complex child abuse trauma, that is, repeated exposure to violence and betrayal, usually at the hands of loved ones and caregivers. Therapy focuses on healing the emotional/attachment injuries perpetrated by particular abusive and/or neglectful others. Before beginning, it is important to specify some of the fundamental assumptions underlying the approach: (a) Recovery from trauma requires some type of re-experiencing trauma feelings and memories. (b) The caveat regarding re-experiencing is that exposure-based procedures require the capacity to regulate intense, negative affect, including anger. (c) There are different types of anger problems associated with complex trauma, including both underregulation and overcontrol, and these require different intervention strategies. (d) Anger intensification is *not* appropriate for individuals with anger control problems. (e) Anger intensification is *only* appropriate for accessing inhibited *adaptive* anger at violation. (f) The purpose of anger intensification is to access the adaptive information associated with healthy anger—this aids in the construction of more adaptive meaning regarding self, others, and traumatic events. Each of these assumptions will be elaborated in the chapter that follows.

One of the hallmarks of emotion-focused therapies is a highly differentiated perspective and approach to treating emotion and emotional processes (Greenberg & Paivio, 1997; Pascual-Leone, Gillis, Singh, & Andreescu, in press). Such a perspective is especially relevant to treating complex posttraumatic stress disorder (PTSD) stemming from child abuse trauma, which involves a complex array of emotional processes and is intertwined with issues of attachment, interpersonal safety and trust, and profound betrayal in intimate relationships. Anger figures prominently in these experiences. This chapter will distinguish between adaptive and maladaptive anger, specify criteria for healthy anger experience and expression in therapy, and describe the role of anger in resolving interpersonal trauma from the past. Clinical examples from emotion-focused therapy for trauma (EFTT; Paivio & Pascual-Leone, 2010) will be used to illustrate constructs and treatment principles.

INTRODUCTION

PTSD is the disorder most often associated with single-episode or type I trauma, and type II (complex) trauma refers to repeated exposure to threat of violence. EFTT focuses mainly on complex interpersonal trauma from childhood emotional, physical, and sexual abuse and neglect in the context of primary relationships with attachment figures. These experiences in childhood typically are associated with a more complex array of disturbances than exposure to a single traumatic event (Courtois & Ford, 2009).

These disturbances include symptom distress (related to PTSD, anxiety, and depression), emotion regulation difficulties (including underregulation, overcontrol, and maladaptive behaviors such as substance abuse and self-harm), and self-related and interpersonal problems (e.g., low self-esteem, poor self-awareness, interpersonal alienation, and distrust). Disrupted affective processes are at the core of this constellation, and problem anger figures prominently among them. Our overview of trauma-related difficulties will focus on those processes directly related to anger problems.

Hyperarousal is central to the aforementioned array of concerns, and although a diagnosis of PTSD typically focuses on fear or anxiety, *complex* posttraumatic stress disorders entail many emotions besides fear (e.g., rage, shame, hopelessness). Chronic irritability and anger are manifestations that can be particularly problematic and can be a priority for intervention. Results of a recent study of the factors associated with the disorders of extreme stress diagnosis further suggested that anger dysregulation is a distinct factor separate from impulse control (Scoboria, Ford, Hsio-ju, & Frisman, 2006). Thus, effective therapy needs to focus on anger, per se, and distinguish this from managing behavior problems, such as substance abuse or self-harm.

Anger regulation problems, irritability, and aggressive behavior also are highly correlated with unresolved trauma, and these can have profoundly deleterious effects on interpersonal relations. For example, there is strong evidence linking early exposure to domestic violence with later interpersonal violence (Wolfe, 2007), as well as a high prevalence of extreme anger and aggressive behavior among combat veterans (Novaco, 2007). Many clients in individual therapy for trauma also experience marital distress and parenting difficulties, and resolving their own attachment injuries and trauma can generalize to improving current relationships.

In contrast, overcontrol of anger also has harmful effects. Chronic inhibition of feelings associated with upsetting or traumatic events results in accumulated stress that contributes to negative health outcomes (Pennebaker & Campbell, 2000). The fear of emerging anger, in particular, is a commonly observed underlying determinant for some forms of anxiety (Barlow, 1988). Furthermore, it is widely accepted that self-injurious behaviors, such as self-cutting, frequently are used to regulate affective states, particularly anger (van der Kolk et al., 1996; Linehan, 1993). Finally, although different types of childhood abuse have been found to have largely overlapping effects, there are a few specific effects related to particular traumatic experiences. Childhood *physical abuse* frequently involves a combination of physical danger and terror as well as distrust and has been hypothesized to be particularly detrimental to self-development and self-regulation (Ford, 2005). A review of the research indicates that the distinct effects of physical abuse center on anger control problems and aggressive behavior, particularly among males. Scoboria et al. (2006) found that anger dysregulation was the only symptom of complex developmental trauma that was more severe for persons who had experienced physical victimization but not sexual victimization. Furthermore, symptom scores were more severe for those who had experienced physical victimization in childhood compared to those who had suffered it in adolescence or adulthood. Anger and aggression are learned responses and ways of coping with prolonged relational trauma. There is also some evidence to suggest that areas of the brain responsible for affect regulation develop in the context of secure attachment relationships, such that failure of brain development may partly account for the "hair trigger" anger response observed in many survivors of child abuse trauma (Ford, 2005).

The anger problems related to complex trauma have a number of treatment implications. Anger at violation is actually a healthy emotion that motivates self-defense, but it becomes problematic when it is overgeneralized, underregulated, used to cover more vulnerable emotional experience, or turned against the self (Paivio & Pascual-Leone, 2010; Pascual-Leone et al., in press). As a case in point, when anger is the dominant emotion in a client's repertoire, he or she does not have access to other more vulnerable feelings. This interferes with optimal functioning. For example, the client who expresses anger in place of hurt, sadness, or fear when perceiving a potential abandonment will have difficulty getting his or her needs for contact, comfort, and support met. Similarly, anger that is underregulated does not serve an adaptive function, even if the anger itself is initially a legitimate and adaptive response to harm (Pascual-Leone et al., in press). High levels of arousal overwhelm both the angry individual and the person being confronted with that anger.

Emotion-focused approaches to the treatment of anger both recognize and address these different anger-related problems. Another distinguishing feature of emotion-focused psychotherapy as contrasted with other treatments is the emphasis on "changing emotion with emotion," rather than with cognition or interpretations (Greenberg, 2002). Information and meaning associated with healthy adaptive emotions, such as anger at maltreatment and sadness at loss, are used to modify the maladaptive meaning associated with emotions such as fear and shame related to trauma (e.g., sense of powerlessness and self-blame). This is particularly relevant to therapy for complex trauma, because many people who have been victimized learn to suppress their feelings of adaptive anger and sadness and consequentially have been unable to assert interpersonal boundaries and grieve important losses. EFTT also draws on a well-developed technology in the humanistic-experiential tradition of psychotherapy (e.g., Gendlin, 1996; Greenberg, Rice, & Elliott, 1993; Perls, 1969; Rogers, 1957). As such, the emotion-focused approach has synthesized person-centered relationship conditions, with a highly developed version of Gestalt chair work, to create moment-by-moment interventions for overcoming experiential avoidance, accessing inhibited emotion, promoting meaning construction processes, and resolving attachment injuries.

THE COMPLEXITY OF ANGER EXPERIENCES: A CASE VIGNETTE

Emotion-focused therapy for complex trauma is a short-term approach (16 to 20 sessions) conducted in phases that are cyclical and reiterative but provide a structured sequence for facilitating trauma resolution (Paivio & Pascual-Leone, 2010). We describe an example of this in the case of "Paul," who had a history of anger and aggression problems. This and other case examples described later in the chapter are composites adapted from cases previously presented in Paivio and Pascual-Leone (2010).

Phase One: Cultivating the Alliance

Paul entered therapy wanting to come to terms with experiences of severe childhood physical abuse by his father and sexual abuse by a male relative. His family history also included the death of his older sister when he was an adolescent. She had been his "protector" and, at the time, he had received no support for dealing with this huge loss. Currently he was in a volatile marriage and had difficulties parenting his three stepchildren. Paul was likeable and intelligent and had a university education and a good job as a manufacturing plant manager. At pretreatment he reported severe symptoms of PTSD and depression, extremely low self-esteem, and high levels of interpersonal distrust. Paul cited his anger as a central problem. When asked about his understanding of his anger problems, Paul stated that his physically abusive father had been "a bad example" and also that he (Paul) used anger "to protect [himself] from ever being hurt again." However, individuals like Paul can experience and express different types of anger (which, as we shall see, is a central tenant of EFTT theory). The complexity of anger experience and the importance of its accurate assessment in EFTT are particularly apparent in this case. So, while Paul's anger at childhood maltreatment can be considered appropriate and *adaptive*, there were problems related to the intensity of these reactions. At the same time (as suggested by his description of anger as a protection against hurt), Paul also frequently experienced anger as a *secondary or defensive* reaction to avoid other feelings, such as shame about having been abused or fear of being hurt. His low self-esteem also suggested that much of his anger could be considered a defense against perceived slights and wounds to his sense of self. Additionally, he held beliefs that children should "respect" their parents, and he would blow up (secondary reaction) at any perceived signs of disrespect from his children. Finally, Paul also had a history of using *instrumental* anger and aggression to control others and prove his masculinity. Because anger was his dominant emotion, promoting the experience and expression of anger with Paul was contraindicated. Rather, therapy would focus on helping him access and explore emotional experiences that were less available to him. Targets of intervention were anger in the therapeutic relationship, anger in his current life, and anger about childhood physical and sexual abuse.

Cultivating a strong therapeutic alliance in the first phase of EFTT requires establishing safety and trust, developing a collaborative understanding of the client's problems, collaborating on the goals and tasks of therapy (how the goals will be achieved), and providing implicit or explicit emotion awareness training. Although Paul was highly motivated to change, he was quick to anger, and not surprisingly, his anger initially dominated therapy sessions. During session two, Paul sarcastically responded to the therapist's empathy by saying, "You don't really care about me. It's your job. I'm just a paycheck to you. You'll keep seeing me no matter what I do." The therapist validated his perceptions but empathically confronted his behavior (Therapist: "Yes it is my job to try and help you open up, and I understand that trust is difficult for you and this will take time. At the same time, this is how you distance yourself from me and therapy, just as you distance yourself in real life, and it hasn't served you well."). Paul softened his stance and agreed that he was afraid of opening up but that he wanted to try. During another early session, the therapist provided the observation that Paul's anger (this time about his wife) threatened to derail the therapy process itself (Therapist: "It's like you get on a roll and it's difficult to stop and there's no room for anything else."). This was also an opportunity for her to educate him on different types of anger (discussed later in this chapter) and collaborate with him on shifting the focus from anger per se to accessing more vulnerable feelings in an effort to expand his emotional repertoire (Therapist: "You know anger well. Growth is going to come from getting to know other parts of Paul. Does that make sense?"). An important aspect of this also involved collaboratively determining that Paul had the necessary ability to monitor and dampen his anger experience in session. He had acquired these skills through previous participation in traditional "anger management" therapy. After this collaboration, whenever Paul reacted to painful material with secondary anger, it served as a mutually recognized marker (a) for the therapist to validate his experience and thereby reduce defensiveness, (b) for Paul to dampen his anger, and (c) for both to explore the underlying meaning (thoughts and feelings) of his anger more deeply.

Phase Two: Reducing Self-Related Difficulties

Self-related difficulties in EFTT concern fear and avoidance of internal experience, shame and self-blame for maltreatment, and maladaptive anger all of which interfere with resolution of interpersonal issues. Thus, therapy increasingly focused on exploring Paul's maladaptive experiences of anger in his current life in order to access underlying thoughts and feelings. During one session he expressed anger toward his wife for using his experience of sexual abuse as a child against him in arguments. Helpful interventions validated Paul's anger at betrayal and also directed his attention to feelings of hurt and sadness (e.g., Therapist: "I hear how angry you are. And at the same time, it must be so hurtful to have her take your trust and use it against you like that."). He was then able to acknowledge that he felt like his wife probably did not love him. This opened the door to not only exploring vulnerable experiences but also acknowledging how his anger had pushed others away and deprived him of the connection and love he actually wanted. Empathic responses were used to evoke and support his sadness, loneliness, and longing for connection and love (e.g., Therapist: "So, under all that anger is a sad and lonely man, hungry for love, and yet pushing others away for fear of being hurt."). Over the course of several sessions, Paul was able to acknowledge and express his more vulnerable experience to the therapist and receive comfort and support from her. By the middle of treatment (session 10), Paul was able to attend to his internal experience and explore the thoughts and feelings that contributed to maladaptive anger and its escalation.

Phase Three: Resolution and Integration of Therapy Experiences

As maladaptive anger is reduced, the final phase of EFTT focuses more on resolving issues with particular perpetrators of abuse and neglect, integrating therapy experiences, and thereby constructing more adaptive meaning regarding self, others, and traumatic events. As the therapist worked with Paul, different anger processes and underlying experiences were identified and explored as they emerged in sessions ("hot" processing). For example, it also became apparent that, in addition to problems with secondary, instrumental, and underregulated anger, Paul also had difficulty acknowledging and expressing feelings of adaptive anger about his father's abuse. Exploration revealed that he feared this would jeopardize the current relationship he had with his father, which he had worked so hard to achieve. In many cases (examples are presented later in the chapter), such inhibition of adaptive anger at abuse can actually interfere with trauma resolution; however, as noted earlier, when anger is the most prevalent or dominant emotion in the client's repertoire, it is more important to focus on alternate emotional experiences that are less available to the client. Therefore, the therapist validated Paul's concern and, again, they decided to focus primarily on helping him access and express more vulnerable feelings. The therapist encouraged Paul to engage in *imaginal confrontations* or dialogues in which he imagined expressing his thoughts and feelings to his father. The eventual resolution of Paul's past trauma involved both acknowledging his contribution to his own pain through maladaptive anger and grieving the many losses he had endured. In particular, he was able to express the deep sadness he felt at having missed out on a healthy and supportive relationship with his father when he was growing up (Therapist: "What would you have wanted most from him?" Client: [*long pause*] "I guess, he never said he loved me." Therapist: "Ah yes, that would have meant so much, to hear 'I love you Paul.'" Client: [*tears well up*] "I guess we both missed out on a lot..."). These experiences, in turn, increased his compassion toward himself and his self-esteem, thus making him less vulnerable to perceived slights and defensive anger, and strengthened his desire to maintain the current relationship with his aging father. At the end of therapy, Paul felt closer to his father while also acknowledging his wrongdoing.

In terms of childhood sexual abuse, Paul did access intense feelings of anger and disgust while re-experiencing one episode of abuse, and the therapist validated these feelings. However, the important part of this process was helping him stay with painful feelings of embarrassment and shame while disclosing details about the abuse, rather than his being stuck in the avoidant and defensive feeling of anger, in addition to accessing other feelings of compassion for himself as an innocent boy who had no one to turn to for support. Again, this helped to strengthen his sense of self, making him less vulnerable to defensive anger.

THEORETICAL APPROACH TO TREATING ANGER IN SURVIVORS OF COMPLEX TRAUMA

Experts agree that recovery from PTSD requires exposure to experiences that directly contradict the emotional helplessness and physical paralysis of trauma (Ford, 2005). In EFTT these contradictory experiences take place through the therapeutic relationship, imaginal confrontation of offenders, and a focus on accessing previously avoided adaptive anger and sadness and associated healthy resources. However, promoting anger experience and expression in therapy is controversial. Anger is a powerful emotion and, when accompanied by aggressive behavior, can have destructive personal, interpersonal, and societal consequences. Moreover, most research has demonstrated that, although increasing anger arousal (venting or catharsis) can produce immediate relief, it does not reduce anger in the long term (Novaco, 2007). The vast majority of treatments for anger, therefore, focus directly on its reduction. However, as already suggested in the previous case vignette, EFTT distinguishes between different types of anger and specifies criteria for adaptive anger experience and expression and the parameters under which anger intensification is appropriate in therapy. In the field of trauma therapy, EFTT is unique in its emphasis, not only on reducing current symptom distress as well as self and interpersonal problems, but also in resolving past issues with particular attachment figures (and offenders) that continue to be sources of distress. Resolving issues with perpetrators of abuse and neglect necessitates at least some focus on acknowledging and expressing adaptive anger at maltreatment.

Types of Anger and Their Appropriate Interventions

A clinician conducting emotion-focused therapy is trained to identify distinct kinds of emotional processes, so that all types of "anger" are not responded to in the same way. In the section that follows, we discuss each of these types of anger and associated intervention principles (also see Paivio & Pascual-Leone, 2010; Pascual-Leone et al., in press).

Adaptive Anger

One of the fundamental assumptions underlying emotion-focused therapies is that emotion is an adaptive orienting system. Thus, *primary adaptive anger*, as a basic affect, is an immediate and direct response to a real environmental threat that is not preceded or mediated by obvious cognitive or other affective components. Anger at interpersonal violation and maltreatment quickly mobilizes self-protective resources and action. It provides energy and a sense of power and readies the individual for self-defense or to protect his or her integrity and boundaries. Interpersonally, anger signals others that an offense has occurred, creates separation and distance, and signals them to "back off." Difficulties here concern modulating its intensity, which can result in either dysregulation or overcontrol. In either case, the information associated with anger is unavailable to guide adaptive action. Negative consequences of anger avoidance include a pervasive sense of victimization, recurrent bouts of depression, and difficulties with assertiveness and with establishing appropriate interpersonal boundaries. Chronic suppression of anger also can result in hypertension and instances of "bottle up—blow up" (Novaco, 2007). The intervention strategy for problems with underregulated or inhibited primary adaptive anger is to either decrease or increase arousal, respectively, in order to access the associated adaptive information.

Criteria for promoting healthy anger. In terms of promoting anger, EFTT defines healthy anger experience and expression according to specific criteria (Paivio & Carriere, 2007) that are consistent with the definition of primary adaptive anger presented earlier. These criteria inform and guide interventions, for example, when imaginally confronting perpetrators of harm. Criteria for healthy anger expression are as follows: (a) Anger must be directed outward to the perpetrator, rather than inward toward the self, and must concern actual and specific harms, transgressions, or violations. (b) Anger must be differentiated from other emotions, such as sadness, guilt, or fear. Anger expression mixed with tears or fear, for example, does not allow the individual full access to the cognitive, motivational, or somatic information specifically associated with anger experience. (c) Anger is expressed assertively with ownership of experience, rather than aggressively, passively, or indirectly. For example, as in other approaches, clients use "I" statements rather than referring to themselves in the third person or blaming and complaining about or hurling insults at others. Anger that is inappropriately expressed does not have the desired effect on the environment, and consequentially adaptive needs for respectful treatment or distance are not met. (d) The intensity of anger expression must be appropriate to the situation. Intense emotional expressions that are a catalyst for change are not the same as catharsis, although relief and release of tension can play a role in both of these. Appropriate intensity is assessed through verbal and nonverbal indicators of arousal, including body posture, vocal quality, and facial expressions that are congruent with anger and with the situation. Inappropriate anger intensity includes both rage that is overwhelming and anger that is lacking in conviction or energy. Again, in both instances, the associated adaptive information is not available to guide one's action, nor is there a clear message communicated to others (Pascual-Leone et al., in press). Finally, (e) anger expressions must include some elaboration and exploration of meaning. This expression is not simply a verbal tirade, but unelaborated meaning must be worked with in an attempt to understand it and the provoking event. This is consistent with the fundamental principle underlying EFTT that client "experiencing," that is, attending to and exploring the meaning of internal experience, is the primary source of new information used in promoting resolution and construction of new meaning.

Maladaptive Anger

In contrast to adaptive anger, most forms of maladaptive anger are inappropriate to the situation and long-lasting, rather than immediate and direct responses to violation.

Primary maladaptive anger is an immediate and direct response to perceived wrongdoing, but it is overgeneralized and frequently associated with posttraumatic stress reactions (Pascual-Leone et al., in press). A rape victim, for instance, reacts with rage at being touched by men, or a survivor of child abuse, whose trust has been betrayed, may react with anger to others' displays of affection. The intervention strategy for primary maladaptive anger is akin to counterconditioning of overgeneralized fear reactions, in which alternative, more adaptive and articulate feelings and meanings are brought into the foreground of experience. Examples of this may include accessing underlying grief over a specific injury and acknowledging underlying shame while accessing self-compassion and more articulate self-affirmations (Paivio & Pascual-Leone, 2011; Pascual-Leone et al., in press).

Secondary anger is a response to maladaptive cognitions that produce, perpetuate, or escalate the anger (e.g., erroneous attributions of malicious intent or dwelling on revenge fantasies). Alternately, defensive anger is secondary to and masks more vulnerable core emotion, such as sadness, fear, or shame. Obvious examples are anger and aggression in response to hurt or shame in the case of Paul presented earlier, or the shame or fear of abandonment as observed in some clients with borderline personality (Linehan, 1993), or some male perpetrators of intimate violence (Holtzworth-Munroe & Clements, 2007). In these instances, secondary anger serves the function of momentarily alleviating painful feelings of vulnerability, and when this is repeatedly successful, it is reinforcing (Pascual-Leone et al., in press). The intervention strategy with secondary anger is to explore it and access the underlying thoughts and feelings.

Instrumental anger and aggressive behavior are used, either intentionally or unconsciously, to control or manipulate others. Appropriate intervention involves confronting and interpreting the instrumental function of this anger and teaching more adaptive ways of getting one's needs met.

Contempt and Disgust: Stepping Stones Toward Adaptive Assertion

Although feelings of contempt and disgust are sometimes problematic and disconcerting aspects of anger experience, they are not necessarily maladaptive at all stages of change. In fact, these emotions can be particularly important early in therapy with survivors of child abuse trauma. Like a poorly articulated (or poorly expressed) albeit *well-directed* impulse of anger, these feelings can usher in adaptive meaning and action tendencies when they are directed in response to legitimate moral transgressions and despicable behaviors (e.g., sexual abuse; Paivio & Pascual-Leone, 2010; Pascual-Leone & Greenberg, 2007). Contempt involves looking down on an object with a sneer or curled lip of disdain ("You worm!"), whereas disgust involves wanting to rid oneself of the object by revulsion or throwing up ("You make me sick!"). Although similar principles apply, accurate intervention with anger, contempt, and disgust first requires therapists to accurately perceive and then empathically respond to nuances in meaning associated with these different emotions.

Treatment Goals: Addressing Anger in the Process of Resolving Complex Trauma

Given the range of difficulties suffered by victims of complex trauma, it is useful to clarify how different anger problems are addressed in EFTT and how these contribute to resolving complex trauma. Doing so clarifies the goals and objectives of this treatment—some of which overlap with and some of which are distinct from other approaches.

With few exceptions, the aim of most trauma therapies when anger is identified as a chief problem is squarely on reducing maladaptive anger (e.g., Linehan, 1993; Novaco, 2007; Zlotnick et al., 1997). However, some recent cognitive-behavioral therapy (CBT) approaches to therapy for complex trauma (e.g., Cloitre, Koenen, Dohen, & Han, 2002) also acknowledge *fear* of anger as a problem among clients who have been exposed to violent childhood abuse. So, those approaches also include skills training in emotion awareness and assertive communication. EFTT criteria for the healthy expression of adaptive anger, presented earlier, are compatible with principles that would be applied in CBT assertiveness training (Kubany et al., 2004). In addition, however, a chief objective in EFTT is to focus on exploring the personal meaning of disavowed anger experience rather than on skills training per se.

Traditional psychodynamic approaches offer another point of comparison as they focus on the meaning associated with defensive anger or "anger turned inward" and aim to help clients acknowledge the underlying feelings or to express anger at an appropriate source. Some psychodynamic models (e.g., Davanloo, 1995) even emphasize increasing arousal as a means of heightening awareness of suppressed anger and *id* impulses. Similarly, EFTT includes anger intensification strategies under specific conditions, and, as stated earlier, increasing arousal is *only* considered appropriate for accessing inhibited adaptive anger so as to then explore its associated adaptive information.

The goal for resolution of relational trauma in EFTT involves developing increased emotional competence, a broader emotional repertoire, and more adaptive views of self and specific others (i.e., perpetrators) who are the focus of therapy. More adaptive emotional processes include reduced negative feelings concerning the other (e.g., hurt, fear, shame, anger, sadness) and an increased ability to acknowledge and attend to one's own needs. When a client continues to be in a relationship with past offenders, as was the case with Paul, this could also mean letting go of the hope that those specific individuals will meet their needs (e.g., for attention, approval, respect) and even letting go of expectations that the other will acknowledge responsibility for harm, apologize, or change. Thus, healthy personal needs are met in new ways—by asserting or soothing oneself, for example, or by reaching out to the therapist or current loved ones for support. As in many schools of therapy, the client does not "give up" on his or her own needs but rather becomes more autonomous and lets go of the longing or insistence that his or her needs be met by unresponsive or even abusive attachment figures.

Resolution also includes increased self-esteem despite the other's opinions, reduced self-blame for one's victimization, increased ability to assert and stand up for oneself, and increased detachment/separation from the other and the traumatic events. Changes in perceptions of the other include a shift from globally negative views of the other (the "bad object") to a more differentiated and realistic perspective, a better understanding of the other's position and actions toward the client, and clearly holding others responsible for the harm they have caused, rather than erroneously blaming oneself. The client may or may not feel more positively toward the other or feel forgiving. Paradoxically, fully acknowledging and working through adaptive anger at maltreatment can contribute to forgiveness (a topic that is also addressed later in this chapter).

INTERVENTION PRINCIPLES AND PROGRESSIONS IN WORKING WITH ANGER

The following sections present the intervention principles that are most relevant to work with anger in each of the phases of EFTT.

Phase One: Emotion Coaching

In early sessions, therapists are attuned and direct client attention to the core emotions and emotional processes that will be the targets of therapy later on. As illustrated earlier in the case of Paul, core adaptive emotions include anger at violation, betrayal, and maltreatment and sadness at losses and neglect, as well as the associated longings, needs, and action tendencies (Therapist: "I hear how angry you are—you needed his support, not his constant put-downs."). Primary maladaptive emotions can include fear, shame, or anger when they are related to trauma and when they entail core negative evaluations about self and others (Therapist: "I imagine such a lot of impotent rage, watching him beat up on her and being utterly powerless to stop it."). Helping clients become aware of these emotional processes contributes to self-development and is the basis for developing a collaborative understanding of disturbance and the goals and tasks of therapy.

Thus, severe problems with emotion awareness and expression (e.g., alexithymia) pose difficulties for clients who are trying to access and articulate their experience. This is especially true for many individuals with histories of complex trauma and anger problems. In these instances, it can be helpful to direct a client's attention to the bodily experiences associated with specific emotions (e.g., energy of anger, tension or trembling of anxiety, heaviness of sadness, hiding or slinking away in shame). Especially in the early phase of therapy, this contributes to client recognition, self-monitoring, and self-control of emotion. As clients recount their reactions to situations, therapists can add directives to attend to bodily experience (e.g., Therapist: "What do you feel in your body as you think about that event?"), combining these with empathic responses that implicitly invite clients to articulate the meaning of their experience (e.g., Therapist: "Butterflies—something scary about it?"). Doing this helps clients attend to their somatic and affective experience as sources of information, which can aid in the construction of personal meaning. A critical aspect of promoting deeper "experiencing" or meaning exploration is helping clients to clearly identify the causes and effects of their maltreatment. In some cases this might be simply identifying the person(s) responsible as perpetrators of trauma (e.g., Client: "His rages terrified me, ruined our family, made me take on a responsibility for the family that was way beyond my years."). Sometimes, as in the case of Paul, clients also must acknowledge how they have harmed themselves and others and express regret.

EFTT can also include explicit teaching about emotions and emotional processes. This is typically integrated into the process of exploring current or past issues rather than presented as a separate stage or exercise. In the case of Paul, for example, the early phase of therapy included educating him about the different types of anger, but this teaching was initiated at in-session markers of instrumental or defensive (secondary) anger that covered feelings of hurt, fear, and shame—emotions he was less aware of in the moment.

Phase Two: Interventions for Changing Maladaptive Anger

Regulating anger. Maladaptive anger interferes with resolution of interpersonal trauma; the client is stuck in an earlier stage of emotional processing, characterized by hostile blaming and rejection rather than assertive anger. Although EFTT has some affinity with CBT in this area, EFTT is not an anger management therapy. Strategies for regulating or reducing underregulated or defensive anger typically are integrated into the process of resolving issues with particular offenders or attachment figures. In many instances, as was illustrated with Paul, it will be more important for clients with chronic anger problems to focus on grief and sadness expression (instead of anger) as a route to healing attachment injuries that stem from child abuse trauma. However, the dilemma is that when trauma involves injustice, violation, and maltreatment, anger is a legitimate response and should not be avoided as a means of control. Thus, therapy must validate clients' experiences of adaptive anger and find ways to help them symbolize and express it appropriately.

Moving beyond secondary anger. The first step in working with chronic anger in EFTT is assessment of the client's capacity to attend to and identify his or her internal experience. This capacity is necessary for clients to identify the factors (internal and external) that contribute to escalating and perpetuating anger. As we have suggested, awareness must be increased for clients to gain control of their anger experience (e.g., Therapist: "So, when you think your kids don't respect you and dwell on that, you feel yourself getting more and more angry."). Additionally, this capacity is essential for clients to expand their emotion repertoire by attending to the core emotions underlying defensive anger experience. The next step is to help clients distinguish between different types of anger experience so they know when to validate, express, modulate, or bypass their own anger and attend to more core vulnerable experience. When clients have limited capacity for emotion regulation, intervention will include the explicit use of emotion regulation strategies such as breathing, relaxation, time-out, or distraction that have been well articulated in the CBT literature (e.g., Deffenbacher, 1999; Fernandez, 2010). Memory evocation strategies can be used to help clarify the triggers for problematic anger reactions. In instances of secondary anger, the underlying cognitive-affective processes need to be brought into awareness and maladaptive aspects must then be explored and changed. EFTT characteristically focuses more on exploring meaning rather than on directly challenging maladaptive cognitions (e.g., Therapist: "What's that all about, this sense that disrespect from your teenage kids is so intolerable?"). Anger at perceived disrespect, in the aforementioned example, also could be understood as a defense against hurt or shame, in which case the therapist directs client attention to the core experience (e.g., Therapist: "So it triggers some sense that you're a bad father, incompetent? That must hurt a lot. Let's stay with that, it's important.").

Phase Three: Promoting Primary Adaptive Anger

Gradual exposure. When clients are afraid of, deny, or believe that anger is socially unacceptable, the change principle is similar to that of gradual exposure to other threatening experiences. Intervention involves successive approximations to the experience (e.g., moving from "feeling annoyed or resentful," to "feeling angry," to "feeling outraged and furious"). When clients deny feeling angry at situations that normally would evoke anger, therapists must use empathic responses, questions, or challenges to elicit a reaction or open a door for acknowledging the experience (e.g., Therapist: "Sounds like you thought that was pretty unfair" or "Did you *like* what she did?"). Here, clients also are implicitly learning the range and appropriate modulation of anger experience, which helps to challenge maladaptive beliefs that all anger is too intense and dangerous. At other times, intervention can focus on client nonverbal behavior that emerges spontaneously and then encourage clients to put words to these actions (e.g., Therapist: "What's in that tone of voice—'how dare you?'"). Secondary or reactive emotions that cover anger (e.g., guilt, fear, defeat, helplessness) are bypassed or explored with the goal of accessing authentic, spontaneous expression of anger at injustice, unfairness, or maltreatment.

Facilitating adaptive anger in the resolution process. EFTT interventions and procedures, such as evocative empathy, promoting experiencing, experiential focusing, imaginal confrontation, and other enactments, are used to promote adaptive anger expression and the resolution of trauma issues. The *imaginal confrontation* (IC) procedure (a modified version of the Gestalt "empty chair" intervention) is a central component of EFTT and requires clients to imagine perpetrators of abuse in an empty chair and express their thoughts and feelings directly to them (for detailed instruction on using this and other interventions see Paivio & Pascual-Leone, 2010). The IC intervention is typically introduced in session four, once a safe therapeutic relationship has been established, and initially can evoke fear and avoidance of internal experience, as well as shame and self-blame (e.g., Client: "I was such a difficult kid, no wonder she lost her temper."). And those complex reactions become the focus of later therapeutic intervention. However, as fear and shame are worked through and desensitization to trauma feelings and memories occurs, clients become better able to freely express previously inhibited feelings directly to the imagined other. Then the client is supported by the therapist in the clear and uninhibited expressions of adaptive emotion, in this case, assertive anger about maltreatment and abuse. The following example of a client, "Julie" (Paivio & Pascual-Leone, 2010), working through sexual abuse in EFTT illustrates these stages in the model. The process begins with blame and complaint toward her imagined father in the empty chair; then moves through overcoming self-interruption, to assertive expression of anger and meaning exploration and entitlement to unmet needs, to letting go of expectations regarding the other; and finally ends with a shift in perceptions of herself and the other.

C: He's [father] such a disgusting pig. Who treats their own daughter like that!?

T: I hear how much you hate him, despise him. Tell him over there [*points to chair*], what you hate, make him understand.

C: Yes, I hate the way you manipulated and corrupted me for your own selfish needs. You perverted everything, I was innocent and you ruined my childhood, you made sex disgusting. I hope you rot in hell! [*sighs, withdraws*]

T: What happened just now, Julie, you sigh and kind of collapse?

C: I don't like it, I sound just like him.

T: But you're not him, you're nothing like him. You're justifiably angry and you want to see him punished for his despicable behavior, for his crimes. Tell him.

C: Yes, I do want to see you punished, you deserve to be punished for all the harm you've done. You fucked me up royally, my life has been such a mess, but I'm not going to let you ruin my life anymore.

T: How do you feel saying that?

C: It feels right, he was the adult, I was just a little kid, I deserved love and security not the twisted life he imposed on me.

T: How do you imagine your father over there would react if he knew how you felt—defensive, remorseful, blaming and angry… ?

C: It's funny—he used to seem so huge and powerful, now I see just a pathetic old man. I don't think he's capable of understanding but it doesn't matter anymore, I know the truth.

In this example, therapist interventions supported the client's adaptive anger at maltreatment and her entitlement to justice, helping her begin to articulate the effects of the abuse and hold the perpetrator accountable for harm. Thus, this process broadens the client's emotional repertoire: guiding her from despair and hate, to assertion, and even later, to accepting personal loss.

Another chief goal here is for clients to begin to have a more realistic perspective of the other. An important step toward this is to elicit the client's understanding of the imagined perpetrator's response to such a confrontation. Enacting or imagining the other can elicit client empathic resources. This can be particularly important in situations when healing attachment relationships is appropriate and important for the client. For example, a client may come to understand that one or both parents had been victims themselves and that they would have regretted their behavior vis-à-vis the client. This was the case with the client Paul, described earlier. In contrast, when healing the attachment relationship is not appropriate, as in the example of Julie, accessing clients' empathic resources by imagining the other's response can help clients view the other as more life-sized and less powerful.

Emotional transformation. Shame and maladaptive self-blame associated with trauma can be transformed by accessing justifiable feelings of anger at the actual perpetrators of harm. The beginning of this pivotal process was illustrated above with Julie. In another example, a woman named "Sally" (Paivio & Pascual-Leone, 2010), diagnosed with depression, describes her relationship with her father, who emotionally abandoned her as a child after her mother had died. The client begins by feeling as though there were something about her that deserved to be rejected. As she explores this feeling there is a sense of anger and, after noticing this, the therapist guides the client's attention toward those aspects of the unfolding experience, thereby transforming her sense of worthlessness into more powerful self-assertion.

C: He was never there for me. All the suffering I put myself through—I guess I have only myself to blame.

T: So, there's this sense of you somehow not deserving love—

C: [*Tears fill her eyes*]. I feel I've had too many losses in my life. It seems so unfair. I had to deal with so much on my own. I hate him for what he did.

T: Tell him what he did. [*Points to empty chair*]

C: [*To her imagined father*] I don't think you realize.… All my relationships, everything has been so much harder…because of the way you treated me. Every single day I've had to fight through that.…

T: What do you resent? Tell him.…

C: I resent you for being so selfish, so inconsiderate and dismissive of me and…and…[*long pause*]…for just never putting me first. [*Pause*] Not that I needed that always.… Oh, I'm just feeling sorry for myself.

T: Ok. Notice that, but try to stay with your resentment for a moment longer.… I know it's difficult but tell him more about your resentment.

C: [*Again, to her imagined father*] It's hard for me to confront you but this I must say: You were not a decent father to me. You abandoned and neglected me...and I'm angry at you for that.

T: So, "I needed your love. And as I child I needed to be put first, at least sometimes."

C: Yes. That's exactly it.

In this example, maladaptive shame undergoes a transformation as subdominant feelings of anger and healthy entitlement are brought to the foreground. Through this process the client eventually expresses adaptive assertive anger, which is supported by the therapist over the course of therapy until it becomes a new healthy part of the client's repertoire.

RESEARCH SUPPORTING THE BENEFITS OF ANGER EXPRESSION IN EMOTION-FOCUSED THERAPY FOR TRAUMA

Several studies support the benefits of adaptive anger expression in EFTT and similar approaches. First, indirect support comes from the results of outcome and process-outcome studies that support the treatment model, in general, with its emphasis on adaptive anger expression (Greenberg & Malcolm, 2002; Paivio & Greenberg, 1995; Paivio, Jarry, Chagigiorgis, Hall, & Ralston, 2010; Paivio & Nieuwenhuis, 2001). Similar results were reported for emotion-focused therapy as a treatment for depression (Greenberg & Watson, 1998; Watson, Gordon, Stermac, Kalogerakos, & Steckley, 2003), in which expression of inhibited anger in loss-related depressions was a key therapy process. Additional support for the benefits of anger expression comes from several studies that specifically examined the role of anger in EFTT.

One study found that upon entering therapy, more than half (64%) of the clients in EFTT identified anger-related problems among the top concerns for which they wanted help (Ralston, 2006). Of these, the most frequently identified were unresolved anger toward perpetrators of abuse and difficulties stemming from limited access to anger experience (e.g., powerlessness, nonassertiveness). Thus, many victims of complex trauma enter therapy with a limited capacity to access anger and its associated healthy strivings. Furthermore, this also indicates that overcoming anger problems is part and parcel of addressing and resolving interpersonal trauma issues.

This speaks to what clients identify as important prior to beginning therapy. Another study (Holowaty & Paivio, 2012) asked clients in EFTT to retrospectively identify aspects of therapy they found most helpful and where these events occurred in therapy. Analyses of videotaped therapy sessions indicated that client-identified helpful events were characterized by high levels of arousal and that in 50% of these events anger was the predominantly expressed emotion. Thus, clients found arousal of anger at maltreatment, in particular, to be helpful. Similarly, in separate research, higher arousal during trauma exploration predicted better outcomes in EFTT, and again, the dominant emotion during those episodes was anger (Ralston, 2006).

Another study directly examined the contributions of anger expression to the resolution of child abuse trauma in EFTT (Paivio & Carriere, 2007). Client dialogues during the imaginal confrontation procedure (99 videotaped episodes taken from 33 different clients) were analyzed using the criteria for healthy anger expression (presented earlier). Results indicated a moderately large relationship ($r > .30$) between healthy anger expression and both the resolution of abuse issues and interpersonal dimensions of change, particularly at 12 months after treatment. Together, these results provide some support for the assertion that healthy anger expression in key therapy situations can have a beneficial effect on outcome in EFTT.

Moreover, treatment principles consistent with EFTT have also recently been applied to the problem of reducing violence, particularly as related to domestic abuse, in a prison population. Research indicated that this approach reduced recidivism rates on par with more established approaches (Pascual-Leone, Bierman, Arnold, & Stasiak, 2011).

Resolution and forgiveness. The construct of forgiveness in EFTT overlaps with, but is not identical to, resolution and is particularly relevant to trauma issues and associated anger problems. Facilitating forgiveness is controversial partly because it sometimes comes with moral and religious imperatives that may seem distasteful to some individuals. It also is unclear whether forgiveness is appropriate when one is confronting situations of extreme cruelty and childhood abuse and whether forgiveness, as a therapeutic outcome, affords additional benefits beyond other forms of resolution (Chagigiorgis & Paivio, 2006). Nonetheless, forgiveness often goes hand in hand with anger and is an important goal for some clients.

Although definitions vary, it is generally accepted that forgiveness does not involve condoning the behavior of offenders and bypassing anger but rather requires acknowledging offenses and working through anger. Widely held definitions also suggest that forgiveness requires both psychological separation from and increased affiliation (i.e., reduced anger) toward the offender. Analyses of interviews with clients who had completed EFTT indicated that, although most clients (82%) reported resolving issues with perpetrators at therapy termination, only a small portion (23%) of those who resolved the trauma issues also reported forgiving their perpetrators (Chagigiorgis & Paivio, 2006). Clients who resolved but did not forgive offenders reported feeling more detached and separate but not less angry (e.g., "I still hate him but I'm not tied up in knots about it anymore. I'm getting on with my life."). Furthermore, it is worth noting that clients more often forgave neglectful, as opposed to abusive, others. These neglectful others tended to be nonprotective mothers. This suggests that clients may be more motivated to forgive primary attachment figures, although this may also be a function of more time in therapy having been spent on issues related to these primary attachment figures. However the case may be, findings show that forgiveness is one of several pathways toward the resolution of troubling anger at perpetrators. For this reason, EFTT does not explicitly advocate forgiveness as a treatment goal but rather leaves this up to the individual client. If forgiveness of the other has been an appropriate and desired goal articulated by the client, then this issue will surface as the client moves closer to resolution and can be supported by the therapist.

CONCLUSION

In conclusion, there is a theoretical and empirical rationale for using an emotion-focused approach to treating some types of anger problems, particularly those associated with complex trauma. Because complex traumatic experiences are intertwined with issues of attachment, interpersonal safety, and profound betrayal, anger in this context is heavily laden with meaning. Changing emotion with emotion is therefore a process that elaborates both feelings and their hereto unarticulated meanings, moment by moment as emotions are experienced and expressed. Working through these issues requires a highly differentiated understanding of different anger processes (productive and unproductive) and goes beyond anger management. It requires helping clients explore the role that anger plays in both obstructing and then facilitating personal change.

REFERENCES

Barlow, D. H. (1988). *Anxiety and its disorders: The nature and treatment of anxiety and panic.* New York, NY: Guilford Press.

Chagigiorgis, H., & Paivio, S. C. (2006). Forgiveness as an outcome in emotion focused therapy for adult survivors of childhood abuse. In W. Malcolm, N. DeCourville, & K. Belicki (Eds.), *Women's perspectives on forgiveness and reconciliation: The complexities of restoring power and connection* (pp. 121–141). New York, NY: Routledge, Taylor & Francis Group.

Cloitre, M., Koenen, K., Dohen, L., & Han, H. (2002). Skills training in affect and interpersonal regulation followed by exposure: A phase-based treatment for PTSD related to childhood abuse. *Journal of Consulting and Clinical Psychology, 70*, 1067–1074.

Courtois, C. A. & Ford, J. D. (Eds.). (2009). *Treatments for complex traumatic stress disorders.* New York, NY: Guilford.

Davanloo, H. (1995). *Unlocking the unconscious: Selected papers of Habib Davanloo.* Oxford, England: John Wiley and Sons.

Deffenbacher, J. L. (1999). Cognitive behavioral conceptualization and treatment of anger. *Journal of Clinical Psychology, 55*, 295–310.

Fernandez, E. (2010). Toward an integrative psychotherapy for maladaptive anger. In M. Potegal, G. Stemmler, & C. Spielberger (Eds.), *The international handbook of anger: Constituent and concomitant biological, psychological, and social processes* (pp. 499–514). New York, NY: Springer.

Ford, J. D. (2005). Treatment implications of altered affect regulation and information processing following child maltreatment. *Psychiatric Annals, 35*(5), 410–419.

Gendlin, E. T. (1996). *Focusing-oriented psychotherapy: A manual of the experiential method.* New York, NY: Guilford.

Greenberg, L. S. (2002). *Emotion-focused therapy: Coaching clients to work through their feelings.* Washington, DC: American Psychological Association.

Greenberg, L. S., & Malcolm, W. (2002). Resolving unfinished business: Relating process to outcome. *Journal of Consulting and Clinical Psychology, 70*(2), 406–416.

Greenberg, L. S., & Paivio, S. C. (1997). *Working with emotions in psychotherapy.* New York, NY: Guilford Press.

Greenberg, L. S., Rice, L. N., & Elliott, R. (1993). *Facilitating emotional change.* New York, NY: Guilford Press

Greenberg, L. S., & Watson, J. (1998). Experiential therapy of depression: Differential effects of client-centered relationship conditions and process experiential interventions. *Psychotherapy Research, 8*, 210–224.

Holowaty, K. A. M., & Paivio, S. C. (2012). Process characteristics of client-identified helpful events in emotion-focused therapy for complex trauma. *Psychotherapy Research, 22*, 56–66.

Holtzworth-Munroe, A., & Clements, K. (2007). The association between anger and male perpetration of intimate partner violence. In T. A. Cavell & K. T. Malcolm (Eds.), *Anger, aggression and interventions for interpersonal violence* (pp. 313–348). Mahwah, NJ: Lawrence Erlbaum Associates Publishers.

Kubany, E. S., Hill, E. E., Owens, J. A., Iannce-Spencer, C., McCaig, M. A., Tremayne, K. J., & Williams, P. L. (2004). Cognitive trauma therapy for battered women with PTSD (CTT-BW). *Journal of Consulting and Clinical Psychology, 72*(1), 3–18.

Linehan, M. M. (1993). *Cognitive-behavioral treatment of borderline personality disorder.* New York, NY: Guilford Press.

Novaco, R. W. (2007). Anger dysregulation. In T. A. Cavell & K. T. Malcolm (Eds.), *Anger, aggression and interventions for interpersonal violence* (pp. 3–54). Mahwah, NJ: Lawrence Erlbaum Associates Publishers.

Paivio, S. C., & Carriere, M. (2007). Contributions of emotion-focused therapy to the understanding and treatment of anger and aggression. In T. A. Cavell & K. T. Malcolm (Eds.), *Anger, aggression and interventions for interpersonal violence* (pp. 143–164). Mahwah, NJ: Lawrence Erlbaum Associates Publishers.

Paivio, S. C., & Greenberg, L. S. (1995). Resolving "unfinished business": Efficacy of experiential therapy using empty-chair dialogue. *Journal of Consulting and Clinical Psychology, 63*(3), 419–425.

Paivio, S. C., Jarry, J. L., Chagigiorgis, H., Hall, I., & Ralston, M. (2010). Efficacy of two versions of emotion-focused therapy for resolving child abuse trauma. *Psychotherapy Research, 20*, 353–366.

Paivio, S. C., & Nieuwenhuis, J. A. (2001). Efficacy of emotion focused therapy for adult survivors of child abuse: A preliminary study. *Journal of Traumatic Stress, 14*(1), 115–133.

Paivio, S. C., & Pascual-Leone, A. (2010). *Emotion focused therapy for complex trauma: An integrative approach.* Washington, DC: American Psychological Association.

Pascual-Leone, A., Bierman, R., Arnold, B., & Stasiak, E. (2011). Emotion-focused therapy for incarcerated offenders of intimate partner violence: A 3-year outcome using a new whole-sample matching method. *Psychotherapy Research, 21*, 331–347.

Pascual-Leone, A., Gillis, P., Singh, T., & Andreescu, C. (in press). Problem anger in psychotherapy: An emotion-focused perspective on hate, rage, and rejecting anger. *Journal of Contemporary Psychotherapy.*

Pascual-Leone, A. & Greenberg, L. S. (2007). Emotional processing in experiential therapy: Why "the only way out is through." *Journal of Consulting and Clinical Psychology, 75*, 875–887.

Pennebaker, J. W., & Campbell, R. S. (2000). The effects of writing about traumatic experiences. *NC-PTSD Clinical Quarterly, 9*, 18–21.

Perls, F. S. (1969). *Gestalt therapy verbatum.* Lafayette, CA: Real People Press.

Ralston, M. (2006). *Emotional arousal and depth of experiencing in imaginal confrontation versus evocative empathy* (Unpublished doctoral dissertation). University of Windsor, Windsor, ON, Canada.

Rogers, C. R. (1957). The necessary and sufficient conditions of therapeutic personality change. *Journal of Consulting Psychology, 21*, 95–103.

Scoboria, A., Ford, J., Hsio-ju, L., & Frisman, L. (May, 2006). *Exploratory and confirmatory factor analysis of the Structured Interview for Disorders of Extreme Stress.*

Paper presented at the Society for the Exploration of Psychotherapy Integration, Los Angeles, CA.

van der Kolk, B., Pelcovitz, D., Roth, S., Mandel, F., McFarlane, A., & Herman, J. (1996). Dissociation, somatization, and affect dysregulation: complexity of adaptation to trauma. *American Journal of Psychiatry, 153*(7 Festschrift Suppl.), 83–93.

Watson, J. C., Gordon, L. B., Stermac, L., Kalogerakos, F., & Steckley, P. (2003). Comparing the effectiveness of Process-Experiential with Cognitive-Behavioral psychotherapy in the treatment of depression. *Journal of Consulting and Clinical Psychology, 71*(4), 773–781.

Wolfe, D. A. (2007). Understanding anger: Key concepts from the field of domestic violence and child abuse. In T. Cavell & K. Malcolm (Eds.), *Anger, aggression and interpersonal violence* (pp. 393–402). Mahwah, NJ: Erlbaum.

Zlotnick, C., Shea, T. M., Rosen, K., Simpson, E., Mulrenin, K., Begin, A., & Pearlstein, T. (1997). An affect-management group for women with posttraumatic stress disorder and histories of childhood sexual abuse. *Journal of Traumatic Stress, 10*(3), 425–436.

4

Regulating Anger in Combat-Related Posttraumatic Stress Disorder

DAVID FORBES, TONY MCHUGH, AND CLAUDE CHEMTOB

Case Vignette

Alan, an unemployed 29-year-old veteran living in a provincial city, is married to Lisa. They have two children, aged 3 and 5. Alan served in Afghanistan, where he experienced a number of contacts with enemy forces, in one of which he and his unit were pinned down by gunfire for a number of hours until reinforcements arrived. Three unit members were killed in this contact. In separate events, Alan also witnessed two explosions of improvised explosive devices (IEDs), one of which resulted in many casualties. Apart from these specific events, Alan described frequent patrolling through towns and villages, during which it was impossible to distinguish "friendly" from "hostile" among the local population. Diagnosed with posttraumatic stress disorder, depression, and alcohol abuse, Alan was medically discharged from the military 2 years previously.

Alan reports marked intrusive memories of his time in Afghanistan, in the form of constant unwanted thoughts and repetitive nightmares. He actively avoids watching the news or reading newspapers due to the distress he experiences when reading about the conflicts in Afghanistan or Iraq. He reports disturbed sleep, poor concentration, significant anxiety, and hypervigilance when driving and when walking among crowds. He feels constantly irritable, is easily frustrated, and is generally negative and angry about most things. Upon discharge from the army, he commenced working as a technician at a local factory but found himself in constant conflict with his employer. Whenever his supervisor asked him to do tasks Alan deemed to be unnecessary, Alan reacted with angry outbursts. He also had altercations with his coworkers when they failed to perform their work to his standard or when they were critical of military action in the Middle East. On a couple of occasions, he was formally reprimanded for making verbal threats of assault. He eventually chose to leave before his employment was terminated.

He describes his marriage as being in crisis, a view shared by Lisa. Although there is an absence of physical violence, there are long periods of withdrawal, marked by intermittent fits of rage, after what he describes as "being nagged endlessly" and feeling cornered by Lisa. Alan also reports rage toward his children when they cry or complain about minor problems. He says he has intrusive images of children killed and injured by the IEDs and "can't stand their whining about nothing." Both particularly occur after a bad night with nightmares.

Alan has no inpatient psychiatric history, but describes a couple of negative experiences with previous therapists and psychiatrists in his local area whom he believed failed to understand the reasons for his anger, as well as his limited capacity to control it and its expression, and blamed and judged him. He subsequently dropped out of these previous attempts at therapy due to anger at the therapists. A recreational user of alcohol prior to deployment, he now drinks a minimum of six cans of beer per weekday and up to two dozen cans per day of the weekend.

THE NATURE OF ANGER IN COMBAT-RELATED POSTTRAUMATIC STRESS DISORDER

Anger features prominently in posttraumatic stress disorder (PTSD), a high-risk problem for combat personnel. It plays an important role in PTSD development, maintenance, and potential response to treatment. In a reciprocal fashion, PTSD plays an important role in the manifestation and expression of anger (Chemtob, Novaco, Hamada, Gross, & Smith, 1997). Anger may also play an important role in the activation of aggressive behavior associated with PTSD. To understand the relationship between these phenomena, this section will outline the nature of PTSD, the relationship between anger and PTSD, and the critical contribution anger makes to PTSD. It will also describe the unique features of the military combat experience that further enhance this relationship.

Posttraumatic Stress Disorder

PTSD is a common psychiatric sequela to exposure to potentially traumatic events. Potentially traumatic events are defined in the *Diagnostic and Statistical Manual of Psychiatric Disorders,* fourth edition (DSM-IV; American Psychiatric Association, 1994), as events the person experienced, witnessed, or was confronted with that involved actual or threatened death or serious injury or a threat to the physical integrity of self or others. Such events include combat, assault, sexual assault, serious accidental injury (most commonly transport injuries), and disasters (both natural and man-made). Exposure rates to such events within the general community are often as high as 60% to 65% (Creamer, Burgess, & McFarlane, 2001; Kessler, Sonnega, Bromet, Hughes, & Nelson, 1995), but these rates increase considerably in past and present members of organizations whose role by definition is to respond to such events, for example, military personnel and members of emergency service organizations, like police, ambulance, and fire services officers.

The prevalence of PTSD following traumatic exposure varies, with lower rates of 5% to 10% reported following noninterpersonal events such as accidental injury and natural disaster and higher rates between 25% and 50% following interpersonal traumas, such as combat and assault, and the highest rates occurring among those exposed to sexual assault (Creamer et al., 2001; Kessler et al., 1995). The likelihood of developing PTSD, however, increases with repeated exposure to such events (Rees et al., 2011).

PTSD is a potentially disabling disorder characterized by three sets of symptoms. The first set reflects a re-experiencing of the traumatic event and includes phenomena such as intrusive thoughts and images of the event, recurrent nightmares, and physical and emotional distress at exposure to reminders of the event. The second set comprises avoidance and numbing symptoms. These include active avoidance of thoughts and feelings of the event and places or activities that act as event reminders and interpersonal detachment and numbing of affect. While the active avoidance and numbing symptoms are included as one symptom cluster in DSM-IV, they are more accurately considered as composing two subclusters and are likely to be separated in the DSM-5, due for release in 2013. The final set comprises hyperarousal symptoms, which include disturbances in sleep and concentration, exaggerated startle, and hypervigilance. This symptom cluster also includes experiencing a lower threshold for irritability and an increased readiness for anger. Data emerging from studies of military personnel serving in Iraq and Afghanistan indicate that anger and aggression are most strongly associated with the hyperarousal cluster of symptoms (Elbogen et al., 2010). Some authors have suggested that PTSD with high anger may be a subtype of PTSD (McHugh, Forbes, Bates, Hopwood & Creamer, 2012; Novaco & Chemtob, 2002).

The Relationship Between Anger and Posttraumatic Stress Disorder

Importantly, a diagnosis of PTSD rarely exists in isolation. Most commonly, PTSD is comorbid with depression, other anxiety disorders, and substance use disorders. Rates of comorbidity in combat veterans have been reported to be as high as 90% (Kulka et al., 1990; O'Toole et al., 1996).

A range of broader psychopathological features are also associated with PTSD. Such features include trauma-related guilt and, importantly, anger and aggression. Although, and as foreshadowed earlier, anger and irritability are symptoms within the hyperarousal cluster of PTSD, the impact of anger on PTSD far exceeds what might be expected from its status as a single PTSD criterion. Illustrative of this, a range of studies describe anger as a key characteristic of PTSD (Frueh, Henning, Pellegrin, & Chobot, 1997; Novaco & Chemtob, 2002; Orth & Wieland, 2006) and a critical predictor of PTSD severity (Andrews, Brewin, Rose, & Kirk, 2000; Frueh et al., 1997; Orth & Maercker, 2009; Orth & Wieland, 2006). In addition, rumination associated with anger also has a substantial effect on PTSD (Orth, Cahill, Foa, & Maercker, 2008), and ruminative style appears closely linked to PTSD's re-experiencing symptom cluster (Orth & Wieland, 2006). Moreover, successful treatment of anger is associated with significant decreases in PTSD symptomatology even among patients with very severe PTSD (Chemtob, Novaco, Hamada, & Gross, 1997; Morland et al., 2010), with some suggesting that up to 40% of PTSD score variance may be attributable to anger (Novaco & Chemtob, 2002).

Problematic anger associated with PTSD has been demonstrated across a broad array of trauma-exposed populations. Most often, it has been reported in military personnel and veterans of various wars, role types (from infantry soldiers to cooks and including combatants, peacekeepers, and peacemakers), and nations and cultures (such as combatants from Holland, Belgium, the United Kingdom, the United States, and Australia; see David et al., 2002; Elbogen et al., 2010; Hovens et al., 1992; Jakupcak et al., 2007; Johnson et al., 1996; O'Toole et al., 1996). Importantly, problematic anger has also been identified as significant in other PTSD populations. These include those occupationally at risk for PTSD, for example, emergency services personnel and disaster relief workers (Evans, Giosan, Patt, Spielman, & Difede, 2006; Mearns & Mauch, 1998), crime victims (Feeny, Zoellner, & Foa, 2000; Zoellner, Goodwin, & Foa, 2000), survivors of torture (Dunnegan, 1997), civilian casualties of war (Toren, Wolmer, Weizman, Magal-Vardi, & Laor, 2002), and transport accidents (Ehlers & Clark, 2000). The largest effect sizes, however, in the association between anger and PTSD (weighted mean effect size $r = .56$) are evident in military veterans (Orth & Wieland, 2006).

From such research, it is clear that problematic anger in PTSD is neither population nor trauma-type specific. In 1994, Lasko and colleagues (Lasko, Gurvits, Kuhne, Orr, & Pitman, 1994) observed, "Increased aggression in war veterans is more appropriately regarded as a property of PTSD, rather than a direct consequence of military combat" (p. 373). Twelve years later, in the first meta-analysis undertaken in the area, Orth and Wieland (2006) re-emphasized this, concluding, "Anger and hostility are substantially related to PTSD among samples who have experienced all possible types of traumatic events, not only in individuals with combat-related PTSD" (p. 704). Consequently, the particular relationship anger has with PTSD is increasingly understood as critical.

The presence of anger has been demonstrated to influence the development of PTSD (Koenen, Stellman, Stellman, & Sommer, 2003), create increased risk of harm to self (Dyer et al., 2009) and others (Barrett, Mills, & Teesson, 2011; Beckham, Moore, & Reynolds, 2000; Finley, Baker, Pugh, & Peterson, 2010), and act as a key factor in PTSD maintenance (Jayasinghe, Giosan, Evans, Spielman, & Difede, 2008). Anger has also been found to negatively influence the outcome of PTSD treatment in combat veterans (Foa, Riggs, Massie, & Yarczower, 1995; Forbes, Creamer, Hawthorne, Allen, & McHugh, 2003; Forbes et al., 2008) and peacekeepers (Forbes et al., 2005) and heighten risk of treatment dropout (Rizvi, Vogt, & Resick, 2009; Stevenson & Chemtob, 2000).

The Combat Veteran Experience

To better understand the nature of anger in combat-related PTSD, it is necessary to understand key elements of the military experience. These extend across the training environment and the battlefield.

Military training. The first issue to consider is the impact of military training. Such training includes a number of elements, which, while critical in forming an effective combat force, increase the salience of anger. An essential component of combat training is to get potential combatants to override their instinctive reactions of fear and avoidance to threat by replacing it with an automatic mobilizing response that includes confrontation with the source of threat. This includes training and language to override or minimize the inhibition against the potential use of lethal force (McGurk, Cotting, Britt, & Adler, 2006). This training may involve careful use of terms to describe the enemy; de-emphasizing the enemy's humanity, for example, by using words like "target" and "source of threat"; or demonizing the enemy (Grossman, 1997). This training also includes reinforcement of the potential life-and-death implications of values and behaviors such as trust, dependability, reliability, punctuality, and attention to detail in the war zone. Such training is, of course, further reinforced in the war zone by "on the job" experience.

Combat exposure. Added to the effect of military training is the impact of the combat service itself. Here we need to consider both the prolonged periods of arousal and vigilance in addition to the burden of often repeated trauma exposure. Modern warfare often offers no "front lines." Whether in Vietnam, Iraq, or Afghanistan, it is difficult to distinguish combatants from noncombatants (Maguen et al., 2010). In the context of the source of threat not being easily identifiable, the veteran may experience prolonged periods of hyperarousal and hypervigilance, driven by the possibility of not only missing the source of a potential threat but also responding in error of action or judgment with lethal force to noncombatants. Either possibility bears potentially catastrophic consequences. Often veterans report the relief they experienced when after days on patrol, enemy contact occurred and a "fire fight" ensued, offering an opportunity for action and discharge of arousal and the replacement of unknown threat by tangible menace. Similarly, in the context of combat errors associated with catastrophic outcomes, mistakes can cause death of friends and place the combatant at risk.

Combat deployments are often associated with multiple potentially traumatic events. These exposures include not only threats to life or physical integrity, potential use of lethal force against enemy combatants, or unintended responsibility for the deaths of civilians but also exposure to the broader horrors of war. This might include witnessing the perpetration or aftermath of atrocities (Litz et al., 2009). Such events lead to cynicism about human nature, anger and its accompanying retribution against perpetrators, and resentment toward authorities perceived as allowing this to happen. In all these contexts, anger serves as a potentially survival-enhancing, priming mechanism. When deregulated, this anger mechanism can make a significant contribution to unacceptable violence, such as that observed in soldiers consumed by "berserk rage" (Shay, 1995).

Malevolent environment. Compounding the aforementioned effects are the impacts of the physical environment. Not uncommonly, the war veteran is deployed in a hostile physical environment. Be it the jungles of Vietnam or the suffocating heat and sandstorms of the Middle East or so-called high-altitude Alpine warfare, the inhospitable physical environment also increases stress and irritability, draining coping resources and posing an increased risk for psychological harm (King, King, Gudanowski, & Vreven, 1995). Included in these environmental factors can also be the "culture shock" experienced by troops from first world countries when fighting battles or conducting peacekeeping missions in developing countries or when exposed to the often impoverished standards of living of the local population. This culture shock may enhance readjustment problems on returning home. Family, friends, and acquaintances may express discontent or complaints at trials and tribulations of daily life that the military veteran regards as trivial, given not only their military experience but also their exposure to the "real" hardships of life in other cultural environments. This may also prompt anger toward people at home who "just don't get it."

Posttraumatic Stress Disorder, Anger, and the Veteran Experience

From this, a picture can be drawn of the combat veteran with PTSD and problematic anger. He or she will typically be experiencing the effects of the following:

- Active PTSD, colored by a strong, current sense of threat, derived from potent intrusive memories of military and combat-related traumatic experiences. For example, this may include persistent sleep disturbance and distressing trauma-related nightmares.
- Chronic irritable hyperarousal diminishing the war veterans' cognitive and emotional coping resources over time. This is due in part to delayed or inadequate treatment.
- Anger of significant frequency, intensity, and prolongation. This propensity for anger is influenced by military training, which primes anger in order to facilitate functioning in the face of not only identifiable threat and stress but also negative affect and confusion.
- Peremptory mobilization of angry and confrontational responses to threat, stress, anxiety, and other dysphoric emotions, resulting in out-of-proportion responses to everyday events, such as what children may or may not eat for dinner
- A loss of conscious awareness of perceptual, cognitive, emotive, and behavioral patterns, such that there is a constant, extremely sensitive, and highly coherent networked response to any and all of a wide range of cues and triggers. Here, any experience of difference or ambiguity may be viewed as threatening,
- A loss of trust in others', and especially authorities', capacity to protect and prevent harm, resulting in an ongoing struggle with responsibility and accountability of the self and others
- An ongoing maintenance of values and actions relevant to military, but not domestic, life, for example, orderliness, dependability, team-honoring and "crisis-averting" punctuality, agreement keeping, and attention to detail
- Feelings of being misunderstood, abandoned, and alienated by the (military included) world, particularly so in the case of conflicts that become unpopular (e.g., Vietnam), where military personnel are ostracized and rejected
- Consequently, a raised propensity for aggressive behavior, especially when first returned home from battle

THEORIES ACCOUNTING FOR ANGER IN COMBAT-RELATED POSTTRAUMATIC STRESS DISORDER AND IMPLICATIONS FOR INTERVENTION

Theories Accounting for Anger in Posttraumatic Stress Disorder

In considering approaches to treatment, it is worth outlining theoretical bases of the relationship between anger and traumatic stress. Three streams of research and theory have considered the causal contribution of anger in PTSD. The first stream emphasizes the role of personality-related variables in the enduring nature of anger in PTSD; the second and third streams examine the role of cognitive and affective variables, respectively. Let us briefly explore each.

Temperament-related theoretical models. One of the more prominent models of the structure of psychiatric comorbidity and its relation to dimensions of temperament was proposed by Krueger (1999). Using the National Comorbidity Survey (NCS) data, Krueger (1999) found that an internalizing/externalizing model, drawn from Achenbach's (1995) internalizing/externalizing model for children, best fit the data. The internalizing factor included the anxiety and mood disorders; the externalizing factor included antisocial behavior and substance abuse disorders. Miller and colleagues (Miller, Greif, & Smith, 2003) drew on the work of Krueger (1999) and sought to test whether clinically meaningful subtypes differing in propensities toward internalizing versus externalizing comorbidity would be observed within a U.S. veteran PTSD sample. They demonstrated that the externalizing personality style, characterized by high negative emotion and low behavioral constraint, was associated with antisociality and aggression in PTSD (Miller et al., 2003; Miller, Kaloupek, Dillon, & Keane, 2004; Miller & Resick, 2007). This model has also been replicated in Australian veteran samples (Forbes, Elhai, Miller, & Creamer, 2010). However, while these temperament-focused studies have identified aggression to be associated with the externalizing subtype, the relationship between anger and the two PTSD subtypes has not been systematically evaluated. Notwithstanding the potential importance of such lines of enquiry, the breadth of such personality-influenced research is relatively limited. Although writing about anger rather than anger in PTSD, Fernandez (2008) pointed out that personality dimensions of anger include not only "internalizing" versus "externalizing" but also at least five other dimensions. Fernandez (2008) further noted that all such notions have been minimally researched.

Cognition-based theoretical models. More common is a second stream of research in which investigators have hypothesized about the influence of cognitive variables on anger in PTSD. There are two current explanatory positions that summarize thinking about this relationship.

One is the *Survival Mode Theory* (Novaco & Chemtob, 1998). Initially posited by Chemtob and colleagues (Chemtob, Roitblat, Hamada, Carlson, & Twentyman, 1988), it hypothesized that the "survival mode" of functioning has an evolutionary base that is activated in the context of threat. This mode of functioning is characterized by a narrowing of attention to threat-related cues, hostile appraisal of ambiguous stimuli, and mobilization of peremptory threat-related responses including anger and aggression. Although such mode is adaptive at times of traumatic threat such as combat, it is maladaptive and inappropriate where it persists in civilian contexts. Loss of self-monitoring, hostile appraisal, rapid escalation of arousal, and consequent antagonistic or aggressive behavior may then serve to maintain the perception of threat, preventing modification of cognitive schema (Novaco & Chemtob, 1998) and sustaining an increased facilitation of reacting to nonsurvival situations as if they were survival-related contexts. Take, for example, the instance of Alan reacting to mistakes made by coworkers with rage and anger. In a civilian context, making errors in most instances is not likely to cause a life-threatening situation. However, in a combat zone failing to follow procedures designed to reduce the risk of triggering an improvised explosive device is critical to saving lives. Thus, a person with PTSD who has an increased readiness to perceive events using a survival mode of perception and response will also be more likely to judge an inconsequential mistake as one involving potential loss of life. In turn, such judgements will trigger anger that will appear highly disproportionate to those who are not functioning in survival mode. Chemtob, Novaco, Hamada, Gross, and Smith (1997) described the interrelationship of anger and PTSD information processing in detail, positing that anger and fear-related networks become intertwined and act to mutually facilitate activation. The theory was used in a study of combat veterans by Taft and colleagues (Taft, Vogt, Marshall, Panuzio, & Niles, 2007) to interpret negative affect in PTSD as connected through associative networks with anger-related feelings, thoughts, memories, and aggressive inclinations.

The second construct derives from Berkowitz's *Neo-Associationist Memory Networking* model of anger. This model hypothesizes the involvement of a constellation of related physiological, motoric, and cognitive "responses" associated with the inclination to defend against or attack a target (Berkowitz, 1990). This is a learning-based theory that holds that aversive stimulation predisposes the individual to negative affect, thereby activating connected feelings, thoughts, memories, and motor impulses to the anger response (Wranik & Scherer, 2010). Berkowitz does not deny the role of appraisals in anger development and maintenance, but he emphasizes that anger is not only driven by "top-down" cognitive processes but is also affected by "bottom-up" processes as permitted in his model. Given the breadth of his neo-associationist model, Berkowitz's theory is capable of accommodating other contemporary models of anger in PTSD theories about anger in PTSD.

Affect-related theory. Another explanatory model to account for the prominence of anger in PTSD is the primary–secondary *Emotion Substitution Proposition.* Most recently described by Feeny and colleagues (Feeny et al., 2000), this has its antecedents in the research of Riggs and colleagues (Riggs, Dancu, Gershuny, Greenberg, & Foa, 1992) into female victims of crime and the anger-as-secondary-emotion understanding of Greenberg and Paivio (1997) and more recently in relation to trauma specifically by Paivio and Pascual-Leone (2010). This theory posits that anger can be experienced as preferential to underlying aversive, dysphoric states. Applied in its original form to explain the relationship of certain forms of anxiety to anger, it has been observed that in PTSD anger deflects sufferers from intrusion-activated fear to a state less associated with feelings of vulnerability.

A Contemporary Understanding of Anger in Posttraumatic Stress Disorder Based on Current Anger-Specific Theorizing

We have synthesized descriptive characteristics from such accounts of anger in PTSD into five groupings in Table 4.1. The first group understands anger in PTSD as characterized by emotional dyscontrol in the absence of self-monitoring, due to lack of awareness or the individual's fear experience. The second views it as involving overarching, pervasive, and persistent intense feelings that are resistant to change. The third emphasizes that anger in PTSD occurs with what we term *an overarching coherence* in which anger is linked with other feelings in an affective memory network. The fourth sees it as characterized by distorted and heightened cognitive processes and angry rumination. The final group considers anger in PTSD as associated with social aggression, alienation, and a loss of social connection.

Table 4.1 KEY CHARACTERISTICS OF ANGER IN POSTTRAUMATIC STRESS DISORDER SUGGESTED BY CONTEMPORARY THEORETICAL MODELS

Characteristic	Product of Characteristic
1. ***A loss of volition***	• Highly automated, disproportionate, and seemingly out of control; cognitive, affective, physiological, and behavioral responses to anger triggers • A diminished ability to monitor the self, thereby resulting in a loss of awareness of the experience and expression of anger (See Chemtob, Novaco, Hamada, Gross, & Smith, 1997; Novaco & Chemtob, 1998)
2. Extreme pervasiveness	• Contemporaneous cognitive, affective, physiological, and behavioral responding that recursively links more and more into a networked response to anger triggers • A tendency for anger to occur secondarily to other emotions, especially anxiety, while existing as superordinate in status to such affects (See Feeny et al., 2000; Taft et al., 2007)
3. Overarching coherence	• A frequency of anger that suggests it to be all-consuming • An intensity of feeling extending to explosiveness, intense cynicism, hatred, or rage • A longevity of feeling marked by preoccupation, a smoldering disposition, and rumination (See Chemtob, Novaco, Hamada, Gross, & Smith, 1997; Novaco & Chemtob, 1998)
4. Distorted and heightened cognitive processes	• A loss of ability to discriminate between significant and insignificant anger triggers • Appraisals and attributions that go beyond mere externalization of cause to fervent blaming, a powerful sense of being wronged, and ruminative preoccupation with what happened and who allowed it to happen (See Feeny et al., 2000; Taft et al., 2007)
5. Loss of connectedness to others	• High negative emotion • Low behavioral constraint • Aggression (See Forbes et al., 2002; Forbes et al., 2008; Forbes, Elhai et al., 2010; Miller, 2003; Miller & Resick, 2007)

Implications for Treatment of Anger in Posttraumatic Stress Disorder

Before detailing interventions for anger in PTSD, it is important to briefly review current evidence-based interventions for PTSD. Descriptions of interventions for anger in PTSD can then be considered in the context of general PTSD treatment. In terms of PTSD treatment, there is consensus in international guidelines that the most effective treatments for PTSD are those that directly address the experience of the traumatic event, what might be called trauma-focused psychological treatment (Forbes, Creamer, et al., 2010). Such trauma-focused interventions stand in contrast to palliative symptom management–focused interventions such as stress, anxiety, or arousal management. Evidence-based trauma-focused interventions include trauma-focused cognitive-behavioral therapy (CBT) interventions. The two trauma-focused CBT interventions with the strongest evidence bases are prolonged exposure (PE; Foa & Rothbaum, 1998) and to a lesser extent cognitive processing therapy (CPT; Resick and Schnicke, 1993). There is also a considerable evidence base for the use of eye movement desensitization and reprocessing (EMDR; Shapiro, 2001) in the treatment of PTSD. These interventions vary in their techniques, but they have three common elements: (a) engagement with and processing of the traumatic memory: This includes accessing the cognitive, affective, and physiological components of the fear structure; promoting habituation to modification(s) of these components; and integrating the memory with broader autobiographical memory; (b) identification and alteration of recovery-impeding and memory-associated maladaptive cognitions and appraisals; and (c) identification and systematic confrontation of currently avoided activities associated with the trauma memory.

These guidelines, and the previously cited empirical and theoretical literature regarding the relationship between anger and PTSD, indicate three "good practice points" in the treatment of anger in PTSD. First, interventions for combat-related PTSD and anger should not be considered in isolation of each other. This is because the cognitive, affective, physiological, and behavioral components of anger are incorporated within the traumatic memories of PTSD. As such, there is a bidirectional relationship between them that is best addressed simultaneously.

Second, it needs to be recognized that, due to a range of factors, effective treatment is necessarily slowed where there is significant anger in PTSD among military personnel and veteran clients (Forbes et al., 2002; Forbes, Creamer, Allen, et al., 2003; Forbes et al., 2005; Forbes et al., 2008a). In general terms, this is because anger undermines the therapeutic alliance so necessary to treatment progress, and as observed by Deffenbacher (2011), the initial treatment task with angry clients is often first and foremost one of keeping them in treatment. Critically, this is partly because anger has the potential to impede or divert the accessing and emotional processing of the fear and vulnerability components of the traumatic memory. Equally critically, it is also because significant anger potentiates such memories (McHugh et al., 2012). Factors that act as a treatment efficacy barrier in this sense might include peremptory hostile appraisal and mobilization for action (Novaco & Chemtob, 1998) or emotion substitution (Riggs et al., 1992). The end result is that, until effectively treated, clients can be caught in an illness labyrinth, where they escape neither the distress and impairment associated with dysfunctional anger and the traumatic memory nor their reciprocal interaction.

Finally, there is potential for mistrust and processing biases toward threat detection and hostile appraisal (Chemtob et al., 1988; Novaco & Chemtob, 2002) associated with anger in traumatized populations to interfere with the development of stabilizing relationships. Such processing biases prevent or impede engagement in the interpersonal alliances required (therapeutic or personal in social support) to offer a sufficiently "safe" environment to facilitate the accessing of and modification (emotional processing) to the traumatic memory and result in premature termination of therapy (Stevenson & Chemtob, 2000).

INTERVENTIONS FOR ANGER REGULATION IN POSTTRAUMATIC STRESS DISORDER

It is not the purpose of this chapter to detail a comprehensive, evidence-based protocol for the treatment of problematic anger. Such protocols are detailed elsewhere in the published literature (e.g., Deffenbacher, 2011) and their content is described in other chapters of this book. Rather, it seeks to illuminate critical facets of treatment that need to be incorporated if effective interventions are to be applied to anger in the context of combat-related PTSD. Two treatment content issues need to be addressed for this to occur. The first relates to necessary modifications of current evidence-based CBT approaches to the treatment of anger to the population of combat veterans with PTSD. The second involves the sometime necessity of sequencing interventions for anger and PTSD. In some respects, some of what follows may appear common sense to experienced treaters of angry clients. However, failure to treat according to these twin treatment facets will be potentially invalidating and alienating of members of the target client group.

In the sections that follow, we will sequentially work through treatment tactics and strategies that fall within each group of issues. To provide tangible and practical illustrations of the means of delivery, we will in several instances refer back to the case vignette described at the chapter's start. Prior to doing so, we wish to again reinforce the importance of understanding the sensitive and cautious approach required to treat anger in PTSD. It has previously been observed that it is difficult to maintain treatment participation in angry, PTSD-affected populations, the military and veteran community included. That this could be an unintended outcome of suboptimally delivered treatment of anger in PTSD would be ironic and most unfortunate, particularly as the need for additional interventions in PTSD where anger is prominent has been well argued elsewhere (see Pitman et al., 1991; Stapleton, Taylor, & Asmundson, 2006).

To return to the starting vignette, the potential client, Alan, described negative experiences with previous treaters whereby he (a) believed the reasons for his anger were not understood, (b) believed his capacity to control his anger and its expression were overestimated, and (c) felt blamed and judged. He subsequently dropped out of treatment due to anger at the therapists. The bedrock of anger treatment is to keep angry clients in treatment, at times almost against their inclination to flee and thereby avoid further hurt (including damage to treaters); Alan's experience was indeed unfortunate and to be actively countered.

Modifications of Cognitive-Behavioral Therapy for Anger in Combat Veterans With Posttraumatic Stress Disorder

There are seven treatment elements that make up the evidence-based CBT approach to the management of problematic anger (Deffenbacher, 2011):

1. Motivational interviewing techniques to identify and enhance levels of treatment readiness
2. Empathic assessment to increase therapeutic engagement and alliance
3. Idiopathic functional assessment, including self-monitoring to determine anger frequency, intensity, and situational triggers; cognitive appraisals; and subsequent anger-related responses and consequences

4. Cognitive interventions to address maladaptive anger-generating thoughts and images, schematic biases in the appraisal, and distorted information processing
5. Relaxation interventions to lower baseline levels of physiological and emotional arousal
6. Behavioral interventions, which include brief interventions to address immediate high-risk situations in addition to skill building to address habitual patterns of responses, including assertiveness and communication skills training and problem solving
7. Generation and incremental processing of a hierarchy of potentially provocative scenarios, via imaginal (and if possible in vivo) exposure

Implicit in these principles, although not always stated, is the importance of separating anger from associated tendencies, such as aggression and violence, and carefully managing risk around them. Accordingly, this chapter, although focused on the affect of anger and its role in PTSD, endorses the need to assess thoroughly for, and effectively address, such tendencies in clients with PTSD-related anger as a matter of practice.

All of these treatment components have a strong evidence base and are relevant for the use of anger management interventions across populations, including those suffering PTSD. On the basis, however, of that described earlier, the following modifications to these interventions are required for effective treatment of anger in combat-related PTSD.

Emphasizing the relationship between anger and military trauma. It is first critical to provide a model whereby anger dysregulation can be understood as strongly influenced by the military and combat trauma context. Regardless of the veracity of their testimony, many, if not most, military personnel and veterans express the belief that anger dysregulation and aggression were not problematic for them before their military service. To provide a model whereby the development of anger can be contextualized within the individual's military and combat trauma experiences can prove critical not only for engagement but also in setting up the focus of the interventions to be provided. Important to this is the introduction of session content underscoring that anger is understandable after the experience of military trauma where malevolence and morally culpable actions are typically part of the experience and a natural element of the general human response to trauma. It is useful here to explain that not all traumas have the same impact and that anger can vary according to trauma type, combat-related trauma being among the most provoking of anger. This learning point can be emphasized by simple visual representations such as those in Table 4.2.

Simultaneously, deploying any or all of the previously described theoretical explanations of anger in PTSD, it can be useful to explain that, although other underlying emotions, such as fear, worry, sadness, guilt, disgust, or grief, are prominent sequelae of trauma, many trauma-affected people default to angry cognition, affect, and behavior on the basis of its psychologically integrating effect. It is again useful here to validate anger conceptually, while not colluding with specific client instances of problematic anger. This is especially true for any tendency toward aggression as an outcome of or means to solving dilemmas and conflicts. Thus, it can be useful to convey that anger is an enabling emotion with positive functions that permits increased functionality in the face of threat, but aggression is

Table 4.2 The Association Between Anger and Traumatic Events

	Cause	Category	Example
↑ ANGER	Human	Intentional (acts of commission)	• Terrorism/atrocities • Warfare • Sabotage/fire setting
		Accidents/failures (acts of omission)	• Mechanical • Human error
	Nature related	Human compounded	• Failure to maintain • Disease • Famine
		Environment only	• Earth, air, fire, and water

unacceptable in the hurt that it typically does to others and (in a key motivational point) the self.

Finally, at this time, it is also important to emphasize that anger can be difficult to recognize for various reasons. These include (a) the impact of military training, where mobilizing responses to confront threat and override or suppress fear and anxiety are intensively instilled; (b) the operation of trauma–sensory–memory–affect networks (which attach to day-to-day sounds, sights, smells, and bodily sensations to trauma-related affects); (c) shifts to survival mode under threatening, stressful, or ambiguous situations and an out-of-conscious-awareness loss of self-monitoring; (d) cognitive (mis)appraisals that tend to confirm the presence of threat and lead to defensive and rapid escalation of arousal, including mobilization of anger and aggression; and, ultimately, (e) developing the acknowledgement that, while adaptive to functioning in the military/combat environment, such combat-related anger is actually maladaptive and ultimately counterproductive outside the combat world.

To briefly return to our vignette about Alan, it is important to recall that he experienced a number of contacts in his combat role, one of which involved the death of three comrades (each of which may have assumed an interpersonal relationship intensity akin to family for Alan); exposure to collateral casualties via improvised explosive devices; and generally being exposed to situations where foe could not be separated from ally. The importance of working through military trauma and at times military culture issues in this sense is axiomatic and not to be overlooked.

Addressing central self-monitoring deficits. It is also critical to establish a base from which interventions aimed at interrupting a self-confirmatory process of threat detection, mobilization, and escalation and consequent responses can be implemented. Although self- monitoring is included in both interventions for anger and PTSD, it needs to be understood that self-monitoring deficits are striking in this population. Consistent with the dominant PTSD theories and those related to anger in PTSD, when the traumatic memory is activated in the context of exposure to triggers and reminders, the PTSD sufferer responds to current context triggers of past event memories as threats. In this context, there is a loss of self-monitoring ability and reduced capacity therefore to intervene and manage their internal state and consequent behavior. Self-monitoring interventions for PTSD and anger (Novaco & Chemtob, 1998) include helping the client to (a) monitor cognitions he or she typically experiences when threatened or provoked; (b) identify signs of arousal in response to the perception of danger or threat; (c) recognize the role anger reactions play, both in response to sensing danger and as behaviors that create danger for others, thereby escalating the potential threat of a situation; and (d) distinguish impulsive actions from controlled responses. Each of these interventions is again most effective when illustrated with some military experience content. This can again be seen in Alan's experience. To recall, he actively avoids watching the news or reading newspapers due to the potential for distress; he reports concentration difficulties, anxiety, and hypervigilance (and, most likely given this array of symptoms, is prone to periods of dissociation); and he feels constantly irritable, easily frustrated, and generally negative and angry about most things. From the nonjudgmental viewpoint as advocated by Deffenbacher (2011), this is a telling example of a man who is profoundly unaware of his experience of anger and its consequences.

Nuancing robust CBT interventions. It is also the case that the efficacy of CBT anger interventions will be enhanced where military and combat-related PTSD-specific themes are woven into the central focus of treatment in the manner we propose. This can be done by exploring how appraisals identified in anger episodes are connected to trauma-related themes, such as threat during military operations, hostility and rejection experienced upon return (particularly for Vietnam veterans), and trust in nonmilitary others.

As part of this treatment thrust, it will also be important to incorporate brief CBT interventions—particularly cognitive disputation and self-instruction training—to reduce misinterpretation of cues and triggers and broaden attention beyond such cues. It is often very useful, as part of this emphasis, to carefully introduce typically crucial anger cost–benefit work for enabling clients to reflect upon and critically review the contingencies associated with operating in a mode where anger-related cognition, affect, physiological responses, and behaviors are networked and there is emotion avoidance and survival focus. Although typically applied early in treatment, this technique can be an important prequel to separating combat enemies from family, friends, associates, and civilian others.

Equally, the benefits of being in charge of one's anger need to be emphasized. Here, it should be stressed from the outset that managing anger does not equate to suppressing anger, keeping a lid on things, or avoiding situations. Furthermore, it is emphasized that functional people do not typically volitionally seek to be angry and that it is in part the seductive and camouflaging nature of anger where the consequences of one's anger cannot be foreseen. As such, anger is viewed positively for its potential benefit prospectively, while any damage it typically causes becomes obvious retrospectively.

Brief physical interventions such as controlled breathing may be helpful in short-circuiting escalations of arousal. It is crucially important to also lower both baseline and in-the-moment levels of hyperarousal for angry military personnel and veterans. Relaxation interventions are a routine but important anger management tactic for lowering baseline levels of physiological and emotional arousal. They are often difficult to implement, because combat veterans with PTSD, following prolonged and possibly multiple tours of duty in hostile environments, often have long histories of above-average levels of physical tension without being aware of this.

It is important to note here that, given the visually intrusive nature of traumatic memories, non-imagery-based relaxation interventions, such as progressive muscle relaxation, minimize the potential for unintended imaginal activation of traumatic memories and dissociation and therefore are strongly preferred. Such physically based interventions also have the added benefit of directly addressing the physical tension associated with hypervigilance and hyperarousal. It needs to be reiterated, however, that specific planning and effort are required to counter the potential for paradoxical reactions to relaxation in military personnel.

To conclude this section on the need to modify CBT anger interventions for anger in combat-related PTSD, we refer to Alan again. The oscillation of feelings from intense arousal to avoidance is palpable in his self-report. He describes his marriage as being in crisis, with long periods of withdrawal, marked by intermittent fits of rage, and high levels of intrusive symptomatology. Helping Alan by emphasizing the relationship between anger and military trauma and increasing his ability to self-monitor his dire levels of anger are of crucial importance here. It is also crucially important that this and other proven CBT interventions are applied with the required finesse. This is nowhere more obvious than in the need to sequence interventions, as this next subsection demonstrates.

Anger and Posttraumatic Stress Disorder: Treatment Sequencing

It is important that treatment of anger in military personnel with PTSD considers the issue of intervention sequencing—that is, the nature and timing of the interventions. As previously outlined, the cornerstone of PTSD treatment is trauma-focused interventions. However, these trauma-focused interventions need to be considered in the context of a broader, phased approach to treatment. A useful model for phased psychological treatment of PTSD was provided by Keane and Kaloupek (1995), who described a five-phased model. The first phase addressed stabilization and education. This includes stabilizing acute psychiatric symptoms, including potential suicidality, severe substance dependence, or acute stressors or crises. Education here focuses on the nature of PTSD and rationale for treatment. The second phase was termed anxiety management. This phase often overlaps with the first and includes introducing a range of anxiety management strategies or broader symptom management skills to provide some immediate symptom relief in addition to aiding the veterans' confidence in addressing the next phase, which is the trauma-focused phase of treatment. Within this phased model trauma-focused work is undertaken in two parts, the first being exposure and the second cognitive restructuring, although a range of trauma-focused interventions beyond prolonged exposure, such as cognitive processing therapy, may also be considered here. Finally, treatment concludes with interventions addressing relapse prevention.

Depending on the nature and prominence of psychopathology associated with the PTSD, there are important clinical decisions to be made about the time, focus, and depth of interventions at this second, symptom management, treatment phase. In this context, it is critical that the severity of anger problems, including the potential for aggression, is taken into account when making decisions about the extent of anger-focused interventions to be provided at this point prior to the delivery of trauma-focused interventions. There is a growing body of literature suggesting that trauma-focused interventions for PTSD also result in improvements in associated anger (Cahill, Rauch, Hembree, & Foa, 2003; Stapleton et al., 2006). In addition, reductions in PTSD symptom severity following trauma-focused treatment can result in fewer triggers for anger-related cognitive, emotional, physiological, and behavioral responses; lower the overall baseline arousal; and release cognitive and emotional resources to be harnessed in regulating residual anger problems.

Therefore, in the context of PTSD associated with mild anger problems, there is a case for the most efficient and parsimonious approach to treatment. This equates to brief inclusion of anger-focused interventions as adjunctive with other arousal management interventions (e.g., anxiety management) in preparation for and in parallel with trauma-focused treatment.

There is, of course, the strong likelihood that in this population there will be presentations involving severe anger problems that will interfere with sustained engagement in treatment and effective emotional processing of the traumatic memory. There are a range of features that would indicate the need to substantively address anger and aggression prior to treating the core PTSD symptoms through trauma-focused interventions.

The first indication is the presence of anger or aggressive behaviors that represent a threat to the individual or others. Although it is not the focus of this chapter, the potential for aggression in angry individuals and groups with PTSD must be assessed. Specific attention should be given to both the presence of and potential for aggression and violence in intimate relationships. Domestically violent perpetrators are well documented as having higher trait levels of anger, insecure attachment that perpetuates anger, and higher levels of personality-related anger (Dutton, 2010). The assessment process should include a session with the partner and, where appropriate, other family members. *This session should not be conducted in the presence of the identified client.* This assessment may act as another source of information about the client's current and past levels of violence, readiness to change, and violence potential. Sessions with the family can only be conducted when the partner and children feel safe in the counseling session, as well as outside the session.

There are a range of measures for assessing patterns and risks of aggression. These are well described in the literature (see, e.g., Eckhardt, Norlander, & Deffenbacher, 2004). Good practice requires that they are applied as part of the anger assessment that must precede treatment commencement and are addressed as a priority and thereby manage extant risks so as to not further potentiate them (e.g., via ill-timed use of trauma-focused interventions that can temporarily increase arousal and distress).

A second indication for anger management prior to trauma-focused treatment is where anger is preventing effective emotional processing of the traumatic memory and inhibiting the activation of cognitive and emotional responses associated with fear, anxiety, horror, or vulnerability. In these contexts, despite repeated intrusive thoughts and nightmares associated with fear and horror responses and facilitated attempts to address these affective states, angry and ruminative responses dominate the trauma-focused therapy, inhibiting effective emotional processing.

The final indication is where cynicism and hostile appraisal are impeding the development of an adequate therapeutic alliance in which to conduct trauma-focused interventions and heightening the risk of premature dropout. In such contexts, the anger is best addressed prior to conducting trauma-focused therapy. Then, safety is increased and there is a stable base for addressing emotional content of the traumatic memory.

OUTCOMES

Unfortunately, although an evidence base for CBT interventions for problematic anger exists, there is a dearth of high-level evidence for the effectiveness of anger interventions in PTSD, with only two randomized controlled trials (RCTs) published to date. Both trials examine the treatment of anger in combat-related PTSD. The first was conducted by Chemtob and colleagues (Chemtob, Novaco, Hamada, & Gross, 1997) on traumatized combat Vietnam veterans. It used aspects of the CBT approaches to anger treatment outlined in this chapter. The study also conceptually drew from the mechanisms purported to underpin the survival mode of trauma response and utilized many of the adaptations described earlier.

The study involved a randomized group design, testing a 12-session anger management intervention against routine care in the treatment of refractory Vietnam veterans with severe combat-related PTSD and severe anger problems. The intervention demonstrated encouraging results, reporting significant improvements (large effect size reductions) in anger control, maintained to 18 months follow-up, and less intense reactions to anger-provoking situations. The groups, however, did not differ at posttreatment or follow-up in measures of trait anger nor on psychophysiological measures.

Only recently has a second RCT been published for this population. This study, conducted by Morland et al. (2010), was a randomized noninferiority trial of CBT-based anger management for combat veterans with PTSD delivered via telemedicine compared to the same treatment delivered in person. In contrast to standard RCTs, where an experimental treatment is examined to demonstrate effectiveness beyond accepted or routine interventions, the aim of a noninferiority trial is to compare a novel modification of an existing evidence-based intervention and potentially demonstrate that this modification, usually one that improves accessibility or efficiency, is at least equivalent in effectiveness to the existing evidence-based intervention.

Consistent with the interventions mentioned previously in this chapter, the anger management intervention utilized self-monitoring of anger and its cues and triggers, development and consolidation of cognitive and behavioral coping strategies for controlling anger, and examination of the relationship between anger and violence. Little was reported in this study, however, about any adaptation of the CBT-based anger management intervention to the features of a population with combat-related PTSD.

In terms of outcomes, participants in both conditions demonstrated significant improvements (moderate to large effect sizes) at posttreatment on measures of anger expression and trait anger, with results maintained to 6 months follow-up. Interestingly, although both conditions demonstrated improvement, mean improvements were slightly larger ($d = .44$ and .21 on measures of anger expression and trait anger, respectively) in the video-teleconferencing condition. In addition, no significant differences were evident in attendance, dropouts (10% overall), or homework completion. The demonstration by this study of the effectiveness of anger management interventions for veterans with PTSD via video-teleconferencing raises considerable opportunity to improve access to effective anger management interventions for veterans across regional and rural communities.

CONCLUSION

Problematic anger and aggression are common features associated with combat-related PTSD. Anger not only plays a significant role in the development and maintenance of PTSD but also is associated with significant distress and impairment in functioning for the war veteran in its own right. In addition, it often activates aggressive behaviors with significant personal and interpersonal consequences. Understanding the nature of anger in veterans with PTSD and developing and disseminating effective treatments are critical in easing the burden associated with this problem. Despite this need, however, studies testing the application of evidence-based anger interventions to this population have been few indeed, with only two high-level RCTs reported to date. Nevertheless, these studies have demonstrated significant positive outcomes and suggest that there is cause for considerable optimism for the potential to deliver effective treatments for combat veterans with problematic anger.

REFERENCES

Achenbach, T. M. (1995). Developmental issues in assessments, taxonomy and diagnosis of child and adolescent psychopathology. In D. Cicchetti & D. J. Cohen (Eds.), *Developmental psychopathology* (Vol. 1, pp. 57–80). New York, NY: Wiley Publishers.

American Psychiatric Association. (1994). *Diagnostic and statistical manual of mental disorders* (4th ed.). Washington, DC: Author.

Andrews, B., Brewin, C. R., Rose, S., & Kirk, M. (2000). Predicting PTSD symptoms in victims of violent crime: The role of shame, anger, and childhood abuse. *Journal of Abnormal Psychology, 109*(1), 69–73. doi:10.1037//0021-843X.1M.I.69

Barrett, E. L., Mills, K. L., & Teesson, M. (2011). Hurt people who hurt people: Violence amongst individuals with comorbid substance use disorder and post traumatic stress disorder. *Addictive Behaviors, 36*(7), 721–728. doi:10.1016/j.addbeh.2011.02.005

Beckham, J. C., Moore, S. D., & Reynolds, V. (2000). Interpersonal hostility and violence in Vietnam combat veterans with chronic posttraumatic stress disorder: A review of theoretical models and empirical evidence. *Aggression and Violent Behavior, 5*(5), 451–466. doi:10.1016/S1359-1789(98)00018-4

Berkowitz, L. (1990). On the formation and regulation of anger and aggression. A cognitive-neoassociationistic analysis. *American Psychologist, 45*(4), 494–503.

Cahill, S. P., Rauch, S. A., Hembree, E. A., & Foa, E. B. (2003). Effect of cognitive-behavioral treatments for PTSD on anger. *Journal of Cognitive Psychotherapy, 17,* 113–131.

Chemtob, C., Roitblat, H. L., Hamada, R. S., Carlson, J. G., & Twentyman, C. T. (1988). A cognitive action theory of post-traumatic stress disorder. *Journal of Anxiety Disorders, 2*(3), 253–275. doi:10.1016/0887-6185(88)90006-0

Chemtob, C. M., Novaco, R. W., Hamada, R. S., & Gross, D. M. (1997). Cognitive-behavioral treatment for severe anger in posttraumatic stress disorder. [Clinical Trial Randomized Controlled Trial Research Support, U.S. Gov't, Non-P.H.S.]. *Journal of Consulting and Clinical Psychology, 65*(1), 184–189.

Chemtob, C. M., Novaco, R. W., Hamada, R. S., Gross, D. M., & Smith, G. (1997). Anger regulation deficits in combat-related posttraumatic stress disorder. *Journal of Traumatic Stress, 10*(1), 17–36.

Creamer, M., Burgess, P., & McFarlane, A. C. (2001). Post-traumatic stress disorder: findings from the Australian National Survey of Mental Health and Well-being. *Psychological Medicine, 31*(7), 1237–1247.

David, A. S., Farrin, L., Hull, L., Unwin, C., Wessely, S., & Wykes, T. (2002). Cognitive functioning and disturbances of mood in UK veterans of the Persian Gulf War: A comparative study. *Psychological Medicine, 32*(8), 1357–1370.

Deffenbacher, J. L. (2011). Cognitive-behavioral conceptualization and treatment of anger. *Cognitive and Behavioral Practice, 18*(2), 212–221.

Dunnegan, S. W. (1997). Violence, trauma and substance abuse. [Review]. *Journal of Psychoactive Drugs, 29*(4), 345–351. doi:10.1080/02791072.1997.10400561

Dutton, D. G. (2010). Anger in intimate relationships. In M. Potegal, G. Stemmler, & C. Speilberger (Eds.), *International handbook of anger* (pp. 535–544). New York, NY: Springer.

Dyer, K. F. W., Dorahy, M. J., Hamilton, G., Corry, M., Shannon, M., MacSherry, A., . . . McElhill, B. (2009). Anger, aggression, and self-harm in PTSD and complex PTSD. *Journal of Clinical Psychology, 65*(10), 1099–1114

Eckhardt, C., Norlander, B., & Deffenbacher, J. L. (2004). The assessment of anger and hostility: A critical review. *Aggression and Violent Behaviour, 9*, 17–43.

Ehlers, A., & Clark, D. M. (2000). A cognitive model of posttraumatic stress disorder. *Behaviour Research and Therapy, 38*(4), 319–345.

Elbogen, E. B., Wagner, H. R., Fuller, S. R., Calhoun, P. S., Kinneer, P. M., & Beckham, J. C. (2010). Correlates of anger and hostility in Iraq and Afghanistan war veterans. *American Journal of Psychiatry, 167*(9), 1051–1058. doi:10.1176/appi.ajp.2010.09050739

Evans, S., Giosan, C., Patt, I., Spielman, L., & Difede, J. (2006). Anger and its association to distress and social/occupational functioning in symptomatic disaster relief workers responding to the September 11, 2001, World Trade Center disaster. *Journal of Traumatic Stress, 19*(1), 147–152. doi:10.1002/jts.20107

Feeny, N. C., Zoellner, L. A., & Foa, E. B. (2000). Anger, dissociation, and posttraumatic stress disorder among female assault victims. *Journal of Traumatic Stress, 13*(1), 89–100. doi:10.1023/A:1007725015225

Fernandez, E. (2008). The angry personality: A representation on six dimensions of anger expression. In G. J. Boyle, D. Matthews, & D. Saklofske (Eds.), *International handbook of personality theory and testing: Vol. 2: Personality measurement and assessment* (pp. 402–419). London, England: Sage Publications.

Finley, E. P., Baker, M., Pugh, M. J., & Peterson, A. (2010). Patterns and perceptions of intimate partner violence committed by returning veterans with post-traumatic stress disorder. *Journal of Family Violence, 25*(8), 737–743. doi:10.1007/s10896-010-9331-7

Foa, E. B., Riggs, D. S., Massie, E. D., & Yarczower, M. (1995). The impact of fear activation and anger on the efficacy of exposure treatment for posttraumatic-stress disorder. *Behavior Therapy, 26*(3), 487–499. doi:10.1016/S0005-7894(05)80096-6

Foa, E. B., & Rothbaum, B. O. (1998). *Treating the trauma of rape: Cognitive-behavioral therapy for PTSD*. New York, NY: Guilford Press.

Forbes, D., Bennett, N., Biddle, D., Crompton, D., McHugh, A., Elliott, P., & Creamer, M. (2005). Clinical presentation and treatment outcome for peacekeeper veterans with PTSD: Preliminary findings. *American Journal of Psychiatry, 162*, 2188–2190.

Forbes, D., Creamer, M., Allen, N., Elliott, P., McHugh, T., Debenham, P., & Hopwood, M. (2002). The MMPI-2 as a predictor of symptom change following treatment for posttraumatic stress disorder. *Journal of Personality Assessment, 79*(2), 321–336. doi:10.1207/S15327752JPA7902_13

Forbes, D., Creamer, M., Allen, N., Elliott, P., McHugh, T., Debenham, P., & Hopwood, M. (2003). MMPI-2 based subgroups of veterans with combat-related PTSD: Differential patterns of symptom change after treatment. *Journal of Nervous and Mental Disease, 191*(8), 531–537. doi:10.1097/01.nmd.0000082181.79051.83

Forbes, D., Creamer, M., Bisson, J. I., Cohen, J. A., Crow, B. E., Foa, E. B.,... Ursano, R. J. (2010). A guide to guidelines for the treatment of PTSD and related conditions. *Journal of Traumatic Stress, 23*(5), 537–552. doi:10.1002/jts.20565

Forbes, D., Creamer, M., Hawthorne, G., Allen, N., & McHugh, T. (2003). Comorbidity as a predictor of symptom change following treatment in combat-related posttraumatic stress disorder. *Journal of Nervous and Mental Disease, 191*(2), 93–99.

Forbes, D., Elhai, J. D., Miller, M. W., & Creamer, M. (2010). Internalizing and externalizing classes in posttraumatic stress disorder: A latent class analysis. *Journal of Traumatic Stress, 23*(3), 340–349. doi:10.1002/jts.20526

Forbes, D., Parslow, R., Creamer, M., Allen, N., McHugh, T., & Hopwood, M. (2008). Mechanisms of anger and treatment outcome in combat veterans with posttraumatic stress disorder. *Journal of Traumatic Stress, 21*(2), 142–149. doi:10.1002/jts.20315

Frueh, B. C., Henning, K. R., Pellegrin, K. L., & Chobot, K. (1997). Relationship between scores on anger measures and PTSD symptomatology, employment, and compensation-seeking status in combat veterans. *Journal of Clinical Psychology, 53*(8), 871–878.

Greenberg, L. S., & Paivio, S. C. (1997). *Working with emotions in psychotherapy.* New York, NY: Guilford Press.

Grossman, D. (1997). *On killing: The psychological cost of learning to kill in war and society.* New York, NY: Black Bay Books.

Hovens, J. E., Op den Velde, W., Falger, P. R., Schouten, E. G., De Groen, J. H., & Van Duijn, H. (1992). Anxiety, depression and anger in Dutch Resistance veterans from World War II. *Psychotherapy and Psychosomatics, 57*(4), 172–179.

Jakupcak, M., Conybeare, D., Phelps, L., Hunt, S., Holmes, H. A., Felker, B.,... McFall, M. E. (2007). Anger, hostility, and aggression among Iraq and Afghanistan War veterans reporting PTSD and subthreshold PTSD. *Journal of Traumatic Stress, 20*(6), 945–954. doi:10.1002/jts.20258

Jayasinghe, N., Giosan, C., Evans, S., Spielman, L., & Difede, J. (2008). Anger and posttraumatic stress disorder in disaster relief workers exposed to the September 11, 2001 World Trade Center disaster one-year follow-up study. *Journal of Nervous and Mental Disease, 196*(11), 844–846. doi:10.1097/NMD.0b013e31818b492c

Johnson, D. R., Rosenheck, R., Fontana, A., Lubin, H., Charney, D., & Southwick, S. (1996). Outcome of intensive inpatient treatment for combat-related posttraumatic stress disorder. *American Journal of Psychiatry, 153*, 771–777.

Keane, T. M., & Kaloupek, D. G. (1995). Cognitive behavior therapy in the treatment of posttraumatic stress disorder. *The Clinical Psychologist, 49*(1), 1–7.

Kessler, R. C., Sonnega, A., Bromet, E., Hughes, M., & Nelson, C. B. (1995). Posttraumatic stress disorder in the National Comorbidity Survey. *Archives of General Psychiatry, 52*(12), 1048–1060.

King, D. W., King, L. A., Gudanowski, D. M., & Vreven, D. L. (1995). Alternative representations of war zone stressors: Relationships to posttraumatic stress disorder in male and female Vietnam veterans. [Research Support, U.S. Gov't, P.H.S.]. *Journal Abnormal Psychology, 104*(1), 184–195.

Koenen, K. C., Stellman, J. M., Stellman, S. D., & Sommer, J. F. (2003). Risk factors for course of posttraumatic stress disorder among Vietnam veterans: A 14-year follow-up of American Legionnaires. *Journal of Consulting and Clinical Psychology, 71*(6), 980–986. doi:10.1037/0022-006x.71.6.980

Krueger, R. F. (1999). The structure of common mental disorders. *Archives of General Psychiatry, 56*(10), 921–926.

Kulka, R. A., Shlenger, W. E., Fairbank, J. A., Hough, R. L., Jordan, B. K., Marmar, C. R., & Weiss, D. S. (1990). *Trauma and the Vietnam War generation*. New York, NY: Brunner/Mazel.

Lasko, N. B., Gurvits, T. V., Kuhne, A. A., Orr, S. P., & Pitman, R. K. (1994). Aggression and its correlates in Vietnam veterans with and without chronic posttraumatic stress disorder. *Comprehensive Psychiatry, 35*(5), 373–381.

Litz, B. T., Stein, N., Delaney, E., Lebowitz, L., Nash, W. P., Silva, C., & Maguen, S. (2009). Moral injury and moral repair in war veterans: A preliminary model and intervention strategy. *Clinical Psychology Review, 29*(8), 695–706. doi:10.1016/j.cpr.2009.07.003

Maguen, S., Lucenko, B. A., Reger, M. A., Gahm, G. A., Litz, B. T., Seal, K. H., . . . Marmar, C. R. (2010). The impact of reported direct and indirect killing on mental health symptoms in Iraq War veterans. *Journal of Traumatic Stress, 23*(1), 86–90. doi:10.1002/jts.20434

McGurk, D., Cotting, D. I., Britt, T. W., & Adler, A. B. (2006). Joining the ranks: The role of indoctrination in transforming civilians to service members. In A. B. Adler, C. A. Castro, & T. W. Britt (Eds.), *Military life: The psychology of serving in peace and combat* (Vol. 2, pp. 13–31). Westport, CT: Praeger Security International.

McHugh, T., Forbes, D., Bates, G., Hopwood, M., & Creamer, M. (2012). Anger in PTSD: Is there a need for a concept of PTSD-related posttraumatic anger? *Clinical Psychology Review, 32*, 93–104.

Mearns, J., & Mauch, T. G. (1998). Negative mood regulation expectancies predict anger among police officers and buffer the effects of job stress. *Journal of Nervous and Mental Disease, 186*(2), 120–125.

Miller, M. W., Greif, J. L., & Smith, A. A. (2003). Multidimensional Personality Questionnaire profiles of veterans with traumatic combat exposure: Externalizing and internalizing subtypes. *Psychological Assessment, 15*(2), 205–215.

Miller, M. W., Kaloupek, D. G., Dillon, A. L., & Keane, T. M. (2004). Externalizing and internalizing subtypes of combat-related PTSD: A replication and extension using the PSY-5 scales. *Journal of Abnormal Psychology, 113*(4), 636–645. doi:10.1037/0021-843X.113.4.636

Miller, M. W., & Resick, P. A. (2007). Internalizing and externalizing subtypes in female sexual assault survivors: Implications for the understanding of complex PTSD. *Behavioral Therapy, 38*(1), 58–71. doi:10.1016/j.beth.2006.04.003

Morland, L. A., Greene, C. J., Rosen, C. S., Foy, D., Reilly, P., Shore, J., . . . Frueh, B. C. (2010). Telemedicine for anger management therapy in a rural population of combat veterans with posttraumatic stress disorder: A randomized noninferiority trial. *Journal of Clinical Psychiatry, 71*(7), 855–863. doi:10.4088/JCP.09m05604blu

Novaco, R. W., & Chemtob, C. M. (1998). Anger and trauma: Conceptualization, assessment, and treatment. In V. M. Follette, J. L. Ruzek, & F. R. Abueg (Eds.), *Cognitive-behavioral therapies for trauma* (pp. 162–190). New York, NY: Guilford Press.

Novaco, R. W., & Chemtob, C. M. (2002). Anger and combat-related posttraumatic stress disorder. *Journal of Traumatic Stress, 15*(2), 123–132. doi:10.1023/A:1014855924072

Orth, U., Cahill, S. P., Foa, E. B., & Maercker, A. (2008). Anger and posttraumatic stress disorder symptoms in crime victims: A longitudinal analysis. [Research Support, Non-U.S. Gov't]. *Journal of Consulting and Clinical Psychology, 76*(2), 208–218. doi:10.1037/0022-006X.76.2.208

Orth, U., & Maercker, A. (2009). Posttraumatic anger in crime victims: Directed at the perpetrator and at the self. *Journal of Traumatic Stress, 22*(2), 158–161. doi:10.1002/jts.20392

Orth, U., & Wieland, E. (2006). Anger, hostility, and posttraumatic stress disorder in trauma-exposed adults: A meta-analysis. *Journal of Consulting and Clinical Psychology, 74*(4), 698–706. doi:10.1037/0022-006X.74.4.698

O'Toole, B. I., Marshall, R. P., Grayson, D. A., Schureck, R. J., Dobson, M., Ffrench, M.,... Vennard, J. (1996). The Australian Vietnam Veterans Health Study: III. Psychological health of Australian Vietnam veterans and its relationship to combat. *International Journal of Epidemiology, 25*(2), 331–340.

Paivio, S. C., & Pascual-Leone, A. (2010). *Emotion focused therapy for complex trauma: An integrative approach.* Washington, DC: American Psychological Association.

Pitman, R. K., Altman, B., Greenwald, E., Longpre, R. E., Macklin, M. L., Poire, R. E., & Steketee, G. S. (1991). Psychiatric complications during flooding therapy for posttraumatic stress disorder. *Journal of Clinical Psychiatry, 52*(1), 17–20.

Rees, S., Silove, D., Chey, T., Ivancic, L., Steel, Z., Creamer, M.,... Forbes, D. (2011). Lifetime prevalence of gender-based violence in women and the relationship with mental disorders and psychosocial function. *Journal of the American Medical Association, 306*(5), 513–521. doi:306/5/513 [pii] 10.1001/jama.2011.1098

Resick, P. A., & Schnicke, M. K. (1993). *Cognitive processing therapy for sexual assault victims: A treatment manual.* Newbury Park, CA: Sage Publications.

Riggs, D. S., Dancu, C. V., Gershuny, B. S., Greenberg, D., & Foa, E. B. (1992). Anger and posttraumatic-stress-disorder in female crime victims. *Journal of Traumatic Stress, 5*(4), 613–625.

Rizvi, S. L., Vogt, D. S., & Resick, P. A. (2009). Cognitive and affective predictors of treatment outcome in Cognitive Processing Therapy and Prolonged Exposure for posttraumatic stress disorder. *Behaviour Research and Therapy, 47*(9), 737–743. doi:10.1016/j.brat.2009.06.003

Shapiro, F. (2001). *Eye movement desensitization and reprocessing (EMDR): Basic principles, protocols, and procedures* (2nd ed.). New York, NY: Guilford Press.

Shay, J. (1995). *Achilles in Vietnam: Combat trauma and the undoing of character.* New York, NY: Simon and Schuster.

Stapleton, J. A., Taylor, S., & Asmundson, G. J. G. (2006). Effects of three PTSD treatments on anger and guilt: Exposure therapy, eye movement desensitization and reprocessing, and relaxation training. *Journal of Traumatic Stress, 19*(1), 19–28.

Stevenson, V. E., & Chemtob, C. M. (2000). Premature treatment termination by angry patients with combat-related post-traumatic stress disorder. *Military Medicine, 165*(5), 422–424.

Taft, C. T., Vogt, D. S., Marshall, A. D., Panuzio, J., & Niles, B. L. (2007). Aggression among combat veterans: Relationships with combat exposure and symptoms of posttraumatic stress disorder, dysphoria, and anxiety. *Journal of Traumatic Stress, 20*(2), 135–145. doi:10.1002/jts.20197

Toren, P., Wolmer, L., Weizman, R., Magal-Vardi, O., & Laor, N. (2002). Retraumatization of Israeli civilians during a reactivation of the Gulf War threat. *Journal of Nervous and Mental Disease, 190*(1), 43.

Wranik, T., & Scherer, K. R. (2010). Why do I get angry? A componential appraisal approach. In M. Potegal, G. Stemmler, & C. Speilberger (Eds.), *International handbook of anger* (pp. 243–266). New York, NY: Springer.

Zoellner, L. A., Goodwin, M. L., & Foa, E. B. (2000). PTSD severity and health perceptions in female victims of sexual assault. *Journal of Traumatic Stress, 13*(4), 635–649.

5

Anger Management Treatment and Substance Use Disorders

MICHAEL S. SHOPSHIRE AND PATRICK M. REILLY

CASE VIGNETTE

Jason Brown was a 41-year-old divorced, African American man with a history of major depressive disorder (MDD). Although he had a history of alcohol abuse, his diagnosis in the currently described treatment episode at a substance abuse outpatient clinic was cocaine and amphetamine use disorder. Jason was hospitalized for MDD when he was 36 and 39 years old. At each hospitalization, he was referred to treatment for SUDs but did not comply with treatment recommendations. Jason reported during individual counseling sessions that he struggled with controlling intense feelings of anger throughout his life. He reported that he had committed several violent assaults, which often occurred while under the influence of either alcohol or stimulants.

Jason reported that his early childhood was uneventful, but during adolescence he was often truant and joined a neighborhood gang and frequently committed physical assaults while engaging in gang-related activities. He dropped out of high school in the 11th grade and enlisted in the U.S. Marine Corps when he was 18 years old. Shortly after entering the Marine Corps, Jason began drinking alcohol heavily. He developed a reputation in his unit as quick-tempered and was disciplined for fighting with other marines.

Jason also began using and selling amphetamines and marijuana upon entering the Marine Corps. During individual counseling sessions, Jason reported that the most violent episode of his life occurred when he was 22 years old while selling illicit drugs while in the Marine Corps. A drug dealer owed him money and Jason attempted to get the money using coercion and violence. Armed with a loaded handgun, he kicked down the door of the drug dealer's house but was soon met with a barrage of gunfire from the drug dealer and his associates. Although shot five times in the abdomen, arms, and legs, Jason reported that "out of pure rage," he was able to flee the scene and drive himself to a local hospital.

Jason recovered from his gunshot wounds and was honorably discharged from the Marine Corps when he was 22 years old. He returned to New York City, found work as an auto mechanic, and married a woman he had known since high school. Although he stopped using amphetamines, he continued to abuse alcohol and began using cocaine. He continued to work periodically as an auto mechanic but lost several jobs as a result of his cocaine and alcohol abuse. After 8 years of unsteady work and substance abuse, Jason's wife divorced him when he was 30 years old. Jason said that to cope with his feelings of loneliness and abandonment after the divorce, he increased his use of alcohol and cocaine. His alcohol use increased to the point of developing an alcohol use disorder. Despite a hospitalization for MDD when he was 36 years old and a successful remission of MDD, Jason continued his problematic drinking and began abusing crack cocaine when he was 37 years old. Although clinical staff diagnosed his SUDs during two inpatient hospitalizations for MDD, Jason refused to enroll in substance abuse treatment.

Jason reported a history of problems with anger and violence throughout his life. As an adolescent, he participated in gang-related violent activities, and between his discharge from the Marine Corps and his second hospitalization for MDD at 39 years old, Jason was arrested five times for assault and numerous times for public intoxication. Interestingly, he denied that he was physically violent toward his wife, but he admitted to attempting to control his wife with verbal threats and verbal abuse.

When he was 40 years old, Jason moved to San Francisco, and a year later, he was admitted to inpatient substance abuse treatment at the San Francisco Veterans Affairs Medical Center (SFVAMC). After completing inpatient treatment, Jason was able to remain abstinent from alcohol and other substances and enrolled in outpatient substance abuse treatment at the SFVAMC.

Jason's first introduction to formal anger management treatment occurred when he was 41 years old at the outpatient substance abuse treatment program. Substance abuse treatment consisted of weekly individual counseling sessions and cognitive-behavioral relapse prevention substance abuse treatment group counseling twice a week. Jason was required to submit weekly urine samples and the results of the urine toxicology screens were discussed during both group and individual counseling. Jason was encouraged to attempt to achieve complete abstinence from all substances. During 6 months of outpatient treatment, Jason had one "slip" in which he smoked crack cocaine. Otherwise, Jason remained drug and alcohol free.

Despite achieving good substance abuse treatment outcomes, Jason reported that he still had trouble controlling his anger. He was proud of his ability to stay clean and sober but was surprised that his frequent and intense states of anger did not subside. Indeed, he reported that he "felt even more angry after getting clean and sober." Jason's problems with anger also indirectly influenced his substance abuse treatment. During group counseling sessions, for example, Jason frequently displayed angry facial expressions and verbally expressed anger toward other clients. Although he was able to control his physical violence during the group sessions, he verbally abused other group members. On one occasion, he was nearly discharged from the program due to threatening behavior toward another client. He also lost a part-time job in a retail store after he threatened a coworker, which interfered with his ability to support himself financially.

Jason's problems with frequent and intense episodes of anger were addressed with manual-guided cognitive-behavioral anger management treatment developed for substance abuse clients (Reilly & Shopshire, 2002). According to this model, which is based on Meichenbaum's (1985) stress inoculation training, clients with anger control problems cope with stressful life events and anger-provoking events with emotion-focused rather than problem-focused coping (Folkman & Lazarus, 1988). In other words, individuals may tend to avoid dealing directly with stressful events with specific action-oriented strategies, such as expressing anger and frustration appropriately or gathering useful information to effectively solve problems in their lives. Rather, they use emotion-focused coping strategies, such as impulsively expressing anger or covering up their feelings with drugs and alcohol. Coping strategies mediate the emotional expression of anger and other emotions. The goal of treatment is to teach clients to switch from using emotion-focused to problem-focused coping strategies. The treatment is similar to other anger management treatments presented in this book, in that clients are taught to monitor the extent to which anger-provoking situations increased arousal of the autonomic nervous system (ANS) and to dampen ANS arousal with the use of specific cognitive and behavioral strategies. Specifically, clients are taught to monitor situations that preceded an episode of anger on an "anger meter," on which "1" was labeled "calm and relaxed" and "10" was reserved for an angry outburst or act of violence. Some clients select a goal of preventing an angry outburst, whereas others decide to prevent a physical act of violence. Jason's personal goal was to prevent an angry outburst, such as verbal abuse or a temper tantrum. Group sessions consisted of psychoeducational material covering specific anger control strategies, such as cognitive restructuring, thought stopping, relaxation training, and assertion training, as well as session time to review individual group members' understanding of concepts, specific anger control plans, and any issues that required clarification. Clients are also encouraged to listen to music, exercise, work on hobbies, or engage in any activity that they find personally calming and relaxing.

Upon entering anger management treatment, Jason reported very high scores on the "anger meter" and questioned whether the group treatment could help him. He did, however, report that he felt a sense of acceptance and support from the other group members. By the fourth session, Jason began to identify the signs and cues that signaled to him that his ANS was aroused and that he would soon have an angry outburst unless he used an anger control strategy. He identified specific situations that tended to frequently provoke his anger, which generally concerned situations when he perceived that others threatened him or showed him a sign of disrespect or when he had to yield to an authority figure. He also began to develop a specific plan for managing his anger. Ideally, an anger control plan should contain cognitive restructuring as an anger management strategy, but Jason had not developed the skills to use this strategy and had to initially rely on thought stopping when he first perceived his ANS begin to increase in arousal. Sometimes he tried to leave the anger-provoking situation to reduce his level of ANS arousal.

Jason came late to the fifth session and announced that he was dropping out of the anger management group treatment because "it wasn't working." He claimed that there were certain people that were always going to "push his buttons" and that he would have to "put them in their place." Jason's announcement was the result of an incident that had occurred on the bus the day before the group session. He had confronted an adolescent on the bus who was talking loudly and, in Jason's opinion, showing disrespect to the other people on the bus. Jason confronted the adolescent and they both raised their voices to the point of shouting and using profanity. Jason was asked to leave the bus by the bus driver.

This incident led to a group discussion on the dangers of trying to justify unreasonable and unrealistic feelings of anger and the negative consequences that can result from this justification. During the session, the therapist discussed cognitive restructuring, and this discussion helped Jason gain awareness of how his beliefs may contribute to his experience of anger. Jason was able to identify his expectations of others that precipitated his feelings of anger, which included the belief that every person absolutely must treat him and others with respect, and that those who failed to meet this expectation must be punished, a common maladaptive belief proposed by Ellis (1973) as precipitating anger. Jason was also able to see that he used this belief to justify his aggressive and violent behavior, how what he perceived as disrespectful was often an exaggeration of the intention of others, and that his desire for punishment and retribution was an overreaction. Jason also saw the negative consequences of his actions. He admitted that he was not acknowledged or congratulated by the other passengers for confronting the adolescent. On the contrary, he was seen as a contributor to an aggressive and potentially dangerous situation.

During the next several sessions, Jason reported moderate levels of anger, which were lower than in prior weeks, and he reported that he was using cognitive restructuring to reduce his level of anger. He realized that he did not have to react angrily to everyone who was not friendly toward him, and that it was neither possible nor desirable to dole out punishment to everyone who offended him. More importantly, he realized that these other people would suffer from the consequences brought on by their own behavior. He said he realized that he did not have to play the role of a policeman or enforce what he viewed as socially acceptable behavior. He felt relieved upon this realization, as if a burden had been lifted.

By the eighth session, Jason had added an exercise program to his anger control plan. Daily walks helped him relieve stress and feel more generally relaxed. He had also developed friendships with two other members in the anger management group and talked regularly with them when he began to feel angry. Jason felt that by listening and supporting group members as they struggled to control their anger, he was better able to manage his own anger.

By the end of anger management treatment, Jason had developed a specific and effective anger control plan. He monitored his hostile self-talk; talked to his friends in the group for social support; walked daily; regularly listened to music in the evening, which helped him relax; and used assertive rather than aggressive behavior, especially when he anticipated a conflict was imminent. He reported lower levels on the "anger meter" and felt that the gains he had made in managing his anger had also improved the quality of his recovery program from drugs and alcohol.

Six months after Jason had completed the anger management group treatment, he continued to report low levels of anger and did not report any further incidents of aggression and violence. He admitted that there had been a couple of occasions where he felt he could have handled a potentially anger-provoking situation more appropriately, but generally, he used his anger control plan effectively and avoided angry outbursts of violent behaviors.

Jason exemplifies the complications associated with the treatment of anger control problems in clients who also misuse substances. Many clients with co-occurring SUDs and anger control problems display outbursts of anger that complicate their substance abuse treatment and their lives. For some clients, ordinary everyday hassles are potentially anger-provoking situations. Similar to other individuals with anger control problems, individuals with co-occurring SUDs with anger problems show a hostility bias (Dodge & Frame, 1982) in which neutral, often benign events are interpreted as very personal and as intentional slights against their sense of self and well-being. The hostility bias is spontaneous and not only influences how situations are perceived but also how they are remembered (Zelli, Huesmann, & Cervone, 1995). And similar to many clients with anger control problems in other populations, clients with SUDs and anger control problems often have unresolved resentments that well up as they cope with anger-provoking situations in their current life. But for many clients with SUDs and anger control problems, the use of substances is an overused emotion-focused coping strategy that has become habitual to the point that the misuse of substances becomes an overriding problem that complicates the treatment of an anger control problem. The challenge in treating the population of clients with co-occurring SUDs and anger control problems is to address these two chronic, long-standing sets of symptoms concurrently.

ANGER PROBLEMS AND SUBSTANCE USE DISORDERS

Some individuals with SUDs have anger control problems, but many do not. Thus, anger is not usually addressed in-depth, if at all, in evidence-based substance abuse treatments. In contrast to other diagnostic categories that may co-occur with anger control problems, such as borderline personality disorder, frequent and intense episodes of anger are not a symptom of the diagnostic category of SUDs. Because anger is not a symptom of SUDs, clinicians may view frequent and intense episodes of anger as secondary to problematic substance use. Substance use may reflect an attempt to cope with unpleasant emotions, however.

SUDs are a set of heterogeneous diagnostic categories. Each substance of abuse has a different profile of psychological effects and physiological dependence. Some substances of abuse have calming effects, whereas other substances stimulate the ANS. The possible causal mechanisms that may initiate substance use and misuse and maintain SUDs are numerous, and many vulnerability factors may interact to lead to the onset of an SUD. The contention of our anger management treatment model for clients with SUDs and anger control problems, nevertheless, is that some individuals with SUDs experience frequent, intense, and unpleasant emotional states of anger, and these episodes of anger may hamper substance abuse treatment by precipitating substance use (Reilly & Shopshire, 2002). Even if anger does not precipitate substance use for some individuals with SUDs, anger control problems may indirectly hamper substance abuse treatment by intimidating staff and other clients, which may in turn lead to a poor working alliance with these clients or expulsion from the treatment program because staff and clients fear angry outbursts and potential violence.

Do frequent and/or intense episodes of anger precede substance use? Is the frequent and intense experience of anger a high-risk situation for relapse? A careful review of the literature shows that very few studies have documented a direct influence between frequent and intense episodes of anger and the tendency to misuse substances, and perhaps this is why the substance abuse treatment research community does not often acknowledge the role of anger problems for SUD treatment. Anecdotal evidence, however, suggests that anger-provoking events may operate as a high-risk situation for relapse to substance abuse. In Alcoholics Anonymous meetings, for example, the acronym HALT is often used to remind members to avoid getting hungry, angry, lonely, or tired because these situations may put them at risk for relapse (Bishop, 2001). Popular books, such as *Of Course You're Angry: A Guide to Dealing With the Emotions of Substance Abuse* (Rosellini & Worden, 1997) and *Anger and Relapse: Breaking the Cycle* (Clancy, 1996), also reflect the common belief that anger plays an important role in the initiation and maintenance of SUDs.

The role of anger in the relapse cycle is not restricted to clinical lore. Indeed, some authors of influential manual-guided, empirically validated substance abuse treatments include brief sessions on anger and frustration tolerance. In their manual for cognitive therapy of SUDs, for example, A. T. Beck, Wright, Newman, and Liese (1993) devote a chapter to anger and frustration tolerance and view this issue as a key component of alcohol and substance abuse treatment. A. T. Beck et al. (1993) note, "Substance abusers are prone to act out hostile impulses when they are under the influence of drugs and alcohol. Although they are particularly prone to use drink to dampen unpleasant feelings of anger, the substance paradoxically may increase the likelihood of the expression of anger via disinhibition" (p. 242). Similarly, in a popular book on cognitive-behavioral substance abuse treatment, Bishop (2001) notes, "Helping people learn to better manage their anger often greatly reduces the frequency, duration, and intensity of both their anger and their lapses and relapses to addictive behavior." These quotations illustrate the complex relation between anger and substance use. Anger, and other negative emotions, may play a role in the initiation and maintenance of SUDs, but the precise relation between anger and substance use is multifaceted and variable.

RESEARCH STUDIES ON ANGER AND SUBSTANCE USE

Prevalence of anger problems. Studies suggest that many clients enrolled in substance abuse treatment experience high levels of anger. Walfish, Massey, and Krone (1990) measured levels of anger in a sample of 268 cocaine-dependent clients enrolled in a residential treatment program. Compared to a normative sample of adults, cocaine-dependent clients reported average State Trait Anger Expression Inventory (STAXI; Spielberger, 1988) trait anger scores in the 85th percentile. In a similar study, we measured STAXI trait anger in 350 consecutive admissions to substance abuse treatment programs at the SFVAMC (Awalt, Shopshire, Reilly, & Hall, 2000). The STAXI trait anger scale was administered at intake. Of the 350 admissions, 45% had clinically significant levels of anger, as indicated by a score at the 85th percentile on the trait anger scale of the STAXI. About 40% of the participants with clinically significant levels of anger also reported subclinical levels of depression as assessed with the Beck Depression Inventory (A. T. Beck, Steer, & Brown, 1996), whereas 20% reported subclinical levels of anxiety as assessed with the State-Trait Anxiety Inventory (Spielberger, Gorssuch, Lushene, Vagg, & Jacobs, 1983). Forty-six percent did not report clinically significant levels of anxiety, depression, or anger. This study illustrated that a substantial number of the veterans seeking treatment for SUDs experienced clinically significant levels of anger. Similarly, Tivis, Parsons, and Nixon (1998) compared a group of individuals with alcohol use disorders that were in remission to a matched community sample comparison group. Individuals with SUDs reported higher scores on the STAXI trait anger scale than the comparison group. Finally, published studies of anger management treatment in samples of clients with SUDs have documented that at least a subset of SUD clients have anger control problems that warrant attention (Fernandez & Scott, 2009; Lin, Mack, Enright, Krahn, & Baskin, 2004; Reilly & Shopshire, 2000).

Anger as a high-risk situation. In their pioneering work on the relapse process, Marlatt and Gordon (1980) asked substance abusers, and individuals who had achieved abstinence from other addictions, to provide retrospective reports of their relapse episodes. These individuals reported that 37% of the episodes involved managing negative emotional states. In a further analysis of negative emotional states, anger and frustration accounted for 85% of relapse episodes where other individuals were involved. Fear and anxiety, in contrast, accounted for 85% of relapse episodes involving intrapsychic experiences. These findings suggest that for individuals with SUDs whose relapse episodes concern interpersonal conflict, feelings of anger are high-risk situations for relapse. The conceptual model proposed by Marlatt and Gordon (1980) provides a framework for understanding the process of relapse. Relapse prevention approaches based on this framework teach clients to identify the high-risk situations that may precipitate drug use and possible relapse and help them develop cognitive and behavioral strategies to cope with these high-risk situations. Frequent and intense episodes of anger may precipitate relapse.

A factor analysis of Marlatt's Reasons for Drinking Questionnaire by Zywiak, Connors, Maisto, and Westerberg (1996) revealed that a negative emotion factor accounted for a substantial proportion of the variance in questionnaire responses. Scores on the negative emotion factor positively correlated with STAXI trait anger. Negative emotion, trait anger, and alcohol use were strongly correlated, suggesting that anger may precipitate relapse for some individuals with SUDs. In the Relapse Replication and Extension Project, Miller, Westerberg, Harris, and Tonigan (1996) examined relapse precipitants based on the Marlatt and Gordon (1980) taxonomy using a prospective design with clients in alcohol treatment. Consistent with Marlatt and Gordon's (1980) original retrospective study, anxiety and depression significantly predicted 6-month relapse to alcohol use, but trait anger did not.

Hall, Havassy, and Wasserman (1991) similarly examined the correlation between negative affect and relapse in a prospective study. Hall et al. (1991) followed a sample of 104 clients with SUDs after they had completed a substance abuse treatment program. Participants were followed for 12 weeks or until they used the target substance for 7 consecutive days. Anger, anxiety, and depression were assessed weekly with self-report questionnaires. Weekly self-reports of substance use were verified biochemically. Consistent with research on the assessment of mood states (Watson & Tellegen, 1985), anger, anxiety, and depression were highly intercorrelated. At each weekly assessment, in which subjects completed retrospective reports for the past week, anger/negative affect was positively correlated with substance use, whereas positive affect was negatively correlated with substance use. That is, individuals with higher levels of anger/negative affect had used the target substance during the past week. Hall et al. (1991) also examined the extent to which self-reports of anger/negative affect for the preceding week prospectively forecasted substance use during the subsequent week. Retrospective reports of anger and negative affect did not prospectively predict substance use during the subsequent week. This finding does not support the contention that anger/negative affect precipitates relapse, but it does not necessarily negate it. Episodes of negative affect as measured by Hall et al. (1991) may have been relatively distal compared to the episodes of cocaine use; an episode of anger/negative affect may not have lasted an entire week, and thus, could not be expected to prospectively forecast substance use a week later.

Many other studies suggest that some individuals use drugs and alcohol to cope with unpleasant emotions, such as anger. Morissette (1994) examined alcohol consumption in a sample of professional women. Participants reported that a main reason for drinking alcohol was to gain control over emotions and relieve negative feelings, including anger and frustration at work. In a study of the correlation of STAXI trait anger and alcohol consumption, Leibsohn, Oetting, and Deffenbacher (1994) reported that students with high trait anger drank more frequently and drank to intoxication more frequently than participants with low trait anger. Hussong and Chassin (1994) have studied the stress–negative affect model, which posits that alcohol and substance use is an attempt to alleviate negative affect resulting from stressful experiences. Anger, anxiety, and depression differentially mediated the relation between stress and alcohol use in a sample of adolescents, with depression accounting for a greater proportion of variance compared to anger and anxiety. Litt, Cooney, and Morse (2000) examined the urge to drink alcohol in a group of participants with alcohol use disorders who completed treatment. Participants who had a stronger urge to take a drink after treatment had higher STAXI trait anger than participants without such an urge.

Anger and substance use may be correlated, but the precise role of anger for substance use is unclear. Anger correlates with substance use, but it may be the result of substance use rather than a precipitant. An argument can be made that when substance use, and its disinhibiting effect, is curtailed, anger and violence will cease to be an issue. This may be the case for some clients with SUDs, but we argue that there is a subgroup of SUD clients who have anger control problems that developed in parallel to SUDs and that anger control problems and SUDs are so closely linked that both problems must be addressed simultaneously in treatment. The disinhibiting effects of substances may produce anger and violence, but also, anger and stressful emotions precipitate substance use. It is possible that a subgroup of individuals with SUDs may have vulnerability factors that predispose them to show hostility and frequently experience intense episodes of anger, and these individuals may, in turn, use substances to manage these unpleasant emotions and the stressful life events that tend to elicit these emotions. For clients with SUDs, frequent and intense episodes of anger may precipitate a relapse episode, and SUD treatment outcomes may be improved if manual-guided anger management treatment is added to evidence-based substance abuse treatment.

Although additional studies of the prevalence of anger control problems in SUD populations are clearly needed, we propose at least three types of SUD clients that may need treatment to control their anger. First, a subgroup of SUD clients may have low frustration tolerance and no other Axis I or Axis II disorders. Second, a subgroup of SUD clients may have co-occurring Axis I disorders (Havassy, Alvidrez, & Owen, 2004) that may in turn co-occur with anger control problems, such as MDD or posttraumatic stress disorder (PTSD; Reilly, Clark, Shopshire, Lewis, & Sorensen, 1994). Third, SUDs may co-occur with Axis II disorders, which may in turn co-occur with anger control problems, such as borderline personality disorder (Linehan et al., 2002).

TREATMENT APPROACHES

Anger management treatments have received a great deal of attention over the past 35 years. Novaco (1975) conducted the first documented study of an anger management treatment in the early 1970s. Since then, over 50 randomized controlled clinical trials of cognitive-behavioral anger management treatments have been conducted (R. Beck & Fernandez, 1998). Anger management treatments examined in clinical trials have been based on established cognitive-behavioral interventions. These treatments share a common theme in that participants are encouraged to self-monitor anger-provoking events and are taught cognitive-behavioral techniques to control anger. Although many studies have used convenience samples of university students or university employees, these studies have identified the "active ingredients" of anger management treatments. It appears that a combination of cognitive restructuring, relaxation training, and communication skills interventions are effective at reducing levels of anger. Fernandez (2010) views these kinds of treatments as integrative psychotherapy approaches to anger management treatment rather than as a stand-alone approach, such as treatments based solely on listening to music, mediation, or exercise.

Relatively few published studies have addressed the efficacy of an anger management treatment for individuals with SUDs. In a recent PsycINFO search using keywords for anger, treatment, substance use, and various drugs of abuse, we found that only four studies addressed anger management treatment in clients with SUDs. We excluded case studies from our review. Despite an interest in the role of anger for substance use disorders, few studies have been published on anger management treatments for SUD clients with anger control problems. Our conclusion is consistent with those of other reviews of the literature (Chermack et al., 2009; Fernandez & Scott, 2009; Korman et al., 2008).

One of the only studies to examine an anger management treatment with SUD clients, using a control group, was conducted by Lin et al. (2004). Lin et al. (2004) recruited individuals from a residential drug treatment program but did not provide specific SUD diagnoses in their article. A sample of 40 participants was randomly assigned to receive either forgiveness therapy or 12-step-based substance abuse treatment matched for time and intensity. Seven participants completed forgiveness therapy and seven participants completed the 12-step-based control group treatment. Forgiveness therapy differs from the typical cognitive-behavioral anger management treatment in that clients examine their own past histories to identify feelings of anger and resentment that were perceived as the result of another person's injustice. Clients were taught that they could make a decision to forgive the person by focusing on reducing resentment and offering benevolence toward the perceived "injurer." The "work phase" of treatment focused on helping the client view the perceived offending person or wrongdoer from a new perspective, in particular, seeing the offending person as "certainly as wrong" but also as "vulnerable or scared" (p. 1116). Across the 12-week treatment, STAXI trait anger decreased significantly across the 12 weeks of treatment, and reductions were sustained at follow-up. Participants in the 12-step control condition, in contrast, showed equally high levels of trait anger at baseline to the experimental group, but trait anger scores did not decrease across time.

The forgiveness therapy of Lin et al. (2004) is new to substance abuse treatment programs and differs from a cognitive-behavioral relapse prevention treatment in that the focus is on the behavior of another person rather than the client's own behavior and what might precede a relapse in a person's life. Although Lin and colleagues (2004) have been cited as the only published randomized controlled trial examining anger management treatment in clients with SUDs only, the study had limitations, including a relatively small sample size of 40 participants and a retention rate of 35%. In addition, the treatment may be restricted to individuals who did indeed experience a past injustice in which a specific person wronged the client. If this were the case, the client may have legitimate feelings of anger from a moral standpoint that require resolution, but a more pressing problem for some individuals with SUDs and anger control problems is what is going on in their current lives that provoke anger. Despite the historical reasons that a person may experience anger, many clients with anger control problems may incorrectly perceive individuals as slighting them, and these misperceptions may precipitate a relapse to substance use. It may be more important to address the immediate consequence of anger for substance use instead of focusing on past injustices.

Korman et al. (2008) conducted a randomized controlled trial of an anger management treatment with 42 problem gamblers with anger control problems; about half of the sample (n = 19) met diagnostic criteria for an SUD. The anger management treatment addressed problem gambling, substance use, and anger concurrently. Participants were randomly assigned to attend either this integrated anger management treatment or usual care. The integrated anger management treatment was based on dialectical behavior therapy (Linehan, 1993) and included functional analysis, skills training, exposure, and response prevention. Participants in the anger management treatment self-reported greater reductions in both STAXI trait anger and days of substance use in the past 90 days.

Fernandez and Scott (2009) studied 58 SUD clients in a 30-day residential substance abuse treatment program and randomly assigned participants to either an anger management condition or a control condition, but attrition in the control condition was high, with only two participants remaining in the 4-week study. Nevertheless, participants receiving an anger management treatment showed statistically and clinically meaningful reductions in STAXI trait anger scores. Mean STAXI trait anger scores above the 85th percentile at the start of treatment decreased to the 50th percentile at the end of treatment, and these levels of anger were sustained at follow-up.

The Fernandez and Scott (2009) 4-week anger management treatment consisted of three phases. The first phase was a psychoeducational phase that presented a conceptual framework for understanding anger control problems. In the second phase, clients were asked to sign a formal contract with group facilitators to encourage commitment to reduce their levels of anger. Clients were encouraged to identify potentially anger-provoking situations and to avoid them when possible. In the event that the avoidance of a potentially anger-provoking situation was impossible, clients rehearsed a plan of action to control their anger. In the third phase of treatment, clients were taught cognitive-behavioral strategies to control their anger when it arose in unavoidable anger-provoking situations. Clients were taught to use thought stopping to reduce their escalation of anger and to use phrases such as "Let it go" to prevent the escalation of anger. Clients were also taught more active cognitive reappraisal of the anger-provoking event, such as reinterpreting the intentionality, responsibility, and blameworthiness of a person who may have provoked anger.

If cognitive reappraisal did not work, clients were taught imagery and relaxation training to reduce their levels of anger. The final phase concerned a more "cathartic" expression of residual, unresolved anger. Participants disclosed their feelings of anger verbally or in writing to a trusted confidant. The treatment of Fernandez and Scott (2009) was integrative in that it combined cognitive-behavioral strategies with more experiential therapies, such as the "empty chair" technique used in Gestalt therapy.

We published one of the first studies examining an anger management treatment for clients with a diagnosis of crack cocaine dependence (Reilly & Shopshire, 2000) and conducted earlier studies that illustrate the usefulness of an anger management treatment for substance abuse treatment patients. Our treatment manual, *Anger Management for Drug Treatment and Mental Health Clients* (Reilly & Shopshire, 2002), and the corresponding workbook (Reilly, Shopshire, Durazzo, & Campbell, 2002) are based on our studies and disseminated by the U.S. Department of Health and Human Services Center for Substance Abuse Treatment.

In our first study, 38 participants with alcohol use disorders reported high levels of trait anger based on published norms for the STAXI trait anger scale (Reilly et al., 1995). All participants were abstinent from alcohol and drugs prior to enrollment in the anger management treatment protocol. Alcohol use was assessed with breathalyzer, and drug use was assessed with urine toxicology screens. Of the 38 participants, 24 (63%) completed the anger management treatment and remained in the drug treatment program after completing anger management treatment. The completers attended 10 sessions ($s = 1.49$) of anger management treatment on average. Levels of trait anger decreased significantly between baseline and the end of treatment, $t(23) = 5.18$, $p < .001$. Reilly, Clark, Shopshire, and Delucchi (1996) studied 25 clients with co-occurring diagnoses of PTSD and alcohol or other substance use disorders who attended a 12-week closed-group anger management treatment. These participants reported significantly higher levels of trait anger than our sample of participants with alcohol use disorders, but levels of anger decreased significantly between baseline and the end of treatment ($p < .05$).

Our largest study consisted of a sample of 59 men who were veterans receiving at least 30 days of outpatient substance abuse treatment at the SFVAMC and 32 women receiving outpatient substance abuse treatment at San Francisco General Hospital (Reilly & Shopshire, 2000). The study was a Stage 1 project as part of the National Institute on Drug Abuse Behavioral Therapies Development Program (Carroll & Onken, 2005), and our goal was to test the feasibility of a cognitive-behavioral anger management treatment in clients with cocaine dependence. The majority of the sample was African American (58%), and 32% reported taking psychiatric medications. Alcohol use was assessed with weekly breathalyzer tests, and illicit substance use was assessed with self-reports and urine toxicology screens. Although meeting criteria for cocaine dependence upon entering substance abuse treatment, 74% reported they had not used any substances during the 30 days prior to beginning anger management treatment. Relapse to substance use was relatively high, with 60% of the participants relapsing to cocaine use during the 12-week study. Among the participants who remained in treatment, the decrease in STAXI trait anger scores during the first month of treatment was statistically significant, although the scores remained relatively high (above the 85th percentile) and problematic based on norms for the trait anger scale. Clinically meaningful differences in levels of trait anger in which participants reached a "normal" mean range (50th percentile) of trait anger did not occur until the last 30 days of treatment. These lower levels of anger were sustained 30 days after treatment. Without random assignment, we could not conclude that the change in trait anger was due to the anger management treatment.

Morland et al. (2010) studied a sample of 125 veterans with PTSD and anger control problems. Although not all participants had SUDs, Moreland et al. (2010) is the largest sample to date to examine the Reilly and Shopshire (2002) anger management treatment. Participants were randomly assigned to receive the Reilly and Shopshire (2002) anger management treatment in either face-to-face sessions or over video conference equipment. Both conditions showed clinically significant reductions in anger, and retention was 90%. This finding suggests that if SUD patients can be retained in treatment and their substance use addressed sufficiently, our anger management treatment may reduce levels of anger in SUD clients.

TREATMENT ISSUES AND RECOMMENDATIONS

Randomized controlled clinical trials are often viewed as essential to establish that a treatment or practice has proven efficacy, but as described previously, only two studies by Lin et al. (2004) and Korman et al. (2008) have randomly assigned participants to either an anger management treatment or control condition in clients with SUDs and anger control problems. Although informative, these studies had relatively small sample sizes. At best, these studies would be viewed as Stage I pilot studies rather than Stage III effectiveness studies, according to the guidelines of Carroll and Onken (2005). Clearly, additional studies are needed to establish the extent to which anger management treatment in SUD clients decreases levels of anger and the extent to which lower levels of anger may improve either treatment retention or substance use outcomes.

Based on the available research studies, we recommend that clinicians meet three prerequisites before delivering an anger management treatment to clients with co-occurring SUDs and anger control problems. First, because only a subgroup of clients with SUDs may have an anger control problem, proper and comprehensive psychological assessment is essential. To identify clients with anger control problems, it is useful to administer the trait anger scale of the STAXI or other measures of trait anger, such as the Novaco Anger Inventory (Novaco, 1975). The advantage of the STAXI trait anger scale is that Spielberger (1988) has extensive norms compared to other measures of trait anger and these norms can be used as a guide to identify clients who may have an anger control problem. In addition, the scale has been used as an outcome measure in many studies of anger management treatments.

It is also necessary to assess a client's potential for violence. This can be determined from intake interviews and standard measures usually administered in public health substance abuse treatment settings, such as the Addiction Severity Index (ASI; McLellan et al., 1992). The ASI is used to assess treatment needs of SUD clients at intake. In the psychiatric status section of the ASI, for example, the intake clinician assesses the extent to which a client has difficulty controlling violent behavior, and in the legal status section, clients are asked about the number of times they have been arrested and charged for assault or charged with disorderly conduct. Although violence potential is self-reported, a preliminary examination of the ASI provides a convenient way to identify SUD clients who may have a history of past violence or self-report a current problem with controlling violence. It is also important to administer a standard violence assessment tool, such as the Revised Conflict Tactics Scales (Straus, Hamby, & Warren, 2003), to assess the potential for violence.

Additional co-occurring Axis I and Axis II disorders should be addressed. As illustrated in our survey of veteran clients with SUDs, many clients with anger control problems may also have a history or current diagnosis of anxiety disorders or major depression, or subclinical symptom levels of these disorders (Awalt et al., 2000). It is important to provide these clients with treatment for these disorders because standard SUD evidence-based treatment and anger management treatment may not address these psychiatric disorders or subclinical symptoms of these disorders. Similarly, a subset of SUD clients may have PTSD and may benefit from an emotional regulation treatment that addresses symptoms of PTSD as well as substance use, such as Seeking Safety (Najavits, 2001). Seeking Safety has been tested in several randomized controlled trials including a multisite trial conducted by the National Institute on Drug Abuse Clinical Trials Network (Hien et al., 2009). Although the influence of Seeking Safety on substance use is unclear, the treatment manual includes sessions on anger management, and the treatment does appear to reduce symptoms of PTSD, which include levels of anger.

It is also important to assess Axis II disorders or personality traits associated with personality disorders. Babcock, Green, Webb, and Yerington (2005), for example, reported that individuals with anger control problems may have different patterns of ANS arousal depending on whether they report personality traits associated with borderline personality disorder versus traits associated with antisocial personality disorder. An assumption of our treatment model, and the treatment model of Fernandez and Scott (2009), is that clients with anger control problems have an ANS that escalates when encountering and initially trying to cope with an anger-provoking event. We teach clients to monitor this escalation phase on an "anger meter," but Babcock et al. (2005) demonstrated that ANS escalation is moderated by antisocial personality traits. Babcock, Canady, Graham, and Schart (2007) recommended that treatments be tailored to fit the client's profile of anger-provoked ANS arousal. For example, clients with borderline personality disorder may benefit from dialectical behavior therapy, which is associated with decreased levels of anger and other negative emotions as well as decreased substance use (Linehan et al., 2002).

Our second recommendation is that anger management treatments should be delivered in conjunction with evidence-based substance abuse treatments with a proven track record of increasing treatment retention and decreasing substance use. Because anger is not necessarily a symptom of SUDs or a precipitator of substance use, it is important to consider anger management treatment as merely an adjunct to effective substance abuse treatment. Of the studies that have been conducted by Fernandez and Scott (2009), Lin et al. (2004), and Reilly and Shopshire (2000), treatment retention was relatively low, and this low retention rate is common in clinical trials of substance abuse treatment. To increase treatment retention and decrease substance use, it is useful to deliver evidence-based substance treatments along with the anger management treatment. For example, in two large multisite effectiveness trials of contingency management, also called "motivational incentives," treatment retention was increased and illicit substance use decreased through the use of rewards for urine screens testing negative for illicit substances (Peirce et al., 2006; Petry et al. 2005). Similarly, a large multisite effectiveness study by Carroll et al. (2006) showed that motivational interviewing (Miller & Rollnick, 1991) increases treatment retention and reduces alcohol use in clients enrolled in substance abuse treatment. The Center for Substance Abuse Treatment Addiction Technology Transfer Centers and the National Institute on Drug Abuse Clinical Trials Network Regional Research and Training Centers disseminate materials for clinicians and administrators to deliver motivational incentives and motivational interviewing. Our recommendation is to provide evidence-based treatments, such as motivational incentives and motivational interviewing, in addition to anger management treatment in order to directly improve retention and decrease substance use.

Third, we suggest that whatever anger management approach clinicians decide to use, the complex role of anger in the initiation of substance use and relapse to substance use should be considered. For clients with SUDs, anger-provoking situations are merely one of many possible high-risk situations that may precipitate substance use. Clinicians must acknowledge that each SUD client may have his or her own high-risk situations that precipitate substance use. Teaching Marlatt and Gordon's (1980) relapse prevention model is useful, and it is important in group and/or individual drug counseling sessions to ensure that clients are aware of the various possible high-risk situations that may lead to substance use or relapse after abstinence is achieved. The relapse prevention model for substance use is consistent with anger management treatments that focus on anger-provoking situations. Clients can be taught to identify which situations precipitate anger, substance use, or both, and clinicians can work with clients to develop specific cognitive and behavioral strategies to cope with these situations. In addition, similar to the Fernandez and Scott (2009) treatment, in our treatment model we regularly work with clients to help them gain awareness of the potentially negative consequences for having an uncontrolled outburst of anger, and we emphasize that angry outbursts not only have implications for their feelings of distress and strained interpersonal relationships but also may lead to the use of substances as a coping mechanism.

CONCLUSION

Despite the common belief among substance abuse treatment practitioners that many clients with SUDs have anger control problems, few studies have clearly established a direct link between frequent, intense episodes of anger and substance use. Many more carefully designed randomized controlled clinical trials in large samples must be conducted to determine the extent to which anger management treatment produces not only reductions in anger but also reduced substance use and increased treatment retention beyond evidence-based substance abuse treatments. We think this is a promising area of research, and it is important for clinicians to continue to see if future studies demonstrate the benefits of anger management treatments in clients with SUDs. For example, Stephen Chermack at the Veterans Affairs (VA) Ann Arbor Health Care System is conducting studies to reduce violence in veterans with SUDs, and Christine Timko and colleagues at the VA Palo Alto Health Care System are currently completing a VA-funded, large-sample, randomized controlled clinical trial examining the efficacy of our anger management treatment model in clients with SUDs. Findings from these researchers and others will hopefully illuminate the precise interplay between the experience of frequent, intense episodes of anger and substance use.

REFERENCES

Awalt, R. M., Shopshire, M. S., Reilly, P. M., & Hall, S. M. (2000). Anger problems in substance abuse treatment. In L. S. Harris (Ed.), *Problems of drug dependence 1999: Proceedings of the 61st Annual Scientific Meeting of the College on Problems of Drug Dependence, Inc.* Washington, DC: U.S. Government Printing Office.

Babcock, J. C., Canady, B., Graham, K. H., & Schart, L. (2007). The evolution of battering interventions: From the dark ages into the scientific age. In J. Hamel & T. Nicholls (Eds.), *Family therapy for domestic violence: A practitioner's guide to gender-inclusive research and treatment* (pp. 215–244). New York, NY: Springer.

Babcock, J. C., Green, C. E., Webb, S. A., & Yerington, T. P. (2005). Psychophysiological profiles of batterers: Autonomic emotional reactivity as it predicts the antisocial spectrum of behavior among intimate partner abusers. *Journal of Abnormal Psychology, 114*, 444–455.

Beck, A. T., Steer, R. A., & Brown, G. K. (1996). *Manual for the Beck Depression Inventory-II.* San Antonio, TX: Psychological Corporation.

Beck, A. T., Wright, F. D., Newman, C. F., & Liese, B. S. (1993). *Cognitive therapy of substance abuse.* New York, NY: Guilford Press.

Beck, R., & Fernandez, E. (1998). Cognitive behavioral therapy in the treatment of anger: A meta-analysis. *Cognitive Therapy and Research, 22*, 3–74.

Bishop, F. M. (2001). *Managing addictions: Cognitive, emotive, and behavioral techniques.* Northvale, NJ: Jason Aronson.

Carroll, K. M., Ball, S. A., Nich, C., Martino, S., Frankforter, T. L., Farentinos, C., … Woody, G. 2006). Motivational interviewing to improve treatment engagement and outcome in individuals seeking treatment for substance abuse: A multisite effectiveness study. *Drug and Alcohol Dependence, 81*, 301–312.

Carroll, K. M, & Onken, L. S. (2005). Behavioral therapies for drug abuse. *American Journal of Psychiatry, 162*, 1452–1460.

Chermack, S. T., Murray, R. L., Winters, J. J., Walton, M. A., Booth, B. M., & Blow, F. C. (2009). Treatment needs of men and women with violence problems in substance use disorder treatment. *Substance Use and Misuse, 44*, 1236–1262.

Clancy, J. (1996). *Anger and relapse: Breaking the cycle.* Madison, WI: International Universities Press.

Dodge, K. A., & Frame, C. L. (1982). Social cognitive biases and deficits in aggressive boys. *Child Development, 53*, 620–635.

Ellis, A. (1973). *Humanistic psychology: The rational emotive approach.* New York, NY: Julian Press.

Fernandez, E. (2010). Toward an integrative psychotherapy for maladaptive anger. In M. Potegal, G. Stemmier, & C. Speilberger (Eds.), *International handbook of anger: Constituent and concomitant biological, psychological, and social processes* (pp. 499–513). New York, NY: Springer.

Fernandez, E., & Scott, S. (2009). Anger treatment in chemically-dependent inpatients: Evaluation of phase effects and gender. *Behavioural and Cognitive Psychotherapy, 37,* 431–447.

Folkman, S., & Lazarus, R. S. (1988). Coping as a mediator of emotion. *Journal of Personality and Social Psychology, 54,* 466–475.

Hall, S. M., Havassy, B. E., & Wasserman, D. A. (1991). Effects of commitment to abstinence, positive moods, stress, and coping on relapse to cocaine use. *Journal of Consulting and Clinical Psychology, 59,* 526–532.

Havassy, B. E., Alvidrez, J., & Owen, K. K. (2004). Comparisons of patients with comorbid psychiatric and substance use disorders: Implications for treatment and service delivery. *American Journal of Psychiatry, 161,* 139–145.

Hien, D. A., Jiang, H., Campbell, A. N., Hu, M. C., Miele, G. M., Cohen, L. R., ... Nunes, E.V. (2009). Do treatment improvements in PTSD severity affect substance use outcomes? A secondary analysis from a randomized clinical trial in NIDA's Clinical Trials Network. *American Journal of Psychiatry, 167,* 95–101.

Hussong, A. M., & Chassin, L. A. (1994). The stress-negative affect model of adolescent alcohol use: Disaggregating negative affect. *Journal of Studies of Alcohol, 55,* 707–718.

Korman, L., Collins, J., Littman-Sharp, N., Skinner, W., McMain, S., & Mercado, V. (2008). Randomized control trial of an integrated therapy for comorbid anger and gambling. *Psychotherapy Research, 18,* 454–465.

Leibsohn, M. T., Oetting, E. R., & Deffenbacher, J. L. (1994). Effects of trait anger on alcohol consumption and consequences. *Journal of Child and Adolescent Substance Abuse, 3,* 17–32.

Lin, W. F., Mack, D., Enright, R. D., Krahn, D., & Baskin, T. W. (2004). Effects of forgiveness therapy on anger, mood, and vulnerability to substance use among inpatient substance-dependent clients. *Journal of Consulting and Clinical Psychology, 72,* 1114–1121.

Linehan, M. M. (1993). *Cognitive behavioral treatment of borderline personality disorder.* New York, NY: Guilford Press.

Linehan, M. M., Dimeff, L. A., Reynolds, S. K., Comtois, K. A., Welch, S. S., Heagerty, P., & Kivlahan, D. R. (2002). Dialectical behavior therapy versus comprehensive validation therapy plus 12-step for the treatment of opioid dependent women meeting criteria for borderline personality disorder. *Drug and Alcohol Dependence, 67,* 13–26.

Litt, M. D., Cooney, N. L., & Morse, P. (2000). Reactivity to alcohol-related stimuli in the laboratory and in the field: Predictors of craving in treated alcoholics. *British Journal of Addiction, 95,* 889–900.

Marlatt, G. A., & Gordon, J. R. (1980). Determinants of relapse: Implications for the maintenance of behavior change. *Behavioral medicine: Changing health lifestyles.* New York, NY: Brunner/Mazel.

McLellan, A. T., Kushner, H., Metzger, D., Peters, R., Smith, L., Grissom, G., ... Argerion, M. (1992). The fifth edition of the Addiction Severity Index. *Journal of Substance Abuse Treatment, 9,* 199–213.

Meichenbaum, D. (1985). *Stress inoculation training.* Elmsford, NY: Pergamon Press.

Miller, W. R., & Rollnick, S. (1991). *Motivational interviewing: Preparing people for change.* New York, NY: Guilford Press.

Miller, W. R., Westerberg, V. S., Harris, R. J., & Tonigan, J. S. (1996). What predicts relapse? Prospective testing of antecedent models. *Addiction, 91,* 155–172.

Morissette, P. (1994). At risk alcohol consumption habits of female professionals and white-collar workers. *Employee Assistance Quarterly, 10,* 47–62.

Morland, L. A., Greene, C. J., Rosen, C., Foy, D., Reilly, P., Shore, J.,... Frueh, B. C. (2010). Telemedicine for anger management therapy in a rural population of combat veterans with posttraumatic stress disorder: A randomized noninferiority trial. *Journal of Clinical Psychiatry, 71*, 855.

Najavits, L. M. (2001). *Seeking safety: A treatment manual for PTSD and substance abuse*. New York, NY: Guilford.

Novaco, R. W. (1975). *Anger control: The development and evaluation of an experimental treatment*. Lexington, MA: Lexington Books.

Peirce, J. M., Petry, N. M., Stitzer, M. L., Blaine, J., Kellogg, S., Satterfield, F.,... Li, R.. (2006). Effects of lower-cost incentives on stimulant abstinence in methadone maintenance treatment: A national drug abuse treatment clinical trials network study. *Archives of General Psychiatry, 63*, 201–208.

Petry, N. M., Peirce, J. M., Stitzer, M. L., Blaine, J., Roll, J. M., Cohen, A.,... Li, R.. (2005). Effect of prize-based incentives on outcomes in stimulant abusers in outpatient psychosocial treatment programs: A national drug abuse treatment clinical trials network study. *Archives of General Psychiatry, 62*, 1148–1156.

Reilly, P. M., Clark, H. W., Shopshire, M. S., & Delucchi, K. L. (1996). Anger management, posttraumatic stress disorder, and substance abuse. In L. S. Harris (Ed.), *Problems of drug dependence; 1995: Proceedings of the 57th Annual Scientific Meeting of the College on Problems of Drug Dependence*. Washington, DC: U.S. Government Printing Office.

Reilly, P. M., Clark, H. W., Shopshire, M. S., Lewis, E. W., & Sorensen, D. J. (1994). Anger management and temper control: Critical components of posttraumatic stress disorder and substance abuse treatment. *Journal of Psychoactive Drugs, 26*, 401–407.

Reilly, P. M., Clark., H. W., Shopshire, M. S., Lewis, E. W., & Sorensen, D. J. (1995). Anger management in substance abuse treatment patients. In L. S. Harris (Ed.), *Problem of Drug Dependence: 1995; Proceedings of the 56th Annual Scientific Meeting of the College on the Problems of Drug Dependence, Inc.* Washington, D.C.: U.S. Government Printing Office.

Reilly, P. M., & Shopshire, M. S. (2000). Anger management group treatment for cocaine dependence. *American Journal of Drug and Alcohol Abuse, 26*, 161–177.

Reilly, P. M., & Shopshire, M. S. (2002). *Anger management for substance abuse and mental health clients: A cognitive behavioral therapy manual*. DHHS Pub. No. (SMA) 02-3661. Rockville, MD: Center for Substance Abuse Treatment, Substance Abuse and Mental Health Services Administration.

Reilly, P. M., Shopshire, M. S., Durazzo, T. C., & Campbell, T. A. (2002). *Anger management for substance abuse and mental health clients: Participant workbook*. DHHS Pub. No. (SMA) 02-3662. Rockville, MD: Center for Substance Abuse Treatment, Substance Abuse and Mental Health Services Administration.

Rosellini, G., & Worden, M. (1997). *Of course you're angry: A guide to dealing with the emotions of substance abuse*. Center City, MN: Hazelden.

Spielberger, C. D. (1988). *Manual for the State-Trait Anger Expression Inventory (STAXI)*. Odessa, FL: Psychological Assessment Resources.

Spielberger, C. D., Gorssuch, R. L., Lushene, P. R., Vagg, P. R., & Jacobs, G. A. (1983). *Manual for the State-Trait Anxiety Inventory*. Palo Alto, CA: Consulting Psychologists Press.

Straus, M. A., Hamby, S. L., & Warren, W. L. (2003). *The conflict tactics scales handout*. Los Angeles, CA: Western Psychological Services.

Tivis, L. J., Parsons, O. A., & Nixon, S. J. (1998). Anger in an inpatient treatment sample of chronic alcoholics. *Alcoholism: Clinical and Experimental Research*, *22*, 902–907.

Walfish, S., Massey, R., & Krone, A. (1990). Anxiety and anger among abusers of different substances. *Drug and Alcohol Dependence*, *25*, 253–256.

Watson, D., & Tellegen, A. (1985). Toward a consensual structure of mood. *Psychological Bulletin*, *98*, 219–235.

Zelli, A., Huesmann, L. R., & Cervone, D. (1995). Social inference and individual differences in aggression: Evidence for spontaneous judgments of hostility. *Aggressive Behavior*, *21*, 405–417.

Zywiak, W. H., Connors, G. J., Maisto, S. A., & Westerberg, V. S. (1996). Relapse research and the Reasons for Drinking Questionnaire. A factor analysis of Marlatt's relapse taxonomy. *Addiction*, *91*, 121–130.

6

Management of Anger in People With Intellectual Disabilities

PAUL WILLNER, ANDREW JAHODA, AND PETER LARKIN

Intellectual disability is the current term for the condition previously known by a variety of names including *learning disability* (still in current U.K. usage) and *mental retardation*. It is defined as a significant impairment of both intellectual and adaptive/functional abilities acquired in childhood, where *significant* is usually interpreted statistically as two standard deviations below the population mean. For intellectual ability this means a Full-Scale IQ of less than 70, and for adaptive behavior it refers, essentially, to people who cannot function effectively without some degree of external support (British Psychological Society, 2000; Fletcher, Loschen, Stavrakaki, & First, 2008; World Health Organization, 1992).

Anger is a frequent problem for many people with intellectual disabilities and is often associated with verbal and/or physical aggression (Taylor & Novaco, 2005). Aggression is the main reason for an adult with a learning disability to be regarded as having severe challenging behavior (Allen & Felce, 1999) and to be referred for resource-intensive intervention (Lowe, Felce, & Blackman, 1995). Left unchecked, aggression resulting from uncontrolled anger can lead to serious consequences, which include exclusion from services, breakdown of residential placements, and, in extreme cases, involvement with the criminal justice system (Allen, Lowe, Brophy, & Moore, 2007; Emerson et al., 2008; Mental Health Foundation, 2008). Aggressive behavior can also have an impact on the psychological well-being of staff (Jenkins, Rose, & Lovell, 1997) and the quality of care they provide (Rose, Jones, & Fletcher, 1998). Community services supporting adults with learning disabilities receive numerous referrals for anger problems: Prevalence estimates for problem anger in the general population of people with intellectual disabilities vary between 11% and 27% (Rose, Dodd, & Rose, 2008). A review of recent studies of aggressive challenging behavior reported that over half of the population of people with intellectual disabilities display some form of aggression (Benson & Brooks, 2008), and anger is highly prevalent in people labeled as having challenging behavior: For example, Lindsay and Law (1999) reported that 60% of clients referred to a community service for people with intellectual disabilities and challenging or offending behaviors presented with clinically significant anger problems.

ANGER PROBLEMS: A DIRECT RESULT OF COGNITIVE DEFICITS?

The prevalence of aggression and dysfunctional anger in people with intellectual disabilities raises the question of whether there are certain underlying factors common to this group that predispose them to aggression. One obvious possibility is that their cognitive deficits per se could make them more likely to be angry and aggressive.

It has been suggested that deficits in several key areas may be linked to aggression, including poor socioemotional understanding and difficulties with interpreting complicated social information (Hunter, Nadany, & Cragg, 2010; Matson & Zeiss, 1978). As a result, people with intellectual disabilities may be more likely to misinterpret aspects of social situations. In turn, opportunities to rectify such misunderstandings may well be diminished by a lack of communicative ability and difficulties in taking the perspectives of others (Carr & Durand, 1985). If individuals also have deficits in emotion regulation, then it may be particularly difficult to prevent anger or frustration, aroused by difficult social situations, from driving them toward an aggressive reaction (Musher-Eizenman et al., 2004). Finally, some people with intellectual disabilities may struggle to generate nonaggressive responses to social situations, making them more likely to respond to challenging situations with aggression (Gardner & Cole, 1989). Individual factors may also contribute to aggression, including cognitive deficits such as poor attention span, impulsivity, and memory impairment (Gardner & Moffatt, 1990), as well as skill deficits in areas such as communication (Antonacci, Manuel, & Davis, 2008).

Given that levels of aggression increase with severity of intellectual disabilities, it is plausible that cognitive deficits themselves may well play some role in aggression in this group (Emerson et al., 1997). However, whether or not deficits partly explain the high levels of aggression in people with intellectual disabilities, there is no reason to think that they offer a comprehensive explanation of aggression in this population. If cognitive deficits do underpin problems of aggression in this group, one might anticipate that the more aggressive individuals would show more marked deficits than their less aggressive peers. However, the few studies to have addressed this question have provided little evidence that aggressive individuals with intellectual disabilities have particular cognitive deficits (e.g., Basquill et al., 2004; Jahoda, Pert, & Trower, 2006). Furthermore, evidence for the efficacy of largely behavioral treatments supported by the deficit model is also far from conclusive (Whitaker, 2001).

In conclusion, existing evidence suggests that "deficit" theories fall well short of explaining aggression in this group. Instead, recent research has begun to demonstrate that the factors underlying aggression in this group may be as varied and multifaceted as those underlying aggression in the wider population. For example, environmental factors, included overcrowding, high turnover of support staff, and inadequate staff training, may also lead to aggression (Gardner & Moffatt, 1990). Thus, the aggressive behavior of people with intellectual disabilities needs to be understood in context.

OTHER RISK FACTORS

A particular source of social threat or conflict is that people with intellectual disabilities are also more likely than the wider population to be ascribed low social status and to encounter stigmatization by their peers (Crocker, Major, & Steele, 1998; Dovidio, Major, & Crocker, 2000). Moreover, they are more likely to be exposed to maltreatment, including increased risk of being bullied and of facing verbal and physical aggression (Emerson, 2005; Fuchs & Benson, 1995; Nabuzoka & Smith, 1993). They also have a greater chance of being physically or sexually abused than do those in the general population (Furey, 1994; Tjaden, Thoennes, National Institute of Justice, & Centers for Disease Control and Prevention, 2000). Crucially, there is evidence that exposure to bullying and other forms of abuse increases the likelihood of an individual becoming aggressive (Burgess, Hartman, & McCormack, 1987; Marini, Dane, Bosacki, & Cura, 2006).

Another potential difficulty might be linked to a lack of autonomy. A defining feature of someone with an intellectual disability is that the person requires a greater degree of support from others to manage in their everyday lives. It is perhaps not surprising, then, that many people with intellectual disabilities, living in the community as well as in residential settings, feel disempowered (Emerson, 2005). This may be accompanied by feelings of anger and frustration, particularly if they feel that others are being controlling or restrictive. Such views might be particularly pertinent for people with milder intellectual disabilities who may be more aware of the limitations of their independence.

Hunter et al. (2010) used data collected from anger management interventions in the United Kingdom to identify the most common social experiences for 10 adults that led to significant feelings of anger. They found that the most widely reported incidents of this type were "minor annoyances" such as "nagging" or being "told off." The incidents rated as being most aggravating were of personal abuse, including being (a) shouted at, (b) physically threatened, and (c) "picked on." MacMahon, Jahoda, and Pert (2006) also investigated common sources of conflict. Fifty-three aggressive and nonaggressive adults with intellectual disabilities were asked to describe a recent situation of conflict that continued to elicit feelings of anger on recall. The most common source of interpersonal anger for both groups was the perception that they were being "belittled" or treated in a condescending manner.

These high levels of exposure to negative life experiences such as stigmatization and abuse may fuel the sense of disempowerment and dissatisfaction expressed by people with intellectual disabilities (Emerson, 2005). In turn, low self-esteem is commonplace in this group (Dagnan & Waring, 2004). With an impoverished quality of life, people with intellectual disabilities may also lack the resources that typically buffer self-esteem from negative comparisons with those around them (Dagnan & Sandhu, 1999). Being poorly equipped to bolster their own self or social identities could make people with intellectual disabilities more sensitive to social threat. It may also explain why they can be sensitive to being rejected or belittled by others. To protect their self-image, individuals in such circumstances may be compelled to resort to aggression (Jahoda, Trower, Pert, & Finn, 2001).

COGNITIVE SOURCES OF AGGRESSION

It appears that a wide range of factors may predispose people with intellectual disabilities to be aggressive. However, to understand why some individuals in this group are frequently aggressive, it is necessary to identify what differentiates them from their peers without problems of aggression. A large body of literature in the general population charts a variety of important cognitive factors in aggression (e.g., Dodge, 1980; Fontaine, Yang, Dodge, Pettit, & Bates, 2009; Lansford et al., 2006). Typically, such research has been approached and discussed from the framework of the Social Information-Processing model. One crucial implication of this evidence is the support it lends to the applicability of cognitive-based therapies for treating problems of aggression. If there are particular biases or cognitive styles that lead to aggression, then it would follow that cognitive interventions that can identify and rectify maladaptive thinking could be of use.

Until quite recently, potential cognitive factors, such as attributional biases, had been overlooked in research into aggression in people with intellectual disabilities. However, recent research has investigated psychosocial factors in the frequent aggression of people with intellectual disabilities. Consequently, it is becoming increasingly apparent that many of the cognitive tendencies thought to underpin aggression in the wider population play similar roles in the aggressive behavior of people with intellectual disabilities.

One finding is that a heightened sensitivity to apparent hostility in others may contribute to anger and aggression. Indeed, several studies have found that frequently aggressive people with intellectual disabilities are more likely to interpret the intent of others as being provocative (Basquill et al., 2004; Jahoda et al., 2006; Pert, Jahoda, & Squire, 1999). Aggressive individuals may also be more likely to attribute negative emotions to facial expressions (Matheson, Jahoda, & MacLean, 2005; Walz & Benson, 1996). Also, in situations of conflict, people with problems of aggression may be motivated by different social goals: Whereas those without problems of aggression often seek a fair outcome, aggressive individuals may be motivated to demonstrate strength (Pert & Jahoda, 2008). On deciding how to deal with conflict, aggressive people may be more likely to come up with aggressive solutions and to have more positive expectations of the consequences of aggression (Basquill et al., 2004; Fuchs & Benson, 1995; Kirk, Jahoda, & Pert, 2008; Pert & Jahoda, 2008). Finally, aggressive individuals may also be less likely to attempt assertive responses in situations of conflict (Jahoda, Pert, Squire, & Trower, 1998).

To bring these theoretical points to life, we will consider the experience and expression of anger and aggression by a person with an intellectual disability. Although this is a heterogeneous population, living in diverse circumstances, there can be commonalities among those with mild intellectual disabilities referred to psychology services with problems of anger and aggression. The composite case study to follow aims to highlight a number of these common features.

Case Study

John is a 38-year-old man who lives in his own apartment, with help provided by a staff team located on the same block. He moved from his family home 6 years ago, following the death of his mother, although there was a history of conflict at home. His two siblings, both older than him, had left the family home a decade before he did.

John has a mild intellectual disability with an IQ score of 65 and is quite independent in many domains of life; he has some literacy skills and can travel independently. However, he has particular difficulties with money and needs weekly help with his finances. John has a history of being financially exploited by people who befriend him. John has little to do during the day, despite the best efforts of his support staff and social worker, because frequent temper outbursts and his dislike of other people "telling me what to do" have led to the breakdown of several supported employment courses and a college course. When angry, he may shout, swear, break objects, and, less frequently, punch and kick out at others. He is also sensitive about being seen as "stupid" and is very aware that his siblings had achieved life goals of work and marriage to which he aspired. He acknowledges that he can lose his temper easily and that he finds it difficult to get "angry thoughts" out of his head, and he obtained a high score on the Provocation Inventory (Novaco, 1994).

John's relationships with other people living on his apartment block are also fraught with frequent conflicts, resulting in his neighbors keeping their distance from him, and he has been banned from a number of communal events and gatherings on the block. Although he recognizes that his behavior has led to his social difficulties, he feels that other people reject him, and he complains of being bored and lonely. His score on the Glasgow Depression Scale for people with intellectual disabilities (Mindham & Espie, 2003) is clinically significant (>13).

He has a tendency to blame other people for incidents of conflict, often thinking his aggression is a justified response to provocation, even where none is intended. Even though he knows that other people can be very frightened of him, he talks about the positive effects of being aggressive and describes it as a way of making sure that other people listen to you. In this sense, he is ambivalent about working on his anger problems, because he does not always share the same prosocial goals for therapy as the staff member who referred him for psychological help.

John's case description reflects a number of the findings outlined in recent studies referred to earlier, which have begun to show how the ways in which aggressive people with intellectual disabilities deal with social situations might contribute to their aggression. Such findings offer insights into the specific psychological mechanisms that lead an individual to become angry and act aggressively. In doing so, they also strengthen the theoretical argument for considering cognitive-behavioral treatments of frequent aggression in people with intellectual disabilities.

COGNITIVE-BEHAVIORAL ANGER INTERVENTIONS FOR PEOPLE WITH INTELLECTUAL DISABILITIES

Cognitive-behavioral therapy (CBT) is a system of psychological therapy that aims to develop more adaptive cognitions and behavior, and so alleviate distress, by changing cognitions such as thoughts, attitudes, and beliefs. The cognitive model of psychopathology was developed initially by Beck (1976) and colleagues. It assumes that people's emotions and behavior are influenced by their perceptions of events (i.e., that thoughts, images, and other cognitive mediating processes affect behavior), that psychological disorders are characterized by distorted or dysfunctional thinking, that how people feel is determined by the way in which they construe situations rather than by the situations per se (or as Shakespeare described it 350 years earlier, "There is nothing either good or bad but thinking makes it so"), and, therefore, that mood and behavior can be improved by working with the client to modify thinking in the direction of more realistic or adaptive evaluations of events.

A number of approaches have been developed by therapists working within a broad CBT framework. The common feature is that treatment is based on a cognitive formulation that (a) seeks to explain the symptoms displayed and (b) guides the choice of therapeutic activities. CBT is typically time limited, problem oriented, and present focused. CBT takes a collaborative approach in which the client is encouraged to take active control of the therapy and uses a scientific method (e.g., behavioral experiments) to examine the evidence relating to thoughts and beliefs. Much of the work is done by the client as "homework." Sessions are structured such that a typical session would involve reviewing the client's state, setting an agenda for the session, reviewing homework, setting session targets, working on them, setting homework, and reviewing the session. When applying CBT to "special populations," such as children or people with intellectual disabilities, these practical aspects of CBT are negotiable: The essential feature of CBT is the cognitive-behavioral formulation and the therapeutic activities that flow from it.

Anger Management

Most of the techniques used to address anger in people with intellectual disabilities are based on an approach by Novaco and colleagues, initially developed for use in an intellectually able population. The approach is recognizably the same as that used in other externalizing disorders: For example, there are close parallels with relapse prevention for substance abuse (Marlatt & Gordon, 1985). It consists of teaching clients to be aware of situations that evoke anger, to be aware of becoming angry, and to develop skills to control and manage anger. Anger is conceptualized as an emotion with physiological, behavioral, and cognitive components, and the program includes a range of coping skills aimed at each of these areas: physiology (relaxation), behavior (distraction, time-out, walking away, help seeking, use of humor and assertiveness), and cognition (cognitive restructuring, problem solving). As is clear from this list, there is an emphasis on behavioral coping skills. Relaxation is also prominent, as it is typically introduced very early in the program and used throughout. Typically, however, cognitive skills are introduced later in the program (Novaco, 1975; Novaco, Ramm, & Black, 2000; see Taylor & Novaco, 2005, for a comprehensive review of the application of these techniques to people with intellectual disabilities).

The anger management program in use in an ongoing randomized controlled trial (Willner et al., 2011) is described here as an example of this approach. The program has been manualized and is delivered within the day services that participants attend by staff working within the same service. The lay therapists receive a one-day training program and fortnightly supervision from a qualified clinical psychologist. We work with groups of, typically, six to nine service users, who have been referred because they express anger in inappropriate ways that cause problems for themselves or others. There are 12 group sessions, which conform to the generic CBT structure described earlier (reviewing the clients' state, setting an agenda for the session, reviewing homework, setting session targets, working on them, setting homework, and reviewing the session). All sessions begin with a warm-up exercise, are punctuated by a tea/coffee break, and end with a relaxation exercise. Topics addressed over sessions include the triggers that evoke anger, physiological and behavioral components of anger, behavioral and cognitive strategies to avoid the buildup of anger and for coping with anger-provoking situations, and acceptable ways of displaying anger (assertiveness). Presentation relies heavily on brainstorming (e.g., "What makes us angry?") and role play. About one third of each session, after the first session, is devoted to discussion of one or two participants' experiences, focusing primarily on ways in which situations might have been handled differently to produce a better outcome, as contributed by facilitators and participants. In addition to simplifying the language used in sessions, we avoid wherever possible the use of written materials, in favor of pictorial representations. Toward the end of every session, participants are asked to undertake a homework assignment, which always consists of working with a staff member to complete a functional analysis ("hassle log") of a situation in which they have been angered that week, which is described, analyzed, and evaluated. The functional analysis involves describing the context, the anger-provoking event, the participant's response, the quality of the outcome, and a consideration of how the anger coping skills taught in the program could have been used to achieve a better outcome. As with the session content, homework is also simplified by using the same homework exercise in every session and presenting the material pictorially, in the form of a workbook.

The assessment of anger is sometimes accomplished using self- or staff-completed recordings of actual incidents of anger, but this is relatively unusual in recent studies of people with intellectual disabilities (see Taylor & Novaco, 2005, Table 5.2). More commonly, anger is assessed using either questionnaires or judgments of what would happen hypothetically in anger-provoking situations. The most commonly used questionnaire is the Novaco Anger Scale (Novaco, 1994, 2003), which includes cognitive, arousal, and behavioral subscales and an anger regulation scale. Two instruments commonly used to assess responses to provocation are the Anger Inventory (Benson & Ivins, 1992) and the Provocation Index (Novaco, 1994), which can be completed either by service users themselves or by carers, or both. Typical items are "You are in a queue to get something and someone pushes in front of you," "You are watching a TV program when someone comes along and switches the channel," and "Someone looks through your things without asking you." Ratings are made on a 4-point scale, from "not angry" to "extremely angry," sometimes using cartoons of increasingly angry faces.

A typical anger management program is based on teaching participants a range of anger coping skills, so it is important to assess the extent to which such skills are acquired. The Profile of Anger Coping Skills (Willner, Brace, & Phillips, 2005) was developed for this purpose. This assessment is based on three brief vignettes, elicited individually from each respondent, of situations in which the respondent often displays anger. For each situation, the respondent is asked to rate the extent to which the service user employed each of eight coping strategies in that specific situation. Summing across all eight strategies gives a score for total strategy usage, and the scores for each of the eight individual coping skills provide a profile of the coping strategies employed by the respondent. A significant correlation has been reported between improvements in anger expression and the acquisition of anger coping skills (Willner & Tomlinson, 2007), which suggests strongly that the acquisition of coping skills plays an important role in anger control. We are currently field-testing a first-person version of this instrument on which service users rate their own usage of anger coping skills (Willner et al., 2011).

There is some evidence that treatment gains following anger management are not confined to the environment in which the intervention was delivered: This comes from studies where the assessment included observer ratings of anger intensity or aggressive incidents in settings other than that in which the intervention was delivered (e.g., King, Lancaster, Wynne, Nettleton, & Davis, 1999; Moore, Adams, Elsworth, & Lewis, 1997; Rose, 1996; Rose & West, 1999; Willner, Jones, Tams, & Green, 2002). To assess the extent to which therapeutic gains transferred across settings, anger management was implemented in a day service, and parallel assessments were undertaken with both day-service staff and home carers. Participants showed decreases in anger and increases in coping skills, which were maintained at 6-month follow-up. Day-service key workers and home carers did not differ significantly, at any time, in their ratings of anger, aggregate coping skills, or individual coping skills. This suggests that there was a high degree of generalization of anger coping skills from day-service to residential settings (Willner & Tomlinson, 2007). However, individuals vary considerably in the particular skills they use to manage anger, and these individual coping styles appear to be stable over time (Willner & Tomlinson, 2007). And although, at the level of the group, similar profiles of coping skills were reported by day-service key workers and home carers, at the level of the individual, coping profiles were different in the two environments, so much so that correlations between the profiles displayed in the two environments were nonsignificant. It is likely that this reflects to some extent the different demands placed on individuals in different environments and the different potential to deploy particular skills. (For example, if a home carer is a significant trigger for anger, then this may decrease the potential to use help seeking as an anger management strategy.) Nevertheless, the fact that participants in an anger management intervention use different skills in different settings suggests that further clinical gains might be available if key workers and home carers share information about the strategies observed in each setting, with the possibility of encouraging service users to utilize their full range of coping skills.

Anger Treatment

Although anger management is usually effective, the effects can sometimes be quite small: For example, Rose, Loftus, Flint, and Carey (2005) reported improvements of around only 10% in anger intensity, with only 20% of participants demonstrating reliable clinical change (Jacobson & Truax, 1991). One reason for this limited effectiveness is likely to be the difficulty within a group format of optimizing treatment for individual participants. There is some scope to design role-plays around a participant's individual triggers, which can be established in the pregroup assessment, but there is little scope in a group program for developing an individual formulation for each participant and building the intervention around it.

A related problem is that anger management assumes a psychoeducational deficit model. The basic assumption is that people who display anger in inappropriate ways do so because they lack the necessary coping skills, and if taught those skills they will be enabled to behave more appropriately. This formulation overlooks the fact that people may possess anger management skills yet fail to use them. People may choose not to control their anger because anger is used instrumentally to achieve positive outcomes, for example, by intimidating others and compelling compliance (Tiedens, 2001). A failure to control anger may also reflect a client's attitudes and beliefs, such as self-righteousness, an inability to take responsibility or a tendency to blame others, and a belief in the cathartic value of expressing anger (DiGiuseppe, 1995). The instrumental use or justification of anger are often seen as clinical counterindications for inclusion in an anger management program (Howells & Day, 2003).

A number of further contraindications to anger management have been identified. For example, anger management may be unsuitable for people with comorbid mental health problems or personality disorders (Howells & Day, 2003). Indeed, for some people with a psychopathic disorder, inclusion in an anger management program may actually increase the risk of recidivism, perhaps because psychopaths learn less about themselves than about new ways of manipulating and deceiving others (Hare, Clark, Thornton, & Grann, 2000). Anger management is also unsuitable for people who are unwilling or unable to function effectively in a group setting.

Anger treatment (Novaco et al., 2000) offers an alternative approach, which to some extent addresses all of these issues. Based on an individual analysis and formulation, anger treatment is delivered individually and aims to modify the cognitive structures that maintain anger, enhance self-monitoring, and develop self-control through graded exposure to provocation. A published manual details the version of anger treatment developed for use with people with intellectual disabilities (Taylor & Novaco, 2005). The intervention begins with a 6-week preparatory phase aimed at developing an understanding of anger and other emotions and establishing motivation to change, followed by a 12-week treatment phase. In contrast to anger management, where cognitive elements are introduced toward the end of the program, cognitive restructuring and problem solving are the major components of anger treatment. Treatment is based on stress inoculation, using therapist-guided graded exposure to a hierarchy of individual triggers for anger. The program includes relaxation and behavioral skills training, but the primary thrust is for cognitive change.

The primary assessment tool used to evaluate anger treatment studies has been the Imaginal Provocation Test (Taylor, Novaco, Guinan, & Street, 2004). This differs from the Provocation Inventory by taking a smaller number of anger-provoking incidents and building scenarios around them: For example, "You come back to the ward/unit after finishing work at tea time. You go into your bedroom to get changed. After a short time you see that someone has been going though your things without asking you." The question "How angry does this make you feel?" is then augmented by questions about what you might do: "swear and shout," "hit the person," and other options. Compared to a waiting-list control condition, participants in anger treatment showed decreases in both anger expression and behavioral responses to provocation. Control measures (clarity of imagery and memory for the provocation scenario) were unaffected, indicating that the potential for provocation remained the same, but the response to provocation was reduced (Taylor et al., 2004). Because anger treatment is heavily weighted toward the cognitive elements of the intervention, this study goes further than the anger management literature in providing evidence to support the potential effectiveness of cognitive therapy in people with intellectual disabilities.

OUTCOMES OF COGNITIVE-BEHAVIORAL ANGER INTERVENTIONS

Following the early demonstration of the effectiveness of CBT for the treatment of depressive disorders, CBT has subsequently been demonstrated to be effective, in the general population, for the treatment of a very wide range of psychological disorders, in both group and individual settings, including anxiety disorders (generalized anxiety disorder, panic, social phobias, obsessive-compulsive disorder, posttraumatic stress disorder), psychosis, eating disorders, relationship problems, personality disorders, forensic issues (aggression and sexual offending), and substance abuse (Hawton, Salkovskis, Kirk, & Clark, 1989; Roth & Fonagy, 2004). In the United Kingdom, CBT is now recommended by the National Institute for Clinical Excellence (NICE) as first-line treatment for a rapidly expanding range of psychological disorders, and widening access to CBT for people with mental health problems is seen as a major policy priority by the U.K. Department of Health, which has allocated £170 million to train 3,600 CBT therapists (Department of Health/Care Service Improvement Partnership, 2007).

It has been estimated that some 25% to 40% of people with intellectual disabilities have additional mental health problems (Department of Health, 2001, 2009), and the U.K. Department of Health has drawn attention to the fact that the National Service Framework for Mental Health applies to all adults, which implies that "a person with a learning disability should be able to access services and be treated in the same way as anyone else, with reasonable adjustments being made" (Department of Health, 2009). This is an enlightened position that until recently was not recognized even within services for people with learning disabilities. As noted by Bender (1993), "therapeutic disdain" has until recently limited the availability of these techniques to clients with intellectual disabilities, who historically have had little or no access to psychotherapeutic interventions. Traditionally, people with learning disabilities have received psychopharmacological or behavioral interventions aimed at controlling their behavior rather than promoting psychological health. Psychotherapists "disdained" to treat people with learning disabilities, who, it was thought, would be unable to benefit (Bender, 1993), and only in the 1990s did this situation start to change (Sinason, 1992; Waitman & Conboy-Hill, 1992). While the limited intellectual abilities of people with intellectual disabilities will clearly constrain the applicability of cognitive techniques to this population, the extensive evidence that children are able to benefit from CBT demonstrates that, with appropriate adaptations, CBT can be used outside the confines of the traditional adult mental health context (Fonagy, Target, Cottrell, Phillips, & Kurtz, 2002). In the years following Bender's (1993) critique, the use of CBT with people who are intellectually disabled has become widespread, at least within British clinical psychology (Nagel & Leiper, 1999). Two particular landmarks along this path were a multiauthor book published in 1997, which acted as a manifesto for clinicians interested in the use of CBT in intellectual disability services (Stenfert-Kroese, Dagnan, & Loumidis, 1997), and a more recent special issue of the *Journal of Applied Research in Intellectual Disabilities* devoted to CBT (Willner & Hatton, 2006).

As a result of this late start, and also because of the difficulty of conducting clinical trials within a small population (Oliver et al., 2002), the evidence of the effectiveness of CBT in people with intellectual disabilities remains sparse. There are a fair number of published case studies and case series describing the application of CBT to a variety of indications, including internalizing disorders such as anxiety (Dagnan & Jahoda, 2006; Lindsay, 1999), depression (Lindsay, 1999; Lindsay, Howells, & Pitcaithly, 1993), posttraumatic stress disorder (Stenfert-Kroese & Thomas, 2006; Willner, 2004), and psychosis (Haddock, Lobbab, Hatton, & Carson, 2004) and externalizing disorders such as sexual offending (Lindsay & Smith, 1998) and arson (Taylor, Thorne, Robertson, & Avery, 2002), as well as anger (reviewed by Taylor & Novaco, 2005). However, there have been very few controlled trials. Indeed, for many years the only controlled trial of CBT in the intellectual disabilities literature was a study that compared a three-component anger management program with each of the separate components (relaxation, self-instruction, and problem solving). The study reported decreases in anger following treatment, with no difference in outcome between the four conditions; however, it did not include an untreated control group and so provided no evidence that the treatments were more effective than no treatment (Benson, Johnson-Rice, & Miranti, 1986).

Recently, however, the evidence base has been substantially augmented through the addition of at least eight studies describing controlled trials comparing intervention for anger problems with a waiting-list control condition. Table 6.1 includes nine studies of anger management groups, two studies of individual therapy in a community setting, and two/three studies of individual anger treatment in a forensic setting. (The numerical ambiguity arises because the study by Taylor, Novaco, Gillmer, Robertson, & Thorne, 2005, includes the participants in their two earlier studies.) All of the studies listed in Table 6.1 reported significant improvements, albeit to varying degrees, following an anger management group or a course of individual anger treatment. Improvements were maintained at 3- to 12-month follow-up in all of the studies that included a follow-up assessment. Effect sizes in the anger management studies were generally large ($d > 1$), with similar effects reported for group and individual formats and for self- and carer ratings. Effect sizes in the anger treatment studies were generally smaller, but large effects were reported on specific measures in two of the three studies. Every study also reported that anger does not decrease spontaneously in the control groups: People who receive anger interventions benefit; however, in the absence of intervention, anger shows little if any spontaneous remission. This area of research constitutes the strongest evidence that CBT can be effective in people with intellectual disabilities.

The anger literature has recently been supplemented by two small controlled trials in depression (McCabe, McGillivray, & Newton, 2006; McGillivray, McCabe, & Kershaw, 2008). These studies demonstrated that, in people with relatively mild (but clinically significant) levels of depression, a brief group-based intervention led to decreases in both depression scores and the occurrence of negative automatic thoughts, confirming that the intervention engendered cognitive change (in addition to clinical improvement). Interestingly, the intervention was as effective when delivered by support staff using a treatment manual (McGillivray et al., 2008) as when delivered by trained therapists (McCabe et al., 2006).

The same technique—training and supervising lay staff to deliver a manualized group-based therapy—has also been used to address anger management problems in people with intellectual disabilities (Willner & Tomlinson, 2007). A large-scale multicenter randomized controlled trial of this intervention is currently in progress (Willner et al., 2011).

Table 6.1 Studies of Anger Interventions Versus Waiting-List Controls[a]

Study	Date	N^b	Format	Sessions	Duration	Rater	Follow-Up
			ANGER MANAGEMENT				
Rose, West, and Clifford	2000	25	Group	16 × 2 h	32 h	Self	12 mo
Willner, Jones, Tams, and Green	2002	16	Group	9 × 2 h	18 h	Self/carer	3 mo
Lindsay et al.	2004	47	Group	40 × 1 h	40 h	Self/carer	3–30 mo
Willner, Brace, and Phillips	2005	17	Group	12 × 2 h	24 h	Self/carer	6 mo
Rose et al.	2005	86	Group	16 × 2 h	32 h	Self	None
Hagiliassis, Gulbenkoglu, Di Marco, Young, and Hudson	2006	29	Group	12 × 2 h	24 h	Self	4 mo
Rose, Dodd, and Rose	2008	41	Individual[c]	16 × ¾ h	12 h	Self	None
Rose, O'Brien, and Rose	2009	64	Group and	16 × 2 h	32 h	Self	None
			Individual[c]	16 × ¾ h	12 h		
Rose	2010	56	Group[c]	16 × 2 h	32 h	Carer	None
Collado-Castillo[d]	2011	36	Group	??	??	Self	None
			ANGER TREATMENT				
Taylor, Novaco, Gillmer, and Thorne	2002	20	Individual	18 × 1 h	18 h	Self	None
Taylor, Novaco, Guinan, and Street	2004	17	Individual	18 × 1 h	18 h	Self	None
Taylor, Novaco, Gillmer, Robertson, and Thorne	2005	36	Individual	18 × 1 h	18 h	Self/carer	4 mo

[a] The table lists all published studies in which a cognitive-behavioral anger management intervention for people with intellectual disabilities has been compared with a waiting-list control group, based on a literature review conducted in February 2012.

[b] The numbers listed are the total number of participants in the study; they may not have been equally distributed between conditions.

[c] Individual participants in the study of Rose et al. (2008) and Rose et al. (2009) received 14 to 18 sessions of 30 to 60 minutes' duration. The figures in the table provide a rough average.

[d] The study of Collado-Castillo (2011) is published in abstract only. Positive results were reported for two interventions, cognitive reappraisal and problem solving, but few further details are available.

Factors Influencing the Effectiveness of Anger Interventions

Two factors have been identified that have a significant impact on the outcome for participants in anger management groups: intellectual ability and the participation of carers in the group. Both factors were first identified in a very small study by Willner et al. (2002) and confirmed in a larger study by Rose et al. (2005).

The relationship between success in anger management and verbal ability (Rose et al., 2005; Willner et al., 2002) is consistent with a body of literature reporting a similar relationship between verbal ability and the cognitive (Dagnan, Chadwick, & Proudlove, 2000; Oathamshaw & Haddock, 2006; Reed & Clements, 1989; Sams, Collins, & Reynolds, 2006) and communication skills (Jahoda, Selkirk, et al., 2009) needed to engage fully in CBT. In two other studies, however, verbal ability did not influence the outcome of individual anger treatment (Rose, 2010; Taylor et al., 2005). This difference may reflect the greater potential for addressing an individual's cognitive limitations in individual treatment, as opposed to the situation in a group, where the facilitator may be unaware of an individual who is losing the plot, or perhaps aware that an individual has disengaged but unable to provide individual support because of the competing demands of other group members. It may also be relevant that the study of Taylor et al. (2005) involved a more able population, with some participants in the "borderline" range of abilities, whereas the participants in the studies of Willner et al. (2002) and Rose et al. (2005) were all clients of learning disability services. Another study also supported the principle that lower intellectual ability confers a disadvantage in a group-based intervention, though in this case, improvement in anger management correlated significantly with nonverbal reasoning ability (assessed using Ravens Coloured Progressive Matrices). The authors speculated that this might reflect the strong emphasis in their program on visual and active learning techniques (Hagiliassis, Gulbenkoglu, Di Marco, Young, & Hudson, 2006).

One strategy that could potentially contribute to a positive outcome is to maximize the involvement of carers by locating the anger management group within the day service attended by the participants and training day-service staff to act as group facilitators. This ensures that the coping skills taught within the group could be reinforced throughout the working week, both by direct input from the group facilitators when the participants were involved in anger events and by the dissemination of the content of the program to other staff. Although there are clear potential benefits to involving carers, this approach is not without its problems (Willner, 2006), and there is no consensus among clinical psychologists over the desirability of carers being present in therapy sessions (Haddock & Jones, 2006). However, the objections to this practice relate primarily to the impact of a carer on the therapeutic relationship in individual therapy and may be of lesser relevance in a group setting.

BARRIERS TO ENGAGEMENT

The recent U.K. Department of Health position paper identified several barriers to people with learning disabilities accessing psychological therapies, including social restriction, challenging behavior, failure of general practitioners to diagnose mental health problems, and resistance from mental health services (Department of Health, 2009). However, assuming that a referral is made, there are also a number of factors that make engagement with therapy difficult for people with learning disabilities. Limited verbal ability, psychological mindedness (particularly in relation to the understanding of emotions and the mediating role of cognitions), and self-efficacy are all likely to present significant barriers. In addition, people with learning disabilities may have had little experience in reporting emotions, giving opinions, or decision making; may be skilled at "covering up" their difficulties; and may have developed the strategy of acquiescing to suggestions made to them with no intention to follow through. There may also be motivational barriers to treatment, including the functionality of some psychological presentations, maladaptive beliefs promoting resistance to change, the intellectually challenging nature of cognitive therapy, and external factors such as inappropriate settings. And although people with learning disabilities do self-refer, the referral is often made under pressure from a third party (Willner, 2006).

The issue of referral is important, because people's views of therapy can have an important impact on clients' engagement and motivation to change (Kilbane & Jahoda, 2011). For example, it is assumed that CBT interventions should be collaborative and time limited. However, individuals with learning disabilities may be looking for a longer term supportive relationship from the therapist. They may also be uncertain whether it is possible to achieve lasting improvement, which is understandable if they have struggled to deal with life's continuing challenges (Pert et al., 2012). A more general therapeutic assumption is that people will be able to apply the skills and insights they have obtained in therapy in their wider lives. Whether or not this happens depends on people being able to generalize their skills, but it also depends on the ability to exercise a degree of control over their lives, which might not always be the case. Learning to control one's anger might involve maintaining a distance from people with whom one is in conflict, and this might be very difficult to achieve in a group-living situation. Moreover, it is not just a matter of practicing new skills. Change is also reinforced when others recognize one's achievements. This is particularly germane to anger interventions, where the aim is reduce interpersonal conflict and improve relationships. Once again, because people with intellectual disabilities have low social status, it may be more difficult for them to change other people's perceptions. A reputation for being difficult and aggressive might be particularly hard to overcome, and where people continue to be treated with suspicion or animosity, conflict is likely to continue.

A useful distinction can be drawn between two sources of difficulty in engaging with cognitive therapy (Dagnan & Lindsay, 2004; Kendall, 1985; Lindsay, Jahoda, Willner, & Taylor, 2013; Willner, 2006). In addition to the cognitive distortions (inaccuracies in the content of thoughts, assumptions, and beliefs) that, in the cognitive model, characterize psychological disorders, people with learning disabilities also have cognitive deficits. These are deficiencies in the processes by which information is acquired and processed, which, in addition to limited intellectual ability (verbal and nonverbal understanding and reasoning), may include limitations of emotional literacy, memory problems, and executive dysfunction (Lindsay, Jahoda, & Willner, 2013). These cognitive deficits create barriers to treatment in two ways: by inhibiting engagement and by increasing the difficulty of psychotherapeutic activities aimed at correcting cognitive distortions, such as challenging thoughts or generating alternative ways of thinking about situations.

As noted earlier, engagement with therapy—for anger in particular—can be promoted by involving carers to support the therapy. There is evidence that the outcome of CBT for anger is improved if clients are accompanied in the therapy session by a carer (Rose et al., 2005), and carers can provide invaluable support for compliance with homework completion, which is a significant problem for CBT therapists (Garland & Scott, 2002) and important for positive outcomes (Rees, McEvoy, & Nathan, 2005). However, carers may themselves display a range of limitations of ability and motivation, similar to those displayed by clients, which need to be recognized, and where possible addressed, in order for their involvement to be effective (Willner, 2006). Carers are aware that their training and experience as therapists are minimal, and some at least would welcome educational input to enable them to improve their ability to support clients in therapy (McVilly, 1997). One criticism of involving carers in the treatment sessions is that clients may be forced to spend time with the very people with whom they feel most angry. This is a legitimate concern, and careful judgements do have to be made about the involvement of carers. On the other hand, bringing clients and carers together in therapy sessions might help to foster better relationships, with a positive impact on anger problems linked to interpersonal difficulties.

If barriers to treatment are recognized, significant steps can be taken to increase accessibility without undermining the underlying principles of CBT (Lindsay, 1999; Lindsay, Jahoda & Willner, 2012; Stenfert-Kroese et al., 1997). Indeed, there are many opportunities to make the therapy more accessible, for example, by using simple language and, wherever appropriate, pictures; by proceeding slowly, with extensive rehearsal; and by supporting homework by providing memory aids or, as discussed earlier, by recruiting carers to provide assistance (Hurley, Tomasulo, & Pfadt, 1998; Lynch, 2004; Royal College of Psychiatrists, 2004; Whitehouse, Tudway, Look, & Stenfert-Kroese, 2006). CBT is not merely about therapeutic dialogue but can use activities that are meaningful for people with intellectual disabilities and take account of their particular social and emotional experience (Jahoda, Dagnan, Stenfert-Kroese, Pert, & Trower, 2009). All of these adaptations are used routinely in anger management work. Indeed, they are standard practice in working therapeutically with people with intellectual disabilities, and although they have not been shown explicitly to improve engagement with and, thereby, the efficacy of CBT, it would be surprising if this were not the case.

REFERENCES

Allen, D., & Felce, D. (1999). Service responses to challenging behaviour. In N. Bouras (Ed.), *Psychiatric and behavioural disorders in developmental disabilities* (pp. 279–294). Cambridge, UK: Cambridge University Press.

Allen, D., Lowe, K., Brophy, S., & Moore, K. (2007). Predictors, costs and characteristics of out of area placements for people with intellectual disability and challenging behaviour. *Journal of Intellectual Disability Research, 51*, 409–416.

Antonacci, D., Manuel, C., & Davis, E. (2008). Diagnosis and treatment of aggression in individuals with developmental disabilities. *Psychiatric Quarterly, 79*, 225–247.

Basquill, M. F., Nezu, C.M., Nezu, A. M., Klein, T. L., & MacLean Jr., W. E. (2004). Aggression-related hostility bias and social problem-solving deficits in adult males with mental retardation. *American Journal on Mental Retardation, 109*, 255–263.

Beck, A. T. (1976). *Cognitive therapy and the emotional disorders*. New York, NY: International Universities Press.

Bender, M. (1993). The unoffered chair: The history of therapeutic disdain towards people with a learning disability. *Clinical Psychology Forum, 54*, 7–12.

Benson, B. A., & Brooks, W. (2008). Aggressive challenging behaviour and intellectual disability. *Current Opinion in Psychiatry, 21*, 454–458.

Benson, B. A., & Ivins, J. (1992). Anger, depression and self-concept in adults with mental retardation. *Journal of Intellectual Disability Research, 36*, 169–175.

Benson, B., Johnson-Rice, C., & Miranti, S. V. (1986). Effects of anger management training with mentally retarded adults in group treatment. *Journal of Consulting and Clinical Psychology, 54*, 728–729.

British Psychological Society. (2000). *Learning disability: Definitions and contexts*. Leicester, UK: British Psychological Society.

Burgess, A. W., Hartman, C. R., & McCormack, A. (1987). Abused to abuser: Antecedents of socially deviant behaviors. *American Journal of Psychiatry, 144*, 1431–1436.

Carr, E. G., & Durand, V. M. (1985). Reducing behavior problems through functional communication training. *Journal of Applied Behavior Analysis, 18*, 111–126.

Collado-Castillo, C. J. (2011). Comparison of a cognitive re-appraisal approach and a problem-solving approach to improve social cognition in adults with intellectual disabilities who exhibit aggressive behavior. *Dissertation Abstracts International Section A: Human and Social Sciences, 71*, 3324.

Crocker, J., Major, B., & Steele, C. (1998). Social stigma. In S. Fiske, D. Gilbert, & G. Lindsey (Ed.), *Handbook of social psychology* (Vol. 2, pp. 504–553). Boston, MA: McGraw-Hill.

Dagnan, D., Chadwick, P., & Proudlove, J. (2000). Towards an assessment of suitability of people with mental retardation for cognitive therapy. *Cognitive Therapy and Research, 24*, 627–636.

Dagnan, D., & Jahoda, A. (2006). Cognitive-behavioural intervention for people with intellectual disability and anxiety disorders. *Journal of Applied Research in Intellectual Disabilities, 19*, 91–98.

Dagnan, D., & Lindsay, W. R. (2004). Research issues in cognitive therapy. In E. Emerson, C. Hatton, T. Thompon, & T. R. Parmenter (Eds.), *The international handbook of applied research in intellectual disabilities* (pp. 517–420). Chichester, UK: Wiley.

Dagnan, D., & Sandhu, S. (1999). Social comparison, self-esteem and depression in people with intellectual disability. *Journal of Intellectual Disability Research, 43*, 372–379.

Dagnan, D., & Waring, M. (2004). Linking stigma to psychological distress: Testing a social-cognitive model of the experience of people with intellectual disabilities. *Clinical Psychology and Psychotherapy, 11*, 247–254.

DiGiuseppe, R. (1995). Developing the therapeutic alliance with angry clients. In H. Kassinove (Ed.), *Anger disorders: Definition, diagnosis and treatment* (pp. 131–150). Philadelphia, PA: Taylor & Francis.

Dodge, K. A. (1980). Social cognition and children's aggressive behavior. *Child Development, 51*, 162–170.

Department of Health. (2001). *Valuing people: A new strategy for learning disability for the 21st century—a white paper*. London, UK: Author.

Department of Health. (2009). *Learning disabilities: Positive practice guide*. London: Author.

Department of Health/ Care Service Improvement Partnership. (2007). *Choices in mental health: Improving access to psychological therapies*. Retrieved from http://www.dh.gov.uk

Dovidio, J. F., Major, B., & Crocker, J. (2000). Stigma: Introduction and overview. In T. F. Heatherton, R. E. Kleck, M. R. Hebl, & J. G. Hull (Eds.), *The social psychology of stigma* (pp. 1–28). New York, NY: Guilford Press.

Emerson, E. (2005). *Adults with learning difficulties in England 2003/2004*. London, UK: Health and Social Care Information Centre.

Emerson, E., Alborz, A., Reeves, D., Mason, H., Swabrick, R., Kiesnan, C., & Mason, L. (1997). *The prevalence of challenging behaviour. The Hester Adrian Research Centre Challenging Behaviour Project, Report 2*. Manchester, UK: Hester Adrian Research Centre, University of Manchester.

Emerson, E., Robertson, J., Dorr, H., Russell, P., Spencer, K., Davies, I., ... Congdon, D. (2008). *Commissioning person centred, cost effective, local support for people with learning difficulties*. London, UK: Social Care Institute for Excellence.

Fletcher, R., Loschen, E., Stavrakaki, C., & First, M. (2008) *Diagnostic manual: Intellectual disability*. Kingston, NY: National Association for the Dually Diagnosed.

Fonagy, P., Target, M., Cottrell, D., Phillips, J., & Kurtz, Z. (2002). *What works for whom? A critical review of treatments for children and adolescents*. New York, NY: Guilford Press.

Fontaine, R. G., Yang, C., Dodge, K. A., Pettit, G. S., & Bates, J. E. (2009). Development of response evaluation and decision (RED) and antisocial behavior in childhood and adolescence. *Developmental Psychology, 45*, 447–459.

Fuchs, C., & Benson, B. A. (1995). Social information processing by aggressive and non-aggressive men with mental retardation. *American Journal on Mental Retardation, 100*, 244–252.

Furey, E. M. (1994). Sexual abuse of adults with mental retardation: Who and where. *Mental Retardation, 32*, 173–180.

Gardner, W. I., & Cole, C. L. (1989). Self-management approaches. *Monographs of the American Association on Mental Retardation, 12*, 19–35.

Gardner, W. I., & Moffatt, C. (1990). Aggressive behaviour: Definition, assessment, treatment. *International Review of Psychiatry, 2*, 91–100.

Garland, A., & Scott, J. (2002). Using homework in therapy for depression. *Journal of Clinical Psychology, 58*, 489–498.

Haddock, K., & Jones, S. P. (2006). Practitioner consensus in the use of cognitive behaviour therapy for individuals with a learning disability. *Journal of Intellectual Disabilities, 10*, 221–230.

Haddock, G., Lobbab, F., Hatton, C., & Carson, R. (2004). Cognitive-behaviour therapy for people with psychosis and mild intellectual disabilities: A case series. *Clinical Psychology and Psychotherapy, 11*, 282–298.

Hagiliassis, N., Gulbenkoglu, H., Di Marco, M., Young, S., & Hudson, A. (2005). The anger management project: A group intervention for anger in people with physical and multiple disabilities. *Journal of Intellectual and Developmental Disability, 30*, 86–96.

Hare, R. F., Clark, D., Thornton, D., & Grann, M. (2000). Psychopathy and the predictive validity of the PCL-R: An international perspective. *Behavioural Sciences and the Law, 18*, 623–645.

Hawton, K., Salkovskis, P. M., Kirk, J., & Clark, D. M. (1989). *Cognitive behaviour therapy for psychiatric problems: A practical guide.* Oxford, England: Oxford University Press.

Howells, M., & Day, A. (2003). Readiness for anger management: Clinical and theoretical issues. *Clinical Psychology Review, 23,* 319–337.

Hunter, C., Nadany, S., & Cragg, R. (2010). The Birmingham provocation hierarchy: For adults with mild to borderline learning disabilities. *Clinical Psychology Forum, 207,* 25–29.

Hurley, A., Tomasulo, D. J., & Pfadt, A. G. (1998). Individual and group psychotherapy approaches for persons with intellectual disabilities and developmental disabilities. *Journal of Developmental and Physical Disabilities, 10,* 365–386.

Jacobson, N., & Truax, F. (1991). Clinical significance: A statistical approach to defining meaningful change in psychotherapy research. *Journal of Consulting and Clinical Psychology, 59,* 12–19.

Jahoda, A., Dagnan, D., Stenfert Kroese, B., Pert, C., & Trower, P. (2009b). Cognitive behavioural therapy: From face to face interaction to a broader contextual understanding of change. *Journal of Intellectual Disability Research, 53,* 759–771.

Jahoda, A., Pert, C., Squire, J., & Trower, P. (1998). Facing stress and conflict: A comparison of the predicted responses and self-concepts of aggressive and non-aggressive people with intellectual disability. *Journal of Intellectual Disability Research, 42,* 360–369.

Jahoda, A., Pert, C., & Trower, P. (2006). Frequent aggression and attribution of hostile intent in people with mild to moderate intellectual disabilities: An empirical investigation. *American Journal on Mental Retardation, 111,* 90–99.

Jahoda, A., Selkirk, M., Trower, P., Pert, C., Stenfert Kroese, B., Dagnan, D., & Burford, B. (2009). The balance of power in therapeutic interactions with individuals who have intellectual disabilities. *British Journal of Clinical Psychology, 48,* 63–77.

Jahoda, A., Trower, P., Pert, C., & Finn, D. (2001). Contingent reinforcement or defending the self? A review of evolving models of aggression in people with mild learning disabilities. *British Journal of Medical Psychology, 74,* 305–321.

Jenkins, R., Rose, J., & Lovell, C. (1997). Psychological well-being of staff working with people who have challenging behaviour. *Journal of Intellectual Disability Research, 41,* 502–511.

Kendall, P. C. (1985). Toward a cognitive-behavioral model of child psychopathology and a critique of related interventions. *Journal of Abnormal and Child Psychology, 13,* 357–372.

Kilbane, A. L., & Jahoda, A. (2011). Therapy expectations: Preliminary exploration and measurement in adults with intellectual disabilities. *Journal of Applied Research in Intellectual Disabilities, 24,* 528–542.

King, N., Lancaster, N., Wynne, G., Nettleton, N., & Davis, R. (1999). Cognitive behavioural anger management training for adults with mild intellectual disability. *Scandinavian Journal of Behavioural Therapy, 28,* 19–22.

Kirk, J. D., Jahoda, A., & Pert, C. (2008). Beliefs about aggression and submissiveness: A comparison of aggressive and nonaggressive individuals with mild intellectual disability. *Journal of Mental Health Research in Intellectual Disabilities, 1,* 191–204.

Lansford, J., Malone, P., Dodge, K., Crozier, J., Pettit, G., & Bates, J. (2006). A 12-year prospective study of patterns of social information processing problems and externalizing behaviors. *Journal of Abnormal Child Psychology, 34,* 709–718.

Lindsay, W. R. (1999). Cognitive therapy. *Psychologist, 12,* 238–241.

Lindsay, W. R., Allan, R., Parry, C., MacLeod, F., Cottrell, J., Overend, H., & Smith, A. H. W. (2004). Anger and aggression in people with intellectual disabilities: Treatment and follow-up of consecutive referrals and a waiting list comparison. *Clinical Psychology and Psychotherapy, 11*, 255–264.

Lindsay, W. R., Howells, L., & Pitcaithly, D. (1993). Cognitive therapy for depression with individuals with intellectual disabilities. *British Journal of Medical Psychology, 66*, 135–141.

Lindsay, W. R., Jahoda, A., & Willner, P. (2013). Techniques in psychological therapy for people with intellectual disabilities II: Adaptation of treatment techniques. In J. L. Taylor, W. R. Lindsay, R. Hastings, & C. Hatton (Eds.), *Psychological therapies for people with intellectual disabilities* (pp. 85–100). London, UK: Wiley.

Lindsay, W. R., Jahoda, A., Willner, P., &Taylor, J. L. (2013). Techniques in psychological therapy for people with intellectual disabilities 1: Assessment and cognitive considerations. In J. L. Taylor, W. R. Lindsay, R. Hastings, & C. Hatton (Eds.), *Psychological therapies for people with intellectual disabilities* (pp. 69–83). London, UK: Wiley.

Lindsay, W. R., & Law, J. (1999, July). *Outcome evaluation of 161 people with learning disabilities in Tayside who have offending or challenging behaviour.* Paper presented to British Association for Behavioural and Cognitive Psychotherapy, 27th Annual Conference, Bristol, UK.

Lindsay, W. R., & Smith, A. H. (1998). Responses to treatment for sex offenders with intellectual disability: A comparison of men with 1- and 2-year probation sentences. *Journal of Intellectual Disability Research, 42*, 346–353.

Lowe, K., Felce, D., & Blackman, D. (1995). People with learning disabilities and challenging behaviour: The characteristics of those referred and not referred to specialist teams. *Psychological Medicine, 25*, 595–603.

Lynch, C. (2004). Psychotherapy for persons with mental retardation. *Mental Retardation, 42*, 399–405.

MacMahon, K., Jahoda, A., & Pert, C. (2006). *Sources of anger-arousal for individuals with mild to moderate intellectual disabilities with and without difficulties with frequent aggression.* Abstract from Seattle Club Conference, Kendal, UK.

Marini, Z. A., Dane, A. V., Bosacki, S. L., & Cura, Y. L. C. (2006). Direct and indirect bully-victims: Differential psychosocial risk factors associated with adolescents involved in bullying and victimization. *Aggressive Behavior, 32*, 551–569.

Marlatt, G. A., & Gordon, J. R. (1985). *Relapse prevention: Maintenance strategies in the treatment of addictive behaviors.* New York, NY: Guilford Press.

Matheson, E., Jahoda, A., & MacLean, J. (2005). Emotional understanding in aggressive and nonaggressive individuals with mild or moderate mental retardation. *American Journal on Mental Retardation, 110*, 57–67.

Matson, J. L., & Zeiss, R. A. (1978). Group training of social skills in chronically explosive, severely disturbed psychiatric patients. *Behavioral Engineering, 5*, 41–50.

McCabe, M. P., McGillivray, J. A., & Newton, D. C. (2006). Effectiveness of treatment programmes for depression among adults with mild/moderate intellectual disability. *Journal of Intellectual Disability Research, 50*, 239–247.

McGillivray, J. A., McCabe, M. P., & Kershaw, M. M. (2008). Depression in people with intellectual disability: An evaluation of a staff-administered treatment program. *Research in Developmental Disabilities, 29*, 524–536.

McVilly, K. R. (1997). Residential staff: How they view their training and professional support. *British Journal of Learning Disabilities, 25*, 18–25.

Mental Health Foundation. (2008). *Boiling point*. Retrieved from http://www.mental-health.org.uk/publications/boiling-point-report/

Mindham, J., & Espie, C. A. (2003). Glasgow Anxiety Scale for people with an Intellectual Disability (GAS-ID): Development and psychometric properties of a new measure for use with people with mild intellectual disability. *Journal of Intellectual Disability Research, 47*, 22–30.

Moore, E., Adams, R., Elsworth, J., & Lewis, J. (1997). An anger management group for people with a learning disability. *British Journal of Learning Disabilities, 25*, 53–57.

Musher-Eizenman, D. R., Boxer, P., Danner, S., Dubow, E. F., Goldstein, S. E., & Heretick, D. M. L. (2004). Social-cognitive mediators of the relation of environmental and emotion regulation factors to children's aggression. *Aggressive Behavior, 30*, 389–408.

Nabuzoka, D., & Smith, D. K. (1993). Sociometric status and social behaviour of children with and without learning difficulties. *Journal of Child Psychology and Psychiatry, 34*, 1435–1448.

Nagel, B., & Leiper, R. (1999). A national survey of psychotherapy with people with learning disabilities. *Clinical Psychology Forum, 129*, 14–18.

Novaco, R. W. (1975). *Anger control: The development and evaluation of an experimental treatment*. Lexington, MA: Lexington Books, D.C. Heath.

Novaco, R. W. (1994). Anger as a risk factor for violence among the mentally disordered. In J. Monahan & H. Steadman (Eds.), *Violence and mental disorder: Developments in risk assessment* (pp. 21–59). Chicago, IL: University of Chicago Press.

Novaco, R. W. (2003). *The Novaco Anger Scale and Provocation Inventory Manual (NAS-PI)*. Los Angeles, CA: Western Psychological Services.

Novaco, R. W., Ramm, M., & Black, L. (2000). Anger treatment with offenders. In C. Hollin (Ed.), *Handbook of offender assessment and treatment* (pp. 281–296). London, UK: Wiley.

Oathamshaw, S., & Haddock, G. (2006). Do people with intellectual disabilities and psychosis have the cognitive skills required to undertake cognitive behavioural therapy? *Journal of Applied Research in Intellectual Disabilities, 19*, 35–46.

Oliver, P. C., Piachaud, J., Done, J., Regan, A., Cooray, S., & Tyrer, P. (2002). Difficulties in conducting a randomised controlled trial of health service interventions in intellectual disability: Implications for evidence- based practice. *Journal of Intellectual Disability Research, 46*, 340–345.

Pert, C., & Jahoda, A. (2008). Social goals and conflict strategies of individuals with mild to moderate intellectual disabilities who present problems of aggression. *Journal of Intellectual Disability Research, 52*, 393–403.

Pert, C., Jahoda, A., & Squire, J. (1999). Attribution of intent and role-taking: Cognitive factors as mediators of aggression with people who have mental retardation. *American Journal on Mental Retardation, 104*, 399–409.

Pert, C., Jahoda, A., Stenfert-Kroese, B., Dagnan, D., Trower, P., & Burford, B. (2012). Cognitive behavioral therapy from the perspective of clients with mild intellectual disabilities: A qualitative investigation of process issues. *Journal of Intellectual Disability Research*. doi:10.1111/j.1365-2788.2012.01546.x [Epub ahead of print]

Reed, J., & Clements, J. (1989). Assessing the understanding of emotional states in a population of adolescents and young adults with mental handicap. *Journal of Mental Deficiency Research, 33*, 229–233.

Rees, C. S., McEvoy, P., & Nathan, P. R. (2005). Relationship between homework completion and outcome in cognitive behaviour therapy. *Cognitive Behaviour Therapy, 34*, 242–247.

Rose, J. (1996). Anger management: A group treatment program for people with learning disabilities. *Journal of Developmental and Physical Disabilities, 8*, 133–150.

Rose, J. (2010). Carer reports of the efficacy of cognitive behavioural interventions for anger. *Research in Developmental Disabilities, 31*, 1502–1508.

Rose, J., Dodd, L., & Rose, N. (2008). Individual cognitive behavioural intervention for anger. *Journal of Mental Health Research in Intellectual Disabilities, 1*, 97–108.

Rose, J., Jones, F., & Fletcher, B. (1998). Investigating the relationship between stress and worker behaviour. *Journal of Intellectual Disability Research, 42*, 163–172.

Rose, J., Loftus, M., Flint, B., & Carey, L. (2005). Factors associated with the efficacy of a group intervention for anger in people with intellectual disabilities. *British Journal of Clinical Psychology, 44*, 305–317.

Rose, J., O'Brien, A., & Rose, D. (2009). Group and individual cognitive behavioural interventions for anger. *Advances in Mental Health and Learning Disabilities, 3*, 45–50.

Rose, J., & West, C. (1999). Assessment of anger in people with intellectual disabilities. *Journal of Applied Research in Intellectual Disabilities, 12*, 211–224.

Rose, J., West, C., & Clifford, D. (2000). Group interventions for anger in people with intellectual disabilities. *Research in Developmental Disabilities, 21*, 171–181.

Roth, A., & Fonagy, P. (2004). *What works for whom? A critical review of psychotherapy research* (2nd ed.). New York, NY: Guilford Press.

Royal College of Psychiatrists. (2004). *Psychotherapy and learning disability.* Council Report CR 116. Retrieved from http://www.rcpsych.ac.uk/files/pdfversion/cr116.pdf

Sams, K., Collins, S., & Reynolds, S. (2006). Cognitive therapy abilities in people with learning disabilities. *Journal of Applied Research in Intellectual Disabilities, 19*, 25–34.

Sinason, V. (1992). *Mental handicap and the human condition: New approaches from the Tavistock*. London, UK: Free Association Books.

Stenfert Kroese, B., Dagnan, D., & Loumidis, K. (Eds.). (1997). *Cognitive-behaviour therapy for people with learning disabilities*. London, UK: Routledge.

Stenfert-Kroese, B., & Thomas, G. (2006). Treating chronic nightmares of sexual assault survivors with an intellectual disability—Two descriptive case studies. *Journal of Applied Research in Intellectual Disabilities, 19*, 75–80.

Taylor, J. L., & Novaco, R. W. (2005). *Anger treatment for people with developmental disabilities: A theory, evidence and manual-based approach*. Chichester, UK: Wiley.

Taylor, J. L., Novaco, R. W., Gillmer, B. T., Robertson, A., & Thorne, I. (2005). Individual cognitive-behavioural anger treatment for people with mild-borderline intellectual disabilities and histories of aggression: A controlled trial. *British Journal of Clinical Psychology, 44*, 367–382.

Taylor, J. L., Novaco, R. W., Gillmer, B., & Thorne, J. (2002). Cognitive-behavioural treatment of anger intensity among offenders with intellectual disabilities. *Journal of Applied Research in Intellectual Disabilities, 15*, 151–165.

Taylor, J. L., Novaco, R. W., Guinan, C., & Street, N. (2004). Development of an imaginal provocation test to evaluate treatment for anger problems in people with intellectual disabilities. *Clinical Psychology and Psychotherapy, 11*, 233–246.

Taylor, J. L., Thorne, I., Robertson, A., & Avery, G. (2002). Evaluation of a group intervention for convicted arsonists with mild and borderline intellectual disabilities. *Criminal Behaviour and Mental Health, 12*, 282–293.

Tiedens, L. Z. (2001). Anger and advancement versus sadness and subjugation: The effect of negative emotion on social status conferral. *Journal of Personality and Social Psychology, 80*, 86–94.

Tjaden, P. G., Thoennes, N., National Institute of Justice, & Centers for Disease Control and Prevention. (2000). *Extent, nature, and consequences of intimate partner violence*. Washington, DC: U.S. Department of Justice, Office of Justice Programs, National Institute of Justice.

Waitman, A., & Conboy-Hill, S. (Eds.). (1992). *Psychotherapy and mental handicap*. London, UK: Sage.

Walz, N. C., & Benson, B. A. (1996). Labeling and discrimination of facial expressions by aggressive and nonaggressive men with mental retardation. *American Journal of Mental Retardation, 101*, 282–291.

Whitaker, S. (2001). Anger control for people with learning disabilities: A critical review. *Behavioural and Cognitive Psychotherapy, 29*, 277–293.

Whitehouse, R. M., Tudway, J. A., Look, R., & Stenfert Kroese, B. (2006). Adapting individual psychotherapy for adults with intellectual disabilities: A comparative review of the cognitive-behavioural and psychodynamic literature. *Journal of Applied Research in Intellectual Disabilities, 19*, 55–66.

Willner, P. (2004). Brief cognitive therapy of nightmares and post-traumatic ruminations in a man with a learning disability. *British Journal of Clinical Psychology, 43*, 469–454.

Willner, P. (2006). Readiness for cognitive therapy in people with intellectual disabilities. *Journal of Applied Research in Intellectual Disabilities, 19*, 5–16.

Willner, P., Brace, N., & Phillips, J. (2005). Assessment of anger coping skills in individuals with intellectual disabilities. *Journal of Intellectual Disability Research, 49*, 329–339.

Willner, P., & Hatton, C. (Eds.). (2006). Cognitive behaviour therapy. *Special Issue: Journal of Applied Research in Intellectual Disabilities, 19*, 1

Willner, P., Jahoda, A., Rose, J., Stenfert Kroese, B., Hood, K., Townson, J., … Felce, D. (2011). Anger management for people with mild to moderate learning disabilities: Study protocol for a multi-centre cluster randomized controlled trial of a manualized intervention delivered by day-service staff. *Trials, 12*, 36.

Willner, P., Jones, J., Tams, R., & Green, G. (2002). A randomised controlled trial of the efficacy of a cognitive-behavioural anger management group for adults with learning disabilities. *Journal of Applied Research in Intellectual Disabilities, 15*, 224–235.

Willner, P., & Tomlinson, S. (2007). Generalization of anger coping skills from day-service to residential settings. *Journal of Applied Research in Intellectual Disabilities, 20*, 553–562.

World Health Organization. (1992). *ICD-10 classification of mental and behavioural disorders: Clinical descriptions and diagnostic guidelines*. Geneva, Switzerland, World Health Organization.

7

Anger Regulation for Psychotic Patients

RAYMOND W. NOVACO AND RICHARD WHITTINGTON

The progressive dissemination of cognitive-behavioral anger treatment over the past several decades has been noteworthy. Various forms of this therapeutic approach to clinical problems of anger/aggression have been applied to diverse client populations in both hospital and community settings. Nine meta-analyses on the effectiveness of psychotherapy for anger have now been published (Beck & Fernandez, 1998; Del Vecchio & O'Leary, 2004; DiGiuseppe & Tafrate, 2003; Edmondson & Conger, 1996; Gansle, 2005; Ho, Carter, & Stephenson, 2010; Saini, 2009; Sukhodolsky, Kassinove, & Gorman, 2004; Tafrate, 1995), which overall have found medium to strong effect sizes. When therapies have been compared, cognitive-behavioral approaches have the greatest efficacy (Dvoskin, Skeem, Novaco & Douglas, 2012). However, many of the studies that qualify for meta-analytic review (by virtue of control group conditions) have not concerned patients with serious clinical problems. Few studies have involved clients with major mental disorder and histories of violent behavior. Very few studies, even those involving case series, have concerned psychotic patients. This chapter casts a background for work on anger and psychosis, provides a review of existing clinical research in this domain, illustrates clinical intervention with a case example, and discusses broader themes associated with delivering clinical care for anger dysregulation in hospital settings.

Anger dysregulation is prototypically transdiagnostic. People beset with psychoses, particularly those who are hospital inpatients, are rarely without comorbidities; thus, anger dysregulation fits eminently with the comorbidity theme highlighted by Harvey, Watkins, Mansell, and Shafran (2004) for transdiagnostic problems. In this transdiagnostic vein, anger is manifested in a wide variety of psychiatric disorders (cf. Novaco, 2010a). In psychotic disorders, anger is associated with delusions and command hallucinations. Anger plays strongly in the functional impairment criterion across diagnostic categories, and, for psychotic patients in hospital settings, it significantly bears on matters of treatment engagement, on the therapeutic milieu, and on the well-being of clinical staff.

ANGER AND MADNESS

The ideas of anger and madness have long been intertwined, which is discussed as a historical theme elsewhere (Novaco, 2010a; Potegal & Novaco, 2010). We briefly encapsulate and expand that theme here for its core relevance to psychotic patients and the treatment of their anger dysregulation. Most noteworthy regarding the association of anger with madness are the writings of the ancient Romans, particularly Seneca and Galen. Before their scholarship, there was, of course, mythology. Anger as a destructive force appeared a millennium earlier in portrayals of the Hindu mythological deity Siva and of the doomsday fiery mare (cf. O'Flaherty, 1971); the wild, frenzied, out-of-control representation of anger occurs with the goddess Kali, Siva's consort (cf. Kinsley, 1975). Also predating the ancient Roman scholars was Greek literary mythology, where there are many fusions of anger and madness, such as in Homer's (2004) *Iliad*, which centrally concerned the "doomed and ruinous" anger of Achilles and highlighted its madness, and Sophocles' portrayal of Ajax's psychotic breakdown, which culminates in suicide.

The scholarship of the Roman Stoics, though, has special status. Seneca (44/1817), the first anger scholar, referred to anger as a "short madness," perhaps stimulated on that point by the writings of the poet Horace decades earlier. Seneca viewed anger as an agitation of the mind and physiognomy. He asserted that not only does anger resemble madness but also it is "many times an irrevocable transition into the thing itself" (p. 222). Seneca, as did other Stoics, Roman and Greek, understood anger as a pernicious and vicious force that makes us destroy one another. Anger's association with mental disorder was also noted by Galen, famous in the history of psychopathology and physician of Marcus Aurelius. Galen saw anger episodes as marked by madness: "You can see that rage is a madness from the things men do . . . " (Galen, 1963, p 42). The special importance of Seneca's writings is that he put forward ideas about anger regulation that predated the formulations of cognitive-behavioral therapy (CBT)—such as the self-generation of anger by cognitive processing, the importance of self-control, the confirmation bias aspects of anger activation, the impulsivity effects, the value of cognitive reframing and attentional shift, and behavioral guidance linkage, that how one behaves affects the course of anger.

Jumping to more contemporary lines of thought, ideas conjoining anger with madness appear in early texts in psychiatry, such as those of Krafft-Ebing (1905) and Tuke (1892), in tagging the condition *excandescentia furibunda*, so named by Platner to designate the "insanity of anger." Tuke defined the condition as a "temporary alteration of the intellect" (p. 474) that accompanies violent rage. Fitting with claims of temporary insanity and the provocation defense, rage episodes were thought to be marked by the loss of mental control or inhibitory central control. Krafft-Ebing saw the condition as indicative of brain abnormalities, some of which originated in trauma, whereas others were due to biochemical agents or grave neuroses or were innately structural. He alternatively called it *iracundia morbosa*. Hall (1899) discussed both terms and their forensic relevance, but he associated the latter with imbecility.

From these classic works—mythical, literary, philosophical, and psychiatric—one easily draws the impression that anger is tenuously contained fury that cannot be moderated, is largely irrational, and is linked to insanity. When one becomes angry, one becomes "mad," and "bedlam" can be the result, both as a product of the anger reaction and as the placement of the angry person. Just as bedlam is a semantic and psychosocial image fusion of anger and madness, so too is "running amok," an eruptive syndrome of frenzied violence in Southeast Asian societies (cf. Spores, 1988). As amok is a psychiatric syndrome, this brings us to a fuller look at the involvement of anger in psychoses.

ANGER AND PSYCHOTIC DISORDERS

Dysregulated anger appears in many psychotic disorders, such as various forms of schizophrenia, schizoaffective disorder, delusional disorders, bipolar disorder, and amok. Major pathways for the activation and maintenance of anger in psychoses are delusions and command hallucinations. Because anger can be understood as linked to threat perceptions (Novaco, 2011), it is a key dynamic in the paranoid, persecutory delusional features of psychotic disorders.

Although amok is formally classified as a culture-bound syndrome (American Psychiatric Association, 2000) of a dissociative, brief psychotic episode and eruption of frenzied violence found predominantly in Southeast Asia, it has ample extension in many societies. It has been observed by both anthropologists and psychiatrists in Micronesia and other Pacific Island societies (Carr & Tan, 1976; Gaw & Bernstein, 1992; Hatta, 1996; Spores, 1988). The term *amok* derives from a Malay word for murderous frenzy with intense rage, manifested primarily by males. Kon (1994) traced its origins on the Malay Archipelago from the mid-16th century and then its appearance in other societies. Psychological precursors to amok are brooding and persecutory ideas, and amnesia commonly occurs afterward. The culture-boundedness of an angry homicidal paroxysm is doubtful. Spree murder is an evident Western cultural parallel, where multiple victims are killed in multiple locations, typically over a period of hours in frenzied, impulsive attacks by someone with serious mental disorder.

Regarding its psychotic features, hallucinatory imaging was noted by Van Loon (1927), who viewed amok as an acute delirium. When diagnostic assessments have been conducted with amok cases, psychotic disorders are typically judged to be present. In Westermeyer's (1972) patients in Laos, psychosis was rare, but his patients lacked the "frenzied" quality that is thought to typify amok—and would serve to differentiate contemporary spree murder from mass murder.

Most of the Malay patients diagnostically classified by Carr and Tan (1976) had delusions or hallucinations or were chronically psychotic. Schmidt, Hill, and Guthrie (1977) diagnosed psychotic disorders in the majority of their sample in Borneo. Ellis's (1893) Singapore amok cases were judged by courts to be insane, although their course of psychopathology seems to have run from depression and brooding to "seeing red" in a dissociated state in mayhem and then amnesia about the episode, with some saying that the "devil entered into me."

Given the historical and philosophical background that we have overviewed on the anger and madness theme and the long-standing anthropological/psychiatric knowledge of culturally infused syndromes of amok and also "wild man" (Clarke, 1973; Newman, 1964), it is puzzling that there has been scant research on anger among psychotic patients. One plausible reason for this neglect is that the pervasive diagnostic category perspective in the psychiatric field has obscured attention to anger per se. It may be that the absence of a diagnostic category defined by anger delegitimizes anger in conceptualizing psychopathology, but arguments for establishing an "anger disorders" category have not been logically or nosologically persuasive. The more simple point, though, is that if one wears diagnostic category glasses, anger episodes are readily viewed as manifestations of the person's "illness"—as a symptom of paranoid schizophrenia, bipolar disorder, major depressive disorder, or posttraumatic stress disorder—rather than as a form of emotional distress meriting clinical attention. Because anger dysregulation, controlling for background and clinical disorder variables, is associated with functional impairments and with violence risk (e.g., Novaco, 2011; Novaco, Swanson, Gonzalez, Gahm, & Reger, 2012), the study of anger among psychotic patients merits sustained focus.

The study of anger among psychotic patients was perhaps pioneered by Landis, Ferrall, and Page (1936). They compared a sample of "normal" college students with "abnormal" patients (119 schizophrenic and 45 manic-depressive patients in two New York hospitals) on anger and fear questionnaire responses. While the students gave higher anger ratings on a provocation inventory, the level of anger among the patients was associated with the number of physical diseases. Soon thereafter, Miller (1939), in the context of examining the effect of "repressed hostile emotion" on blood pressure, studied 60 paranoid and 23 other schizophrenic patients, along with 33 depressed patients and 77 controls, and found that the repressed hostility/anger paranoid patients and depressive patients had the highest blood pressure.

Among psychotic disorders, anger is most relevant to paranoid schizophrenia, delusional disorder (persecutory type), and schizoaffective disorder, and it is hypothetically a key dynamic in the paranoid processes that occur in psychotic disorders. Psychiatric hospital studies involving psychotic patients that have assessed anger for its relationship to violence typically have not examined anger in its relationship to psychotic symptoms (e.g., Doyle & Dolan, 2006a, 2006b; Kay, Wolkenfeld, & Murrill, 1988). However, there are a number of studies that have linked anger to psychotic symptoms bearing on violent behavior. Kennedy, Kemp, and Dyer (1992) reported that in the month prior to a violent offense, anger and fear were pervasive in the persecutory delusions of their sample of people with paranoid schizophrenia. McNeil, Eisner, and Binder (2003) found anger to be significantly related to threat/control-override symptoms (i.e., thoughts of people wishing to do you harm and of personal control being overridden by external agents and other paranoia symptoms). Importantly, after controlling for multiple sets of psychotic symptoms and other diagnostic and background variables, anger was the strongest predictor of violent behavior. In the national antipsychotic drugs effectiveness trials project, Swanson et al. (2009) found that, in conjunction with other positive psychotic symptoms, "hostility" increased the odds of serious violence by a factor of 1.65. Most impressively from a methodological standpoint, Skeem et al. (2006), who analyzed weekly interview data on high-risk patients in the community over a 26-week period and discovered that anger was the strongest predictor of violence the following week, reported that anger was strongly correlated (.74) with threat/control-override symptoms.

Delusional systems have long been known to feature anger. Cameron's (1943) idea of the "paranoid pseudo community" represented the paranoid person's systematized delusions of discrimination and persecution as a product of social learning deficits and insulations from reality checks. Being insecure and self-deprecating, the paranoid person is susceptible to slights and inclined toward attributing hostility to others. Having poor communications skills, the paranoid person is unable to check his or her suspicions for accuracy when they arise. Anger reactions prompt antagonistic behavior, which then elicits rejection and counteraggression, thus reinforcing paranoid beliefs.

The idea of confirmation bias and its manifestation in delusional systems can be found in Shakespeare's Othello, who is tormented by false beliefs implanted by his adversary Iago about his wife's unfaithfulness. Characteristically "very sudden in choler," Othello's heightened suspiciousness and jealousy ("the green-eyed monster") induce him to interpret all information in accord with his persecutory delusion—"Trifles light as air are to the jealous conformations strong as holy writ" (Act II, Scene III, lines 364–366). Anger dysregulation and progressively disordered thought led the otherwise valiant Moor of Venice to kill his wife. In case records of 8,134 psychiatric inpatients in Munich hospitals, Soyka, Naber, and Volcker (1991) found the prevalence of delusions of jealousy to range from 2.5% to 7% across categories of psychotic disorder. Although violence is often the subject of investigations on delusional jealousy, anger has been neglected. Enoch and Trethowan (1967), who proposed the term *Othello syndrome*, do refer to rage in their presentation, but they give no systematic attention to anger dimensions.

Threat/control-override (TCO) symptoms have been linked with violence (e.g., Link & Stueve, 1994; Swanson, Borum, Swartz, & Monahan, 1996; Link, Stueve, & Phelan, 1998; Teasdale, Silver, & Monahan, 2006), although there have been disconfirming findings (e.g., Appelbaum, Robbins, & Monahan, 2000; Stompe, Ortwein-Swoboda, & Schanda, 2004). Pertinent to anger, Appelbaum et al. (2000) found that TCO symptoms were related to anger and that controlling for anger and impulsivity eliminated the association between TCO symptoms and violence. McNeil et al. (2003) reported that anger was correlated with TCO symptoms (r = .32) and with symptoms of paranoia (r = .42). The relationship of TCO symptoms to anger is unclear, but the long-standing Aristotelian idea that anger results from "perceived wrongdoing" fits here, along with one function of anger being to suppress fear. Nederlof, Muris, and Hovens (2011), in their study of aggressive behavior by psychotic patients, also found a .32 correlation between TCO symptoms and anger, both of which were associated with self-reported aggressive behavior, but anger disposition had the higher magnitude correlation with aggression.

Pertinent to paranoia, anger is directed by attention, and what receives attention is guided by integrated cognitive structures or schemas, which incorporate rules about environment–behavior relationships. The cognitive network assigns meaning to events and the complex stimuli that configure them. Associated with high anger reactivity is an interpretive bias to infer malevolence or "wrongdoing" that feeds the reciprocal connection between anger and aggression. One function of anger is social distancing (Novaco, 1976, 2007). That is, the expression of anger (in face, posture, words, and deeds) signifies an antagonistic posture or "combat mode," which serves to deter the closing of distance (physical and psychological) by others. Anger maintains distance from those who threaten us, energizes preparedness for counterattack, and defends self-worth by externalizing attributions of blame for misfortune. Yet, paranoia has been conjectured by Trower and Chadwick (1995) to be of two types: "bad me" and "poor me," which are differentiated by their self-evaluative beliefs and their characteristic emotional response to threat.

The "poor me" type is inclined to anger and other-blaming. Fornells-Ambrojo and Garety (2009), improving upon some prior studies with insufficient measurement of anger, found that anger differentiated patients with persecutory delusions from depressed patients and from normals, and that anger was associated with the attributional bias characterized by blaming others instead of oneself.

Anger has also been identified as a prevalent prodromal feature of first episode psychoses among young adults in the community (Yung & McGorry, 1996) and military servicemen (Tan & Ang, 2001). It has also been found to be related to self-harm physical health problems of community-residing psychotic patients (Fassino, Amianto, Gastaldo, & Leombruni, 2009).

THE PROBLEM OF VIOLENCE IN PSYCHIATRIC INPATIENT SERVICES

Psychotically disturbed people often find themselves in long-term care hospitals, which house forensic and/or civil commitment patients. In these facilities, anger and assaultive behavior are salient problems. For example, in the five California State Hospitals where over 4,000 patients were detained, approximately 14% of patients had assaulted someone in the hospital in a 30-day period, and about 35% were rated by their primary clinician as someone who "gets angry and annoyed easily" (Novaco, 1997). The importance of anger for patient assaultiveness was established in early studies by Craig (1982) and by Kay et al. (1988), who respectively found anger to be the strongest variable associated with physical aggression before hospital admission and during hospitalization.

Anger is an emotion that is frequently encountered within inpatient services. This is partly due to the aversive and sometimes coercive nature of psychiatric treatment and partly to it being a by-product or accompaniment of the mental health problems that may have led to an admission in the first place. Once on the ward, patients often control their anger, despite their distress and the aversiveness of everyday institutional life. The complex interactions between anger propensity, acute or chronic mental illness, and the restrictive environment of the psychiatric ward present major challenges for clinical staff in these settings.

The involvement of anger in psychopathology has been examined previously in this chapter and elsewhere (Novaco, 2010a), but the links between psychopathology and violence are not straightforward (e.g., Choe, Teplin, & Abram, 2008). Moreover, not all violent incidents in psychiatric units or elsewhere are motivated by anger, whether impulsively reactive or vengeful. Many are driven rather by fear, which may be rational or delusional, or are motivated by predatory and largely instrumental goals (e.g., Cornell et al., 1996). Conversely, high levels of anger do not automatically lead to physically aggressive outbursts, although it is likely that a person's normal inhibitions against acting aggressively when angered may be reduced or impaired during periods of illness.

Psychiatric hospitals have been known for decades to have long-standing problems with assaultive behavior by patients against other patients and against staff (e.g., Depp, 1976; Foster, Bowers, & Nijman, 2007; Fottrell, 1980; Haller & Deluty, 1988; National Audit Office, 2003; Nijman, Bowers, Oud, & Jansen, 2005; Whittington & Richter, 2005). The scale of violence, though, should not be exaggerated, as many psychiatric units will rarely experience more than the occasional episode of verbal aggression. Even on units with higher levels of aggression, usually less than 20% of admitted patients actually act aggressively (Cornaggia, Beghi, Pavone, & Barale, 2011). As with most forms of aggression, a relatively small proportion of perpetrators are involved in a large proportion of incidents (e.g., Rutter, Gudjonsson, & Rabe-Hesketh, 2004). But this minority of violent patients can cause extensive physical and psychological damage to other patients and staff on the ward, disturb the therapeutic climate in general, and have a knock-on effect in terms of social and economic consequences beyond the ward itself. Very large proportions of staff, particularly nurses, are exposed to violence at some point in their working lives (Bowers et al., 2009) and have to learn to deal with the emotions they experience as a result.

The profile of patients who are violent in mental health services is in some respects not significantly different from that in other settings (Monahan & Steadman, 2012). Many studies reviewed by Cornaggia et al. (2011) confirm that violent patients are likely to be relatively young, single males who are unemployed, from deprived backgrounds with a history of violence and childhood physical or sexual abuse, and at high risk of suicide. Other characteristics of perpetrators, in mental health settings, include early onset of illness, longer duration of illness, longer hospitalizations, involuntary admission, high number of admissions, and high levels of "impulsiveness/hostility" compared to other patients. The latter term, however, is often a misnomer for "anger," which one can see was quite specifically assessed in some of the studies reviewed.

A number of studies with control variables have now shown that anger, a dynamic variable amenable to treatment, is predictive of violence prior to hospitalization (Craig, 1982; McNeil et al., 2003; Novaco, 1994), during hospitalization (Doyle & Dolan, 2006a; Linaker & Busch-Iversen, 1995; Novaco, 1994; Novaco & Taylor, 2004; Wang & Diamond, 1999), and in the community after discharge (Doyle & Dolan, 2006b; Doyle, Carter, Shaw, & Dolan, 2012; Monahan et al., 2001; Skeem et al. 2006; Swogger, Walsh, Homaifar, Caine, & Conner, 2012). However, anger as a risk factor for violence in psychiatric settings must be considered within the context of a wide range of relevant variables in an overall biopsychosocial approach to the problem, particularly when patients are medically compromised (e.g., Johansson, Jamora, Ruff, & Pack, 2008). Violence by people with mental health problems is sometimes viewed as "unpredictable," driven by apparently unintelligible aspects of an illness. However, many "normal" people would feel angry and act antagonistically if they were exposed to the indignities and frustrations associated with much institutional mental health care. What is distinctive about violence in mental health settings from the biopsychosocial point of view is the toxic combination of this often aversive social environment (i.e., the regulated and disciplined milieu of the psychiatric ward) with the presence of acute and severe psychopathology. When ward staff experience high levels of work strain, there is heightened volatility in the mixture.

About half of all violent incidents in mental health settings are directly preceded by aversive stimulation of some sort (Whittington & Richter, 2005). Other patients are an important source of these provocations, but the single most important antecedent, present in 39% of incidents, is staff–patient interaction, as found in the meta-analysis by Papadopoulos et al. (2012). Friction is heightened when coercion or request denial is involved. The importance of these interpersonal communication factors in patient aggression is increasingly recognized (Daffern, Day, & Cookson, 2012). Staff are responsible for implementing treatment decisions, and communication of these decisions is a frequent precursor of violence. Typical conflict situations include denial of services, extending commitment/detention, and enforcing medication (Flannery, Staffieri, Hildum, & Walker, 2011). Intrusive physical care when people are confused is another common flashpoint. The implementation of unwelcome treatment decisions and the delivery of intrusive personal care require the highest level of communication skills from staff. Although this might seem obvious, there is still a tendency among staff to underestimate the impact of their own behavior on patients when compared to how patients view such situations. Illness factors predominate in staff explanations of violence, whereas patients, in contrast, tend to emphasize issues around poor communication (Duxbury & Whittington, 2005; Ilkiw-Lavalle & Grenyer, 2003). Because staff behavior is amenable to change and improvement through training and supervision, this minimization by staff of the importance of their own behavior is a missed opportunity for addressing the problem of violence. Given that assaultive behavior by patients seriously impairs treatment milieu, results in restrictions and diminished chances for discharge, constitutes risk for harm among staff, and has considerable financial cost in workers' compensation claims and employee turnover, the involvement of anger in staff–patient interaction merits further attention.

ANGER AND THE THERAPEUTIC RELATIONSHIP WITH WARD STAFF

Anger has been studied as a hospital ward atmosphere variable (Friis, 1986; Rossberg & Friis, 2003) that is unsettling to both psychotic patients and hospital staff. When patients are informed of unwelcomed treatment decisions (e.g., the requirement to take unwanted medication, denial of telephone usage, or denial of leave), such aversive events often activate patient anger. These circumstances inevitably raise issues for staff about their own personal safety, and their anxiety may override professional concerns for the needs of the patient. Unresolved emotional aspects of a staff member's relationship with the patient may become entangled with the professional dimension and interfere with effective resolution of the conflict. One unresolved aspect may be hostility, or even anger itself, toward the patient as an individual or as a "typical case." This is heightened by the patient having a history of assaultiveness.

A constant theme in patient accounts of conflict situations, especially those triggering coercive interventions (i.e., restraint and seclusion), is the patient's anger in response to the way in which staff impose restrictions on his or her behavior. Being subject to restrictions (e.g., access to telephone, grounds privileges, making noise, etc.) will frequently have irritating and even humiliating qualities; the aversiveness can be minimized by the skilful and respectful deployment of words and tone of voice. What staff perceive as weaknesses in colleagues' approach to managing a conflict situation include their way of speaking, being rude and shouting, making personal comments, staring, pointing their fingers, getting into confrontations easily, responding to anger with anger, and getting into arguments (Spokes et al., 2002). Others have described a tendency toward "going in strong" when faced with an angry and aroused patient (Whittington & Wykes, 1994).

Working face to face with people who have serious mental disorder inevitably generates a wide range of emotional reactions in staff. These reactions can include feeling manipulated, inadequate, disappointed, overwhelmed, and suspicious, all of which pull for anger. Attributions for patient behavior are a key element influencing staff reaction. Forsyth (2007) found that staff anger was associated with their attributions for patients' behavior. When patient negative behavior, such as disengagement and noncompliance, was viewed as controllable and based on choice, anger was more likely to be experienced by staff. To be sure, clinical levels of angry dyscontrol are unlikely to be present in mental health staff, as that would lead to exclusion from the system at a very early stage, but subclinical levels are plausible. They may be present as a chronic, low-level feature of the person's mental state at work and of a general interpersonal style with patients, producing flare-ups in particularly demanding situations or with particularly unfavored patients. Effective practitioners are able to identify their own anger reactivity and will have self-control strategies when working with patients, enhanced by good training, reflection on previous experience, and effective ongoing supervision.

High levels of anger in the therapeutic relationship may occur at particular flashpoints. Anger is a very common reaction following exposure to patient violence, with more than 40% reporting this response in some studies (Åström, Bucht, Eisenmann, Norberg, & Saveman, 2002; Ryan & Poster, 1989), although this may include anger with colleagues or the organization for not providing sufficient support. However, when assessing postassault anger using a validated measure, levels of anger are unremarkable and rapidly dissipate (Wykes & Whittington, 1998). Anger is also one of the strong reactions nurses report after a patient suicide (Midence, Gregory, & Stanley, 1996). The way staff manage their anger can influence whether patient violence reoccurs (Daffern et al., 2012), and detachment from anger can improve de-escalation attempts (Finfgeld-Connett, 2009).

When assaultive behavior by a patient is manifest or imminent, staff must intervene to manage the situation. On such occasions, anger may underpin overcontrolling reactions, such that highly coercive interventions are sometimes used when more collaborative, less provocative interventions might be appropriate (Whittington & Wykes, 1994). Although intended by the practitioner as a therapeutic intervention to preserve the safety of others or as self-defense, staff actions can be experienced by the patient as a provocation. This then fuels a deviation-amplifying cycle of anger dysregulation and violent behavior (Novaco, 2007).

Improving anger control among patients in inpatient settings can have two benefits. First, in terms of short-term violence management, aggressive outbursts on the ward can be reduced, making the environment safer, calmer, and more therapeutic for all. Second, in terms of longer term treatment, the period of inpatient admission is an opportunity for focused intervention to improve anger regulatory capacity after discharge, thereby reducing the likelihood of hospital readmission or of incarceration.

Case Illustration

John is a 25-year-old who was admitted to an inpatient mental health service after being arrested for assaulting a passerby from whom he had aggressively requested money on a city street. When the person refused, John became angry, claiming that the person had looked down on him and had scarred his face "using x-ray vision." He had to be restrained by several police officers. Following assessment and a brief admission to a psychiatric intensive care unit, he was detained under the Mental Health Act in a forensic secure unit.

John has a long history of recreational substance and alcohol misuse, including reliance on prescribed drugs, mephedrone (a legal high), steroids, amphetamines, and cocaine. On multiple previous admissions to mental health services, he has been diagnosed as being schizophrenic or having a psychotic illness, with an unspecified personality disorder.

He was brought up in foster care from the age of 9 when his mother died. He left school at age 16 with a credential in information technology, having failed his other exams. He had a number of brief jobs in the first few years after school, including fixing computers, but has not worked for at least 3 years. He has lived off state benefits, begging and occasionally shoplifting since then. He has one sister who has "disowned" him and whom he never sees.

Structured clinical assessments indicate a high risk for future violence, based on social instability, poor history of compliance with therapy, significant impulsivity, and lack of empathy for others. However, he has a number of protective factors and strengths, particularly above-average intelligence (IQ 115), an interest in computer games, a small social network based around football (soccer), and a strong relationship with a particular uncle. When not in the hospital, he plays football with friends about once a month and meets his uncle in a pub every week. He says this is the only person in his family "who hasn't given up on me—the rest are bastards."

In the first few months of his admission, he was prescribed 10 mg olanzapine daily for his psychotic symptoms and 7.5 mg procyclidine daily for the extrapyramidal side effects of the olanzapine. The procyclidine gives him feelings of euphoria, and he regularly angrily demands PRN doses when there is no obvious sign of tremor or rigidity. This demand is a continuous source of conflict with staff. To ensure medication adherence, there are plans to start him on an olanzapine depot regimen with an intramuscular injection of 200 mg every 2 weeks. He has reluctantly agreed to this to hasten his discharge.

During his 3 months on the unit, he has frequently lost his temper with other patients. There is constant conflict with staff when they try to enforce unit rules, particularly around smoking, which is restricted to specific times and places. If his request to smoke is denied by staff, John becomes extremely agitated, abusive, and intimidating, shouting and swearing at the staff member, threatening violence, and hitting in some instances. This regularly leads to restraint and seclusion.

Although much of his psychotic symptomatology has been reduced, some paranoid delusional ideas continue. He believes that the Russian mafia are watching him, which is rooted in a drug deal a few years ago with a local petty criminal. He is obsessed by media reports of death from plutonium poisoning and is hypersensitive to "invisible agents" that can breach his "skin boundary." These ideas have diminished with the pharmacological treatment, but his delusions return at times when his mood is low and particularly intensify at times of stress. Beyond these delusions, his general attitude conveys a sense of entitlement in which "your stupid rules don't apply to me" and a sense of superiority to both staff and patients on the ward.

In a typical recent incident, he had spent the morning in an agitated state, having been confronted by staff when caught intimidating a vulnerable patient for a cigarette. In the afternoon, he approached one of the nurses who was talking to another patient and asked to speak alone with her. He wanted more procyclidine. She said she was busy but would certainly make time to talk to him later. He then started shouting at her abusively, as he particularly resents having restrictions placed on him by female staff. When the nurse stood up, John became more agitated and asserted that her wristwatch was a radio-transmitter, and she was using it to "call in the Russian boys." When she folded her arms in front of her, he thought that showed contempt for him and his concerns. A senior nurse who had been alerted by the noise and who had a good relationship with him informed him of the procyclidine regimen, and John walked away, angrily but without lashing out.

In another incident, John was watching television in the dayroom when another patient began shouting at the screen. It was clear that the other patient had bizarre ideas of reference about the content of the program. John angrily told him to "shut up." When the other patient ignored him and carried on shouting, John stood up, marched over to him, and grabbed him by the collar, barking obscenities. He verbally abused him about being "crazy" and "stupid" and then shoved him, causing the other patient to fall to the floor. When staff responded, John was arrogant and contemptuous and complained bitterly about being locked up with "crazies."

Initial assessments indicate that his anger episodes occur one to two times a day. They are brief in duration and escalate in a matter of minutes, usually consisting of shouting and threats and ending with him walking away without actual violence. Sometimes he instead lashes out and damages property. About one episode a week escalates to a degree where restraint and PRN medication are required. He expresses little remorse after episodes, and when he does convey regret, staff feel that it is unconvincing. Given his overall improvement in terms of psychosis, he is referred to an anger management program within the unit.

CASE FORMULATION AND ANGER ASSESSMENT

In the absence of anger assessment with standardized psychometric instruments, it is evident that John has high anger reactivity that disposes him toward physical aggression, direct and indirect. How forthcoming he would be in endorsing anger items on questionnaires or disclosing his anger experiences in a clinical interview is another matter, as people can "mask" their anger, particularly in forensic settings. In the clinical context, though, what is needed from an anger assessment procedure is not merely to establish someone's level of anger, but to identify the anger problem domains and the psychological deficits associated with the anger dysregulation. All too often, anger assessment by practitioners stops with scores on a scale. It is also important to look for convergence across instruments and across modes of assessment—self-report, staff rated, archival records, and even physiological measures. Many instruments have been constructed for the assessment of anger, hostility, and aggression, and two reviews provide valuable coverage. Eckhardt, Norlander, and Deffenbacher (2004) give attention to the range of anger and hostility self-report scales, and Suris et al. (2004) deal with aggressive behavior measures. Novaco (2010b) addresses anger assessment in the forensic context, discussing measures, issues, and guiding principles. The Novaco Anger Scale and Provocation Inventory

(NAS-PI; Novaco, 2003) is a dual instrument, whereby the NAS is constructed to identify anger disposition in cognitive, arousal, and behavior domains and thematic content areas (e.g., justification, somatic tension, physical antagonism) embedded within each domain. The PI assesses anger level in response to a range of provoking situations, and it can also be used to conduct a structured interview to assess provocation appraisal structures and strengths in coping.

What we see in the case report is that John is impulsively aggressive, verbally and physically. His physical aggressivity has required that he be restrained, which was done by police on the street, as well as staff in the hospital. His anger and aggression are often associated with paranoid ideation, and his delusions are of the "poor me" paranoid type that blames others for his misfortunes and circumstances. A strong sense of entitlement sparks many of his anger reactions and creates the conflict situations in which his anger arises. He is a hot responder, very reactive to being thwarted, and resents being restricted. Although his eruptions are said to be brief in duration, it is unlikely that his anger dissipates quickly, so angry rumination might be in play. His perceptual system is strongly set for threat detection and is biased for confirmation, as he rapidly tags incidental objects and gestures as malevolent. His aggressive behavior rapidly escalates, but he does on occasion show inhibitory control, as when he walks away from conflict and when he processes explanations for being denied a request.

There has been consistency over time in his diagnosis of (paranoid) schizophrenia with comorbid personality disorder (not otherwise specified [NOS]) and substance abuse. The latter significantly raises the risk for violence among mentally disordered patients in the community (Steadman et al., 1998), so that aspect must be added to the risk factor tally. His medication regimen has somewhat stabilized his psychotic symptoms, and these should be systematically assessed by semistructured interview procedures that rate positive and negative psychotic symptoms. The medication adherence plan is reassuring, but his motivated need for the procyclidine must be evaluated.

The meaning structures underlying his anger reactions require further examination. His family history is characterized by neglect, trauma, and insecure attachment. He experienced abandonment with the death of his mother and by being disowned by his sister. Those relationships may bear on his conflicts with female staff. His father's role in his life is unknown and must be ascertained. School failure and being jobless have added to his history of frustration and disappointment.

Aside from this array of adversities, deficits, and risk factors, John has some strengths that can be utilized in treatment and engaging his involvement in anger therapy. His above-average intelligence and information technology background will facilitate his understanding of early treatment goals and procedures, such as the central importance of self-monitoring. That he enjoys football with friends indicates that he seeks belonging, has a sense of social reciprocity, and get satisfaction from things other than drugs. His relationship with his uncle is a major asset, the full meaning of which must be explored therapeutically. In addition to him having a trusted, loved, and socially supportive family member, it also indicates that John wants to be valued by people. Lastly, that John does sometimes exercise self-control in provocation situations can be used to bolster his sense of worth.

ANGER TREATMENT APPLICATION

Anger Costs: Prompting Motivation for Treatment

Treatment engagement follows from recognition that the costs of staying the same outweigh the costs of trying to be different. How sensitized a client is to the costs of recurrent anger reactions can be assessed from three lines of inquiry: (a) the degree to which he or she is aware of personal anger pattern features, (b) the degree of investment in anger habits, and (c) the degree to which the client is troubled by the experiential correlates and social products of his or her anger reactions. Heightening recognition of anger costs is part of the anger treatment "preparatory phase" that has been developed to facilitate treatment engagement, which is fully described in Taylor and Novaco (2005). It was first implemented with psychotic patients at the State Hospital Scotland (Novaco, 1997; Renwick, Black, Ramm, & Novaco, 1997), although it was predated by the "stages of change" model put forward by Prochaska and DiClemente (1983) and the motivational interviewing approach of Miller and Rollnick (1991, 2002). Adopting a supportive mode that would explore and acknowledge John's intellectual strengths, his social interests, and his capacity to sometimes control anger reactions, the therapist would help John construct a "decision matrix" that explores the costs and benefits of anger and aggression, in both the short and longer term. The functions served by his anger and aggressive behavior would be explored, with an eye toward helping him understand that the benefits of developing anger control outweigh the believed benefits of his customary routines.

An essential part of the preparatory work will be to boost his self-monitoring capacity. This would be accomplished at the outset by conducting psychometric assessments of his anger and reviewing those with him. In addition to identifying the domains and themes of his anger reactions, the therapist would involve John in a discussion about situations, learned from his Provocation Inventory response, that make other people quite angry but do not make him angry. The aim here is to learn what works for him in anger control and to boost his sense of self-worth. John would be encouraged to maintain an anger log that recorded his anger experiences with regard to the triggering event, thoughts he had when the event occurred, his somatic and affective arousal states, and his behavior.

Another key part of the preparatory phase is to build arousal reduction skills. This is accomplished by centering arousal reduction on breathing regulation, as breathing is the core rhythm of the body. Slow, deep breathing techniques derived by ancient qigong practices and yoga are very valuable. The training in breathing regulation would be combined with deep muscle relaxation, based on the Jacobson (1939) procedure (systematically tensing and then relaxing muscle groups in progression) that has long been used in behavior therapy. John's involvement in sports activities would be a good avenue for engagement here. Relaxation imagery would also be used to enhance his capacity to regulate troublesome internal states, and he would be encouraged to build a set of tranquil images.

As multiple assessments of his anger are completed, his case formulation would be constructed and discussed with him so as to enlist his collaboration on designating treatment targets. The preparatory phase is thus constructed to "prime" the patient motivationally and to establish basic skills of emotion identification, self-monitoring, communication about anger experiences, and arousal reduction. It serves to build trust for the therapist, providing an atmosphere conducive to the disclosure and collaboration required by this therapeutic approach (see also Howells & Day, 2003). The preparatory phase can be pitched in a sleight of hand as a "trial period," with its conclusion then leading to a more explicit and informed choice about starting the "real treatment," which of course has already started.

Stress Inoculation Approach to Anger Treatment

This cognitive-behavioral approach to anger treatment involves the following key components: (a) client education about anger, stress, and aggression; (b) self-monitoring of anger frequency, intensity, and situational triggers; (c) construction of a personal anger provocation hierarchy, created from the self-monitoring data and used for the practice and testing of coping skills; (d) arousal reduction techniques of progressive muscle relaxation, breathing-focused relaxation, and guided imagery training; (e) cognitive restructuring by altering attentional focus, modifying appraisals, and using self-instruction; (f) training behavioral coping in communication and respectful assertiveness as modeled and rehearsed with the therapist; and (g) practicing the cognitive, arousal regulatory, and behavioral coping skills while visualizing and role playing progressively more intense anger-arousing scenes from the personal hierarchies. Here is how some of these components would be implemented in John's case.

Cognitive restructuring is fundamental to CBT. Much of John's anger is driven by his thoughts and beliefs. The therapist first would introduce the idea of "thought catching"—that is, monitoring his automatic thoughts that occur at the time of provocation. His anger logs would supply self-recorded information about his thoughts at the time of an incident. These thoughts, and their role in experience and expression of anger, would be fully explored. How those thoughts are approached hinges on how his anger schemas have been formulated, involving his appraisal (malevolence/wrongdoing) and expectation (entitlement) structures. Much attention would be given to a meaning analysis bearing on sensitivity to threat. He would be encouraged to try to think differently about the situation by putting himself in the shoes of the person with whom he was angry, as, for example, when staff do their jobs and apply rules. Day, Howells, Mohr, Schall, and Gerace (2008) offer several techniques to enhance perspective taking.

To the extent that his anger-activating appraisals are based on mistaking "what was" for "what is" (e.g., staff do not really care about me and will abandon me), these will be explored as information-processing errors, but it would be done in a way that supportively learns about his early traumatic experiences and helps him identify and integrate the distressed emotions. The therapist must be sure to provide a context of safety and support throughout. This was fundamental to anger treatment with combat veterans with severe posttraumatic stress disorder (Chemtob, Novaco, Hamada, & Gross, 1997; Novaco & Chemtob, 1998).

The development of arousal reduction skills would be enhanced in each session. The breathing and muscle relaxation techniques require steady refinement, and John's proficiency would be monitored in each session. Other classic methods, such as autogenic procedures (Schultz & Lutne, 1959), emphasizing images of heaviness and warmth, are good supplements or substitutes for physically impaired clients (e.g., spinal cord injury patients) or for someone who is averse to muscle tensing (e.g., of the face). Guided relaxation imagery would also be used, vividly portraying tranquil scenes to the client to induce a light somnambulistic state. John's personal interests and institutional resources would be marshaled (e.g., music, art, horticulture) to bolster arousal reduction efforts and encourage him to engage in practices having arousal reduction aims, such as meditation, exercise, yoga, or aesthetic appreciation. Because deep breathing is easily exportable, he would be coached to use it when confronted with provocation. These arousal reduction techniques are consonant with a Buddhist perspective (Hanh, 2001).

John's anger episodes are marked by escalation. This can be curtailed by the development of behavioral coping skills. Three main types of skills would be inculcated: (a) *diplomacy*, whereby he learns to effectively convey a conflict-neutralizing sentiment, offer a modicum of empathy, and seek a mutually satisfying solution; (b) *strategic withdrawal*, whereby he removes himself from high-conflict situations, especially with staff when resolution is not immediately feasible, followed by cool-down techniques, and later constructive re-engagement; and (c) *respectful assertiveness*, whereby he maintains poise and control with a repertoire of verbal skills and courteous firmness. Therapist-directed role play is the principal mode for teaching behavioral skills.

In the stress inoculation approach to CBT anger treatment (Novaco, 1976), provocation hierarchy work is a central platform by which cognitive restructuring, arousal reduction, and behavioral coping skills are rehearsed with the therapist and are then applied and tested. Provocation is simulated in the therapeutic context by imaginal and role-play exposure to anger incidents anchored in the client's life experiences. The provocation incidents are graduated in anger intensity and are arranged as a hierarchy, which is produced collaboratively. This graduated, hierarchical exposure, done in conjunction with the teaching of coping skills across sessions, is the basis for the "inoculation" metaphor. The therapist helps the client to arrange a gradation of personally provoking situations, constructing scenes providing sufficient detail to generate a good imaginal image. The scenarios are described in matter-of-fact terms but incorporate wording that captures the client's perceptual sensitivities on provoking elements, such as the antagonist's tone of voice or nuances of facial expression. Each scenario ends with provocative aspects of the situation, not denoting the client's reaction, so that it serves as a stimulus scene. An example of a hierarchy scene for John would be:

> *You are sitting in the day room, watching your favorite television program. You are really enjoying it. Another person comes in, and without asking, walks up to the TV, switches to another channel, and then sits down to watch a different program.*

In constructing hierarchy items, the therapist would identify moderating variables that will exacerbate or buffer the magnitude of the anger reaction, should any of John's scenes need to be intensified or attenuated. Prior to the presentation of a scene, whether in imaginal or role-play mode, anger control coping is rehearsed and arousal reduction is induced through deep breathing and muscle relaxation. Imaginal presentation would occur before role play is attempted. If John experienced anger while imagining the scene (30-second exposure), he would signal that by raising a finger. The therapist would note the latency and firmness of the finger raising as information about degree of anger experienced and scene appropriateness for its hierarchy position. Details about the procedure for individual treatment are given in a therapist manual (Novaco, 2001) and are elaborated further in Taylor and Novaco (2005). Treatment in effect concludes when the hierarchy is successfully completed. In the 20-session anger treatment with psychotic patients at the State Hospital Scotland (Walker, Novaco, O'Hanlon, & Ramm, 2009), 4 sessions are devoted to relapse prevention, reprogramming, and enhancing generalization. After the completion of treatment, a "postvention" phase could be implemented, such as is done by Fernandez and Scott (2009) with chemically dependent inpatients (see also Fernandez, 2010).

RESEARCH FINDINGS ON ANGER TREATMENT WITH PSYCHOTIC PATIENTS

Few studies have evaluated the efficacy of anger treatment for psychotic people, and most have been conducted in the United Kingdom, where CBT has been commonly applied to remedy psychotic symptoms (Haddock & Shaw, 2008). Anger, though, has been neglected as a treatment target in that genre of clinical research. The first study was a case series by Renwick et al. (1997), which was conducted with four male patients at the State Hospital Scotland, a maximum security facility. Three had diagnoses of schizophrenia, and one was neurologically impaired. All had severe violence histories. The anger treatment was an extension of the stress inoculation approach, delivered in a 20-session procedure with the preparatory phase. Significant improvement in anger control on multiple dimensions was achieved, as evaluated by ratings by each patient's psychiatrist and key member of ward staff.

Two sequenced studies were then conducted by Haddock and her colleagues; the initial study was a case series, which was followed by a randomized controlled trial (RCT). In the first study, Haddock, Lowens, Brosnan, Barrowclough, and Novaco (2004) implemented a cojoined CBT for psychosis and CBT for anger protocol, applying it to three young adult males with long-standing histories of psychoses who were inpatients on a high-dependency psychiatric ward. The psychotic symptoms of one patient were predominantly delusions, and the other two had both delusions and hallucinations, the latter being both visual and auditory for one of them. They all had substance abuse problems. Their attitude and behavior toward ward staff was angry, hostile, and assaultive. Treatment was conducted for 30 sessions. Psychometric assessments of psychotic symptoms and anger (self-report and staff rated) were done at baseline, end of treatment, and 1-year follow-up. Psychotic symptoms and anger appreciably declined across measures, and all three patients were discharged into supportive hostels in the community.

That case series then led to an RCT of the CBT for psychosis and anger treatment compared with social activity therapy (Haddock et al., 2009). The participants were 72 people (57 inpatients) with schizophrenia and schizoaffective disorder and having a history of violence. They were randomly assigned to treatment conditions, with assessors blind to those conditions. The CBT group had a significantly lower number of physical aggression incidents during the treatment and follow-up periods. Although self-reported and staff-rated anger declined during treatment and follow-up, the treatment groups did not differ in the anger reductions. Significant treatment group differences in favor of the CBT condition were obtained for delusions on one of two measures. Assessment of general functioning did not differ between treatment conditions, but the CBT group had significantly greater decreases in security risk management scores. Although the results of that study were mixed in showing differential clinical gains, the positive findings provide an optimistic springboard for continued development of the treatment.

A fourth CBT anger treatment was conducted with schizophrenic patients at a day care ward in Taiwan by Chan, Lu, Tseng, and Chou (2003). They implemented Novaco's (1978) procedures in a group-based format over 10 hourly sessions with 35 patients. Compared to a matched control group of 43 patients, those receiving the anger treatment significantly improved in State-Trait Anger Expression Inventory-2 (STAXI) anger expression, particularly anger control, from pretreatment through a 2-week follow-up.

The fifth study of anger treatment with psychotic patients involved an innovative drama therapy program by Reiss, Quayle, Brett, and Meux (1998). Their treatment incorporated some principles of CBT, but it was not implemented in a CBT-structured format. The study was conducted at a high-security hospital in England with 12 male patients, all having violent histories, but only 5 of whom had schizophrenia diagnoses, the remainder having personality disorder classifications. Reiss et al. found posttreatment reductions in anger on two psychometric measures. Theater has been relevant to the psychology of anger and anger dyscontrol since the plays of Seneca and Shakespeare noted earlier, and this study suggests a new platform for anger treatment for people with serious mental disorder.

SUMMARY AND CONCLUSION

The cognitive-behavioral treatment of anger has been shown to have applicability to a wide range of client populations, but treatment studies with psychotic patients are scarce. Anger dysregulation is associated with many clinical disorders, and in addition to it being indicative of subjective distress, self-report of anger is predictive of violent behavior. There are many aspects of psychosis that engender anger dysregulation. Hospitalized psychotic patients with long-standing aggression histories, mental disorder, and even intellectual disabilities can be engaged in CBT anger treatment and have been shown to benefit. Although the robust clinical gains have not yet been established for persons with psychoses, nor has their sustainability or generalizability been demonstrated, we are optimistic in seeking further advances in providing remedies for anger dyscontrol with this important clinical population.

REFERENCES

American Psychiatric Association. (2000). *Diagnostic and statistical manual of mental disorders* (4th ed., text rev.). Arlington, VA: Author.

Appelbaum, P. S., Robbins, P. C., & Monahan, J. (2000). Violence and delusions: Data from the MacArthur violence risk assessment study. *American Journal of Psychiatry, 157*, 566–572.

Åström, S., Bucht, G., Eisenmann, M., Norberg, A., & Saveman, B-I. (2002). Incidence of violence towards staff caring for the elderly. *Scandinavian Journal of Caring Sciences, 16*, 66–72.

Beck, R., & Fernandez, E. (1998). Cognitive-behavioral therapy in the treatment of anger: A meta-analysis. *Cognitive Therapy and Research, 22*, 63–74.

Bowers, L., Allan, T., Simpson, A., Jones, J., Van der Merwe, M., & Jeffrey, D. (2009). Identifying key factors associated with aggression on acute inpatient psychiatric wards. *Issues in Mental Health Nursing, 30*, 260–271.

Cameron, N. (1943). The paranoid pseudo-community. *American Journal of Sociology, 49*, 32–38.

Carr, J. E., & Tan, E. K. (1976). In search of the true amok: Amok as viewed within the Malay culture. *American Journal of Psychiatry, 133*, 1295–1299.

Chan, H-Y., Lu, R-B., Tseng, C-L., & Chou, K-R. (2003). Effectiveness of the anger-control program in reducing anger expression in patients with schizophrenia. *Archives of Psychiatric Nursing, 17*, 88–95.

Chemtob, C. M., Novaco, R. W., Hamada, R. S., & Gross, D. M. (1997). Cognitive-behavioral treatment for severe anger in posttraumatic stress disorder. *Journal of Consulting and Clinical Psychology, 65*, 184–189.

Choe, J. Y., Teplin, L. A., & Abram, K. M. (2008). Perpetration of violence, violent victimization, and severe mental illness: Balancing public health concerns. *Psychiatric Services, 59*, 153–164.

Clarke, W. C. (1973). Temporary madness as theatre: Wild man behaviour in New Guinea. *Oceania, 43*, 198–214.

Cornaggia, C., Beghi, M., Pavone, F., & Barale, F. (2011). Aggression in psychiatry wards: A systematic review. *Psychiatry Research, 189*, 10–20.

Cornell, D. G., Warren, J., Hawk, G., Stafford, E., Oram, G., & Pine, D. (1996). Psychopathy in instrumental and reactive violent offenders. *Journal of Consulting and Clinical Psychology, 64*, 783–790.

Craig, T. J. (1982). An epidemiological study of problems associated with violence among psychiatric inpatients. *American Journal of Psychiatry, 139*, 1262–1266.

Daffern, M., Day, A., & Cookson, A. (2012). Implications for the prevention of aggressive behavior within psychiatric hospitals drawn from interpersonal communication theory. *International Journal of Offender Therapy and Comparative Criminology, 56*, 401–419.

Day, A., Howells, K., Mohr, P., Schall, E., & Gerace, A. (2008). The development of CBT programmes for anger: The role of interventions to promote perspective taking. *Behavioural and Cognitive Psychotherapy, 36*, 299–312.

Del Vecchio, T., & O'Leary, K. D. (2004). Effectiveness of anger treatments for specific anger problems: A meta-analytic review. *Clinical Psychology Review, 24*, 15–34.

Depp, F. C. (1976). Violent behavior on psychiatric wards. *Aggressive Behavior, 2*, 295–306.

DiGiuseppe, R., & Tafrate, R. C. (2003). Anger treatment for adults: A meta-analytic review. *Clinical Psychology: Science and Practice, 10*, 7084.

Doyle, M., Carter, S., Shaw, J., & Dolan, M. (2012). Predicting community violence from patients discharged from acute mental health units in England. *Social Psychiatry and Psychiatric Epidemiology, 47*, 627–637.

Doyle, M., & Dolan, M. (2006a). Evaluating the validity of anger regulation problems, interpersonal style, and disturbed mental state for predicting inpatient violence. *Behavioral Sciences and the Law, 24*, 783–798.

Doyle, M., & Dolan, M. (2006b). Predicting community violence from patients discharged from mental health services. *British Journal of Psychiatry, 189*, 520–526.

Duxbury, J., & Whittington, R. (2005). Causes and management of patient aggression and violence: Staff and patient perspectives. *Journal of Advanced Nursing, 50*, 469–478.

Dvoskin, J., Skeem, J. L., Novaco, R. W., & Douglas, K. S. (2012). *Applying social science to reduce violent offending*. New York, NY: Oxford University Press.

Eckhardt, C., Norlander, B., & Deffenbacher, J. (2004). The assessment of anger and hostility: A critical review. *Aggression and Violent Behavior, 9*, 17–43.

Edmondson, C. B., & Conger, J. C. (1996). A review of treatment efficacy for individuals with anger problems: Conceptual, assessment, and methodological issues. *Clinical Psychology Review, 16*, 251–275.

Ellis, W. G. (1893). The amok of the Malays. *Journal of Mental Science, 39*, 325–338.

Enoch, M. D., & Trethowan, W. H. (1967). *Some uncommon psychiatric syndromes*. Bristol, England: John Wright & Sons.

Fassino, S., Amianto, F., Gastaldo, L., & Leombruni, P. (2009). Anger and functioning amongst inpatients with schizophrenia or schizoaffective disorder living in a therapeutic community. *Psychiatry and Clinical Neurosciences, 63*, 186–194.

Fernandez, E. (2010). Toward an integrative psychotherapy for maladaptive anger. In M. Potegal, G. Stemmler, & C. Spielberger (Eds.), *Handbook of anger* (pp. 499–513). New York, NY: Springer.

Fernandez, E., & Scott, S. (2009). Anger treatment in chemically-dependent inpatients: Evaluation of phase effects and gender. *Cognitive and Behavioural Psychotherapy, 37*, 431–447.

Finfgeld-Connett, D. (2009). Model of therapeutic and non-therapeutic responses to patient aggression. *Issues in Mental Health Nursing, 30*, 530–537.

Flannery, R., Staffieri, A., Hildum, S., & Walker, A. P. (2011). The violence triad and common single precipitants to psychiatric patient assaults on staff: 16-year analysis of the assaulted staff action program. *Psychiatric Quarterly, 82*, 85–93.

Fornells-Ambrojo, M., & Garety, P. A. (2009). Understanding attributional biases, emotions and self-esteem in "poor me" paranoia: Findings from an early psychosis sample. *British Journal of Clinical Psychology, 48*, 141–162.

Forsyth, A. (2007). The effects of diagnosis and non-compliance attributions on therapeutic alliance processes in adult acute psychiatric settings. *Journal of Psychiatric and Mental Health Nursing, 14*, 33–40.

Foster, C., Bowers, L., & Nijman, H. (2007). Aggressive behaviour on acute psychiatric wards: Prevalence, severity and management. *Journal of Advanced Nursing, 58*, 140–149.

Fottrell, E. (1980). A study of violent behaviour among patients in psychiatric hospitals. *British Journal of Psychiatry, 136*, 216–221.

Friis, S. (1986). Characteristics of a good ward atmosphere. *Acta Psychiatrica Scandinavica, 74*, 469–473.

Galen, C. (1963). *On the passions and errors of the soul* (P. W. Harkins, Trans.). Columbus, OH: Ohio State University Press.

Gansle, K. A. (2005). The effectiveness of school-based anger interventions and programs: A meta-analysis. *Journal of School Psychology, 43*, 321–341.

Gaw, A. C., & Bernstein, R. L. (1992). Classification of amok in DSM-IV. *Hospital and Community Psychiatry, 43*, 789–793.

Haddock, G., Barrowclough, C., Shaw, J., Dunn, G., Novaco, R., & Tarrier, N. (2009). Randomised control trial of CBT for psychosis and anger in people with schizophrenia at risk for violence. *British Journal of Psychiatry, 194*, 152–157.

Haddock, G., Lowens, I., Brosnan, N., Barrowclough, C., & Novaco, R. W. (2004). Cognitive behaviour therapy for inpatients with psychosis and anger problems within a low secure environment. *Behavioural and Cognitive Psychotherapy, 32*, 77–98.

Haddock, G., & Shaw, J. J. (2008). Understanding and working with aggression, violence, and psychosis. In K. T. Mueser & D. V. Jeste (Eds.), *Clinical handbook of schizophrenia* (pp. 398–410). New York, NY: Guilford.

Hall, G. S. (1899). A study of anger. *American Journal of Psychology, 10*, 516–591.

Haller, R. M., & Deluty, R. H. (1988). Assaults on staff by psychiatric in-patients. *British Journal of Psychiatry, 152*, 174–179.

Hanh, T. N. (2001). *Anger: Wisdom for cooling the flames*. New York, NY: Riverhead Books.

Harvey, A. G., Watkins, E., Mansell, W., & Shafran, R. (2004). *Cognitive behavioural processes across psychological disorders*. Oxford, England: Oxford University Press.

Hatta, S. M. (1996). A Malay crosscultural worldview and forensic review of amok. *Australian and New Zealand Journal of Psychiatry, 30*, 505–510.

Ho, B. P. V., Carter, M., & Stephenson, J. (2010). Anger management using a cognitive-behavioural approach for children with special education needs: A literature review and meta-analysis. *International Journal of Disability, Development and Education, 57*, 245–265.

Homer. (2004). *The Iliad* (R. Fitzgerald, Trans.). New York, NY: Farrar, Straus and Giroux.

Howells, K., & Day, A. (2003). Readiness for anger management: Clinical and theoretical issues. *Clinical Psychology Review, 23*, 319–337.

Ilkiw-Lavalle, O., & Grenyer, B. F. S. (2003). Differences between patient and staff perceptions of aggression in mental health units. *Psychiatric Services, 54*, 389–393.

Jacobson, E. (1939). *Progressive relaxation*. Chicago, IL: University of Chicago Press.

Johansson, S. H., Jamora, C. W., Ruff, R. M., & Pack, N. M. (2008). A biopsychosocial perspective of aggression in the context of traumatic brain injury. *Brain Injury, 22*, 999–1006.

Kay, S. R., Wolkenfeld, F., & Murrill, L. M. (1988). Profiles of aggression among psychiatric patients II. Covariates and predictors. *Journal of Nervous and Mental Disease, 176*, 547–557.

Kennedy, H. G., Kemp, L. I., & Dyer, D. E. (1992). Fear and anger in delusional (paranoid) disorder: The association with violence. *British Journal of Psychiatry, 160*, 488–492.

Kinsley, D. (1975). Freedom from death in the worship of Kali. *Numen, 22*, 183–207.

Kon, Y. (1994). Amok. *British Journal of Psychiatry, 165*, 685–698.

Krafft-Ebing, v. R. (1905). *Textbook of insanity* (C. G. Chaddock, Trans.). Philadelphia, PA: F. A. Davis.

Landis, C., Ferrall, S., & Page, J. (1936). Fear, anger, and disease: Their inter-correlations in normal and abnormal people. *American Journal of Psychology, 48*, 585–597.

Linaker, O. M., & Busch-Iversen, H. (1995). Predictors of imminent violence in psychiatric inpatients. *Acta Psychiatrica Scandinavia, 92*, 250–254.

Link, B. G., & Stueve, A. (1994). Psychotic symptoms and the violent/illegal behavior of mental patients compared to community controls. In J. Monahan & H. J. Steadman (Eds.), *Violence and mental disorders*. Chicago, IL: Chicago University Press.

Link, B. G., Stueve, A., & Phelan, J. (1998). Psychotic symptoms and violent behaviors: Probing the components of "threat/control override" symptoms. *Social Psychiatry and Psychiatric Epidemiology, 33*, S55–S60.

McNeil, D. E., Eisner, J. P., & Binder, R. L. (2003). The relationship between aggressive attributional style and violence by psychiatric patients. *Journal of Consulting and Clinical Psychology, 71*, 399–403.

Midence, K., Gregory, S., & Stanley, R. (1996). The effects of patient suicide on nursing staff. *Journal of Clinical Nursing, 5*, 115–120.

Miller, M. L. (1939). Blood pressure in relation to inhibited aggression in psychotics. *Psychosomatic Medicine, 1*, 162–167.

Miller, W. R., & Rollnick, S. (1991). *Motivational interviewing: Preparing people to change addictive behavior.* New York, NY: Guilford Press.

Miller, W. R., & Rollnick, S. (2002). *Motivational interviewing: Preparing people for change* (2nd ed.). New York, NY: Guilford.

Monahan, J., & Steadman, H. (2012). Extending violence reduction principles to justice- involved persons with mental illness. In J. Dvoskin, J. Skeem, R. Novaco, & K. Douglas (Eds.), *Applying social science to reduce violent offending* (pp. 245–261). New York, NY: Oxford University Press.

Monahan, J., Steadman, H. J., Silver, E., Appelbaum, P. S., Robbins, P. C., Mulvey, E. P.,... Banks, S. (2001). *Rethinking risk assessment: The MacArthur study of mental disorder and violence.* Oxford, England: Oxford University Press.

National Audit Office. (2003, March 27). *A safer place to work: Protecting NHS hospital and ambulance staff from violence and aggression.* London, England: Comptroller & Auditory General.

Nederlof, A. F., Muris, P., & Hovens, J. E. (2011). Treat/control-override symptoms and emotional reactions to positive symptoms as correlates of aggressive behavior in psychotic patients. *Journal of Nervous and Mental Disease, 199*, 342–347.

Newman, P. L. (1964). "Wild man" behavior in a New Guinea highlands community. *American Anthropologist, 66*, 1–19.

Nijman, H., Bowers, L., Oud, N., & Jansen, G. (2005). Psychiatric nurses' experiences with inpatient aggression. *Aggressive Behavior, 31*, 217–227.

Novaco, R. W. (1976). The functions and regulation of the arousal of anger. *American Journal of Psychiatry, 133*, 1124–1128.

Novaco, R. W., Stress inoculation: A cognitive therapy for anger and its application to a case of depression. *Journal of Consulting and Clinical Psychology, 45*, 600–608.

Novaco, R. W. (1978). Anger and coping with stress: Cognitive-behavioral interventions. In J. P. Foreyt & D. Rathjen (Eds.), *Cognitive behavior therapy: Research and application* (pp. 135–173). New York, NY: Plenum Press.

Novaco, R. W. (1994). Anger as a risk factor for violence among the mentally disordered. In J. Monahan & H. Steadman (Eds.), *Violence and mental disorder: Developments in risk assessment* (pp. 21–59) Chicago, IL: University of Chicago Press.

Novaco, R. W. (1997). Remediating anger and aggression with violent offenders. *Legal and Criminological Psychology, 2*, 77–88.

Novaco, R. W. (2001). Stress inoculation treatment for anger control: Therapist procedures. Unpublished treatment manual (revised).

Novaco, R. W. (2003). *The Novaco Anger Scale and Provocation Inventory (NAS-PI).* Los Angeles, CA: Western Psychological Services.

Novaco, R. W. (2007). Anger dysregulation: Its assessment and treatment. In T. A. Cavell & K. T. Malcolm (Eds.), *Anger, aggression, and interventions for interpersonal violence* (pp. 3–54). Mahwah, NJ: Erlbaum.

Novaco, R. W. (2010a). Anger and psychopathology. In M. Potegal, G. Stemmler, & C. Spielberger (Eds.), *Handbook of anger* (pp. 465–498). New York, NY: Springer.

Novaco, R. W. (2010b). Anger assessment in forensic settings. *Forensic Update, 100*, 42–47.

Novaco, R. W. (2011). Anger dysregulation: Driver of violent offending. *Journal of Forensic Psychiatry and Psychology, 22*, 650–668.

Novaco, R. W., & Chemtob, C. M. (1998). Anger and trauma: Conceptualization, assessment, and treatment. In V. M. Follette, J. I. Ruzek, & F. Abueg (Eds.), *Cognitive-behavioral therapies for trauma* (pp. 162–190). New York, NY: Guilford.

Novaco, R. W., Swanson, R. D., Gonzalez, O. I., Gahm, G. A., & Reger, M. D. (2012). Anger and postcombat mental health: Validation of a brief anger measure with U.S. soldiers postdeployed from Iraq and Afghanistan. *Psychological Assessment, 24*, 661–675.

Novaco, R. W., & Taylor, J. L. (2004). Assessment of anger and aggression in offenders with developmental disabilities. *Psychological Assessment, 16*, 42–50.

O'Flaherty, W. D. (1971). The submarine mare in the mythology of Siva. *Journal of the Royal Asiatic Society, 103*, 9–27.

Papadopoulos, C., Ross, J., Stewart, D., Dack, C., James, K., & Bowers, L. (2012). The antecedents of violence and aggression within psychiatric in-patient settings. *Acta Psychiatrica Scandinavica, 125*, 425–439.

Potegal, M., & Novaco, R. W. (2010). A brief history of anger. In M. Potegal, G. Stemmler, & C. Spielberger (Eds.), *Handbook of anger* (pp. 9–24). New York, NY: Springer.

Prochaska, J. O., & DiClemente, C. C. (1983). Stages and processes of self-change of smoking: Toward an integrative model of change. *Journal of Consulting and Clinical Psychology, 51*, 390–395.

Reiss, D., Quayle, M., Brett, T., & Meux, C. (1998). Dramatherapy for mentally disordered offenders: Changes in levels of anger. *Criminal Behaviour and Mental Health, 8*, 139–153.

Renwick, S., Black, L., Ramm, M., & Novaco, R. W. (1997). Anger treatment with forensic hospital patients. *Legal and Criminological Psychology, 2*, 103–116.

Rossberg, J. I., & Friis, S. (2003). Do the spontaneity and anger and aggression subscales of the Ward Atmosphere Scale form homogeneous dimensions? A cross-sectional study of 54 wards for psychotic patients. *Acta Psychiatrica Scandinavica, 107*, 118–123.

Rutter, S., Gudjonsson, G., & Rabe-Hesketh, S. (2004). Violent incidents in a medium secure unit: The characteristics of persistent perpetrators of violence. *Journal of Forensic Psychiatry and Psychology, 15*, 293–302.

Ryan, J., & Poster, E. (1989). The assaulted nurse: Short-term and long-term responses. *Archives of Psychiatric Nursing, 3*, 323–331.

Saini, M. (2009). A meta-analysis of the psychological treatment of anger: Developing guidelines for evidence-based practice. *Journal of the American Academy of Psychiatry and the Law, 34*, 473–488.

Schmidt, K., Hill, L., & Guthrie, G. (1977). Running amok. *International Journal of Social Psychiatry, 23*, 264–274.

Schultz, J., & Lutne, W. (1959). *Autogenic training*. New York, NY: Grune & Stratton.

Seneca, L. (44/1817). *Seneca's morals*. New York, NY: Harper & Brothers.

Skeem, J. L., Schubert, C., Odgers, C., Mulvey, E. P., Gardner, W., & Lidz, C. (2006). Psychiatric symptoms and community violence among high risk patients: A test of the relationship at the weekly level. *Journal of Consulting and Clinical Psychology, 74*, 967–979.

Soyka, M., Naber, G., & Volcker, A. (1991). Prevalence of delusional jealousy in different psychiatric disorders: An analysis of 93 cases. *British Journal of Psychiatry, 158*, 549–553.

Spokes, K., Bond, K., Lowe, T., Jones, J., Illingworth, P., Brimblecombe, N., & Wellman, N. (2002). HOVIS—The Hertfordshire/Oxfordshire violent incident study. *Journal of Psychiatric and Mental Health Nursing, 9*, 199–209.

Spores, J. C. (1988). *Running amok: An historical inquiry.* Ohio University Monographs in International Studies, Southeast Asia Series, No. 82. Athens, OH: Ohio University Press.

Steadman, H., Mulvey, E., Monahan, J., Robbins, P. C., Appelbaum, P. S., Grisso, T. Roth, L., & Silver, E. (1998). Violence by people discharged from acute psychiatric inpatient facilities and by others in the same neighborhoods. *Archives of General Psychiatry, 55*, 393–401.

Stompe, T., Ortwein-Swoboda, G., & Schanda, H. (2004). Schizophrenia, delusional symptoms, and violence: The threat/control-override concept reexamined. *Schizophrenia Bulletin, 30*, 31–44.

Sukhodolsky, D. G., Kassinove, H., & Gorman, B. S. (2004). Cognitive-behavior therapy for anger in children and adolescents: A meta-analysis. *Aggression and Violent Behavior, 9*, 247–269.

Suris, A., Lind, L., Emmett, G., Borman, P. D., Kashner, M., & Barratt, E. S. (2004). Measures of aggressive behavior: Overview of clinical and research instruments. *Aggression and Violent Behavior, 9*, 165–227.

Swanson, J. W., Borum, R., Swartz, M. S., & Monahan, J. (1996). Psychotic symptoms and disorders and the risk of violent behaviour in the community. *Criminal Behaviour and Mental Health, 6*, 309–329.

Swanson, J. W., Swartz, M. S., Van Dorn, R. A., Elbogen, E. B., Wagner, H. R., Rosenheck, R. A., . . . Liberman, J. A. (2009). A national study of violent behavior in persons with schizophrenia. *Archives of General Psychiatry, 63*, 490–499.

Swogger, M. T., Walsh, Z., Homaifar, B. Y., Caine, E. D., & Conner, K. R. (2012). Predicting self- and other-directed violence among discharged psychiatric patients: The roles of anger and psychopathic traits. *Psychological Medicine, 42*, 371–379.

Tafrate, R. C. (1995). Evaluation of treatment strategies for adult anger disorders. In H. Kassinove (Ed.), *Anger disorders: Definition, diagnosis, and treatment* (pp. 109–129). Washington, DC: Taylor & Francis.

Tan, H-Y., & Ang, Y-G. (2001). First-episode psychosis in the military: A comparative study of prodromal symptoms. *Australian and New Zealand Journal of Psychiatry, 35*, 512–519.

Taylor, J. L., & Novaco, R. W. (2005). *Anger treatment for people with developmental disabilities.* Chicester, England: John Wiley & Sons.

Taylor, J. L., Novaco, R. W., Guinan, C., & Street, N. (2004). Development of an imaginal provocation test to evaluate treatment for anger problems in people with intellectual disabilities. *Clinical Psychology and Psychotherapy, 11*, 233–246.

Teasdale, B., Silver, E., & Monahan, J. (2006). Gender, threat/control-override delusions and violence. *Law and Human Behavior, 30*, 649–658.

Trower, P., & Chadwick, P. (1995). Pathways to defense of the self: A theory of two types of paranoia. *Clinical Psychology: Science and Practice, 2*, 263–278.

Tuke, D. H. (1892). *A dictionary of psychological medicine.* London, England: J & A Churchill.

Van Loon, F. H. G. (1927). Amok and lattah. *Journal of Abnormal and Social Psychology, 21*, 434–444.

Walker, C., Novaco, R. W., O'Hanlon, M., & Ramm, M. (2009). *Anger treatment protocol.* The State Hospital, Scotland.

Wang, E. W., & Diamond, P. M. (1999). Empirically identifying factors related to violence risk in corrections. *Behavioral Sciences and the Law, 17*, 377–389.

Westermeyer, J. (1972). A comparison of amok and other homicide in Laos. *American Journal of Psychiatry, 129*, 79–85.

Whittington, R., & Richter, D. (2005). Interactional aspects of violent behaviour on acute psychiatric wards. *Psychology, Crime and Law, 11*, 377–388.

Whittington, R., & Wykes, T. (1994). "Going in strong": Confrontive coping by staff. *Journal of Forensic Psychiatry, 5*, 609–614.

Wykes, T., & Whittington, R. (1998). Prevalence and predictors of early traumatic stress reactions in assaulted psychiatric nurses. *Journal of Forensic Psychiatry, 9*, 643–658.

Yung, A. R., & McGorry, P. D. (1996). The initial prodromae in psychosis: Descriptive and qualitative aspects. *Australian and New Zealand Journal of Psychiatry, 30*, 587–599.

8

Dialectical Behavior Therapy for Maladaptive Anger in Borderline Personality Disorder

SHIREEN L. RIZVI, LAUREN M. STEFFEL, AND AMANDA CARSON-WONG

Case Vignette

Jane[1] was a 36-year-old, unmarried, unemployed Caucasian woman who was living by herself in her family's home. She had not worked consistently for 3 years and was supporting herself by collecting unemployment benefits, working odd jobs, and using some savings that were left to her when her parents died. She was self-referred to a dialectical behavior therapy (DBT) clinic after being told by an ex-boyfriend that she probably had borderline personality disorder (BPD) and needed help. Jane described a history of suicidal thoughts but no suicide attempts. She also regularly injured herself by making cuts with a razor on her upper arms and inner thighs, areas she believed she could mostly keep hidden. She stated that her goals for treatment were to learn how to manage her emotions more effectively and to stop her self-injurious behavior, about which she felt tremendous shame.

A structured diagnostic interview indicated that, at the time she presented for treatment, she met criteria for BPD, major depressive disorder, alcohol abuse, panic disorder, and avoidant personality disorder. In terms of BPD, Jane met seven out of nine criteria: (a) strong fears of abandonment and frantic efforts to avoid being abandoned; (b) a pattern of unstable relationships with friends and romantic partners; (c) identity disturbance; (d) impulsive behaviors including alcohol abuse and promiscuity; (e) recurrent suicidal ideation and frequent self-injury; (f) emotional lability, alternating between depression, anxiety, and irritability; and (g) chronic feelings of emptiness. At the time of the intake, Jane denied that anger was a problem, but she did report frequent irritability at "little things," such as misplacing her keys or accidentally dropping items, which then led to him yelling at friends or family.

Jane began treatment with a DBT therapist and simultaneously began attending a weekly skills training group. She initially presented as quite anxious and withdrawn in both individual and group therapy, but over the course of a few weeks, she began to seem more comfortable and participative. When discussing her goal of better emotion regulation more extensively, Jane did not name anger as a problem. Rather, she stated that she had problems with intense anxiety, sadness, and shame, all of which left her feeling paralyzed. Even though Jane initially did not consider anger a problem, further discussion with the therapist revealed that Jane frequently experienced intense and easily-triggered anger. Jane would often respond angrily to people she felt were "glaring" at her or displaying facial expressions she felt were threatening. In addition, Jane also often interpreted benign comments as insulting. When feelings of anger were provoked, Jane believed she was unable to regulate anger and would attempt to distance herself from (or avoid) the emotion. She spent much of each day in bed or in front of the television, and she avoided stimuli likely to evoke negative emotion such as job searching, contact with relatives, and dating. Despite her active attempts to avoid cues that elicit negative emotion, she could not avoid all emotional experiences and her history of avoidance left her ill-equipped to manage negative emotions when they did arise. A relatively minor cue such as receiving a credit card bill in the mail or noticing a neighbor glancing at her "suspiciously" would produce paniclike symptoms (e.g., sweaty palms, rapid heartbeat, difficulty breathing), feelings of intense anger, and urges to confront and yell at the offending person, followed by urges to withdraw or shut down, drink excessively, or otherwise "escape." Due to deficits in effective emotion regulation strategies, when emotional intensity was high for Jane she would also experience strong urges to harm herself, which she felt unable to resist. She would cut herself with a razor, feel immediate relief from the paniclike state, and then, within moments, feel intense anger at herself for being a "screw-up."

Following DBT protocols (discussed later in this chapter), Jane's self-injury was the primary target of treatment. Although she had stated that one of her goals was to eliminate self-injury, she was extremely reluctant to discuss self-harm at any length in treatment. When the clinician brought up the topic in order to conduct a detailed analysis of the factors that contributed to self-injury and determine effective solutions, Jane would respond that it was unnecessary to analyze the matter because she "just shouldn't do it." When the therapist would note an absence of self-injury and attempt to praise Jane for developing alternate behaviors, Jane would irritably say, "I'm not proud of that at all. I shouldn't be doing it in the first place, so why should I be proud of it?" Jane's nonverbal behavior (glaring, upright posture, pounding his fist on his knee) during these encounters would indicate anger or irritability and the therapist would experience an urge to back away from the topic.

About a month into therapy, Jane's first significant anger episode occurred. She called her therapist following an episode of self-injury, although this was a violation of the "24-hour rule" in standard, outpatient DBT. The 24-hour rule states that a client is not to reach out to his or her therapist for additional help in the 24 hours following an episode of intentional self-injury. The rationale for the rule is to prevent inadvertent positive reinforcement of suicidal and self-injurious behavior and to communicate to the client that, because self-injury is a (maladaptive) attempt at problem solving, the client has already solved the problem and does not need more help from the therapist. Jane knew the rule and had already had a lengthy discussion with her therapist about it, at which time she expressed understanding of both the rule and the reason for it. However, on this particular night, she called her therapist to say that she was feeling "out of control" because she cut herself and needed her help. The therapist quickly assessed immediate risk of further injury (there was none) and then stated that she had to get off the phone and would speak to Jane the next day. Jane started screaming into the phone: "How can you do this to me? You are an awful therapist; you can't do anything right! I hate you and I'm going to quit!" She hung up. The therapist was quite shocked, having never heard Jane raise her voice before or express any displeasure with her.

Jane showed up at the next regularly scheduled session looking sheepish and demoralized. She said that she was sorry for "losing my cool" on the phone. The therapist suggested that together, they complete a detailed behavioral chain analysis about what happened in order to better understand Jane's emotional experience and how it related to her cognitions and behaviors. Jane grew quiet and then said, "What's done is done. I already apologized. Let's leave it alone." The therapist then used DBT validation strategies to convey understanding of Jane's reluctance to talk about her anger while also gently insisting on a chain analysis and thus blocking avoidance. She observed Jane's discomfort and asked what she was feeling. When the latter refused to answer, the therapist wondered aloud if Jane was feeling shame about her anger outburst, and whether that shame was leading to her in-session shut down. Jane acknowledged that she did feel ashamed for yelling at the therapist and embarrassed to discuss "my tantrum." The therapist said, "I can understand why you would feel frustrated and angry if you felt desperate for support over the phone and I ended the call to adhere to the 24-hour rule. However, I think that's why it's especially crucial for us to do a chain analysis on that night to figure out a more effective way for you to get the support you needed rather than leave you feeling even worse off, angry, and ashamed ... and I have to admit, I felt hurt as well. Do you think it might be helpful to talk about that night and identify some other skills you could have used so that, if something similar happens in the future, we can avoid that outcome?" Jane nodded and said, "I guess so."

Jane and the therapist then completed a detailed assessment of the chain of events, including thoughts, feelings, behaviors, and external events that occurred before, during, and after the call. She said that the therapist's signal to end the call was perceived as "You don't care about me! I finally reached out for help when I felt out of control, and you rejected me." She and the therapist noted that using the DBT skill "check the facts" to assess this interpretation (i.e., asking herself if evidence supported her interpretation and actively generating alternative interpretations) might have helped, because she might have remembered that the therapist was bound to uphold the 24-hour rule and had otherwise been very accessible over the phone and collaborative in helping identify more effective behaviors in crisis situations. They also identified certain physiological reactions, such as flushing in her face and muscle tension, that were clues to her anger and the need to take a break and downregulate her intense emotional arousal by using skills such as a mindful breathing exercise or intense physical exercise. Jane stated that her plan for the future would be to notice her arousal, end the call, and use a breathing exercise or a hot shower to reduce emotional arousal, and then check the interpretation that had led to anger when in a less aroused state.

DIAGNOSTIC APPROACHES TO EMOTIONS AND BORDERLINE PERSONALITY DISORDER

In the diagnostic system of the *Diagnostic and Statistical Manual of Mental Disorders*, fourth edition, text revision (DSM-IV-TR; American Psychiatric Association [APA], 2000), BPD is one of the few psychological disorders that has problems with anger as one of its criteria. BPD is a polythetic disorder in which an individual must meet at least five out of nine criteria to receive the diagnosis. One of the possible criteria specifies that the person experiences "inappropriate, intense anger or difficulty controlling anger (e.g., frequent displays of temper, constant anger, recurrent physical fights)" (APA, 2000, p. 710).

The term *borderline* was first introduced by psychoanalyst Adolf Stern in 1938 when referring to a group of patients he considered to be on the border between neurosis and psychosis (Paris, 1999). Stern labeled this group as having a "borderline group of neuroses," which he described as a constellation of symptoms consisting of narcissism, psychic bleeding, inordinate hypersensitivity, psychic rigidity, negative therapeutic reactions, feelings of inferiority, masochism, wound licking, somatic anxiety, projection, and difficulties in reality testing (Paris, 1999). Anger was not listed as a symptom in this early description of BPD. Although the term *borderline* was introduced in 1938, the operational definition of BPD was not developed until 1975 and was not considered to be a discrete diagnosis until 1978, when a study showed that BPD could be reliably distinguished from affective and other Axis I disorders (Gunderson & Kolb, 1978; Gunderson & Singer, 1975). At this time, "problems with anger" was included as a symptom associated with this disorder. The definition of BPD and its diagnostic criteria were further defined in the DSM-III by the editor, Spitzer, who reviewed BPD research and consulted with therapists who specialized in the treatment of people with these characteristics (Bradley, Conklin, & Fowler, 2007). Spitzer's research resulted in the development of a potential diagnostic set for BPD that was then evaluated nationally by psychiatrists, which led to the first inclusion of BPD as a distinct diagnosis in the DSM-III in 1980. Despite some revisions of the BPD diagnostic criteria in the DSM-IV and DSM-IV-TR, anger as a criterion for BPD remained the same. Proposed changes to the criteria for BPD for DSM-V alter the anger criterion, which is defined in the DSM-IV-TR as "inappropriate, intense anger or difficulty controlling anger" (APA, 2000, p. 710) to "antagonism, characterized by hostility: persistent or frequent feelings of anger; anger or irritability in response to minor slights or insults" (APA, 2011). This proposed revision makes the role of anger more specific to interpersonal contexts and emphasizes the role of anger in response to minor triggers. Linehan (1993a) proposed an alternative organization to the disorder that focuses on five areas that are frequently dysregulated in people with BPD: emotion dysregulation, interpersonal dysregulation, behavioral dysregulation, cognitive dysregulation, and self dysregulation. Linehan further specified that emotion dysregulation is at the core of this disorder and that the other areas of dysregulation can be conceptualized as ineffective ways to regulate emotions (e.g., behavioral dysregulation such as self-harm or impulsive substance use to alleviate intense emotions) or inevitable consequences of chronically dysregulated emotions (e.g., unstable sense of self due to inability to predict one's own emotional reactions to different emotional cues). This formulation guided the development of DBT (discussed in-depth later in this chapter) for the treatment of BPD, which emphasizes the treatment of emotion dysregulation across all emotions, including, but not limited to, anger.

RESEARCH ON EMOTIONS AND BORDERLINE PERSONALITY DISORDER

Empirical research supports the concept that emotional dysregulation is a core feature of the diagnosis of BPD. For example, Levine, Marziali, and Hood (1997) found that people with BPD experience problems with emotional awareness, decreased capacity to coordinate mixed affective states, decreased accuracy at identifying the emotional facial expressions of others, and a higher intensity of response to negative emotion. With reference to anger, individuals with BPD may be more aware of behaviors in the environment that trigger anger or may be less able to accurately identify anger in others (i.e., more likely to misperceive anger in facial expression), less capable of regulating anger when it arises, and more likely to react with extreme expressions of anger such as verbal or physical aggression. Notably, the study by Levine and colleagues (1997) found no difference between a BPD and a non-BPD group in intensity of positive emotions experienced.

There is evidence that individuals with BPD have higher levels of trait anger or hostility when compared to controls and other personality disorders (Gardner, Leibenluft, O'Leary, & Cowdry, 1991; Koenigsberg et al., 2002). However, another study found that when anger was induced in both BPD and healthy controls, there was no difference in the reaction of anger between groups, although anger was more prolonged within the BPD group (Jacob et al., 2008). In a study in which both positive and negative emotions were examined (e.g., anger, shame, joy, anxiety, and sadness), people with BPD and major depressive disorder (MDD) both had higher levels of anger and sadness in comparison to healthy controls, and people with BPD endorsed higher levels of anxiety and shame than did those with MDD or healthy controls. No differences were found between the groups in the ratings of joy (Jacob et al., 2009), which is consistent with findings by Levine et al. (1997). The overall higher ratings of negative emotions in BPD led Jacob et al. (2009) to suggest that BPD may be better characterized by problems with extreme negative affect rather than a general emotional hyperactivity.

A limitation of traditional studies of negative emotion and BPD is that they have primarily relied on the use of self-report data gathered in a controlled environment (i.e., retrospective reporting). Self-monitoring, on the other hand, is a method by which individuals record data about emotions, behaviors, and thoughts anywhere and throughout the day. More recently, a form of self-monitoring known as ecological momentary assessment (EMA) has been used to gather data on emotional lability immediately and throughout the day, within the person's natural environment, such that a person rates the intensity of various emotions as they occur. EMA may be particularly important in data gathering on emotions, as emotions can be highly context specific and difficult to recall after they have passed (Shiffman, Stone, & Hufford, 2008). Providing tools that allow individuals to report immediate emotions and intensity of emotions increases the validity of the reporting and eliminates problems with recall. Most EMA studies on BPD and emotions to date have focused on general negative mood instability rather than on anger specifically. These studies have found that individuals with BPD experience more negative emotions, a greater intensity of negative emotions, and problems with identifying emotions when compared to healthy controls (Ebner-Priemer et al., 2007; Stein, 1996; Stiglmayr, Grathwol, & Bohus, 2001; Zeigler-Hill & Abraham, 2006). However, recent studies utilizing EMA to investigate specific types of negative emotion, including anger, found that participants with BPD or BPD features experienced more emotional change than non-BPD participants in a limited period of time. Those with BPD symptoms experienced more frequent shifts from euthymic mood to anger or from anxiety to anger and often reported that anxiety preceded anger (Reisch, Ebner-Priemer, Tschacher, Bohus, & Linehan, 2008; Tragesser & Robinson, 2009). These outcomes offer further support for the core role of negative emotional lability within BPD and may be important to consider when addressing problems with anger, in terms of both the frequency with which anger is experienced and the identification of emotions that might precede or trigger anger.

THE ROLE OF ANGER IN INTERPERSONAL DIFFICULTIES IN BORDERLINE PERSONALITY DISORDER

Externalized anger may be even more problematic for others who are in contact with the individual with BPD than for the individual. Anger can play a significant role in another feature of BPD: volatile interpersonal relationships. Relationships with family, romantic partners, and friends may be strained by frequent or intense arguments or verbal or physical conflict. Extreme displays of temper are likely to be perceived as particularly aversive by observers. Individuals with BPD struggle significantly with emotion regulation and may use maladaptive strategies as a way to reduce or cope with intense negative emotions. However, maladaptive attempts to reduce anger through "release," such as throwing or breaking things, slamming doors, or punching walls, and impulsive behaviors meant to reduce anger, such as substance use, reckless driving, or self-injury, may anger or frighten observers. Angry or fearful reactions from family or friends might then lead to an escalation in anger.

In addition, because the individual with BPD supposedly has more sensitivity to emotions, greater emotional reactivity, and a slower return to baseline (Linehan, 1993a), others might perceive his or her anger as disproportionate to the situation. Individuals with BPD are often told things like "Don't be so mad," "It's not a big deal," or "You're blowing things out of proportion." Such statements, though intended to be calming or perspective giving, are likely to be received as invalidating, particularly when the individual is already emotionally aroused. They can trigger further anger or other problematic negative emotions like shame and guilt. This is not to say that the individual's interpretation of a situation is always wholly accurate or the behavioral dyscontrol appropriate (see later for information about how DBT addresses this lack of congruence). However, high emotional arousal generally interferes with perspective taking and results in more impulsive, emotion-specific reactions. Hence, anger may escalate following minor slights or statements intended to be calming.

In some cases, anger related to BPD can also lead to impulsive actions like substance use, shoplifting, and reckless driving that in the short term are used as a way to reduce anger but ultimately lead to more severe problems and perhaps even legal consequences. Legal problems such as fines, lawsuits, incarceration, and job loss take an obvious toll on the individual with BPD, but they also take a substantial toll on family, partners, and friends who are affected by legal proceedings, related financial costs, and the emotional strain of watching a loved one engaged in the legal system. Displays of anger that break laws or cause harm to another person or property may be more likely to motivate others to take action in a variety of forms. Some might strongly encourage treatment after extreme displays, especially in the context of self-injury. Others might bring legal charges following destruction of property or verbal or physical assault. Some might cut ties entirely. Individuals with BPD are plagued by on-and-off relationships, and severed ties may leave them isolated and without support as time passes.

DIALECTICAL BEHAVIOR THERAPY FOR EMOTION DYSREGULATION IN BORDERLINE PERSONALITY DISORDER

DBT is a comprehensive, cognitive-behavioral treatment that was originally developed by Linehan (1993a) for individuals with BPD and problems of suicidal and self-injurious behavior in an outpatient environment. Since its development, DBT has been used to address a range of problems and disorders that are related to problems with emotion regulation and has been adapted to a number of settings, such as inpatient units, schools, and forensic settings (see Rizvi, Steffel, & Carson-Wong, in press). Comprehensive DBT consists of four treatment modalities: individual therapy, skills training (typically in a group format), phone coaching as needed, and consultation meetings specifically for the DBT therapist team. The treatment has five primary functions: to increase the client's motivation to change (typically through individual psychotherapy), enhance the client's capabilities (via skills training), generalize the client's skills use to the broader environment (via phone coaching), structure the environment to reinforce adaptive behaviors (via phone coaching and individual therapy), and increase therapist motivation and competence (via therapist team consultation meetings).

Biosocial Theory of Dialectical Behavior Therapy

The practice of DBT and its formulation of BPD are guided by the biosocial theory (Linehan, 1993a), which posits that pervasive emotion dysregulation is the core feature of BPD and stems from the transaction between a biologically based predisposition to emotion dysregulation and an invalidating environment. Emotion dysregulation consists of heightened emotional sensitivity, greater emotional reactivity, slower return to baseline, and childhood impulsivity (Crowell, Beauchaine, & Linehan, 2009; Linehan, 1993a). Notably, although DBT specifically addresses problems of emotion regulation, including problems with anger, it does not place any particular emphasis on addressing anger over any other emotion. The biosocial theory defines an invalidating environment as one in which a person's communication of internal experiences, particularly emotions, is either invalidated, not tolerated, or only intermittently reinforced (such that small emotional expressions are ignored and only extreme expressions are responded to). When this happens, individuals learn, sometimes without awareness, that their emotional experiences are not to be trusted and that heightened emotional responses are necessary to communicate effectively. In the invalidating environment, effective emotion regulation skills are not modeled, such that the individual does not develop the skills to understand, label, tolerate, or regulate emotions. Imagine a child being given a bicycle for the first time and having a parent watch her fumble and say, "That's all wrong; you don't ride a bicycle like that," without modeling the proper way to ride a bicycle. The child is left knowing that her technique is wrong but is no closer to learning how to effectively ride a bicycle. In the same way, a child who experiences high levels of emotion dysregulation and is told to stop feeling a certain way without being taught effective ways to regulate strong negative emotions will learn to invalidate his or her own emotional experience without learning the tools necessary to manage these emotions. The transactional model of the biosocial theory proposes that biologically based emotion dysregulation interacts with the invalidating environment to produce a vicious cycle in which the child experiences high levels of emotional dysregulation that elicit invalidation from people in the child's environment. The emotional invalidation, in turn, increases the likelihood of strong emotionality in the child, and so on.

Anger, in particular, may be an emotion that people are less likely to tolerate and more likely to invalidate when expressed. Consider a child born more sensitive to perceived attacks or threats from others, more likely to react with a loud tantrum, and slower to return to a peaceful state. Perhaps this child screams and kicks things when he is hungry, bored, or otherwise unhappy. The parents might repeatedly tell the child, "Don't be so temperamental" or "There's nothing to be so upset about" or might try to ignore the tantrums, though they might respond positively (e.g., provide soothing) when the tantrums get sufficiently violent. This occasional positive response likely reinforces the behavior, making it more likely to occur again under similar conditions. Over the course of time, the child learns that his experience of anger is not valid and also learns that only extreme displays of anger are effective in order to receive what he wants. Rather than learning how to effectively regulate anger or problem solve in scenarios that elicit anger, the child attempts to suppress anger until the emotion is too overwhelming and then has even larger temper tantrums. As these tantrums escalate, the parents might react with frustration or attempts to ignore the child in a way that only exacerbates the child's anger. It is important to note that often these processes occur outside of both the child's and parents' awareness. That is, the parents may be unaware that by responding only when the child's behavior is escalated, they are making it more likely to occur again rather than less likely. Similarly, the child, who may be labeled "manipulative," may respond with more tantrums because this behavior has been reinforced in the past and the child may not know another way to respond.

According to the biosocial theory and the DBT formulation of emotional experiences, anger is often conceptualized as a secondary emotion that is experienced following a more subjectively aversive primary emotion, such as shame or sadness. Primary emotions are the initial emotions elicited by a situation. A significant loss, such as the death of a close friend, would elicit the primary emotion of sadness.

A threat to future well-being would elicit the primary emotion of fear. Secondary emotions are responses to primary emotions or other primary internal processes and are often attempts to lessen aversive emotional experiences (Greenberg & Pascual-Leone, 2006). For example, one might initially be saddened by someone who has rejected him or her, and that sadness might immediately lead to anger, if the emotion of anger is less aversive to the individual than the feeling of sadness. Anger may be less aversive because it is often associated with a sense of power or control, which is the opposite of a sense of powerlessness associated with emotions like sadness and anxiety. Anger may be an attempt to suppress feelings of vulnerability or desperation. For example, an individual might lack the skills or experience to cope with a situation, say, a job interview. Feelings of vulnerability elicited by difficult questions in the interview might trigger intense anger and an outburst if the individual cannot tolerate feeling vulnerable. An outside observer might see the outburst as uncalled for when in fact the self-directed anger at one's vulnerability makes perfect sense to the individual. It is important to determine whether anger is a primary or secondary emotion to a situation as this has important treatment implications (see later).

Behavioral Theory

DBT, at its core, is a behavioral treatment that conceptualizes behavior as anything an individual does, including thinking, feeling, or acting. The DBT conceptualization of anger thus would include not only overt angry behaviors such as yelling, verbal threats, throwing things, or physical fights but also anger at the level of sensation and at the level of cognition (i.e., thoughts that elicit or arise from anger). Each of these "behaviors" would be considered relevant targets for intervention. Under the guidance of behavioral theory, DBT employs interventions that aim to increase the frequency of adaptive behaviors and decrease the frequency of maladaptive behaviors. The primary assessment tool to aid in these interventions is behavior chain analysis, which is a sequential functional analysis employed in traditional behavior therapy to identify antecedents or triggers of a problem behavior; the sequence of thoughts, emotions, and behaviors that led up to the problem behavior; and the consequences of said behavior that reinforce the behavior via operant conditioning. For example, an assessment of Jane's phone outburst at her therapist would include an assessment of thoughts/interpretations that preceded yelling (perhaps, "She won't help me" and "She should help me"), physiological anger response (e.g., muscle tension, flushing), what was actually said ("You're an awful therapist ... "), and consequences (perhaps shame for yelling at the therapist or perhaps a sense of being in control when verbally attacking the therapist, who was perceived as refusing help). The chain analysis used in DBT is also similar to a SORCK analysis (Kanfer & Philips, 1970). This analysis is used to describe the relationship between variables by identifying the stimulus ("S"), organismic variables that may mediate effects of the stimulus ("O"), response ("R"), consequences ("C'), and the ratio of consequences to the frequency of the response ("K").

As a behavioral therapy, DBT conceptualizes the development and maintenance of behaviors based on principles of classical and operant conditioning, as well as modeling. Anger outbursts are more likely to occur if a person's previous communications of anger have been responded to in a positive way. This is an example of operant conditioning. A therapist who agrees to extend a session or ignore the 24-hour rule after a client's angry outburst, for example, is probably increasing the likelihood that an outburst will occur again. Similarly, specific situations or manners of communication may become classically conditioned to elicit an anger response. For example, if in the past an important person would offer to help the individual with BPD and also accuse the individual of being incompetent, the offer to help might become paired with a message of incompetence (i.e., an insult) and elicit anger, such that any offer to help from any individual might elicit anger even without any implied insult or message of incompetence.

Anger responses may also be learned via modeling by important figures in an individual's environment. If Jane witnessed her mother gain attention from her father only when she screamed or made threats, she may have learned that intense expressions of anger are effective forms of communication. Behavior change thus requires looking at factors that contribute to or maintain behavior and then breaking those associations, changing the consequences of the behavior, and/or teaching new ways of responding. In Jane's case, if in fact she had learned that screaming at a therapist will help extend the phone call and get the help sought, prolonging the call or offering her advice about how to cope in his situation would reinforce the outburst of anger. To break this association, the therapist has to gently but firmly end the call. The therapist can also work to reinforce more adaptive behaviors, such as responding to gentle and specific requests for help quickly and enthusiastically, and also highlighting verbally how the client has used a more gentle and effective approach so that the client clearly understands that this manner of communication is effective.

It is also often the case that behavior problems are the result of skills deficits and deficiencies in emotional and cognitive processing. Thus, the therapist must work with Jane to identify emotion regulation techniques that help her better manage and tolerate anger, as well as alternative behavioral skills that are more likely to secure help and support, such as effective interpersonal communication skills. In conjunction with the skills training groups, the therapist might use contingency management, exposure, or cognitive restructuring techniques to fill skills deficits and help Jane develop effective behavioral alternatives to outbursts. Examples of emotion regulation skills include behaviors that aim to downregulate intense emotional and physiological arousal, such as vigorous exercise, hot showers, or mindful diaphragmatic breathing. Emotion regulation skills also include cognitive techniques that aim to reduce emotion via cognitive reappraisal, such as "check the facts" (Linehan, in press), similar to the theory behind rational emotive therapy (Ellis & Dryden, 1987), which teaches individuals to generate a range of interpretations about a situation and then weigh evidence for and against the interpretations in order to dispute distorted interpretations. Other DBT techniques, specifically Eastern mindfulness practices (primarily Zen), help individuals develop skills to assess situations in a more objective and nonjudgmental manner (Linehan, 1997).

Dialectical Theory

Dialectical theory is the third guiding theory of DBT and states that reality is made up of opposing and ever-changing forces. A person can have two opposing viewpoints that both hold truths. Dialectical strategies can be particularly important when working with clients who find certain emotions intolerable or who consistently invalidate their own emotional experiences. For example, a person may feel intense anger about certain life circumstances and believe that events are unjust, and yet also believe that he is overreacting and should just "get over it" and not feel angry. As such, the client is essentially invalidating his own point of view by vacillating between feeling intense anger at a perceived injustice and dismissive of his own perception and resultant emotions. In Jane's case, she would have to accept the experience of disappointment and anger when her therapist does not provide support in a given moment while also learning to regulate her emotion and behave more effectively to meet her own needs. If she rejects reality, such as circumventing the 24-hour rule by calling her therapist, Jane only feels more anger at the therapist, who ends the call. Acceptance would be likely to lead to less anger as well as consideration of alternative methods of coping with her distress. In addition, her angry outburst at the therapist triggered feelings of shame, which led Jane to try to avoid discussion of the phone call rather than discuss the incident and think about ways she can more effectively communicate disappointment in the future (see interpersonal skills description later). In addition, effective emotion regulation techniques to change her behavior are crucial, so that as she accepts that certain situations will elicit the feeling of anger, she learns that she can tolerate the experience of anger without acting on it.

DIALECTICAL BEHAVIOR THERAPY STRATEGIES THAT BEST TARGET ANGER

Given the high degree of focus on emotion dysregulation in DBT, there are a number of strategies available to a DBT therapist for addressing problems with emotions in general and anger specifically. The full set of strategies in DBT for emotion dysregulation cannot be described here (interested readers are referred to the treatment manuals; Linehan, 1993a, 1993b). Instead, details will be provided on major interventions for assessing and treating emotion dysregulation in DBT—emotion-focused behavioral analyses and the emotion regulation skills—as well as an overview of skills designed to increase interpersonal effectiveness.

Behavioral analysis is the assessment tool used in DBT to more fully understand problem behaviors (Linehan, 1993a). It is essentially a step-by-step analysis of all the events (both external and internal) that led up to a problem behavior as well as the short-term and long-term consequences of the behavior. A behavioral analysis includes attention to thoughts, feelings, and behaviors that compose the chain of events. The idea is that the more thoroughly a clinician understands the problem from a behavioral point of view, the more likely he or she is to come up with solutions that are both relevant and likely to be effective. Key components of a behavioral analysis include (in temporal order) vulnerability factors, the prompting event, (cognitive, emotional, and behavioral) links between the prompting event and the problem behavior, the nature of the problem behavior itself, and consequences (Linehan, 1993a).

Problem behaviors that are likely to occur as a result of anger include verbal or physical attacks on others or damaging an object. Conducting a behavioral analysis on such a behavior would usually first involve a detailed account of the behavior itself, in terms of topography (i.e., what the behavior "looks like"), frequency, and intensity. The clinician wants to get as clear a picture as possible in order to best understand how and why the behavior occurred. This assessment involves a nonjudgmental stance toward the individual and the behavior. The clinician would identify the prompting event that set the behavior off, in other words, what event led to the problem behavior, such that if the event had not occurred, the problem behavior would not have occurred. For example, the prompting event of being "cut off" by a car in traffic may have ultimately led to a client initiating a physical fight with the other driver. Vulnerability factors refer to factors that made the individual more vulnerable to the effects of the prompting event on the particular day or in that particular moment. For example, the client may have been ruminating about a fight she had with her ex-partner the night before when she got cut off in traffic, such that the rumination and resultant negative mood intensified her reaction to being cut off. Links such as emotions (fear then anger), cognitions ("What a jerk," "They shouldn't even be allowed to drive," "I can't believe they cut me off"), and other behaviors (tailgating the car, flashing lights) would be assessed. Finally, consequences for the problem behavior are explored. A client may say that immediately following the angry behavior, she felt powerful and strong (positive short-term consequence), but that initial feeling of power turned into shame over losing control of her behavior (negative longer term consequence). The thorough behavior chain analysis reveals contingencies between behavior and controlling factors (i.e., positive or negative reinforcers), which then opens up opportunities to think about intervention: What could the client have done differently at every step to prevent the problem behavior from occurring? Although there are likely to be as many solutions as there are links in the chain of events, a DBT therapist is most often going to offer specific DBT skills as possible interventions.

As described earlier, skills training is a core component of DBT. Skills training is composed of a specified set of skills that fall into four separate modules: mindfulness, interpersonal effectiveness, distress tolerance, and emotion regulation. Although all DBT skills are likely to have an effect on emotion regulation, if practiced regularly and effectively, the set of skills that compose the emotion regulation module are specifically designed to help individuals gain better control over their emotional experiencing. These skills are described fully in the skills training manual (Linehan, 1993b) and summarized here.

Broadly construed, the emotion regulation skills are "sold" to individuals as skills that will help them be less likely to experience negative emotions and more likely to experience positive emotions. It is also made clear that the goal is not to get rid of negative emotions completely. The first steps to emotion regulation in DBT are to learn to accurately identify emotions and to understand the function of emotions when they occur. Clients are taught a model of emotions that describes emotions as full-system responses to prompting events and include biological, cognitive, behavioral, and sensory components (including action urges—what one has the urge to do when experiencing a specific emotion—such as fleeing when afraid). Emotions organize our thoughts, motivate behavior quickly, and communicate information to others and to ourselves (Lazarus, 1991). Many clients respond quite positively to this model, recognizing for the first time that they experience emotions for a reason and that emotions are not "all in their heads," as many of them have been told. Participants are then taught skills to work on reducing vulnerability to negative emotions, including attention to balancing sleep, eating, exercise, and physical illness, which many individuals with BPD have trouble regulating successfully. At the same time, individuals are taught skills for increasing positive emotions in both the short and long term. Many clients have the mistaken belief that if they simply remove all the negative aspects of their life, they will be happy; they do not see the importance of adding positive, pleasurable activities into their lives.

Three critical skills for emotion regulation are "mindfulness of current emotion," "check the facts" (which is similar to cognitive reappraisal), and "opposite-to-emotion action" (also called "opposite action"). Mindfulness of current emotion emphasizes the value of just "riding out" an emotional experience with nonjudgmental awareness, without doing anything to change it, stop it, or amplify it. Most clients with BPD rarely just observe their emotions objectively. Rather, they will usually report that when an emotion reaches a certain level of intensity, they engage in a behavior meant to change the nature of the emotion (e.g., self-injury, drug use, lashing out at someone, avoidance). In the short term, these behavioral strategies "work" by decreasing the intensity of the emotion, which then increases the likelihood that that behavior will be practiced again in a similar scenario in the future. The downside is that the individuals never learn that if they just observe without acting on the emotion, the emotion will naturally lessen in intensity even without action (Bishop et al., 2004). This skill is also taught with the message that emotions are not something to always run away from and avoid. Simply noticing the emotion could change one's relationship to the experience of the emotion.

Finally, opposite action is the primary skill suggested by DBT for what to do when individuals want to change the emotion they are currently experiencing. Opposite action was informed by exposure treatments for fear (i.e., reducing fear involves approaching rather than avoiding feared objects) and proposed by Linehan to work for all emotions (Linehan, 1993a; Rizvi & Linehan, 2005). It is proposed to work most effectively when the emotion, or the intensity of the emotion, is neither warranted nor effective in the context. In essence, the skill involves identifying the action urge associated with the current emotional experience and acting in ways that are opposite to that urge. For example, if someone experiences anger at a boss for assigning her an unappealing project, she might have the urge to verbally attack the boss. However, if verbally attacking the boss is ineffective for the client (i.e., by creating a worse working environment or impeding promotional opportunities), then she might want to change the anger through opposite action. Engaging in opposite action might be acting kind to the boss, throwing herself wholeheartedly into expressing kindness, making eye contact, and refraining from verbal attacks. Using opposite action "all the way" would also involve thinking decent or kind thoughts about the boss, because holding on to negative appraisals would only serve to prolong feelings of anger. It is suggested that the person continue to practice the skill until the intensity of her original emotion decreases noticeably.

As mentioned previously, the emotion of anger is not given more attention than any other emotion in DBT, including in DBT skills training. All emotion regulation skills are taught with regard to a myriad of emotions. However, if someone has specific problems with anger, then efforts are made to help a person determine whether anger is a primary or secondary emotional response to a prompting event (through the model of emotions). Individuals are taught to identify factors that make them vulnerable to angry outbursts (e.g., being tired, being in physical pain, experiencing an aversive primary emotion such as shame) and possible ways to reduce those factors are generated. Action urges most associated with anger are to lash out or attack the person eliciting the anger (physically or verbally). Thus, the standard "opposite actions" for anger are to either *gently* avoid the person or to "be decent," which means to approach the person with decency and compassion (and kindness if possible; Linehan, 1993b). For example, if a client is angry at her sister, whom she perceives as having favored another sibling over her, and that anger has the potential to ruin a family event because the behavioral urge associated with anger is to verbally attack the sister, then an effective choice might be to practice opposite action. In this case, the client might gently avoid the sister and engage with other relatives, or in being "decent," she might respond civilly to the sister's questions, pay her sister a compliment, or even hug her. DBT therapists are always cautious to differentiate between the validity of feelings and the efficacy of certain behaviors. The client's anger at her sister is not necessarily described as invalid, but what is important for the client to consider is what behavior and which emotions are most effective in a given context. Thus, reducing her anger at her sister might be the most effective thing for the client to do at this family event. The idea is that throwing oneself into acting opposite to the behavioral urges will not only reduce the intensity of the emotion but also, if the person acts opposite "all the way," actually serve to change the emotion (Rizvi & Linehan, 2005).

DBT interpersonal effectiveness skills are also likely to be helpful in the context of anger, particularly for individuals who tend to argue, accuse, or threaten others when asking for something or when saying no. To effectively use interpersonal effectiveness skills, DBT clients are first taught to identify and prioritize their goals in interpersonal situations, in terms of their objective (desired outcome), relationship goal (how they want the other person to feel about them), and self-respect goal (how they want to feel about themselves). Often, clients with difficulty regulating anger become focused on an immediate outcome or on "being right" rather than considering broader goals or longer term consequences. Perhaps they have learned that others will comply when they make a request by yelling or making threats. Or perhaps they simply lack the skill to say no to someone else's request. By clearly identifying and prioritizing the objective, relationship, and self-respect goals, the client can then determine the intensity with which to say yes or no. If the relationship is very important, the client might practice ways to lower the intensity of the communication (making a request rather than demanding, offering to reciprocate, using a softened tone).

In addition, the "DEAR MAN, GIVE FAST" skills describe *what* to say and *how* to say it. The skills emphasize the importance of objectively describing the situation ("D") and then expressing emotion or preference ("E") rather than making judgments about the other person or the scenario, next asserting a specific request or no statement ("A"), and finally reinforcing the other person (e.g., with gratitude or an offer for a reciprocal exchange; "R"). The how skills describe being gentle or gently assertive ("G"), acting interested ("I"), validating the other person's point of view ("V"), and having an easy manner ("E"). Helping clients practice, in advance, objectively and nonjudgmentally describing situations, expressing emotions, and asserting requests in a gentle but specific manner can be helpful to clients who have difficulty managing anger or lack effective communication skills. Completing interpersonal scripts in advance can be particularly useful, so that clients learn how to communicate effectively before they experience an interpersonal crisis and feel intense emotion. Similarly, discussing how to appear gentle, interested, validating, and easygoing can help clients think about how to change their presentation and replace angry signals (furrowed brow, clenched fists) with those that are better received by others (open hands, relaxed posture).

DIALECTICAL BEHAVIOR THERAPY OUTCOMES

BPD is a disorder frequently encountered in both inpatient and outpatient treatment settings. Many therapists find that work with BPD can be stressful, because the disorder is commonly associated with nonsuicidal self-injury (NSSI) and suicide attempts (Widiger & Frances, 1989). In individuals with BPD, rates of NSSI range from 69% to 80%, up to 75% attempt suicide at least once, and approximately 8% to 10% die by suicide (Black, Blum, Pfohl, & Hale, 2004; Gunderson, 1984; Linehan, Rizvi, Welch, & Page, 2008). DBT is considered an evidence-based and empirically supported treatment for BPD and suicidal and self-injurious behaviors (American Psychiatric Association, 2006). To date, there have been more than a dozen randomized controlled trials (RCTs) examining efficacy of DBT for BPD. Due to the high rates of self-injury and suicide attempts in this population, early efficacy studies of standard DBT focused on pre- and posttherapy rates of NSSI, suicidal behaviors, and use of medical facilities. These studies found that DBT, when compared to treatment as usual (TAU), was associated with greater reductions in frequency and medical severity of self-injurious behaviors, frequency and length of inpatient hospitalization, and treatment dropout (Linehan, Armstrong, Suarez, Allmon, & Heard, 1991). Later studies found that DBT is also effective in the reduction of depression, hopelessness, suicidal ideation, NSSI, and alcohol abuse (Linehan et al., 1991; Linehan et al., 1999; van den Bosch, Koeter, Stijnen, Verheul, & van den Brink, 2005; Verheul et al., 2003). A study comparing DBT to a more active condition, community treatment by experts (CTBE), found that those in the DBT condition committed half as many suicide attempts, were twice as likely to stay in treatment, had reduced emergency department and inpatient psychiatric care use, demonstrated lower medical risks in suicide attempts, and were more likely to achieve partial or full remission from substance abuse (Harned et al., 2008; Linehan et al., 2006).

Few studies have focused on the effect of DBT on anger, with mixed findings. When comparing DBT to TAU in a BPD population, studies have found that there is a significant decrease in anger over treatment, but no significant difference between the DBT and TAU groups (Bohus et al., 2004; Feigenbaum et al., 2011; Linehan et al., 1999; McMain et al., 2009). Conversely, two studies have found that DBT significantly reduces anger when compared to TAU with a BPD population (Koons et al., 2001; Linehan, Heard, & Armstrong, 1993). In addition, Evershed and colleagues (2003) compared DBT to TAU for a forensic population of clients with BPD and also found a significant reduction in hostility, the more cognitive aspects of anger (thoughts that are elicited or arise from anger, such as covert rumination, justification, or suspicion), expression of anger, and anger experienced in the DBT group. Two other studies that examined the efficacy of the DBT skills group only (no individual therapy) found that participants demonstrated a significant decrease in ratings of anger, as well as depression, anxiety, irritability, and affective instability, when compared to a standard group therapy (Koons et al., 2006; Soler et al., 2009). A study by Linehan, McDavid, Brown, Sayrs, and Gallop (2008) examined the effect of DBT and medication (olanzapine) on anger in BPD by comparing DBT plus olanzapine to DBT plus placebo. This study found that participants in the olanzapine condition experienced a faster reduction in anger. The researchers concluded that the addition of olanzapine to treatment was more effective in the reduction of anger than DBT alone.

The evidence just described generally supports DBT as an effective treatment to reduce anger, although we cannot determine whether DBT is more effective than other therapies in the treatment of anger, and further study is required to determine how to best reduce anger and aggression within a BPD population. In most of these studies, trait and state anger were measured using the State-Trait Anger Expression Inventory (STAXI; Spielberger, 1988). The STAXI is a self-report measure that has been shown to have good internal consistency and test–retest reliability (Forgays, Forgays, & Spielberger, 1997) and measures items such as state anger, trait anger, anger expression-out, anger expression-in, anger control-out, and anger control-in. Despite the general use of the STAXI across studies, it is possible that the mixed findings in studies of DBT for anger occurred because the STAXI is a self-report measure, and self-report measures have inherent limitations due to their sole reliance on the participant's understanding of the questions as well as accuracy of recall. A further problem with the STAXI is its limited subscales and lack of measurement of styles of anger besides the direction of anger (in vs. out), such as the locus of anger, modality of anger (e.g., verbal), impulsivity (controlled vs. not), and objective of anger (i.e., punitive or restorative; Fernandez, 2008). It would be useful for future studies to use a clinician-administered measure for anger to account for possible problems in participant interpretation or recall. Further research on the role of anger in BPD and the effect of DBT on anger is warranted to better understand the mixed findings that have been published thus far.

CONCLUSION

BPD is a disorder characterized by significant emotion dysregulation, and although problems specifically with anger are not required to diagnose the disorder, BPD is one of the few disorders in which anger is a specific diagnostic criterion. From a DBT perspective, problems regulating anger and other emotions are defined as heightened sensitivity to emotions, greater reactivity to emotional stimuli, and slower return to emotional baseline. Anger may be easily triggered, more explosive in its display, and slower to dissipate in individuals with BPD. In addition, anger is often considered a secondary emotion, in which it arises following the experience of a more aversive primary emotion, such as shame or guilt. In the case of Jane as described at the start of this chapter, a feeling of betrayal when the therapist ends the phone coaching call turns to anger (secondary emotion), which is quickly triggered and intense in its display ("I hate you!"). To intervene with problems of anger, a DBT clinician would first use an emotion-focused behavioral analysis of the chain of events that triggered anger, determine whether it is the primary or secondary emotion, and then generate points of intervention in the chain. The emotion regulation skills "mindfulness of emotion" and "opposite action" are designed to increase awareness of an emotion without action and to change the emotion, respectively, while interpersonal skills help reduce angry forms of communication by outlining precisely what to say and how to say it. To date, a number of studies have indicated that DBT is a beneficial treatment in the reduction of anger in clients with BPD, although there is not yet sufficient data to determine if DBT is more effective than other forms of treatment for anger.

NOTE

1. This vignette is a composite of clients with BPD currently being seen in our clinic, with steps taken to remove any identifying information.

REFERENCES

American Psychiatric Association. (2000). *Diagnostic and statistical manual of mental disorders* (4th ed., text rev.). Washington, DC: Author.

American Psychiatric Association. (2006). *American Psychiatric Association practice guidelines for the treatment of psychiatric disorders: Compendium 2006* (pp. 1223–1314). Washington, DC: American Psychiatric Association.

American Psychiatric Association. (2011, June 21). *APA DSM-V development proposed revisions*. Borderline personality disorder. Retrieved June 19, 2012, from http://www.dsm5.org/proposedrevision/Pages/proposedrevision.aspx?rid=17

Bishop, S. R., Lau, M., Shapiro, S., Carlson, N. D., Anderson, N. D., Carmody, J., ... Devins, G. (2004). Mindfulness: A proposed operational definition. *Clinical Psychology: Science and Practice, 11*, 230–241.

Black, D. W., Blum, N., Pfohl, B., & Hale, N. (2004). Suicidal behavior in borderline personality disorder: Prevalence, risk factors, prediction, and prevention. *Journal of Personality Disorders, 18*, 226–239.

Bohus, M., Haaf, B., Simms, T., Limberger, M. F., Schmahl, C., Unckel, C., ... Linehan, M. M. (2004). Effectiveness of inpatient dialectical behavioral therapy for borderline personality disorder: A controlled trial. *Behaviour Research and Therapy, 42*, 487–499.

Bradley, R., Conklin, C. Z., & Fowler, K. A. (2007). Borderline personality disorder. In W. T. O'Donohue & K. A. Fowler (Eds.), *Personality disorders: Toward the DSM-V* (pp. 167–202). Thousand Oaks, CA: Sage Publications.

Crowell, S. E., Beauchaine, T. P., & Linehan, M. M. (2009). A biosocial developmental model of borderline personality: Elaborating and extending Linehan's theory. *Psychological Bulletin, 135*, 495–510.

Ebner-Priemer, U. W., Welch, S. S., Grossman, P., Reisch, T., Linehan, M. M., & Bohus, M. (2007). Psychophysiological ambulatory assessment of affective dysregulation in borderline personality disorder. *Psychiatry Research, 150*, 265–275.

Ellis, A., & Dryden, W. (1987). *The practice of rational-emotive therapy*. New York, NY: Springer.

Evershed, S., Tennant, A., Boomer, D., Rees, A., Barkham, M., & Watson, A. (2003). Practice-based outcomes of dialectical behavior therapy (DBT) targeting anger and violence, with male forensic patients: A pragmatic and non-contemporaneous comparison. *Criminal Behaviour and Mental Health, 13*, 198–213.

Feigenbaum, J. D., Fonagy, P., Pilling, S., Jones, A., Wildgoose, A., & Bebbington, P. E. (2011). A real-world study of the effectiveness of DBT in the UK National Health Service. *British Journal of Clinical Psychology, 51*(2), 1–21.

Fernandez, E. (2008). The angry personality: A representation of six dimensions of anger expression. In G. J. Boyle, D. Matthews, & D. Saklofske (Eds.), *International handbook of personality theory and testing: Vol. 2: Personality measurement and assessment* (pp. 402–419). London, England: Sage Publications.

Forgays, D. G., Forgays, D. K., & Spielberger, C. D. (1997). Factor structure of the state-trait anger expression inventory. *Journal of Personality Assessment, 69*, 497–507.

Gardner, D. L., Leibenluft, E., O'Leary, K. M., & Cowdry, R. W. (1991). Self-ratings of anger and hostility in borderline personality disorder. *Journal of Nervous and Mental Disease, 179*, 157–161.

Greenberg, L. S., & Pascual-Leone, A. (2006). Emotion in psychotherapy: A practice-friendly research review. *Journal of Clinical Psychology, 62*, 611–630.

Gunderson, J. G. (1984). *Borderline personality disorder.* Washington, DC: American Psychiatric Press.

Gunderson, J. G., & Kolb, J. E. (1978). Discriminating features of borderline patients. *American Journal of Psychiatry, 135*, 792–796.

Gunderson, J. G., & Singer, M. T. (1975). Defining borderline patients: An overview. *American Journal of Psychiatry, 132*, 1–10.

Harned, M. S., Chapman, A. L., Dexter-Mazza, E. T., Murray, A., Comtois, K. A., & Linehan, M. M. (2008). Treating co-occurring axis I disorders in recurrently suicidal women with borderline personality disorder. *Journal of Consulting and Clinical Psychology, 76*, 1068–1075.

Jacob, G. A., Guenzler, C., Zimmerman, S., Scheel, C. N., Rusch, N., Leonhart, R., … Lieb, K. (2008). Time course of anger and other emotions in women with borderline personality disorder: A preliminary study. *Journal of Behaviour Therapy and Experimental Psychiatry, 39*, 391–402.

Jacob, G. A., Hellstern, K., Ower, N., Pillmann, M., Scheel, C. N., Rüsch, N., & Lieb, K. (2009). Emotion reactions to standardized stimuli in women with borderline personality disorder: Stronger negative affect, but no differences in reactivity. *Journal of Nervous and Mental Disease, 197*, 808–815.

Kanfer, E. H., & Philips, J. S. (1970). *Learning foundations of behavior therapy.* New York, NY: Wiley.

Koenigsberg, H. W., Harvey, P. D., Mitropoulou, V., Schmeidler, J., New, A. S., Goodman, M., … Siever, L. J. (2002). Characterizing affective instability in borderline personality disorder. *American Journal of Psychiatry, 159*, 784–788.

Koons, C. R., Chapman, A. L., Betts, B. B., O'Rourke, B., Morse, N., & Robins, C. J. (2006). Dialectical behavior therapy adapted for the vocational rehabilitation of significantly disabled mentally ill adults. *Cognitive Behavioral Practice, 13*, 146–156.

Koons, C. R., Robins, C. J., Tweed, J. L., Lynch, T. R., Gonzalez, A. M., Morse, J. Q., … Bastian, L. A. (2001). Efficacy of dialectical behavior therapy in women veterans with borderline personality disorder. *Behavior Therapy, 32*, 371–390.

Lazarus, R. S. (1991). Progress on a cognitive-motivational-relational theory of emotion. *American Psychologist, 46*(8), 819–834.

Levine, D., Marziali, E., & Hood, J. (1997). Emotion processing in borderline personality disorders. *Journal of Nervous and Mental Disease, 185*, 240–246.

Linehan, M. M. (1993a). *Cognitive-behavioral treatment of borderline personality disorder.* New York, NY: Guilford Press.

Linehan, M. M. (1993b). *Skills training manual for treating borderline personality disorder*. New York, NY: Guilford Press.

Linehan, M. M. (1997). Validation & psychotherapy. In A. Bohart & L. Greenberg (Eds.), *Empathy reconsidered: New directions in psychotherapy*. Washington, DC: American Psychiatric Association.

Linehan, M. M. (in press). *Skills training manual for disordered emotion regulation*. New York, NY: Guilford Press.

Linehan, M. M., Armstrong, H. E., Suarez, A., Allmon, D., & Heard, H. L. (1991). Cognitive-behavioral treatment of chronically parasuicidal borderline patients. *Archives of General Psychiatry, 48*, 1060–1064.

Linehan, M. M., Comtois, K. A., Murray, A. M., Brown, M. Z., Gallop, R. J., Heard, H. L., ... Lindenboim, N. (2006). Two-year randomized controlled trial and follow-up of dialectical behavior therapy vs therapy by experts for suicidal behaviors and borderline personality disorder. *Archives of General Psychiatry, 63*, 757–766.

Linehan, M. M., Heard, H., & Armstrong, H. E. (1993). Naturalistic follow-up of a behavioral treatment for chronically parasuicidal borderline patients. *Archives of General Psychiatry, 50*, 971–974.

Linehan, M. M., McDavid, J. D., Brown, M. Z., Sayrs, J. H. F., & Gallop, R. J. (2008). Olanzapine plus dialectical behavior therapy for women with high irritability who meet criteria for borderline personality disorder: A double blind, placebo-controlled pilot study. *Journal of Clinical Psychiatry, 69*, 999–1005.

Linehan, M. M., Rizvi, S. L., Welch, S. S., & Page, B. (2008). Psychiatric aspects of suicidal behavior: Personality disorders. In K. Hawton & K. van Heeringen (Eds.), *The international handbook of suicide and attempted suicide* (pp. 147–178). West Sussex, England: John Wiley & Sons.

Linehan, M. M., Schimidt, H., III, Dimeff, L. A., Craft, J. C., Kanter, J., & Comtois, K. A. (1999). Dialectical behavior therapy for patients with borderline personality disorder and drug-dependence. *American Journal on Addictions, 8*, 279–292.

McMain, S. F., Links, P. S., Gnam, W. H., Guimond, T., Cardish, R. J., Korman, L., & Streiner, D. L. (2009). A randomized trial of dialectical behavior therapy versus general psychiatric management for borderline personality disorder. *American Journal of Psychiatry, 166*, 1365–1374.

Paris, J. (1999). Borderline personality disorder. In T. Millon, P. H. Blaney, & R. D. Davis (Eds.), *Oxford textbook of psychopathology* (pp. 628–673). New York, NY: Oxford University Press.

Reisch, T., Ebner-Priemer, U. W., Tschacher, W., Bohus, M., & Linehan, M. M. (2008). Sequences of emotions in patients with borderline personality disorder. *Acta Psychiatrica Scandinavica, 118*, 42–48.

Rizvi, S. L., & Linehan, M. M. (2005). The treatment of maladaptive shame in borderline personality disorder: A pilot study of "opposite action." *Cognitive and Behavioral Practice, 12*(4), 437–447.

Rizvi, S. L., Steffel, L. M., & Carson-Wong, A. C. (in press). An overview of Dialectical Behavior Therapy for professional psychologists. *Professional Psychology: Research and Practice*.

Shiffman, S., Stone, A. A., & Hufford, M. R. (2008). Ecological momentary assessment. *Annual Review of Clinical Psychology, 4*, 1–32.

Soler, J., Pascual, J. C., Tiana, T., Cebria, A., Barrachina, J., Campins, M. J., ... Perez, V. (2009). Dialectical behavior therapy skills training compared to standard group therapy in borderline personality disorder: A 3-month randomized controlled clinical trial. *Behaviour Research and Therapy, 47*(5), 353–358.

Spielberger, C. D. (1988). *Manual for the state-trait anger expression scale (STAX).* Odessa, FL: Psychological Assessment Resources.

Stein, K. F. (1996). Affect instability in adults with a borderline personality disorder. *Archives of Psychiatric Nursing, 10*, 32–40.

Stiglmayr, C., Grathwol, T., & Bohus, M. (2001). *States of aversive tension in patients with borderline personality disorder: A controlled field study in progress in ambulatory assessment.* Seattle, WA: Hogrefe and Huber.

Tragesser, S. L., & Robinson, R. J. (2009). The role of affective instability and UPPS impulsivity in borderline personality disorder features. *Journal of Personality Disorders, 23*, 370–383.

van den Bosch, L. M. C., Koeter, M. W. J., Stijnen, T., Verheul, R., & van den Brink, W. (2005). Sustained efficacy of dialectical behavior therapy for borderline personality disorder. *Behaviour Research and Therapy, 43*, 1231–1241.

Verheul, R., van den Bosch, L. M., Koeter, M. W. J., Ridder, M. A. J., Stijnen, T., & van den Brink, W. (2003). Dialectical behavior therapy for women with borderline personality disorder: 12-month randomized clinical trial in the Netherlands. *British Journal of Psychiatry, 182*, 135–140.

Widiger, T. A., & Frances, A. J. (1989). Epidemiology, diagnosis, and comorbidity of borderline personality disorder. In A. Tasman, R. E. Hales, & A. J. Frances (Eds.), *American Psychiatric Press review of psychiatry* (Vol. 8, pp. 8–24).Washington, DC: American Psychiatric Publishing.

Zeigler-Hill, V., & Abraham, J. (2006). Borderline personality features: Instability of self-esteem and affect. *Journal of Social and Clinical Psychology, 25*, 668–687.

9

Targeting Anger in Forensic Populations

ANDREW DAY AND JAMES VESS

The problems that are commonly associated with poor anger regulation are well documented throughout this book. They include a wide range of behavioral, psychological, and physical health problems, including cardiovascular disease (Rainville, Bechara, Naqvi, & Damasio, 2006), personality disorders (Howells, 2009), substance abuse (Eftekhari, Turner, & Larimer, 2004), posttraumatic stress disorder (Andrews, Brewin, Rose, & Kirk, 2000), and organic brain disorders (McDonald, Hunt, Henry, Dimoska, & Bornhofen, 2010). Anger is, however, considered to be a particularly important antecedent to aggression (Novaco, Ramm, & Black, 2001), and one of the most common reasons for referring someone for treatment in the forensic setting is to reduce the risk of violent behavior occurring. Although all acts of violence are aggressive, not all acts of aggression are violent, with the distinction between aggressive and violent behavior being largely based on the extent of physical harm inflicted (Anderson & Bushman, 2002). The term *violent offending* is used in this chapter to refer to a subcategory of violence that pertains to acts of violence that contravene the legal code and thus is often the primary therapeutic target in forensic settings. It would, however, be a mistake to see anger management programs as a therapeutic solution to all violent offending, as contemporary violent offender treatment programs aim to also address a range of other needs in addition to anger control (Serin, 1994).

In this chapter we illustrate the role that anger can play in violent behavior in a hypothetical case vignette. The vignette depicts the type of person who is commonly referred for treatment in a forensic setting and is then used to introduce some of the clinical issues that can arise in treating anger problems in violent offenders.

Case Vignette

Mr. Smith is a 32-year-old man of European descent who is serving a sentence of 10 years imprisonment. His offenses involve one count of breaking and entering with a weapon and two counts of wounds with intent to cause great bodily harm, but he was referred for "anger management" by prison staff following a series of incidents in the prison. These involved altercations with other prisoners and were triggered by what Mr. Smith believed to be derogatory comments made about his family. He was observed to have reacted with intense anger, to have made verbal threats, and, on two occasions, to have responded with physical aggression. Concerns were also expressed about his risk of further violent offending after his release and whether he would be suitable for early release into the community on parole.

Mr. Smith was polite and cooperative throughout the initial assessment sessions but asserted that he did not have a problem with anger and that his behavior was both appropriate and justified. He was nonetheless willing to attend further sessions, reporting that this was likely to assist him in his efforts to gain parole. History taking was complicated by his apparently poor recall of events, and although this did not appear to be a deliberate attempt to mislead, it did seem that Mr. Smith had some difficulties remembering and accessing information clearly. His thinking, as reflected in his speech, was very literal, and some indications of mild to moderate cognitive limitations were apparent. However, his thought process was coherent, with no indication of thought disorder associated with psychosis, delusions, or hallucinations.

Background information. Mr. Smith was one of five siblings, with an older brother and sister and two younger brothers. His father was described as a heavy drinker who was both verbally and physically abusive to the children and their mother. The father left the family when Mr. Smith was 8 years old, and Mr. Smith reported that he had no contact with him since that time. His mother worked steadily to support the family, but all of the boys became associated with antisocial and gang-affiliated peers. Mr. Smith reported that most of his friends in childhood were economically marginalized kids who engaged in petty offending and were often truant from school. He stated that he was often picked on, both by his older brother and by older boys on his block. In the words of Mr. Smith: "I learned early that it is a dog-eat-dog world." He believed that he needed to become "tougher than the other guy" to command respect and avoid being victimized.

Mr. Smith did not attend school after eighth grade, and behavioral difficulties at home resulted in a placement in social welfare care. He remembers running away from the placement because of physical abuse. Records indicate that Mr. Smith became a solvent abuser at the age of 14, and he now has a 12-year history of serious alcohol abuse. He describes a pattern of heavy drinking an average of 3 days a week in which he would "drink until I drop" and occasionally experience alcohol-related blackouts. He also reported cannabis use on a daily basis. One of the most noteworthy aspects of Mr. Smith's developmental history, however, was the death of two of his brothers. It appears that a younger brother hung himself at age 17 and his older brother later died in a drug-related shooting.

Mr. Smith reported having a number of brief sexual relationships until age 20, when he began his first long-term relationship with the woman who is the mother of his two children. They have separated since his current imprisonment, although Mr. Smith expresses the desire to renew the relationship and restore contact with the children when he is released from prison. His work history is marginal, according to both his self-report and available documentation from ex-employers. Mr. Smith has had periods of employment ranging from 2 weeks to over a year in various low-skilled jobs, including packaging in a factory, sorting material at a recycling company, janitorial work, and casual work as a bouncer at a bar. He has been fired several times for failing to report to work, and this usually appears to be related to his drinking and drug use. During his extended periods of unemployment he would live temporarily with various extended family members or acquaintances.

Violence history. Mr. Smith has a history of violence from an early age. The first aggressive incident occurred at school when he was 8 years old when he threw a desk over the head of a fellow student. He is also reported to have assaulted a teacher when he was 13, following which he was expelled from the school. Reports also indicate that Mr. Smith's relationship with the mother of his children has involved substantial conflict and that some of his violent convictions have been for offenses against her. In fact, his formal criminal history includes six convictions for domestic violence, which occurred prior to the offenses for which he is serving his current sentence. Mr. Smith at some points has indicated that all of his previous violence is limited to assaulting his partner but at other times has acknowledged a history of street fighting. He has occasionally recognized that he has a "bad temper."

Mr. Smith had been drinking heavily prior to his current offending, which occurred after he was informed by his sister that his brother-in-law had struck Mr. Smith's mother. Witnesses reported that Mr. Smith became enraged, picked up a hand axe, and proceeded to the brother-in-law's house. He then struck him in the head with the blunt end of the axe, stating it was in retaliation for the assault of his mother. The second victim, a cousin, then attempted to call the police, at which point Mr Smith stabbed him with a knife.

Psychometric assessment. The Violence Risk Scale (VRS; Wong & Gordon, 1999) was administered as part of the initial assessment. The VRS is widely used to inform the assessment, prediction, and treatment of violence, and scores have been shown to be highly correlated with violent recidivism. Mr. Smith was assessed as demonstrating risk factors associated with five static (unchanging) variables associated with violence, including age of first violent offense, number of juvenile convictions, violence throughout life span, prior release failures/escapes (he was arrested while on parole from a previous conviction), and stability of family upbringing. The VRS also assesses a range of dynamic (changeable) factors that are associated with risk of violence. These include items relating to a violent lifestyle, criminal personality and attitudes, emotional control, insight into violence, interpersonal aggression, weapons use, impulsivity, and cognitive distortions. These are all identified as possible target areas for interventions that have the potential to reduce the risk of future violence occurring. Mr. Smith was given the highest rating (indicating more significant difficulties) in the areas of substance abuse, stability of relationships, community support, release back into high-risk situations, and a clear cycle of violence in the context of his domestic relationship. Mr. Smith was given a total score on the VRS that places him in the group described as having a "medium" risk of violence. This group has been reported as having a violent recidivism rate of 32.8% over a period of 4.4 years following release from prison[1] (Wong & Gordon, 2006).

The State-Trait Anger Expression Inventory (STAXI-2; Spielberger, 1999) is a 57-item self-report measure that purports to assess state anger, trait anger, and styles of anger expression and control. It is one of the most widely used and best validated measures of anger currently available. The trait anger subscale of the STAXI-2 measures an individual's general propensity to experience anger and its concomitant components over time. This scale is the most important in determining whether an individual has an anger problem or not. Respondents are asked to indicate their general anger experience with a number of items, with 1 ("almost never") and 4 ("almost always") the endpoints. Mr. Smith's score was above the normal range, and people with this score typically experience angry feelings to a degree that they interfere with optimal functioning. They frequently express angry feelings and often feel that they are treated unfairly by others. Mr Smith also scored over the 75th percentile on the anger expression-out subscale, indicating that he frequently expresses his anger through aggressive behavior directed toward other persons or objects in the environment. His score on the anger control-out subscale was also high, suggesting that he spends a great deal of energy in monitoring and preventing the outward experience and expression of anger.

The Anger Disorders Scale: Short Form (DiGiuseppe & Tafrate, 2004) is a scale that has been designed to assess aspects of anger that may lead to impairments in functioning. It is based on a model of anger that identifies a number of different domains in which anger may be experienced and expressed (e.g., cognitive, behavioral) and has been well validated with clinical populations. The Short Form provides a total score, along with three subscale scores: reactivity/expression, anger-in, and vengeance. Mr. Smith's profile was above the 75th percentile for each of these subscales, suggesting that he is above average in his reactivity, expressiveness of anger, and vengeance. His profile suggests that he has significant anger pathology, according to the test manual.

The Personality Assessment Inventory (Morey, 1991) is a 344-item self-report measure of psychopathology that has been designed to assess specific aspects of personality and mental health functioning. The measure contains 4 validity scales, 11 clinical scales, 5 treatment scales, and 2 interpersonal scales but was administered here primarily as a measure of invalid responding (the tendency to present an overly positive or negative impression of oneself in a self-report measure) and to determine the likely level of engagement with psychological treatment. Mr Smith scored above average (T = 70) on the interpersonal scales of dominance and warmth, suggesting that he is likely to be assertive, although not distant, in his relationships. These scores should, however, all be interpreted in light of a slightly elevated score (T = 66) on the positive impression subscale. This subscale purports to measure an overly positive self-presentation, although high scores may also reflect careless responding. As such, it is likely that his self-report of anger problems provides a slightly overpositive picture of his actual functioning.

In sum, the results of the assessment suggest that Mr. Smith is at some risk of acting violently in the future, and, although not all of his violence occurs in the context of anger arousal, he does have particular difficulties in regulating his anger, and this has led him to react aggressively and violently in response to perceived provocation. His patterns of behavior in such circumstances are long-standing, with their origins in early childhood and sustained by the belief that it is essential to act aggressively to avoid being victimized by others. Mr. Smith also sees himself as responsible for protecting those whom he cares for and whom he believes are less able to care for themselves. He does, however, get angry with his intimate partner when she does not conform to his wishes and he has a history of acting violently against her. He does not recognize the need for treatment but is willing to attend further sessions or an anger management program because he sees this as promoting his chances of early release from prison. This preliminary formulation provides the basis for the discussion of treatment issues that follows.

ISSUES IN TREATING ANGER IN FORENSIC POPULATIONS

Assessing the Risk of Violence

When working in the forensic setting, an initial task is to carefully consider the risk of the client acting violently in the future. In the case just described, the VRS classifies Mr. Smith as someone who is of "medium" risk of reoffending, suggesting that there is a reasonable likelihood that he will act violently again in the future. It is, however, important to recognize that risk is always contingent on a range of different factors, and that even "high-risk" offenders will not be at high risk at all times or in all situations. In other words, even for highly aggressive individuals, violent acts do not occur randomly but are a response to particular events and situations (see Megargee, 2010). The VRS identifies a number of different areas of need that are potentially relevant to Mr. Smith's treatment and suggests that effective risk management strategies will seek to address not only the way in which he controls anger arousal but also a range of other factors including a violent lifestyle, criminal personality and attitudes, weapons use, and impulsivity.

Considering the Nature of the Relationship Between Anger and Violence

It is particularly important to note that not all of Mr. Smith's violent behavior occurs in response to angry emotion. There is evidence from his history that violence can occur in the absence of emotional arousal or perceived wrongdoing, with violence also being used as a means of commanding respect or avoiding victimization. This is not unusual for violent offenders and highlights the danger that is associated with assuming that all violence is mediated by anger. Although Mr. Smith does experiences problems with anger regulation and, at times, expresses his anger through aggressive behavior, at other times he acts violently without feeling angry. Learning to control his anger more effectively is unlikely to effectively reduce the risk of further offending in these circumstances.

Aggression that occurs when the perpetrator is in a state of high anger arousal is typically, but not always,[2] elicited by events that are in some way aversive for the individual, often when he or she is blocked from achieving important goals or when expected rewards fail to eventuate (Berkowitz & Harmon-Jones, 2004). It follows that treatment should begin with a careful examination of the situations in which the client feels angry and the strength of feeling that results. For Mr. Smith, the assessment suggests that he will present at particularly high risk for violence when he is intoxicated and perceives that he has been provoked. In this example, the most significant provocations center around threats, both real and perceived, to his family, particularly his mother. For other violent offenders, aggression more typically occurs in situations in which there are perceived threats to social status. In such circumstances the offender attributes malevolent intent to others, experiences intense feelings of anger, and then seeks to effect change in others through force. Much less is known about the triggers for Mr. Smith's domestic violence, and it will be important to consider domestic violence further when developing a treatment plan for this client, in relation to both treatment needs (e.g., beliefs that are misogynistic or self-entitled) and the need to ensure the ongoing safety of family members.

Unlike Mr. Smith, some violent offenders have personality characteristics that differ from those of the angry, highly impulsive individual. Fernandez (2008), for example, described how the expression of passive-aggressive anger may not be impulsive, and Tsytsarev and Grodnitsky (1995) have described what they refer to as prolonged anger arousal and an "accumulation of affective tension which turns into an explosion of anger and rage, and is usually accompanied, or preceded, by intense feelings of humiliation and despair" (p. 104). The treatment of the individual who is generally low in anger but then unexpectedly and unpredictably acts aggressively has generally received limited attention (see Blackburn, 1993; Megargee, 1966) but is nonetheless important to consider when offering treatment to violent individuals. Davey, Day, and Howells (2005), for example, have argued that teaching specific anger management strategies to those who already overuse these strategies is likely to be, at best, ineffective and, at worst, counterproductive insofar as it is likely to reinforce and entrench the problem. There is also evidence to suggest that experiences of trauma are associated as much with the inhibition of anger as they are with outward emotional expression (see Orth & Weiland, 2006). Such findings, although to be expected when one considers the similarities that exist between angry rumination and the re-experiencing of traumatic symptoms (which are characteristic of posttraumatic stress disorder), mean that improving emotional control may not always be the most appropriate treatment target for those who overregulate angry emotion. Once again, a careful review of a number of recent anger-provoking situations is needed to identify which regulation strategies are routinely employed by a particular individual (and whether they are effective) before any decision can be made to treat.

Promoting Therapeutic Engagement

One of the most challenging aspects of working in the forensic setting is finding ways to engage clients in the treatment process. In the forensic setting, clients such as Mr. Smith often feel pressured to attend treatment and are sometimes legally coerced. This can create hostility and resentment, which leads to low levels of therapeutic engagement. Even when clients agree to participate in treatment, they may not see their behavior as particularly problematic and their goal is often to change the source of frustration, irritation, or annoyance rather than to engage in treatment that requires them to change their feelings or behavior. For others, the goal is to fulfill a legal requirement or to facilitate release from the criminal justice system. Mr. Smith's presentation is not atypical in this respect; although he acknowledges his offending, he is reluctant to identify anger as a major problem and believes he was justified in both his violence and his response to provocation from other prisoners (which he sees as protective of his mother). He was keen to defend this position and sought the endorsement of the therapist for these views, expressing frustration when the therapist challenged his behavior. At the same time, Mr. Smith was also clear that he was only participating in treatment because he believed that this would advantage him when he appears before the parole board.

Treatment-incompatible personal goals and dysfunctional client inferences about the nature of a problem have been identified by Howells and Day (2003) as a common cause of low treatment readiness that prevents forensic clients from engaging effectively in anger treatment. A number of ways to address low levels of readiness, such as that which relates to goals of treatment, have been identified (Ward, Day, Howells, & Birgden, 2004). These include making efforts to increase problem awareness or to instill confidence in the type of treatment that is offered. There may be a need to address feelings of shame (that are thought to inhibit treatment engagement), as well as to promote opportunities to access support for treatment from others and develop the skills that allow the client to function in a group. It is recommended that low levels of motivation to change be addressed using problem recognition and decision-making techniques that have been developed in motivational interviewing (Miller & Rollnick, 1991), although motivation may be increased in other ways in the forensic setting, such as by educating offenders about the impact of their offenses. Techniques that facilitate what has been referred to as "emotional deepening" may also be useful, particularly when clients seem to be defensive (Constantino, Castonguay, & Schut, 2001). Finally, Hemphill and Hart (2002) have proposed that interventions that reduce the status of criminal behavior, help the offender to feel in control, and emphasize self-sufficiency can all play a role in motivating those offenders who have psychopathic traits to engage in treatment. Beyko and Wong's (2005) suggestion of using behavioral contracts would also seem to be sensible in this regard.

There may, of course, be other reasons why an individual may be reluctant to engage in treatment that is offered in a forensic setting. It may be important to consider modifying the treatment that is offered to better suit the needs of the client and the context in which treatment is offered. This might, for example, involve amending program content such that it better suits the literacy levels of the client or involve changing treatment materials so they are more culturally appropriate. It is also possible to modify some of the structural components of the treatment, such as the intensity of treatment—some offenders may not be willing to commit to a program that lasts for over a year but may be more inclined to engage in a briefer program.

Attending to Comorbidity

Issues of comorbidity are particularly common in forensic populations and can have a profound influence on treatment. Despite the various accounts Mr. Smith has offered regarding his violent behavior, one factor that clearly emerges is the disinhibiting effect of alcohol upon his judgment and self-control. Mr. Smith himself has acknowledged that his past violence has been precipitated by alcohol, and he has been described by his partner as a "good provider" and a "nice person" when he is sober. During the assessment interview, Mr. Smith was able to reflect on the problems that he experiences with alcohol, identifying these as relevant to his anger and violence. For example, he stated that when he is drinking, he feels like a "he-man" and wants to "act tough" when provoked. Such provocation is apparently easily handled when he is intoxicated.

It is worth noting here that chronic abuse of solvents has particularly destructive effects on brain functioning over time and that this effect seems especially pronounced during childhood and adolescence when the brain is undergoing important developmental change. Severe alcohol abuse may also have long-term effects on brain functioning that are associated with cognitive impairment. Recent medical research also suggests that excessive use of cannabis, especially during adolescence and early adulthood, may be associated with impairment of memory and general cognitive functioning (Montgomery, Seddon, Fisk, Murphy, & Jansari, 2012). This may moderate the extent to which Mr. Smith is able to successfully implement the skills that he learns in treatment in everyday life.

THEORETICAL UNDERPINNINGS OF TREATMENT

Social learning is widely accepted to be important to the onset and maintenance of aggressive behavior. Imitation (observing acts of aggression) and vicarious reinforcement (perceiving aggression to be rewarded) are important here (Bandura, 1977), as are broader mechanisms involved in the learning of aggressive scripts during childhood and adolescence (Huesmann & Miller, 1994). Social learning theories are particularly helpful in identifying *distal* variables that can help to explain aggressive and violent behavior, but there is also a need to consider *proximal* variables, that is, those that affect the individual's behavior at the time that the violence occurs. In our case vignette, it is easy to identify a number of distal variables that are present in his background (e.g., abusive father, affiliation with antisocial peer groups, death of brothers, etc.) that are likely to have influenced his social learning and how he sees the world and responds to threat or provocation (e.g., it is a "dog-eat-dog" world and you need to become "tougher than the other guy" to survive).

Violent offenders have been shown to hold similar sets of core beliefs about themselves, the world, and their violence that can help to explain their aggressive behavior as well as inform attempts at intervention (Beech, Fisher, & Ward, 2006). These have been described in relation to what have been termed *implicit theories* (Ward, 2000), or networks of beliefs that support, facilitate, or legitimize violence, and are thus considered to be key risk factors for offending. They are implicit as individuals may not recognize them as hypothetical, seeing them as truths about the world and how people should behave. For example, Gilchrist (2009) has proposed that men who are violent toward their intimate partners subscribe to the theories that violence is "normal," that women are essentially "unknowable," and that events in the world are often "uncontrollable."

One of the most important proximal variables in aggression, however, is anger arousal. It has been well established that habitually aggressive individuals have a tendency to display a hostile attribution bias; that is, they perceive the intentions of others as counter to their goals and experience intense feelings of anger—particularly when feeling under threat or in circumstances where the situation is ambiguous (see Dodge & Crick, 1990). Theoretically, some of the most profound differences between aggressive and nonaggressive individuals lie in the ability of the individual to self-regulate anger arousal following a perceived provocation. Novaco's (1997) approach emphasizes the importance of affective instigators (anger, rage, annoyance) and the cognitive structures, propositions, operations, and products that give rise to affective states (see also Novaco & Welsh, 1989; Power & Dalgleish, 1999). Thus Howells, Daffern, and Day (2008) suggest that although poor self-regulation may function as a long-term trait (e.g., the trait of impulsivity), state variables (either internal or external to the person, but including angry arousal) can override the broad dispositions to self-regulate.

In line with our earlier observations about the relationship between violence and overcontrolled angry emotion, Baumeister, Heatherton, and Tice (1994) have drawn attention to the fact that much previous research on motives for violent and aggressive behavior emphasizes the strength of instigation (e.g., overpowering feelings of anger) and neglects self-regulatory and -inhibitory aspects of aggression. Baumeister et al. identify other processes serving to diminish self-regulation of violence, including desensitization through repetition of violent acts, escalation (mutual retaliation between perpetrator and victim), and excitation transfer in the course of escalatory encounters.

TREATING ANGER IN FORENSIC CLIENTS

Cognitive-behavioral therapy has become the preferred method of treating anger in violent offenders. Four key features of the cognitive-behavioral method are thought to be central to change. First, exposure to provocation (either overt or covert) appears to be important, as means of both reducing arousal through habituation and facilitating the implementation of other strategies. Exposure is a common feature of the cognitive-behavioral approach more generally and has been shown to be effective in the treatment of a variety of other disorders (Shapiro, Carlson, Astin, & Freedman, 2006). Second, cognitive change is required, given that anger is commonly understood as mediated by the presence of automatic thoughts and irrational beliefs (DiGiuseppe, Tafrate, & Eckhardt, 1994) and a consequence of rumination (Simpson & Papageorgiou, 2003). In working with violent offenders, a particular focus of any intervention is on changing what are commonly referred to as cognitive distortions. This is a term that has become widely used in forensic settings to refer to particular beliefs that are considered to be important causal antecedents to offending (i.e., criminogenic) and have been classified in terms of either primary (self-centered attitudes, thoughts, and beliefs) or secondary (blaming others, minimizing/mislabeling, and assuming the worst of others). The latter can be understood in terms of post hoc rationalizations and justifications of the violent behavior (see Gibbs, Potter, & Goldstein, 1995). Improving self-management skills is a third component of treatment, with interventions encouraging the development of appropriate coping skills when under stress. Finally, relaxation has been suggested as an effective way of reducing physiological arousal.

Programs that are offered in forensic settings are typically delivered in small group settings by psychologists and social workers, and participants are encouraged to use the Socratic method to confront and challenge each other when comments are made that suggest the presence of cognitive distortions. For example, the client's beliefs concerning the intentions and motives of other people involved in anger-provoking incidents may be the focus of intervention, especially when these beliefs appear unrealistic, unhelpful, or self-serving. The client is encouraged to examine these beliefs carefully and conduct experiments to establish the extent to which they are justified. Typically clients will then be given homework tasks in which they are asked to practice disputation across a range of different situations. The final part of therapy typically involves generating alternative beliefs and practicing using these in the situations in which provocations are perceived, often in conjunction with methods that help control physiological arousal (see DiGiuseppe & Tafrate, 2003).

What is described in the previous paragraph is a relatively standard approach to treating problematic anger, and the focus on self-management and improving emotional control will be familiar to those who treat anger in other populations. Mr. Smith was subsequently referred to a prison anger management group, which was delivered using cognitive-behavioral treatment methods. He was asked to describe to the group the situations in which he experienced anger and to reflect on what was going through his mind at the time. In giving feedback to Mr. Smith, the group remarked on his need to appear tough and suggested that he had a tendency to react too quickly, and before he had established whether any threat was indeed real. Mr. Smith took the position that his behavior was unproblematic and reacted aggressively when challenged by other members of the group, criticizing them, the quality of the program, and how it was being delivered. He was described by facilitators as being disruptive and interpersonally dominant, and he did not comply with requests to complete self-monitoring tasks given as group homework. After three sessions he was asked to leave the group.

Kozar and Day (2012) in their recent review of the role of the therapeutic alliance in violent offending behavior programs have argued that therapists should pay particular attention to ruptures in therapy. These may come in the form of clients communicating negative sentiments, disagreeing about the tasks and goals of treatment, not complying, avoiding, and not utilizing the therapeutic techniques that are offered. For example, a key indication of an alliance rupture is client anger and hostility toward the therapist. Castonguay, Constantino, and Holtforth's (2006) review of research relating to this issue suggests that the manner in which clinicians respond to anger in treatment (such as expressing their own feelings rather than turning them inward) will have a significant impact on whether such ruptures are resolved or not. As Kozar and Day suggest, if therapists are to be effective in treating violent offenders, they need to not only deliver material that assists the client in his or her understanding of the offending but also observe and reflect on any behavior that occurs during treatment that is representative of the offense process. In our experience in working with violent offenders, however, although ruptures are to be expected and do offer important therapeutic opportunities, it is also the case that treatment is likely to be ineffective for some and in such circumstances it becomes appropriate to withdraw clients. This is particularly the case in settings in which there are limited treatment opportunities and high levels of demand.

For Mr. Smith, cognitive-behavioral treatment delivered in a group setting was not effective. The method depends on the client having some introspective ability and self-awareness,[3] and it appeared that Mr. Smith had limited skills in this area and would require additional support before he was ready to engage in group treatment. The concrete thinking style of Mr. Smith made it difficult for him to consider alternative (conscious) responses to anger-provoking triggers, and he perceived the group's cognitive challenges as attacks on his status. Thus, there was a need to either provide more support to him before inviting him to join a group (focusing, for example, on raising problem awareness and motivation to change; see earlier) or offer alternative methods of treatment.

In our work we have also become increasingly interested in how experiential approaches to intervention might be used to overcome problems that arise in treating violent offenders. Although these suggestions are preliminary and are in need of further empirical investigation, they offer the possibility of providing a more engaging experience for those clients who might be considered resistant. The experiential methods that we have discussed are all consistent with the cognitive-behavioral model of change but focus primarily on the development of perspective-taking skills through forgiveness training, two-chair work, and video feedback (see Day, Howells, Mohr, Schall, & Gerace, 2008). An alternative therapeutic modality is psychological acceptance (Hayes, Jacobsen, Follette, & Dougher, 1994; Hayes, Wilson, Gifford, & Follette, 1996). Derived from the word meaning "to take or receive what is offered," psychological acceptance is the active process of taking in an event or situation that seems potentially useful in managing provocation. In a therapeutic context, acceptance-based approaches attempt to teach clients to feel emotions and bodily sensations more fully and without avoidance and to notice fully the presence of thoughts without following, resisting, believing, or disbelieving them.[4]

An example of an acceptance-based approach to intervention with anger-related disturbances is provided by mindfulness-based approaches. As taught in most clinical interventions, mindfulness is a collection of meditation practices and skills that are designed to enhance an individual's ability to remain immersed nonjudgmentally in the present moment (Kabat-Zinn, Massion, Hebert, & Rosenbaum, 2003). Concentrative meditation involves bringing one's attention to a single focus (i.e., a mantra); mindfulness meditation involves an ongoing process of receptive attention where attention is much less differentiated (Shapiro, 1982). Typical mindfulness practices focus attention on the breath and then on each section of the body in turn, with the accompanying instruction to simply observe bodily sensations without any judgment or evaluation. Other formal practices include observing the breath, sitting and walking meditations, and yoga. In addition, practitioners are encouraged to apply the principles of mindfulness informally in their everyday life, applying awareness and a nonjudgmental attitude toward everyday activities such as eating and driving (Kabat-Zinn, 1994).

The utility of such approaches with violent offenders has yet to be established, but they represent alternative approaches to treatment that may be particularly useful for those, such as Mr. Smith, who do not respond to more conventional anger management methods. Not only are acceptance-based approaches particularly relevant to the reduction of negative affect, but also, by their nature, they reduce impulsive responding by increasing awareness of mental states and their role in eliciting behavior that is perceived as automatic. In addition, this type of treatment is low cost, easy to implement in an institutional setting, and, in some circumstances, more culturally appropriate. Furthermore, the evidence supporting their efficacy in nonforensic populations is persuasive (e.g., Brown, Ryan, & Cresswell, 2007; Grossman, Niemann, Schmidt, & Walach, 2004; Kuyken et al., 2008), offering grounds for some optimism in relation to their application with these types of clients.

TREATMENT EFFICACY

There is now a reasonably robust evidence base to support the idea that treating problematic anger is effective, especially when cognitive-behavioral methods are employed. Meta-analytic reviews of treatment effectiveness (e.g., DiGiuseppe &

Tafrate, 2003; Edmondson & Conger, 1996) have consistently suggested that although the effect sizes associated with treatment are moderate, program outcomes are sufficiently positive to be considered as producing reliable clinical change (see Deffenbacher, Oetting, & DiGiuseppe, 2002). Indeed, Beck and Fernandez (1998), in their meta-analysis of 50 outcome studies, concluded that individuals receiving cognitive-behavioral anger management therapy were 75% better off in terms of anger reduction than the average untreated control. In a more recent meta-analysis of anger management outcomes, DiGiuseppe and Tafrate (2003) found that the effects of anger management were most marked on posttreatment measures of aggression.

Even though anger management programs have been administered on a very large scale internationally within criminal justice and forensic mental health systems, there have been relatively few studies that have evaluated their effects with forensic populations. In the DiGiuseppe and Tafrate (2003) meta-analysis, for example, only 8 of the 57 studies reviewed were conducted with offender participants, and although other evaluations of offender treatment have been conducted (e.g., Smith, Smith, & Beckner, 1994; Valliant, Jensen, & Raven-Brook, 1995; Valliant & Raven, 1994), most of these suffer from methodological problems (such as a lack of control groups or an absence of behavioral measures), which limit the extent to which their findings can be considered to be robust.

Two large-scale evaluations have been reported with offender populations that warrant specific mention. First, Dowden, Blanchette, and Serin (1999) found that a 50-hour anger management program offered to adult male offenders in Canada produced reductions in recidivism over a 3-year period, though only for those offenders who were categorized as "high risk." A follow-up study by Dowden and Serin (2002) found that while anger management program participants were no less likely to be involved with institutional incidents than those who had not received any treatment, there were marked differences in subsequent recidivism between those who completed treatment and those who dropped out. Over the 3-year follow-up period, the violent recidivism rates for the dropout, control (untreated), and treatment groups were 40%, 17%, and 5%, respectively.

A second set of studies by Howells and colleagues in Australia on the effects of a briefer (20-hour) anger management program with offenders produced less encouraging results (Heseltine, Howells, & Day, 2010; Howells et al., 2005; Watt & Howells, 1999). These studies found no differences between the treatment groups and untreated controls on a range of dependent measures, including anger experience, anger expression, prison misconduct, and observational measures of aggressive behavior. One of the main conclusions of Howells et al. (2005) was that although treated participants consistently showed improvements on a range of anger measures, these effects were very small in absolute terms and, generally, were hardly greater than the changes observed in the control group. The one exception to this general picture was that anger knowledge improved more in treated participants than in the controls.

There is a surprisingly limited evidence base from which to draw any firm conclusions about the effectiveness of multimodal treatments to reduce risk of violent behavior in violent offenders (McGuire, 2008). Jolliffe and Farrington (2007), in their systematic review of violent offender treatment conducted for the Ministry of Justice in the United Kingdom, were only able to identify 11 outcome studies that met the required methodological criteria. They cautiously concluded that "interventions with violent offenders were effective both at reducing general and violent re-offending, with a difference in percentage re-convicted of about eight to eleven per cent for general re-offending measures and seven to eight per cent for violent re-offending measures" (p. iv). They did note, however, that effectiveness varied considerably according to factors such as the content of the intervention, the delivery of the intervention, and the methodology of the study.

More recently, Serin, Gobeil, and Preston (2009) have published an evaluation of a persistently violent offender treatment program offered to Canadian offenders. They compared program completers to two control groups (those who completed an alternative program and those who failed to complete) but identified few differences between the groups on a range of measures (including change on measures of treatment targets, institutional misconduct, and postrelease returns to custody). Serin and colleagues suggested that this may mean either that the program is effective with only certain groups of violent offenders or that it did not meet some of the criteria that are usually associated with the more effective programs (e.g., program integrity and intensity).

Collectively, these rather inconsistent findings suggest that much can be done to improve the ways in which violent offender treatment is both conceptualized and delivered. In particular, the findings of the studies by Howells and colleagues (see earlier) require explanation. It may be, for example, that the anger programs they evaluated were too brief (approximately 20 hours delivered in group sessions) to produce change in the actual experience or behavior of a group who typically have long-term and multiple psychological difficulties. An alternative explanation, related to issues of low treatment readiness, is that many offenders are not sufficiently engaged in the process of behavior change to benefit from treatment and that more attention should be given to only offering treatment to those who are considered "treatment ready" (Day, Casey, Ward, Howells, & Vess, 2010). Finally, it has been suggested that prisons do not typically provide environments that are conducive to successful rehabilitation, with qualitative and ethnographic research consistently identifying ways in which the institutional social climate can act in countertherapeutic ways (Day, Casey, Vess, & Huisy, 2012). There is also an obvious need for more rigorously designed and controlled evaluation research to be conducted.

CONCLUSION

This chapter has explored the treatment of anger in forensic settings. It is suggested that the primary aim of treatment in this context is often to manage the risk of further violence occurring. However, there are a number of different ways in which anger regulation problems can impact upon risk and, as such, careful assessment is required before offering anger management programs that aim to modify risk. In addition, many offenders are not well equipped to benefit from such interventions and transfer these skills to life outside prison due to the presence of comorbid mental health problems, substance use issues, or problems with neuropsychological functioning. Furthermore, they may not recognize the need to change or attend treatment as a means of improving their chances of release from custody. A key aim of any treatment is to meaningfully engage the client in the process of behavior change, and the focus of risk management strategies should be to help them do this by managing both psychological risk (through treatment) and environmental risk (through structured programs of external supervision and support). Utilizing alternative approaches to treatment, such as those that draw on acceptance-based approaches, may have particular value in working with forensic clients.

NOTES

1. This compares to those in a "low" scoring group with a violent recidivism rate of 8.4% and a "high" scoring group with a violent recidivism rate of 51.1% over the same period.
2. For example, anger in response to moral transgression or wrongdoing.
3. Fehrer (2002) has further suggested that cognitive-behavioral interventions are not always effective when individuals react too quickly to apply an alternative behavior or thought and, as such, may not work well with highly impulsive individuals. Other critiques of cognitive-behavioral treatment methods have suggested that clinical improvement often occurs before the presumptively key features have been adequately implemented (Ilardi & Craighead, 1994) and that changes in cognitive mediators often fail to explain the impact of treatment (Burns & Spangler, 2001; Morgenstern & Longabaugh, 2000).
4. It should be noted that psychological acceptance does not refer to toleration or the acceptance of an event in an effort to control or minimize it. Instead, acceptance refers to the willingness to remain in contact with, and to actively experience, particular private experiences (bodily sensations, emotions, thoughts, memories, behavioral predispositions) that seem to accompany functionally useful overt behaviors.

REFERENCES

Anderson, C. A., & Bushman, B. J. (2002). Human aggression. *Annual Review of Psychology, 53*, 27–51.

Andrews, B., Brewin, C. R., Rose, S., & Kirk, M. (2000). Predicting PTSD symptoms in victims of violent crime: The role of shame, anger, and childhood abuse. *Journal of Abnormal Psychology, 109*, 69–73.

Bandura, A. (1977). *Social learning theory.* Englewood Cliffs, NJ: Prentice-Hall.

Baumeister, R. F., Heatherton, T. F., & Tice, D. M. (1994). *Losing control: How and why people fail at self-regulation.* San Diego, CA: Academic Press.

Beck, R., & Fernandez, E. (1998). Cognitive-behavioral therapy in the treatment of anger: A meta-analysis. *Cognitive Therapy and Research, 22*, 63–74.

Beech, A., Fisher, D., & Ward, T. (2006). Sexual murderers' implicit theories. *Journal of Interpersonal Violence, 20*, 1366–1389.

Berkowitz, L., & Harmon-Jones, E. (2004). Towards an understanding of the determinants of anger. *Emotion, 4*, 107–130.

Beyko, M. J., & Wong, S. C. P. (2005). Predictors of treatment attrition and indicators for program improvement not offender shortcomings: A study of sex offender treatment attrition. *Sexual Abuse: A Journal of Research and Treatment, 17*, 375–389.

Blackburn, R. (1993). *The psychology of criminal conduct: Theory, research and practice.* New York, NY: Wiley & Sons.

Brown, K. W., Ryan, R. M., & Cresswell, J. D. (2007). Mindfulness: Theoretical foundations and evidence for its salutary effects. *Psychological Inquiry, 18*, 211–237.

Burns, D. D., & Spangler, D. L. (2001). Do changes in dysfunctional attitudes mediate changes in depression and anxiety in cognitive-behavioral therapy? *Behavior Therapy, 32*, 337–369.

Castonguay, L. G., Constantino, M. J., & Holtforth, M. G. (2006). The working alliance: Where are we and where should we go? *Psychotherapy: Theory, Research, Practice, Training, 43*, 271–279.

Constantino, M. J., Castonguay, L. G., & Schut, A. J. (2001). The Working Alliance: A flagship for the "scientist-practitioner" model in psychotherapy. In G. S. Tryon (Ed.), *Counseling based on process research: Applying what we know* (pp. 81–131). Boston, MA: Allyn and Bacon.

Davey, L., Day, A., & Howells, K. (2005). Anger, overcontrol and violent offending. *Aggression and Violent Behavior, 10*, 624–635.

Day, A., Casey, S., Vess, J., & Huisy, G. (2012). Assessing the therapeutic climate of prisons. *Criminal Justice and Behavior, 39*, 156–168.

Day, A., Casey, S., Ward, T., Howells, K., & Vess, J. (2010). *Transitions to better lives: Offender readiness and rehabilitation.* Cullompton, England: Willan Press.

Day, A., Howells, K., Mohr, P., Schall, E., & Gerace, A. (2008). The development of CBT programmes for anger: The role of interventions to promote perspective-taking skills. *Behavioural and Cognitive Psychotherapy, 36*, 299–312.

Deffenbacher, J. L., Oetting, E. R., & DiGiuseppe, R. A. (2002). Principles of empirically supported interventions applied to anger management. *The Counselling Psychologist, 30*, 262–280.

DiGiuseppe, R., Tafrate, R., & Eckhardt, C. (1994). Critical issues in the treatment of anger. *Cognitive and Behavioral Practice, 1*, 111–132.

DiGiuseppe, R., & Tafrate, R. (2003). Anger treatment for adults: A meta-analytic review. *Clinical Psychology: Science and Practice, 10*, 70–84.

DiGiuseppe, R., & Tafrate, R. (2004). *Anger Disorders Scale (ADS): Technical manual.* Toronto, Ontario, Canada: MultiHealth Systems.

Dodge, K. A., & Crick, N. R. (1990). Social information-processing bases of aggressive behaviour in children. *Personality and Social Psychology Bulletin, 16*, 8–22.

Dowden, C., & Serin, R. (2002). *Anger Management Programming for federal male offenders: The impact of dropouts and other program performance variables on recidivism.* Ottawa, Ontario, Canada: Research Branch, Correctional Service Canada.

Dowden, C., Blanchette, K., & Serin, R. (1999). *Anger Management Programming for federal male offenders: An effective intervention.* Ottawa, Ontario, Canada: Research Branch, Correctional Service Canada.

Edmondson, C., & Conger, J. (1996). A review of treatment efficacy for individuals with anger problems: Conceptual, assessment and methodological issues. *Clinical Psychology Review, 16*, 251–275.

Eftekhari, A., Turner, A. P., & Larimer, M. E. (2004). Anger expression, coping, and substance use in adolescent offenders. *Addictive Behaviors, 29*, 1001–1008.

Fehrer, F. C. (2002). The awareness response: A transpersonal approach to reducing maladaptive emotional reactivity. Unpublished doctoral dissertation. Institute of Transpersonal Psychology, Palo Alto, CA.

Fernandez, E. (2008). The angry personality: A representation on six dimensions of anger expression. In G. J. Boyle, D. Matthews, & D. Saklofske (Eds.), *International handbook of personality theory and testing: Vol. 2: Personality measurement and assessment* (pp. 402–419). London, England: Sage Publications.

Gibbs, J. C., Potter, G. B., & Goldstein, A. P. (1995). *The EQUIP Program: Teaching youth to think and act responsibly through a peer-helping approach*. Champaign, IL: Research Press.

Gilchrist, E. (2009). Implicit thinking about implicit theories in intimate partner violence. *Psychology, Crime and Law, 15*, 131–145.

Grossman, P., Niemann, L., Schmidt, S., & Walach, H. (2004). Mindfulness-based stress reduction and health benefits: A meta-analysis. *Journal of Psychosomatic Research, 57*, 35–43.

Hayes, S. C., Jacobsen, N. S., Follette, V. M., & Dougher, M. J. (1994). *Acceptance and change: Content and context in psychotherapy*. Reno, NV: Context Press.

Hayes, S. C., Wilson, K. G., Gifford, E. V., & Follette, V. M. (1996). Experiential avoidance and behavioural disorders: A functional dimensional approach to diagnosis and treatment. *Journal of Consulting and Clinical Psychology, 64*, 1152–1168.

Hemphill, J. F., & Hart, S. D. (2002). Motivating the unmotivated: Psychopathy, treatment and change. In M. McMurran (Ed.), *Motivating offenders to change: A guide to enhancing engagement in therapy* (pp. 193–219). Chichester, England: Wiley.

Heseltine, K., Howells, K., & Day, A. (2010). Brief anger interventions with offenders may be ineffective: A replication and extension. *Behaviour Research and Therapy, 48*, 246–250.

Howells, K., & Day, A. (2003). Readiness for anger management: Clinical and theoretical issues. *Clinical Psychology Review, 23*, 319–337.

Howells, K. (2009). Angry affect, aggression and personality disorder. In M. McMurran & R. Howard (Eds.). *Personality, personality disorder and violence: An evidence based approach* (pp. 191–211). London, England: Wiley-Blackwell.

Howells, K., Daffern, M., & Day, A. (2008). Aggression and violence. In K. Soothill, M. Dolan, & P. Rogers (Eds.), *The handbook of forensic mental health* (pp. 351–374). Cullompton, England: Willan.

Howells, K., Day, A., Williamson, P., Bubner, S., Jauncey, S., Parker, A., & Heseltine, K. (2005). Brief anger management programs with offenders: Outcomes and predictors of change. *Journal of Forensic Psychiatry and Psychology, 16*, 296–311.

Huesmann, L. R., & Miller, L. S. (1994). Long-term effects of repeated exposure to media violence in childhood. In L. R. Huesmann (Ed.), *Aggressive behavior: Current perspectives* (pp. 153–186). New York, NY: Plenum.

Ilardi, S. S., & Craighead, W. E. (1994). The role of non-specific factors in cognitive-behavior therapy for depression. *Clinical Psychology: Science and Practice, 1*, 138–156.

Jolliffe, D., & Farrington, D. P. (2007). *A systematic review of the national and international evidence on the effectiveness of interventions with violent offenders*. Series 16/07. London, England: Ministry of Justice Research.

Kuyken, W., Byford, S., Taylor, R. S., Watkins, E., Holden, E., White, K., … Teasdale, J. D. (2008). Mindfulness-based cognitive therapy to prevent relapse in recurrent depression. *Journal of Consulting and Clinical Psychology, 76*, 966–978.

Kabat-Zinn, J. (1994). *Full catastrophe living: Using the wisdom of your body and mind to face stress, pain, and illness*. New York, NY: Delacorte.

Kabat-Zinn, J., Massion, A. O., Hebert, J. R., & Rosenbaum, E. (2003). Meditation. In J. C. Holland (Ed.), *Textbook on psycho-oncology* (pp. 767–779). Oxford, England: Oxford University Press.

Kozar, C., & Day, A. (2012). The therapeutic alliance in offending behavior programs: A necessary and sufficient condition for change? *Aggression and Violent Behavior, 17*, 482–486.

McDonald, S., Hunt, C., Henry, J. D., Dimoska, A., & Bornhofen, C. (2010). Angry responses to emotional events: The role of impaired control and drive in people with severe traumatic brain injury. *Journal of Clinical and Experimental Neuropsychology, 32*, 855–864.

McGuire, J. (2008). A review of effective interventions for reducing aggression and violence. *Philosophical Transactions of the Royal Society B, 363*, 2577–2597.

Megargee, E. (1966). Undercontrolled and over-controlled personality types in extreme anti-social aggression. *Psychological Monographs, 80*, 1–611.

Megargee, E. (2010). Using the algebra of aggression in forensic practice. *British Journal of Forensic Practice, 13*, 4–11.

Miller, W. R., & Rollnick, S. (1991). *Motivational interviewing: Preparing people to change addictive behaviour.* New York, NY: Guilford.

Montgomery, C., Seddon, A. L., Fisk, J. E., Murphy, P. N., & Jansari, A. (2012). Cannabis—related deficits in real—world memory. *Human Psychopharmacology: Clinical and Experimental, 27*, 217–225.

Morey, L. (1991). *The Personality Assessment Inventory.* Lutz, FL: PAR.

Morgenstern, J., & Longabaugh, R. (2000). *Cognitive-behavioral treatment for alcohol disorder.* New York, NY: Guilford.

Novaco, R. W., & Welsh, W. N. (1989). Anger disturbances: Cognitive mediation and clinical prescription. In K. Howells & C. R. Hollin (Eds.), *Clinical approaches to violence* (pp. 39–60). Chichester, England: Wiley.

Novaco, R. W. (1997). Remediating anger and aggression with violent offenders. *Legal and Criminological Psychology, 2*, 77–88.

Novaco, R. W., Ramm, M., & Black, L. (2001). Anger treatment with offenders. In C. R. Hollin (Ed.), *Handbook of offender assessment and treatment (pp. 281–296).* Chichester, England: Wiley.

Orth, U., & Wieland, E. (2006). Anger, hostility, and posttraumatic stress disorder in trauma-exposed adults: A meta-analysis. *Journal of Consulting and Clinical Psychology, 74*, 698–706.

Power, M., & Dalgleish, T. (1999). *Cognition and emotion: From order to disorder.* Hove, England: Psychology Press.

Rainville, P., Bechara, A., Naqvi, N., & Damasio, A. R. (2006). Basic emotions are associated with distinct patterns of cardio-respiratory activity. *International Journal of Psychophysiology, 61*, 5–18.

Serin, R. C., Gobeil, R., & Preston, D. L. (2009). Evaluation of the persistently violent offender treatment program. *International Journal of Offender Therapy and Comparative Criminology, 53*, 57–73.

Serin, R. C. (1994). *Treating violent offenders: A review of current practices.* Research Report R-38. Ottawa, Ontario, Canada: Correctional Service of Canada.

Shapiro, D. H. (1982). Overview: Clinical and physiological comparisons of meditation with other self-control strategies. *American Journal of Psychiatry, 139*, 267–274.

Shapiro, S. L., Carlson, L. E., Astin, J. A., & Freedman, B. (2006). Mechanisms of mindfulness. *Journal of Clinical Psychology, 62*, 373–386.

Simpson, C., & Papageorgiou, C. (2003). Metacognitive beliefs about rumination in anger. *Cognitive Behavioral Practice, 10*, 91–94.

Smith, L. L., Smith, J. N., & Beckner, B. M. (1994). An anger-management workshop for women inmates. *Families in Society, 75*, 172–175.

Spielberger, C. D. (1999). *STAXI-2 professional manual.* Odessa, FL: Psychological Assessment Resources.

Tsytsarev, S., & Grodnitsky, G. (1995). Anger and criminality. In H. Kassinove (Ed.), *Anger disorders* (pp. 91–108). Philadelphia, PA: Taylor and Francis.

Valliant, P. M., & Raven, L. M. (1994). Management of anger and its effect on incarcerated assaultive and non-assaultive offenders. *Psychological Reports, 75*, 275–278.

Valliant, P. M., Jensen, B., & Raven-Brook, L. (1995). Brief cognitive behavioural therapy with male adolescent offenders in open custody or on probation: An evaluation of management of anger. *Psychological Reports, 76*, 1056–1058.

Ward, T. (2000). Sexual offenders' cognitive distortions as implicit theories. *Aggression and Violent Behavior, 5*, 491–507.

Ward, T., Day, A., Howells, K., & Birgden, A. (2004). The multifactor offender readiness model. *Aggression and Violent Behavior, 9*, 645–673.

Watt, B., & Howells, K. (1999). Skills training for aggression control: evaluation of an anger management programme for violent offenders. *Legal and Criminological Psychology, 4*, 285–300.

Wong, S. C. P., & Gordon, A. (1999). *Manual for the Violence Risk Scale (version 2).* Regional Psychiatric Centre (Prairies) & University of Saskatchewan.

Wong, S. C. P., & Gordon, A. (2006). The validity and reliability of the Violence Risk Scale: A treatment friendly violence risk assessment tool. *Psychology, Public Policy and Law, 12*, 279–309.

10

Anger Management in Schools

The Coping Power Program for Children and Early Adolescents

JOHN E. LOCHMAN, NICOLE P. POWELL,
CAROLINE L. BOXMEYER, MEGHANN KELLY,
CASEY DILLON, AND CATHERINE BRADSHAW ■

Coping Power—Case Vignette

James was 13 years old and a seventh grader at Rosevale K-8 School. He had numerous disciplinary actions for talking back to teachers and for getting into verbal and physical altercations with classmates. He was recently reported to the truancy board due to repeated unexcused absences. James had a long history of disruptive behavior and academic difficulty. He had been diagnosed with attention-deficit/hyperactivity disorder (ADHD), taken stimulant medication, and received behavioral support with a Section 504 plan. Although James's intelligence was estimated to be in the low-average range, he had nearly failed several grades due to poor completion of assignments. James had recently begun refusing to take medication for ADHD and resisting going to school. When he attended school, he often put his head on his desk and refused to do his work. He also tended to overattribute hostile intent in others and lashed out in response to even the slightest provocation.

James's teacher and school psychologist were very concerned about his deteriorating behavior and felt that he was at risk of dropping out of school. They were particularly concerned because his mother, Vanessa, was busy working two jobs and trying to support her family as a single parent. She seemed to care deeply about James but had difficulty supporting his academic learning and behavioral needs. The school psychologist, Ms. Alvarez, was about to begin a new group for students with anger management and disruptive behavior problems. She planned to use the Coping Power curriculum as the basis for the group content. Ms. Alvarez thought that the group would be beneficial for James but was uncertain whether he and his mother would be willing to participate.

James had been suspended from school for 3 days for fighting with a classmate. The school required parents to attend a meeting with the principal and school psychologist when a student returned to school following a suspension. When James's mother came to check him back in to school, Ms. Alvarez and the principal met with her. They took a motivational enhancement approach and began the meeting by asking Vanessa how things were going for her family and what her concerns were for James. Vanessa became very emotional and said that she was feeling overwhelmed and was concerned about James. She was aware that he was having difficulty at school; however, she did not know how to help him. She shared that James barely talked to her and spent most of his time in his room or else "hanging out" in the neighborhood. She was hardly able to spend any time with him because she worked long hours and also had two younger children and elderly parents to care for. Vanessa shared that she was almost too scared to talk to James anymore for fear that he would become angry and aggressive.

Ms. Alvarez empathized with Vanessa and described how Coping Power could help James with his anger and social skills. Vanessa was appreciative of the potential services and said she would like for James to participate. Ms. Alvarez met with James and described the program. He was not particularly enthusiastic about a group that seemed to be for students who had "problems," but he agreed to participate because it would at least get him out of class.

At the start of the Coping Power group, Ms. Alvarez guided the group members in identifying long-term and short-term personal goals. James had difficulty thinking of goals because no one had ever spent time encouraging him to think about his future. The only thing he could come up with was that he would like his teachers and mother to "get off his back." Ms. Alvarez praised him for sharing this concern and helped him identify short-term goals that would help him reach this long-term goal (e.g., stay out of fights, participate in class). When prompted to select one goal for the week, James decided that he would try to keep his head off his desk during class.

James missed the next two sessions after he was suspended for fighting. He had become extremely volatile and aggressive when an opponent bumped into him during a game. When James returned to the group, the students were learning to use an imaginary thermometer to measure their anger and to become more attentive to the bodily changes that serve as "clues" to their anger. Ms. Alvarez asked James how his body felt when the opponent bumped into him. He said that his hands balled into fists and his face got hot. Ms. Alvarez explained that these changes were important clues that James's body had given him about his onset of anger. Next, the group discussed whether one is able to handle anger-provoking situations better at high, medium, or low levels of anger. Most of the group members agreed that they handled situations better when they were just a little bit angry, rather than very angry. However, James said that his anger was like a light switch and that it was impossible for him to keep from getting really angry once someone upset him. Ms. Alvarez praised James for sharing this insight and let him know that, over the next few weeks, they were going to practice catching the early signs of anger and using coping strategies to keep their anger under control.

Even though James began to show reasonably good engagement in Coping Power, he continued to act out in class, which was frustrating to his teachers. Ms. Alvarez made assertive attempts to communicate to James's teachers the concept of shaping behavior in small steps. Ms. Alvarez encouraged them to be on the lookout for times that James showed good participation and remained calm rather than responding in anger. She recommended that James's teachers praise him for small improvements in these target behaviors. During the next few sessions, James learned to identify the internal thoughts that contributed to his impulsive anger (e.g., "he did that to me on purpose") and to use alternate coping thoughts (e.g., "I won't be a fool, I'll keep my cool"). During anger induction activities conducted in session, James was very quick to anger and needed additional coaching to utilize coping self-statements to manage his anger. In a follow-up session, James was proud to share an example from his week in which he remained calm when his teacher put his name on the board for talking. James said he kept his cool by reminding himself that his teacher "was probably just trying to do her job."

Ms. Alvarez praised James for taking what he learned in group and applying it outside. James said he was glad he was not getting into trouble as much, but he did not want others to think that he could not stand up for himself. Ms. Alvarez acknowledged this valid concern and explained that keeping your anger arousal at a manageable level was just the first step. She explained to the group that they would be learning a set of steps that they could use to solve social problems effectively. She told them these steps included (a) identifying the problem as specifically as possible (from your own perspective and from the perspective of each person involved), (b) brainstorming a range of different solutions (being sure to include socially desirable solutions such as verbal assertion, bargaining, and compromise as options), (c) thinking ahead about the likely consequences of each solution, (d) picking the solution likely to result in the best outcome for all parties involved, and (e) reviewing the actual outcome of the solution after it is enacted.

During one of the sessions on this topic, James and another group member got into a shoving match about whose turn it was to sit in a favorite chair. Ms. Alvarez separated them and suggested that they use the problem-solving steps they were learning to address the situation. Ms. Alvarez then helped them brainstorm choices (e.g., no one sits in the favorite chair; one person sits in it today and the other person waits until the next meeting). They decided that they would each sit in the chair for half the time that day and that James could sit in it first because he had arrived at group first. At the end of the session, James and the other student both agreed that the solution they picked worked out better than fighting, which could have resulted in disciplinary action for both of them. After the group spent several weeks learning this problem-solving process, James and his fellow group members made a public service video teaching others how to solve social problems effectively. James really enjoyed the video production process and for the first time could visualize a positive long-term goal for himself of trying to become a video producer.

Toward the end of the Coping Power intervention, Ms. Alvarez led the group members in a series of activities intended to help them recognize that the people with whom we spend time can have an impact on our behavior and personal goal attainment. In a monthly individual check-in with Ms. Alvarez, James admitted that he had been spending time with some older kids in his neighborhood who were pressuring him to use drugs and to get involved in their theft ring. Ms. Alvarez helped James anticipate some of the negative consequences of continuing to spend time with these kids. In the next group session, the students practiced specific ways that they could resist peer pressure (e.g., by saying no thanks, finding other friends to spend time with). They also practiced specific social skills for making and maintaining friendships with positive peers and for resolving interpersonal conflicts using assertive communication techniques. Outside of group, James tried to spend more time with Malcolm, a neighbor who was well liked and who was involved in producing the school's daily telecast. As their friendship developed, Malcolm helped James join the school's telecast crew, which further improved James's feelings of connectedness to school.

As the group neared completion, Ms. Alvarez helped the students identify specific behavioral improvements they had made. James said he was proud of himself for becoming more involved in school and for fighting less. He realized that these changes had helped him reach his long-term goal of getting his mother and teachers "off his back," while also helping him to make friends. Ms. Alvarez praised James for these improvements and helped him anticipate how to continue to apply the skills he had learned, even in the face of likely challenges in the future. The group ended with a pizza party that the members had earned by successfully working as a team.

Parent component. While James was participating in the Coping Power student group, his mother met with Ms. Alvarez several times for parenting support, using the Coping Power curriculum. Recognizing how overwhelmed Vanessa was, Ms. Alvarez started by helping Vanessa learn to implement some relaxation and time management strategies. Vanessa committed to going for a walk with a friend two times a week to help her take care of herself and gain some social support. She also committed to spending more quality one-on-one time with James. Because he had shown an interest in cooking, she invited James to start fixing supper with her. After several weeks, Vanessa noticed that James spent less time in his room and had started sharing what was on his mind while they were cooking. Next, Ms. Alvarez encouraged Vanessa to oversee James's use of a planner or notebook to keep track of his assignments and tests. Because Vanessa was not home in the afternoon, she asked her father (who had recently moved in with the family) to check over James's work. This helped improve James's assignment completion and fostered a bond with his grandfather. During two additional meetings, Ms. Alvarez talked with Vanessa about how she could help James practice managing his anger at home. Ms. Alvarez also invited James to teach his mother about the problem-solving approach he had learned. Together, they planned to use the same approach to solve problems at home. Finally, Ms. Alvarez encouraged Vanessa to continue to monitor James's free-time activities and to use a consistent approach for increasing his compliant behavior at home. At their last meeting, Ms. Alvarez helped Vanessa and James celebrate the gains they had made as a family and encouraged a discussion of how they could maintain these gains through future life transitions.

ANGER AND ITS OUTCOMES

Anger and aggression are common to many individuals, representing clinically significant problems only when frequent and severe enough to disrupt family, school, or community functioning, or when the anger is connected to the individual's serious antisocial behavior, delinquency, substance abuse (Lochman, Barry, Powell, & Young, 2010; Lochman, Powell, Clanton, & McElroy, 2006; Powell, Lochman, Boxmeyer, Barry, & Young, 2010), or cardiovascular problems (Fernandez, 2008).

When individuals perceive themselves as endangered or provoked, they have common physiological responses at two levels (Goleman, 1995) and can have two types of anger (Larson & Lochman, 2011; Lochman et al., 2006). The first type follows amygdala activation after a perceived threat or frustration and results in a quick, impulsive, and intense anger response. In the second type of anger, the thalamus signals the neocortex, which then processes the perceived causes and possible responses to the provocation. The result can be a deliberate, calculated anger response. The action of the amygdala on the adrenocortical branch of the nervous system can create a general background state of action readiness, which can last for hours or for days. This activation can be stimulated by stress of all kinds, and individuals become more prone to serious anger arousal if they are already activated by mild to moderate irritation and frustration. When a person is in this state of readiness, even minor triggers can produce highly intense anger responses. Thus, anger can build on anger (Goleman, 1995). Escalating anger can be the result of a series of perceived provocations, each of which triggers further arousal, which dissipates slowly.

Aggressive anger has been described as a negative, phenomenological feeling that motivates actions (usually against others) that aim to warn, intimidate, control, attack, or gain retribution (Kassinove & Tafrate, 2006); in contrast, passive anger involves resistance (e.g., evasiveness, manipulation, secretive behavior) rather than retaliation (Fernandez, 2008). Associated features of anger may include characteristic cognitive distortions when the anger is not justified (e.g., blaming), physiological changes (e.g., increased heart rate), and distinctive behavioral displays (e.g., scowling, raised voice). The types of stimuli that tend to trigger an anger response are broad in scope and can be physical or psychological provocations that may cause hurt to a person's pride or dignity. Anger can be adaptive by heightening awareness and energizing an individual to take action against the offending entity (Goleman, 1995). However, anger is an emotion that is often difficult to control due to the intense physiological reactions involved in the fight response often triggered by anger.

Although anger, aggression, and violence are not isomorphic (Fernandez, 2008), aggression is generally defined as a behavioral act intended to harm or hurt (Larson & Lochman, 2011; Lochman et al., 2006; Lochman, Barry, et al., 2010). However, there are numerous types of aggression depending on the intentions of the aggressor and the situation that stimulated the aggressive response. One distinction, between proactive and reactive aggression, is relevant because of its association with anger (Dodge, Lochman, Harnish, Bates, & Pettit, 1997; Fite, Rathert, Colder, Lochman, & Wells, 2012; Hubbard, Morrow, Romano, & McAuliffe, 2010). Proactive and reactive aggression peak in early adolescence (Fite, Colder, Lochman, & Wells, 2008) and are highly correlated in children, but the behavioral types do have distinctly different purposes and associated features (Polman, Orobio de Castro, Koops, van Boxtel, & Merk, 2007). Proactive aggression is typically used to meet a goal, including secondary gains such as money. In contrast, reactive aggression is not associated with seeking to meet secondary goals through aggressive behavior. Instead, reactive aggression is associated with negative reactions to perceived or actual wrongdoing and with ready irritation when provoked. Children with higher levels of reactive aggressive display higher levels of anger, have greater anxiety and depression, and have poorer views of their social competence (Dodge et al., 1997) in comparison to children with relatively higher levels of proactive aggressive display. Reactive aggression, which is characterized by "hot blooded" anger and is more emotionally driven, is likely to occur with visible displays of anger, while proactive overt aggression, which is more calculated and "cold blooded," is accompanied by lower levels of simmering anger or by no anger at all, parallel to the types of anger described previously (Lochman et al., 2006).

Reactive and proactive aggression also have differential relations to an individual's social skills and social relations. In terms of peer relations, reactive aggression is associated with peer rejection and peer victimization, while proactive aggression is associated with involvement with delinquent peers and is less associated with peer rejection (Dodge et al., 1997). The effect of proactive aggression on youths' subsequent substance abuse has been mediated by increasing involvement in deviant peer groups, while the effect of children's reactive aggression on subsequent substance use has been mediated by both being rejected by peers and by deviant peer involvement (Fite, Colder, Lochman, & Wells, 2007). In comparison to reactive aggression, proactive aggressive behavior is more affected by neighborhood poverty and crime (Fite, Wynn, Lochman, & Wells, 2009) and is more predictive of later serious antisocial behavior such as delinquency and delinquency-related violence (Fite et al., 2008).

Problems With Anger and Aggression

Although some problems with anger and aggression are expected during childhood and adolescence, what is typical versus atypical is a matter of degree. Increases in the severity and frequency of aggression lead to disruptions in the youth's functioning and, in extreme cases, may cause damage to others. Aggression that is serious enough to meet the criteria for conduct disorder is estimated to occur in 6% to 16% of males under age 18 and in 2% to 9% of females in this age range (American Psychiatric Association, 2000). A diagnosis of conduct disorder is often one part of a developmental trajectory that starts with aggression during early childhood and continues into adolescence and adulthood in the form of antisocial behavior (Schaeffer, Petras, Ialongo, Poduska, & Kellam, 2003). For example, longitudinal research has shown that aggression in childhood, especially when it is associated with peer rejection and related emotional distress, predicts problems in later adolescence including substance abuse and delinquent behavior (Coie, Lochman, Terry, & Hyman, 1992). Children who demonstrate problems with anger and aggression are at increased risk for a number of negative outcomes.

Children who are prone to anger tend to exhibit higher levels of aggressive behavior in cross-sectional research (e.g., Bohnert, Crnic, & Lim, 2003; Eisenberg et al., 2001) as well as in longitudinal studies (e.g., Eisenberg et al., 2009). In adolescents, anger is related to substance use both contemporaneously (e.g., Colder & Stice, 1998; Hussong & Chassin, 1994) and longitudinally (e.g., Pardini, Lochman, & Wells, 2004) and also predicts delinquency in prospective and cross-sectional research (e.g., Colder & Stice, 1998). Anger has also been associated with internalizing problems such as anxiety and depression in children (e.g., Eisenberg et al., 2009; Zeman, Shipman, & Suveg, 2002) and adolescents (e.g., Oldehinkel, Hartman, Ferdinand, Verhulst, & Ormel, 2007), and some researchers have hypothesized that the relation between anger and internalizing problems may strengthen over time as internalizing youth experience increasing problems in social relationships and, as a result, higher levels of anger (e.g., Eisenberg et al., 2005).

Aggression is related to mental health problems in children, including problems with depression and anxiety (Knox, King, Hanna, Logan, & Ghaziuddin, 2000). Aggressive children and adolescents demonstrate higher levels of academic problems, are more likely to be retained in a grade at school, and are more likely to prematurely drop out of school (Risi, Gerhardstein, & Kistner, 2003). Early aggression has also been related to social problems in adolescence and adulthood, including substance abuse, delinquency, and incarceration (Brook & Newcomb, 1995).

Reactive aggression, which is particularly associated with unregulated anger, has been found to predict adolescent substance use (Fite et al., 2007). The relation between reactive aggression and substance use has been found to be complex. As expected, Fite et al. (2007) found that reactive aggression was associated with peer rejection, which was marginally significant in predicting delinquent peer affiliations, which in turn predicted substance use. This is consistent with previous research that has found that rejected aggressive children affiliate with other rejected aggressive children, and such affiliations provide an environment that is reinforcing of aggression and other antisocial behavior (Dishion, Patterson, & Griesler, 1994).

CONTEXTUAL SOCIAL-COGNITIVE FACTORS CONTRIBUTING TO PROBLEMS WITH ANGER AND AGGRESSION

A contextual social-cognitive framework can be useful in the conceptualization of youth anger and aggression (e.g., Dodge, Laird, Lochman, Zelli, & Conduct Problems Prevention Research Group, 2002; Lochman & Wells, 2002a). The social information–processing model (SIP; Crick & Dodge, 1994) presents six stages through which an individual progresses in responding to a social problem. As a group, aggressive youth have been shown to have deficits in each of these stages, although on an individual level, youths' deficits are likely to be limited to certain steps (Orobio de Castro, Veerman, Koops, Bosch, & Monshouwer, 2002).

Children's Social-Cognitive Processes

In the first three stages (Lochman, Fitzgerald, & Whidby, 1999), children encode pertinent details from their surroundings, generate interpretations regarding the nature of the situation, and formulate a social goal that will determine their response to the situation at hand. During the encoding stage, aggressive children demonstrate a bias toward information or "cues" perceived as hostile and appear to be less thorough in their initial processing. In comparison to nonaggressive peers, aggressive children are more likely to attend to and recall anger-related information rather than neutral information, to remember fewer relevant cues about a situation overall, and to recall more of the most recent cues in a sequence than those occurring at the beginning or middle (Crick & Dodge, 1994). In the second stage, aggressive children are thought to have trouble interpreting encoded information, due to the fact that increased levels of aggression are linked to a greater inclination to perceive others' actions as offensive or provocative (Dodge, Pettit, McClaskey, & Brown, 1986). When formulating interpersonal goals, aggressive children are more likely than their nonaggressive peers to endorse goals associated with dominance and revenge (Erdley & Asher, 1996; Lochman, Wayland, & White, 1993; McDonald & Lochman, 2012). This remains true even when the conflict in question is fairly minimal (Lochman, Boxmeyer, Powell, Barry, & Pardini, 2010).

The final three stages of the SIP model include creating a mental list of possible behavioral responses, methodically assessing the quality of each potential response, and putting into action the chosen response. As with the first three stages of the SIP model, as a group, aggressive children have been shown to have difficulties at each of the final three stages (Lochman & Dodge, 1994). In the fourth stage, aggressive children generally come up with fewer solutions to interpersonal problems than their nonaggressive peers, and they are likely to generate more direct-action solutions and fewer verbal assertion, bargaining, and compromise solutions than their nonaggressive peers (see Larson & Lochman, 2011). As aggressive youth evaluate their potential solutions in the fifth stage, they are likely to view aggressive choices as less negative (Deluty, 1983) and more positive (Crick & Werner, 1998) as compared to nonaggressive children, and to believe that aggression will result in positive outcomes (Lochman & Dodge, 1994). Unfortunately, even in situations when aggressive children do choose to move forward with positive responses, evidence indicates that they are less adept than nonaggressive children at carrying them out (Dodge et al., 1986). This process is commonly thought of as cyclical in nature, as the outcome of the chosen and enacted response likely impacts upon future response choices (Lochman, Boxmeyer, et al., 2010).

Contextual Risk Factors

Parenting. A substantial body of research indicates that aggressive behavior in children and adolescents is also influenced by certain problematic parenting practices (e.g., Gershoff, 2002; McKee, Colletti, Rakow, Jones, & Forehand, 2008). Parenting practices that may play a role include harsh or irritable discipline (e.g., Chang, Swartz, Dodge, & McBride-Chang, 2003) and physical abuse (e.g., Jaffee, Caspi, Moffitt, & Taylor, 2004). In contrast, an indulgent, overly permissive parenting style has also been associated with children's aggression (e.g., Xu, Farver, & Zhang, 2009). Research by Patterson and colleagues (e.g., Patterson, Reid, & Dishion, 1992) indicates that parenting behaviors that can place a child at risk for aggression can be identified early in the child's life. For example, problems with the consistency and timing of parental responses to 1-year-old children's needs are a risk factor for later childhood aggression. Starting when their children are toddlers, parents may also respond to noncompliance with increasingly harsh demands, initiating a cycle whereby children's negative behaviors and parents' harsh responses escalate, often ending with parents withdrawing in frustration and serving to reinforce the child's problem behavior. Inconsistent discipline, vague commands, low levels of warmth and involvement, and problems with supervision and monitoring of children and young adolescents are also risk factors for aggressive behavior (Patterson et al., 1992). The link between poor parenting and hostile behavior in children is viewed as bidirectional, as poor parenting can contribute to children's increasingly negative behaviors and vice versa (Fite, Colder, Lochman, & Wells, 2006).

Peer and neighborhood factors. Peer relationships can also serve as a source of risk for children's aggressive behavior. Aggression places children at risk for rejection by peers (Cillessen, Van IJzendoorn, Van Lieshout, & Hartup, 1992), and aggressive children who are also socially rejected tend to demonstrate more serious behavior problems than children who are either aggressive only or rejected only (Lochman & Wayland, 1994). Research also shows that aggressive children are likely to associate with other aggressive children, increasing the probability that problem behaviors will be maintained or exacerbated through reinforcement and modeling (e.g., Dishion, Andrews, & Crosby, 1995).

Children who are exposed to neighborhood violence are at risk for engaging in aggressive behaviors themselves, and other neighborhood factors such as high crime rates, low levels of social cohesion, and poverty also predict children's aggressive behavior as well as their beliefs about aggression (e.g., Guerra, Huesmann, & Spindler, 2003). These effects tend to increase during middle childhood, as children gain increased independence and experience lower levels of adult supervision (Ingoldsby & Shaw, 2002).

THE COPING POWER PROGRAM

Coping Power (Lochman, Wells, & Lenhart, 2008; Wells, Lochman, & Lenhart, 2008) was designed as a secondary prevention program for children whose aggressive behavior places them at risk for developing serious problems in adolescence. Using the contextual social-cognitive model described earlier as a framework, the program targets skills deficits that contribute to anger/aggressive behavior in children, including social-cognitive deficiencies and distortions, difficulty with management of strong emotions, and problems with social skills. A corresponding parent component addresses effective skills for managing children's disruptive behavior, as well as strategies for improving family functioning.

Coping Power Program Child Component

The Coping Power Child Component includes 34 sessions designed to be implemented with small groups of four to six students in the school setting. The program has also been used in clinic settings and can be delivered individually. The content targets fourth through sixth graders, though the program can be modified for use with slightly younger and slightly older students, and an early adolescent version is currently in development. Typically, meetings are held weekly for 45 to 60 minutes and are run by two coleaders. The sessions are highly structured, including consistent opening and closing activities as well as content-specific activities and exercises. Unstructured individual meetings are also scheduled on a monthly basis to promote students' engagement in the program, to allow time for individualization of program concepts, and to encourage generalization of skills outside of the group setting.

Behavior management. Coping Power takes a proactive approach to behavior management, setting up a consistent structure for rewards and consequences at the outset. Based on compliance with group rules and participation during activities, students earn points, which can be redeemed for privileges or prizes. Leaders also use selective ignoring, redirection, and differential reinforcement to discourage disruptive behaviors and encourage prosocial behaviors. When disruptive behaviors continue, leaders give up to three verbal warnings ("strikes") after which students fail to earn points and/or may be asked to leave the meeting.

Goal setting. Each Coping Power session incorporates material related to the identification and attainment of behavioral goals. In the initial sessions, students are introduced to goal setting and learn to use written goal sheets to record personal goals and to monitor their progress. Goals are stated in clear and observable terms (e.g., "Use appropriate language during recess") and are meant to be challenging but attainable. Teachers or parents provide daily feedback on the goal sheets, and students earn points when their goal is reached. The goal sheets are a key element for promoting generalization of skills across settings as well as for informing and involving teachers and/or parents in students' experience with Coping Power.

Opening activities. Coping Power meetings open with a review of students' goal sheets during which successes are rewarded and, when goals have not been reached, challenges are discussed and obstacles are identified. Based on a student's progress, a more or less challenging goal may be set for the following week. After goals have been set, material from the previous session is reviewed in a discussion or question-and-answer format.

Closing activities. All 34 Coping Power sessions close with the same set of activities. During positive feedback, each student compliments another student, with leaders shaping the process to focus on appropriate behaviors and use of positive coping skills (e.g., "Eddie stayed calm when Chris called him a name"). Next, points are tallied and students are given the opportunity to spend them or to save them for more valuable rewards. A free-time period is optional, if time permits. It is important for leaders to carefully monitor students' interactions during free time, as a reduction in structure can lead to an increase in problem behaviors, which may be reinforced by peers (i.e., deviancy training). With leader supervision and involvement, free time can serve as a useful reinforcer and can provide leaders with opportunities to assess students' social interactions and to coach and reinforce use of appropriate problem solving and social skills.

Emotion awareness and anger management. Emotion awareness is covered early in the Coping Power curriculum, as this topic is an important prerequisite to several other skills (e.g., anger management, social problem solving) addressed later in the program. Students learn to observe their individual cognitive, behavioral, and physiological signs of affective arousal and to differentiate one feeling state from another (e.g., anger vs. fear). A thermometer analogy is used to help students recognize variations in the intensity of their feelings, and vocabulary is introduced to help students verbalize the range of their feelings (e.g., "annoyed" to "furious"). Emphasis is placed on recognition of anger at its earliest and most manageable stages. A recurring message throughout this unit is that "all feelings are acceptable, but some behaviors are not," which helps to normalize emotional experiences while also sending a message that students are responsible for controlling their actions. A similar purpose is served by helping students to recognize the environmental cues of their anger arousal ("triggers"), as awareness of these precipitating factors can help students to prepare their responses in advance.

Cognitive self-control. Subsequent sessions involve training in cognitive self-control strategies to manage anger. Students are taught about the impact of cognitions on increasing or decreasing anger arousal and learn how they can use internal coping statements to manage their emotions. For example, students may recognize that internal self-talk such as "He can't talk to me like that" is likely to increase their anger, whereas a self-statement such as "It's too bad he has to act that way" is likely to help them maintain emotional control. A set of activities that become increasingly more personal and challenging provide opportunities for practice. Initially, students act out teasing scenarios with puppets and take turns verbalizing coping self-statements. Subsequent activities involve group members directly taunting each other in a controlled way, again with students verbalizing their self-statements and processing their reactions with leaders.

Students also learn several other self-control strategies to provide options for managing their strong feelings. To teach distraction, students engage in a challenging concentration task (e.g., memorization or building) while being taunted by other group members. Through processing after the game, students recognize that they were able to stay in control of their anger by focusing on the task rather than on the other students. Other strategies that are presented and rehearsed include guided imagery, breathing exercises, and progressive muscle relaxation.

Perspective taking. As noted earlier, aggressive children commonly display problems in their social-cognitive processing, including a tendency to excessively attribute hostile intent to others' actions as well as a tendency to minimize or misunderstand the impact of their aggressive behaviors on others. Such problems with perspective taking place students at risk for social conflicts; for example, a student who assumes that his or her teacher assigns extra homework "to be mean" may feel justified in taking an argumentative stance with him or her. Several Coping Power activities target students' abilities to accurately infer others' thoughts, intentions, and feelings. In one such activity, students view a picture of an ambiguous interpersonal situation and are asked to generate ideas for what may have happened and how the characters might feel. As group members share their ideas, differences in perspectives become apparent and leader-guided discussion is used to validate all viewpoints. Another activity involves a student performing a brief role-play of an ambiguous situation (e.g., ignoring another person, breaking an item), after which other group members are asked to guess the motives for the "actor's" behavior. The activity highlights the difficulties involved in trying to infer another person's intentions.

Social problem solving. Children or adolescents who are angrily aggressive lack the ability to effectively resolve interpersonal conflicts because of characteristic problem-solving deficits, particularly in generating a range of developmentally appropriate solutions for social problems. In Coping Power, students are taught to approach problem solving in a step-wise manner with the PICC model, first focusing on accurate Problem Identification, then generating a range of Choices, and finally evaluating the Consequences associated with each choice. The PICC model shifts students' focus away from impulsive responding and encourages recognition of the numerous response options available in a given situation. Leaders seek to expand students' often limited repertoire of potential behavioral choices, guiding them toward responses such as assertiveness, negotiation, and compromise when students suggest less effective solutions (e.g., aggression, help seeking). In addition to discussions and role-plays involving the PICC model, session activities include a video-making exercise in which students demonstrate their understanding of and ability to apply the model by developing and filming a PICC model advertisement.

Peer relationships. At the conclusion of the Coping Power program, sessions focus on social skills important for developmental tasks on the horizon for students about to transition to middle school or high school. Through discussions and role-plays, students learn about and practice a set of skills designed to assist them with developing positive peer relationships in a new setting. Students identify and rehearse ways to skillfully introduce themselves and to join with a group of unfamiliar peers. Session activities encourage students to identify qualities that they seek in friends, such as trustworthiness, similar goals, and shared interests, and students also identify the positive attributes that they can contribute to a friendship. Finally, peer pressure to engage in potentially harmful activities is discussed, and students learn and actively practice a range of refusal skills to use in peer pressure situations.

Coping Power Program Parent Component

Parents of Coping Power students are invited to participate in the Parent Component, a 16-session skills-based intervention. Meetings are typically 90 minutes long and occur during the same time frame, but separate from the child sessions. During meetings, parents receive information about skills students are learning in their sessions, and parents are encouraged to reinforce their children's use of these skills at home. Social learning techniques form the basis of much of the program, with topics including reinforcing children's appropriate behaviors, establishing expectations and house rules, delivering effective instructions, and ignoring minor disruptive behaviors. Parents also learn strategies for managing children's misbehavior, including time-out, privilege removal, and work chores. In addition to these standard parenting skills, material on topics relevant to behavior management and family functioning is also presented. For example, parents learn strategies to actively support their children's academic progress, stress management techniques, and ways to promote family communication.

ADAPTATIONS FOR EARLY ADOLESCENTS

There is a dearth of research on evidence-based prevention or intervention programs targeting early to midadolescents. As a result, we are developing a version of Coping Power with colleagues in Baltimore and New Orleans that will extend the program through early- to midadolescence. Focus groups and discussions with clinicians who have used Coping Power indicated that approximately 85% to 90% of the existing Coping Power program content was perceived to be appropriate for the early adolescent years. Nevertheless, a series of developmental adaptations were made to create Coping Power for Early Adolescents (CP-EA), in order to address early adolescents' greater autonomy and independent thinking and functioning, their need for more discussion and collaborative problem solving, and their increased emphasis on self-evaluation and monitoring. To follow we outline some of the key changes that were made in creating the CP-EA program.

Structural Changes for Coping Power in Early Adolescence

Certain structural changes in the delivery of the program have been found to be useful for early adolescents' needs and abilities to be more involved in decisions about their lives, and these structural changes include preprogram meetings, journaling, self-evaluation on goal sheets, having a more structured summarization of the session at the end of each meeting, and including a challenge task at the end of each session. Prior to the beginning of the program, each adolescent meets individually with a clinician to review what Coping Power is about, to collaboratively discuss the purpose of the program, and to make a personal commitment to attend sessions. This initial affirmation of commitment by the adolescent is a motivational strategy to enhance youths' engagement and anticipated attendance.

Another key structural change has involved the inclusion of a journaling activity at the beginning of each session. As youths arrive for each session, and before the group begins, they keep a journal of questions related to reactions about activities from the prior session. Journaling provides another opportunity for adolescents' self-expression and is particularly useful for introspective adolescents who otherwise can be quiet in sessions. Journaling also can reinforce adolescents' retrieval and recall of information provided in earlier sessions, making it more likely that they will use that information more actively in their daily life.

As children move into adolescence, their abilities to be self-aware and to monitor themselves typically increase. In an effort to enhance these abilities, we ask adolescents to rate their own goal attainment on their weekly goal sheets. As with younger children, teacher or parent reports are still obtained, but adolescents have an opportunity to see how much their self-perceptions agree with the perceptions of the adults around them. Improved self-monitoring can lead adolescents to better sustain the behavioral changes that they begin to make during CP-EA.

As they develop, we aim to help adolescents increasingly and actively process information that they have been exposed to in CP-EA. To promote this, we have included a summary time at the end of each session, when adolescents respond to questions about what they would tell someone else about the content of that day's session and what they anticipate that they will remember about this meeting when they come back next week.

To increase the likelihood of adolescents' active transfer of skills learned during a session, CP-EA includes Challenge Tasks at the end of most sessions, as adolescents are challenged in different ways to use the skills in real life. An example of a Challenge Task in one of the sessions on goal setting is to encourage students to interview adults about the role that goal setting has played in their life, particularly how the adults overcame barriers to their goals.

Content Changes

Because of adolescents' development socially, emotionally, and in decision making, CP-EA has added content throughout to focus on how adolescents can take personal responsibility for work to be completed in sessions. In addition, CP-EA has new sessions and activities on age-related topics, including relationship development, cyber bullying and social aggression, and repairing damaged relationships.

More advanced relationship-building skills involve active listening, use of "I" messages, and assertive communication. Active listening is introduced by noting that of course adolescents want people to listen to them, but that listening to others makes it more likely that others will listen reciprocally. Adolescents are informed that three steps involved in being an active listener are to look at the person who is talking, to show that you are listening by nodding, and to repeat back what the person told you in your own words. Leaders model poor active listening, and then the adolescents role-play poor and good active listening, as they demonstrate the three steps.

Adolescents are introduced to the idea that "I" messages permit them to express their feelings and can help avoid misunderstandings, improve relationships, and prevent angry reactions. Adolescents are asked whether there is a difference between these two sentences: "You make me really mad when you are rude to me" versus "I am really mad because the things you said sounded rude to me and hurt my feelings." They are then led to discuss how the second sentence permits adolescents to express their feelings, but in a way that is less reactive and less likely to elicit aggressive reactions. Adolescents practice using "I" messages during role-plays, which are periodically "frozen" so they can discuss what the "I" message was and how effective it was.

Assertiveness is another communication skill that adolescents can be expected to further refine during the middle and high school years. One reason that youths resort to aggression is that they lack the skills to be assertive in a competent way. When discussing this skill with adolescents, we note than when their rights are being violated, they can and should stand up for themselves. However, they have to be able to do this without hurting others. Example situations are discussed, including reasonable requests that an adolescent cannot fulfill (e.g., a friend asks to borrow a math book at a time when the adolescent needs it). In such situations, adolescents can be assertive by (a) giving their negative answer to the request, (b) expressing their understanding of the other person's problem, and (c) giving their reason for declining. Thus, the adolescent could say: "No, I can't lend you the book over the weekend. I understand that you need it, but I have to use it over the same time." The therapist models how situations can be handled in a wimpy way, then in a cranky way, and finally in an assertive way, and the adolescents practice the skills during role-plays.

The topic of relational aggression is introduced by noting that "social aggression" hurts other people by getting others to turn on them, by embarrassing them, or by making them feel bad about themselves. Examples of psychological aggression are provided (e.g., telling others not to interact with someone as a way to get back at that person), and adolescents use the PICC model to generate alternate solutions (and consequences for various solutions) when faced with social aggression. Social aggression issues are problem solved from the viewpoint both of the victim and of the aggressor. A related topic for adolescents involves cyber-bullying. Cyber-bullying involves insulting someone, sending embarrassing pictures, sharing personal information without permission, and spreading rumors through electronic means. These situations are problem solved from the vantage point of being a victim (e.g., ignoring, talking to a trusted adult) or of a bystander (e.g., not forwarding mean messages, not supporting peers who cyber-bully).

Another issue of particular importance for adolescents is how they can repair important relationships with friends, parents, and romantic partners that have been damaged by arguments and conflicts. Adolescents write a letter (that is typically not actually sent) in which they apologize to someone they have been close to, indicating how they feel now and what they would like to have happen, including rebuilding the friendship. Adolescents then decide if they wish to actually send such a letter and role-play how to handle this type of apology in person.

THE COPING POWER PROGRAM: OUTCOME EFFECTS

Coping Power was designed to target individual risk factors, along with risk factors in the family, peer, neighborhood, and classroom contexts. Ultimately, the goal of this preventive intervention is to affect the trajectory of at-risk youth. The efficacy and effectiveness of the Coping Power program have been evaluated through a number of randomized controlled trials. Additionally, factors affecting successful dissemination have been explored.

Efficacy

A study conducted by Lochman and Wells (2004) evaluated the efficacy of Coping Power with boys at the transition from elementary to middle school. Participants in the study were 183 boys (61% African American, 39% Caucasian) in either fourth or fifth grade who received high teacher ratings of aggression. The participants were randomly assigned to either the Coping Power Child Component, the Coping Power Child and Parent Components, or an untreated control condition. The intervention conditions were implemented across either fourth and fifth grades or fifth and sixth grades.

Results from a 1-year follow-up indicated boys in the intervention conditions had lower levels of self-reported covert delinquent behavior, lower levels of substance use (as reported by parents), and greater teacher-rated behavioral improvement at school compared to the untreated control group. In comparison to the untreated control group, results suggest the condition with both child and parent components produced significantly greater reduction on parent-rated substance use by the child than the treatment condition with the child component alone. However, boys in the child-component-only condition emerged with the greatest increase in teacher-rated behavioral improvement, suggesting the child component was the primary influence in behavioral gains within the school context.

The treatment and control conditions were also compared to a normative sample of 63 nonrisk boys. At the 1-year follow-up, the normative sample and treatment groups did not significantly differ on rates of self-reported covert delinquency, parent-reported substance use, and teacher-rated behavioral improvements. In contrast, when the control and normative samples were compared, the control group had higher levels of covert delinquency and weaker levels of behavioral improvement at school. These results suggest the intervention moved the aggressive boys' risk for delinquency and school behavioral problems from a nonnormative into a normative range. Path analyses indicate that for both intervention groups, the intervention effects on delinquency, substance use, and school behavior were at least partially mediated through intervention-produced improvements in child and parent variables that were targets for the intervention. These targets include children's internal locus of control, their perceptions of their parents' consistency, children's attributional biases, and children's expectation that aggression would not produce positive outcomes (Lochman & Wells, 2002a).

Effectiveness

Given the emergence of empirical support for the efficacy of the Coping Power program, the effectiveness of the program was evaluated to determine whether similar positive effects would be observed in real-world contexts. A study was conducted examining whether a universal preventative intervention could enhance the effects of Coping Power when delivered to fifth- and sixth-grade students (Lochman & Wells, 2002b). The study was conducted in a greater proportion of inner-city, high-poverty schools as compared to the efficacy study, and the intervention was implemented by personnel more equivalent to counselors and social workers in school settings. Participants were 245 male (66%) and female (34%) students identified as being at risk based on their fourth-grade teachers' ratings of aggressive behavior. The participants (78% African American, 20% Caucasian) were randomly assigned to one of four conditions: Coping Power (CP) + Universal Intervention, CP + Universal Control, Treatment Control + Universal Intervention, and Treatment Control + Universal Control. The universal intervention consisted of an in-training service day for teachers and parent meetings for parents of children in a universal intervention classroom. At postintervention, the interventions produced lower rates of self-reported substance use, lower teacher-rated aggression, higher perceived social competence, and greater teacher-rated behavioral improvement. The group that received only Coping Power displayed reduced parent-rated proactive aggression, lower activity level by children, better teacher-rated peer acceptance of target children, and increased parental supportiveness (Lochman & Wells, 2002b). At the 1-year follow-up, in comparison to the control condition, all intervention groups produced lower levels of substance use and delinquency and lower levels of teacher-reported aggression (Lochman & Wells, 2003).

Another study was conducted in Dutch outpatient clinics with children aged 8 to 13 years at the time of enrollment, who had been diagnosed with oppositional defiant disorder or conduct disorder (van de Wiel et al., 2007). At the 4-year follow-up, results suggest the children who received the Dutch version of Coping Power (Utrecht Coping Power Program [UCPP]) had reductions in cigarette and marijuana use as compared to a care-as-usual group. The rates of substance use by the UCPP group were within the normative range of typically developing Dutch adolescents (Zonnevylle-Bender, Matthys, van de Wiel, & Lochman, 2007). In terms of cost-effectiveness, van de Wiel and colleagues (2003) found that the UCPP produced reductions in conduct problems at the end of intervention for 49% less cost than in the care-as-usual condition.

Dissemination

A dissemination study was conducted to evaluate whether counselor and school characteristics along with type of training were related to the implementation of Coping Power. In this study, school counselors were randomly assigned to one of three conditions: Coping Power—training plus feedback (CP-TF), Coping Power—basic training (CP-BT), or care-as-usual comparison. There were nineteen schools in each condition, with 168 children in the CB-TF condition, 183 children in the CB-BT condition, and 180 in the control group. Students participated in the Coping Power program during the spring of fourth grade and for the majority of fifth grade.

Counselors in the training conditions (CB-TF and CB-BT) attended a 3-day workshop prior to beginning the intervention and participated in monthly training sessions. Counselors in the CB-TF condition participated in two additional training components. The counselors in the CB-TF condition had access to an e-mail address and hotline where they could contact the trainer and seek individualized consultation to address barriers of implementation. In addition, researchers coded the audiotaped child and parent group sessions in order to provide counselors in the CB-TF condition with feedback on completion of objectives and quality of implementation. School-level characteristics and interventionist characteristics were examined in relation to treatment fidelity and outcomes. Counselors' agreeableness and conscientiousness were positively associated with number of sessions scheduled and the quality of engagement with children and parents. Conversely, counselors who were cynical about organizational change and in schools with rigid managerial control and little autonomy for school professionals were less likely to display a high level of fidelity to the treatment protocol (Lochman, Powell, et al., 2009).

In terms of outcome effects, children in the CP-TF condition experienced reductions in parent, teacher, and youth ratings of externalizing behavior relative to the control condition. Additionally, children in the CP-TF condition showed improvements in social and academic skills in comparison to the control and CP-BT conditions. CP-BT children did not display significant behavioral improvements. This study highlights the impact training has on successful implementation of the Coping Power program (Lochman, Boxmeyer, et al., 2009).

CONCLUSION

High levels of anger and aggression can place children and adolescents at risk for serious problems later in their development. An understanding of the contextual social-cognitive factors that contribute to childhood aggression has led to the development of the Coping Power program, in which children, and more recently with CP-EA, young adolescents, learn a variety of ways to cope with anger and to solve social problems in a constructive manner. In the companion parent component, parents learn to manage their children's disruptive behaviors and to promote children's prosocial development. In a variety of outcome studies, Coping Power has repeatedly demonstrated success in helping children to make behavioral improvements and reduce their risk for problems with delinquency and substance use. Further information regarding the Coping Power program and the steps to obtaining training is available at http://www.copingpower.com or by contacting the authors directly.

AUTHOR NOTE

The preparation of this chapter has been supported by a grant from the National Institutes on Drug Abuse (DA 023156).

REFERENCES

American Psychiatric Association. (2000). *Diagnostic and statistical manual of mental disorders* (4th ed., text rev.). Washington, DC: American Psychiatric Press.

Bohnert, A. M., Crnic, K. A., & Lim, K. G. (2003). Emotional competence and aggressive behavior in school-age children. *Journal of Abnormal Child Psychology, 31*, 79–91.

Brook, J. S., & Newcomb, M. D. (1995). Childhood aggression and unconventionality: Impact on later academic achievement, drug use, and workforce involvement. *Journal of Genetic Psychology, 156*, 393–410.

Chang, L., Swartz, D., Dodge, K. A., & McBride-Chang, C. (2003). Harsh parenting in relation to child emotion regulation and aggression. *Journal of Family Psychology, 17*, 598–606.

Cillessen, A. H., Van IJzendoorn, H. W., Van Lieshout, C. F., & Hartup, W. W. (1992). Heterogeneity among peer-rejected boys: Subtypes and stabilities. *Child Development, 63*, 893–905.

Coie, J. D., Lochman, J. E., Terry, R., & Hyman, C. (1992). Predicting early adolescent disorder from childhood aggression and peer rejection. *Journal of Consulting and Clinical Psychology, 60*, 783–792.

Colder, C. R., & Stice, E. (1998). A longitudinal study of the interactive effects of impulsivity and anger on adolescent problem behavior. *Journal of Youth and Adolescence, 27*(3), 255–274.

Crick, N. R., & Dodge, K. A. (1994). A review and reformulation of social information-processing mechanisms in children's social adjustment. *Psychological Bulletin, 115*(1), 74–101.

Crick, N. R., & Werner, N. E. (1998). Response decision processes in relational and overt aggression. *Child Development, 69*, 1630–1639.

Deluty, R. H. (1983). Children's evaluations of aggressive, assertive, and submissive responses. *Journal of Clinical Child Psychology, 12*, 124–129.

Dishion, T. J., Andrews, D. W., & Crosby, L. (1995). Antisocial boys and their friends in early adolescence: Relationship characteristics, quality, and interactional process. *Child Development, 66*, 139–151.

Dishion, T. J., Patterson, G. R., & Griesler, P. C. (1994). Peer adaptation in the development of antisocial behavior: A confluence model. In L. R. Huesmann (Ed.), *Aggressive behavior: Current perspectives* (pp. 61–95). New York, NY: Plenum Press.

Dodge, K. A., Laird, R., Lochman, J. E., Zelli, A., & Conduct Problems Prevention Research Group. (2002). Multidimensional latent-construct analysis of children's social information processing patterns: Correlations with aggressive behavior problems. *Psychological Assessment, 14*(1), 60–73.

Dodge, K. A., Lochman, J. E., Harnish, J. D., Bates, J. E., & Pettit, G. S. (1997). Reactive and proactive aggression in school children and psychiatrically impaired chronically assaultive youth. *Journal of Abnormal Psychology, 106*, 37–51.

Dodge, K. A., Pettit, G. S., McClaskey, C. L., & Brown, M. M. (1986). Social competence in children. *Monographs of the Society for Research in Child Development, 51*(2, Serial No. 213).

Eisenberg, N., Cumberland, A., Spinrad, T. L., Fabes, R. A., Shepard, S. A., Reiser, M., … Guthrie, I. K. (2001). The relations of regulation and emotionality to children's externalizing and internalizing problem behavior. *Child Development, 72*(4), 1112–1134.

Eisenberg, N., Sadovsky, A., Spinrad, T. L., Fabes, R. A., Losoya, S. H., Valiente, C., … Shephard, S. A. (2005). The relations of problem behavior status to children's negative emotionality, effortful control, and impulsivity: Concurrent relations and prediction of change. *Developmental Psychology, 41*, 193–211.

Eisenberg, N., Valiente, C., Spinrad, T. L., Cumberland, A., Liew, J., Reiser, M., ... Losoya, S. H. (2009). Longitudinal relations of children's effortful control, impulsivity, and negative emotionality to their externalizing, internalizing, and co-occurring behavior problems. *Developmental Psychology, 45*(4), 988–1008.

Erdley, C. A., & Asher, S. R. (1996). Children's social goals and self-efficacy perceptions as influences on their responses to ambiguous provocation. *Child Development, 67*, 1329–1344.

Fernandez, E. (2008). The angry personality: A representation on six dimensions of anger expression. In G. J. Boyle, D. Matthews, & D. Saklofske (Eds.), *International handbook of personality theory and testing: Vol. 2: Personality measurement and assessment* (pp. 402–419). London, England: Sage Publications.

Fite, P. J., Colder, C. R., Lochman, J. E., & Wells, K. C. (2006). The mutual influence of parenting and boys' externalizing behavior problems. *Journal of Applied Developmental Psychology, 27*, 151–164.

Fite, P. J., Colder, C. R., Lochman, J. E., & Wells, K. C. (2007). Pathways from proactive and reactive aggression to substance use. *Psychology of Addictive Behaviors, 21*, 355–364.

Fite, P. J., Colder, C. R., Lochman, J. E., & Wells, K. C. (2008). Developmental trajectories of proactive and reactive aggression from 5th to 9th grade. *Journal of Clinical Child and Adolescent Psychology, 37*, 412–421.

Fite, P. J., Rathert, J., Colder, C. R., Lochman, J. E., & Wells, K. C. (2012). Proactive and reactive aggression: Implications for adolescent adjustment. In R. J. R. Levesque (Ed.), *Encyclopedia of adolescence* (pp. 2164–2170). New York, NY: Springer.

Fite, P. J., Wynn, P., Lochman, J. E., & Wells, K. C. (2009). The effect of neighborhood disadvantage on proactive and reactive aggression. *Journal of Community Psychology, 37*, 542–546.

Gershoff, E. T. (2002). Corporal punishment by parents and associated child behaviors and experiences: A meta-analytic and theoretical review. *Psychological Bulletin, 128*(4), 539–579.

Goleman, D. (1995). *Emotional intelligence*. New York, NY: Bantam Books.

Guerra, N. G., Huesmann, L. R., & Spindler, A. (2003). Community violence exposure, social cognition, and aggression among urban elementary school children. *Child Development, 74*, 1561–1576.

Hubbard, J. A., Morrow, M. T., Romano, L. J., & McAuliffe, M. D. (2010). The role of anger on children's reactive versus proactive aggression: Review of findings, issues of measurement, and implications for intervention. In W. Arsenio & E. Lemerise (Eds.), *Emotions, aggression, and moral development* (pp. 201–217). Washington, DC: American Psychological Association.

Hussong, A. M., & Chassin, L. (1994). The stress-negative affect model of adolescent alcohol use: Disaggregating negative affect. *Journal of Studies on Alcohol, 55*, 707–718.

Ingoldsby, E. M., & Shaw, D. S. (2002). Neighborhood contextual factors and early-starting antisocial pathways. *Clinical Child and Family Psychology Review, 5*(1), 21–55.

Jaffee, S. R., Caspi, A., Moffitt, T. E., & Taylor, A. (2004). Physical maltreatment victim to antisocial child: Evidence of an environmentally mediated process. *Journal of Abnormal Psychology, 113*(1), 44–55.

Kassinove, H., & Tafrate, R. C. (2006). Anger-related disorders: Basic issues, models, and diagnostic considerations. In E. L. Feindler (Ed.), *Anger-related disorders: A practitioner's guide to comparative treatments* (pp. 1–27). New York, NY: Springer.

Knox, M., King, C., Hanna, G. L., Logan, D., & Ghaziuddin, N. (2000). Aggressive behavior in clinically depressed adolescents. *Journal of the American Academy of Child and Adolescent Psychiatry, 39*, 611–618.

Larson, J., & Lochman, J. E. (2011). *Helping school children cope with anger: A cognitive-behavioral intervention* (2nd ed.). New York, NY: Guilford.

Lochman, J. E., Barry, T. D., Powell, N., & Young, L. (2010). Anger and aggression. In D. W. Nangle, D. J. Hansen, C. A. Erdley, & P. J. Norton (Eds.), *Practitioner's guide to empirically based measures of social skills* (pp. 155–166). New York, NY: Springer.

Lochman, J. E., Boxmeyer, C. L., Powell, N. P., Barry, T. D., & Pardini, D. A. (2010). Anger control training for aggressive youths. In J. R. Weisz & A. E. Kazdin (Eds.), *Evidence-based psychotherapies for children and adolescents* (2nd ed., pp. 227–242). New York, NY: Guilford Press.

Lochman, J. E., Boxmeyer, C., Powell, N., Qu, L., Wells, K., & Windle, M. (2009). Dissemination of the Coping Power program: Importance of intensity of counselor training. *Journal of Consulting and Clinical Psychology, 77*(3), 397–409.

Lochman, J. E., & Dodge, K. A. (1994). Social-cognitive processes of severely violent, moderately aggressive and nonaggressive boys. *Journal of Consulting and Clinical Psychology, 62*, 366–374.

Lochman, J. E., Fitzgerald, D. P., & Whidby, J. M. (1999). Anger management with aggressive children. In C. Schaefer (Ed.), *Short-term psychotherapy groups for children* (pp. 301–349). Northvale, NJ: Jason Aronson.

Lochman, J. E., Powell, N. P., Boxmeyer, C., Qu, L., Wells, K. C., & Windle, M. (2009). Implementation of a school-based prevention program: Effects of counselor and school characteristics. *Professional Psychology: Research and Practice, 40*(5), 476–482.

Lochman, J. E., Powell, N., Clanton, N., & McElroy, H. (2006). Anger and aggression. In G. Bear & K. Minke (Eds.), *Children's needs III: Development, prevention, and intervention* (pp. 115–133). Washington, DC: National Association of School Psychologists.

Lochman, J. E., & Wayland, K. K. (1994). Aggression, social acceptance and race as predictors of negative adolescent outcomes. *Journal of the American Academy of Child and Adolescent Psychiatry, 33*, 1026–1035.

Lochman, J. E., Wayland, K. K., & White, K. J. (1993). Social goals: Relationship to adolescent adjustment and to social problem-solving. *Journal of Abnormal Child Psychology, 21*, 135–151.

Lochman, J. E., & Wells, K. C. (2002a). Contextual social-cognitive mediators and child outcome: A test of the theoretical model in the coping power program. *Development and Psychopathology, 14*(4), 945–967.

Lochman, J. E., & Wells, K. C. (2002b). The Coping Power program at the middle-school transition: Universal and indicated prevention effects. *Psychology of Addictive Behaviors, 16*(4, Suppl), S40–S54.

Lochman, J. E., & Wells, K. C. (2003). Effectiveness study of Coping Power and classroom intervention with aggressive children: Outcomes at a one-year follow-up. *Behavior Therapy, 34*, 493–515.

Lochman, J. E., & Wells, K. C. (2004). The Coping Power Program for preadolescent aggressive boys and their parents: Outcome effects at the 1-year follow-up. *Journal of Consulting and Clinical Psychology, 72*(4), 571–578.

Lochman, J. E., Wells, K. C., & Lenhart, L. A. (2008). *Coping Power child group program: Facilitator guide*. New York, NY: Oxford University Press.

McDonald, K. L., & Lochman, J. E. (2012). Predictors and outcomes associated with trajectories of revenge goals from fourth grade through seventh grade. *Journal of Abnormal Child Psychology, 40*, 225–236.

McKee, L., Colletti, C., Rakow, A., Jones, D. J., & Forehand, R. (2008). Parenting and child externalizing behaviors: Are the associations specific or diffuse? *Aggression and Violent Behavior, 13*, 201–215.

Oldehinkel, A. J., Hartman, C. A., Ferdinand, R. F., Verhulst, F. C., & Ormel, J. (2007). Effortful control as modifier of the association between negative emotionality and adolescents' mental health problems. *Development and Psychopathology, 19*, 523–539.

Orobio de Castro, B., Veerman, J. W., Koops, W., Bosch, J. D., & Monshouwer, H. J. (2002). Hostile attribution of intent and aggressive behavior: A meta-analysis. *Child Development, 73*, 916–934.

Pardini, D., Lochman, J. E., & Wells, K. C. (2004). Negative emotions and alcohol use initiation in high-risk boys: The moderating effect of good inhibitory control. *Journal of Abnormal Child Psychology, 32*, 505–518.

Patterson, G. R., Reid, J. B., & Dishion, T. J. (1992). *Antisocial boys*. Eugene, OR: Castalia.

Polman, H., Orobio de Castro, B., Koops, W., van Boxtel, W. W., & Merk, W. M. (2007). A meta-analysis of the distinction between reactive and proactive aggression in children and adolescents. *Journal of Abnormal Child Psychology, 35*, 522–535.

Powell, N. P., Lochman, J. E., Boxmeyer, C. L., Barry, T. D., & Young, L. (2010). Anger and aggression in children: The role of arousal and cognition. In W. Arsenio & E. Lemerise (Eds.), *Emotions, aggression, and moral development* (pp. 239–258). Washington, DC: American Psychological Association.

Risi, S., Gerhardstein, R., & Kistner, J. (2003). Children's classroom peer relationships and subsequent educational outcomes. *Journal of Clinical Child and Adolescent Psychology, 32*, 351–361.

Schaeffer, C. M., Petras, H., Ialongo, N., Poduska, J., & Kellam, S. (2003). Modeling growth in boys' aggressive behavior across elementary school: Links to later criminal involvement, conduct disorder, and antisocial personality disorder. *Developmental Psychology, 39*, 1020–1035.

Van de Wiel, N.M.H., Matthys, W., Cohen-Kettenis, P., & van Engeland, H. (2003). Application of the Utrecht Coping Power program and care as usual to children with Disruptive Behavior Disorders in outpatient clinics: A comparative study of cost and course of treatment. *Behavior Therapy, 34*, 421–436.

Wells, K. C., Lochman, J. E., & Lenhart, L. A. (2008). *Coping Power parent group program: Facilitator guide*. New York, NY: Oxford University Press.

Xu, Y., Farver, J. M., & Zhang, Z. (2009). Temperament, harsh and indulgent parenting, and Chinese children's proactive and reactive aggression. *Child Development, 80*(1), 244–258.

Zeman, J., Shipman, K., & Suveg, C. (2002). Anger and sadness regulation: Predictions to internalizing and externalizing symptoms in children. *Journal of Clinical Child and Adolescent Psychology, 31*(3), 393–398.

Zonnevylle-Bender, M. S., Matthys, W., van de Wiel, N. H., & Lochman, J. E. (2007). Preventive effects of treatment of disruptive behavior disorder in middle childhood on substance use and delinquent behavior. *Journal of the American Academy of Child and Adolescent Psychiatry, 46*(1), 33–39.

11

Treatments for Anger Regulation and Reactive Aggression in Young Children

JULIE A. HUBBARD AND LAUREN E. SWIFT

Case Vignette

Bobby is a 10-year-old boy in the fourth grade at his local elementary school, and he and his classmates are playing basketball on the playground. The other boys do not usually let Bobby play with them, but they are short of a player and have allowed him to join. At first, Bobby is excited to be included, but his excitement quickly turns to frustration when he realizes that the other boys are not passing him the ball. When he is open for a shot, no one seems to notice, even when he yells the other boys' names. Red-faced and scowling, Bobby steals the ball from his own teammate, throws it across the playground, and runs away. He completely forgets about his open shot or his team's chances of winning the game.

Unfortunately, incidents such as this one happen to Bobby often. He is frequently the target of jokes, and he is rarely included in the games and activities of the other children unless a teacher steps in to help. Even then, after a few minutes, Bobby often gets angry and explodes by tossing board games, ripping notebooks, or throwing a tantrum. After these episodes, Bobby's peers are even less inclined to include him in their play. As Bobby grows more aware of his exclusion, he begins to avoid school, complain to the school nurse that he doesn't feel well, or cry until his parents allow him to stay home. As Bobby's grades start to slip, he begins feeling irritable and sad about himself and the future.

Fortunately, Bobby's teacher recognizes his distress and refers him to a school-based program designed to teach social skills, problem solving with peers, emotion identification and understanding, and emotion regulation. Over time, Bobby's ability to manage his angry feelings slowly improves, his aggressive behaviors slowly diminish, and his peers begin to include him in their play with greater enthusiasm.

This chapter concerns our theoretical understanding of anger in young children, as well as intervention approaches for young children's anger, with a particular focus on the peer context. All young children get angry and frustrated when things do not go their way (Fabes & Eisenberg, 1992). These feelings are developmentally normative and appropriate and do not require intervention. In fact, interventions for young children's anger often emphasize the mantra that "angry feelings are okay." However, young children's anger becomes more concerning when it frequently results in aggressive behaviors. A second adage common to intervention programs for young children is "but aggressive behaviors are not okay." Concern about aggressive behaviors toward peers increases when these behaviors do not decline as children progress from preschool age into middle childhood (NICHD Early Child Care Research Network, 2004).

Moreover, frequent reactive aggression may set a child on a pathway toward peer rejection, school avoidance, academic difficulties, and depression (see, for review, Hubbard, McAuliffe, Morrow, & Romano, 2010). As described in the case vignette, Bobby's pattern of reactive aggression cost him his friends, his interest in school, and his self-esteem. This chapter will describe what we understand about young children's anger from a theoretical perspective and what we know about evidence-based treatment options for these children. The first section of the chapter will focus on the theory underlying anger and aggression in young children, and the second section will examine current intervention approaches and their outcomes. Finally, the third section will include recommendations for future directions in intervention development, implementation, and evaluation.

THEORETICAL PERSPECTIVES ON ANGER AND AGGRESSION IN CHILDREN

Social Information–Processing Model

The social information–processing (SIP) model is the best known theoretical approach to understanding young children's aggression. Interestingly, in the original version of this model, no mention was made of the construct of anger. Rather, Dodge, Pettit, McClaskey, and Brown (1986) proposed that children progress through five steps as they take in information about a social situation and formulate a behavioral response. These steps include (a) encoding social cues, (b) interpreting these cues, (c) generating potential responses to the situation, (d) evaluating the possible consequences of these responses, and (e) selecting a response to enact.

In their reformulation of the SIP model, Crick and Dodge (1994) described briefly how emotion may interact with or influence the SIP steps. Subsequently, Lemerise and Arsenio (2000) developed a more thorough theory of the interplay of emotion and cognition in children's SIP. Both of these perspectives suggest that children progress through the five SIP steps differently, and perhaps less adaptively, at times when they are emotionally aroused, perhaps because emotion tends to compromise judgment.

However, neither Crick and Dodge (1994) nor Lemerise and Arsenio (2000) considered the role of the particular emotion of anger in the SIP steps. Experiencing anger likely affects children's SIP in specific ways (Bierman, 2007; Snyder, Schrepferman, Brooker, & Stoolmiller, 2007). For example, in the encoding step, children may notice fewer social cues if they are angry, or they may disproportionately perceive negative social cues. In the interpretation step, when children are angry, they may more easily attribute negative intentions or hostility to their peers' behavior than they would otherwise. In the generation and evaluation steps, when children are angry, they may consider more aggressive solutions to problems with peers, and they may be less concerned with the negative social consequences of these solutions (e.g., "It doesn't matter if he doesn't like me, because I don't like him either!"). In combination, these examples suggest some reasons that children may be more likely to behave aggressively when they are angered, within the context of an SIP model.

In a previous chapter (Hubbard & Dearing, 2004), we reviewed literature suggesting that aggressive children are more likely than their peers to struggle with emotion regulation, and perhaps anger regulation especially. In brief, we found strong empirical support for the hypothesis that aggressive children have difficulties with emotion regulation, in that they are more likely than their peers to be physiologically reactive to emotion-evoking social situations, to express negative emotions, and to display high levels of negative emotionality. These findings suggest that one possible reason aggressive children may often struggle to progress through the SIP steps adaptively is that they become angered more easily than their peers, and this anger negatively impacts upon their SIP processing.

Integration of anger into the SIP model is clearly an important goal for our field. Such an integrated model may more adequately describe the multiple mechanisms driving children's aggression. However, this approach implies that anger is only important in understanding children's aggression to the extent that it interacts with cognitive mechanisms. In contrast, it is our belief that we also need to "think outside the SIP box" in considering how anger and aggression may relate. Anger may influence children's aggression in ways that are unrelated to SIP. Consideration of the relation between anger and aggression, independent of SIP, has been called for by several researchers and interventionists (e.g., Denham & Burton, 2004; Greenberg, Kusche, & Speltz, 1991). Additionally, the work of prominent emotions theorists supports the idea that emotion is not inherently intertwined with cognition. For example, in a highly influential paper, Izard (1993) posited that emotion is not always activated by cognition, and he specified three systems (neural, sensorimotor, and motivational) he believes activate emotion independent of cognition.

For example, children who anger more easily are likely to experience physiological overarousal more quickly than other children when provoked by peers. High levels of physiological arousal may increase the challenge that these children face when trying to regulate angry feelings and curb aggressive behaviors (Scarpa & Raine, 1997). In addition, children who anger easily may find themselves in more negative interactions with their peers (Hubbard, 2001), and these interactions may provide increased opportunities to engage in aggressive behavior. These are just a few examples of ways in which the tendency to anger easily may negatively influence children's aggressive behavior, beyond its negative impact on children's SIP.

Reactive and Proactive Aggression

Many years ago, Averill (1982) succinctly described the complex relationship between anger and aggression when he stated that all anger does not lead to aggression, and all aggression is not the result of anger. This thinking has led to the theory that aggression may be driven by two different functions, one reactive and the other proactive (Dodge, 1991; Vitaro & Brendgen, 2005). Reactive aggression is anger driven, defensive, retaliatory, and in response to real or perceived provocation. Conversely, proactive aggression is displayed to reach a goal, whether the goal involves material or territorial gain (proactive instrumental aggression) or social dominance (proactive bullying aggression). Thus, reactive aggression is closely theoretically tied to anger, whereas proactive aggression is not.

A growing empirical literature suggests that reactive aggression is propelled by different social-cognitive and emotional processes than proactive aggression. In the following paragraphs, we will review this literature briefly (see Table 11.1 for a summary of the differences between reactive and proactive aggression).

Social cognition. Convergent research across diverse samples (e.g., elementary, middle, and high school children and adolescents in several countries; low-socioeconomic-status [SES] African American boys; behavior-disordered Dutch boys; incarcerated adolescents) demonstrates that different SIP steps predict children's tendency to engage in reactive versus proactive aggression. More specifically, reactive aggression, but not proactive aggression, is positively related to difficulty encoding social cues (Dodge et al., 1997), the tendency to attribute hostile intent to peers in ambiguously provocative situations (Crick & Dodge, 1996; De Castro, Merk, Koops, Verrman, & Bosch, 2005; Dodge & Coie, 1987; Kempes, Matthys, Maassen, van Goozen, & van Engeland, 2006; Nas, Orobio de Castro, & Koops, 2005; Schippell, Vasey, Cravens-Brown, & Bretvald, 2003; Schwartz et al., 1998), and the generation of aggressive responses to social conflicts (De Castro et al., 2005; Dodge & Coie, 1987; Dodge, Lochman, Harnish, Bates, & Pettit, 1997). These findings suggest that the SIP steps of encoding social cues, interpreting social cues, and generating potential responses to social situations may be particularly influenced by children's anger.

Three other social-cognitive processes appear more closely linked to proactive aggression. Particularly, proactive aggression, but not reactive aggression, is positively related to self-efficacy in enacting aggressive behaviors (Crick & Dodge, 1996; Dodge et al., 1997), prioritizing instrumental goals over social

Table 11.1 Key Differences Between Reactive and Proactive Aggression

	Reactive Aggression	**Proactive Aggression**
Definition	Defensive, retaliatory, following provocation	Goal directed, instigated
Emotional profile	Driven by anger High physiological arousal	Unemotional Low physiological arousal
Social-cognitive difficulties	Encoding social cues Hostile attributional biases Aggressive solutions to social problems	Self-efficacy about aggression Prioritizing instrumental over social goals Positive outcome expectations for aggression

goals in peer interaction (Crick & Dodge, 1996), and expecting that aggressive behavior will result in positive outcomes and not in negative outcomes (Arsenio, Gold, & Adams, 2004; Crick & Dodge, 1996, Dodge et al., 1997; Hubbard, Dodge, Cillessen, Coie, & Schwartz, 2001; Schwartz et al., 1998; Smithmyer, Hubbard, & Simons, 2000). Interestingly, this last body of research has shown links to a diverse range of expected positive outcomes, from the belief that aggression will result in material or territorial gain, to the belief that it will lead to respect and liking by others (Smithmyer et al., 2000), and even to the belief that it will make one feel happier (Arsenio et al., 2004). Thus, whereas reactive aggression seems more closely tied to the first three SIP steps, proactive aggression seems more related to the last two SIP steps.

Emotional and physiological processes. As described earlier, theorists conceptualize reactive aggression as emotionally driven, whereas they view proactive aggression as quite unemotional. Furthermore, the emotion that is most often invoked when characterizing reactive aggression is anger. The hypothesis that reactive but not proactive aggression is related to difficulties with anger and its regulation has garnered support across a number of studies (De Castro et al., 2005; Dodge & Coie, 1987; Little, Brauner, Jones, Nock, & Hawley, 2003; Little, Jones, Henrich, & Hawley, 2003; McAuliffe, Hubbard, Rubin, Morrow, & Dearing, 2007; Price & Dodge, 1989; Raine et al., 2006). The samples used in these studies were diverse and included elementary school children, low-SES African American boys, German adolescents, and antisocial adolescents.

However, in all of these studies, anger was assessed in a traitlike way through self-report, peer report, or hypothetical vignettes. None of the studies included laboratory-based observational measures of children's anger or measures of the physiological arousal that likely accompanies anger. This is particularly important because episodes of reactive aggression are thought to be characterized by high levels of physiological arousal, whereas episodes of proactive aggression are consistent with a profile of low physiological arousal (Dodge, 1991; Vitaro & Brendgen, 2005). Yet, we have preciously little data along these lines.

In fact, only one study of the associations between the subtypes of aggression and physiological arousal has been published to date. In this large-scale study (Hubbard et al., 2002; Hubbard et al., 2004), teacher ratings of reactive and proactive aggression were gathered on 272 second-grade children. These children then participated in a laboratory procedure in which they lost a board game to a peer confederate who cheated. Physiological data on children's skin conductance reactivity (SCR) and observational data on children's anger expression were collected during each turn of the game. Findings revealed that reactive aggression, but not proactive aggression, was positively related to SCR and observed anger expression. Moreover, these relations held not only when SCR and anger expression were aggregated across the game but also in terms of rate of increase over the time span of the game. That is to say, children higher in teacher-rated reactive aggression had steeper increases in their SCR and anger expression over the course of the game, whereas these increases were not related to proactive aggression.

This project (Hubbard et al., 2002; Hubbard et al., 2004) was an important starting point in understanding the role of physiological factors in anger arousal and aggression likelihood. Still, more information is needed about whether children's physiological and emotional profiles differ *in the moment* when they are engaging in episodes of reactive versus proactive aggression. To address this question, Hubbard and colleagues (2010) developed laboratory-based measures of reactive and proactive aggression involving the use of virtual peers. They assessed physiological arousal and anger expression simultaneously with measurements of the subtypes of aggression. Interestingly, observed anger expression correlated positively with children's levels of reactive aggression during the laboratory tasks, but not their levels of proactive aggression. These findings provide further support for the idea that reactive aggression is driven by anger and initial evidence that proactive aggression is not. Furthermore, children's physiological arousal was positively related to their levels of reactive aggression in the lab, but negatively related to their levels of proactive aggression. These data provide the first empirical support of theory suggesting that proactive aggression is literally "cold blooded," in that it is displayed when children are particularly calm and unaroused.

Differential treatment approaches for reactive versus proactive aggression. The literature previously reviewed suggests that it may make sense to develop differential interventions for reactive aggression and proactive aggression in young children. Separate interventions for reactive and proactive aggression have been suggested by numerous researchers (e.g., Brown & Parsons, 1998; Crick & Dodge, 1996; Dodge, 1991; Dodge & Coie, 1987; Dodge & Schwartz, 1997; Larson, 1994; Little et al., 2003; McAdams, 2002; Phillips & Lochman, 2003; Poulin & Boivin, 1999; Salmivalli & Nieminen, 2002; Vitaro & Brendgen, 2005; Vitaro, Brendgen, & Tremblay, 2002; Waschbusch, Willoughby, & Pelham, 1998; Weinshenker & Siegel, 2002). These treatment packages could target the specific correlates of each subtype of aggression. For example, a reactive aggression intervention could emphasize anger regulation training, hostile attributional bias reduction, and social problem solving. In contrast, treatment for proactive aggression could stress the negative consequences of aggressive behavior, the importance of social goals, and the development of empathy for others. Aggressive behavior may be decreased more effectively if the specific behavioral, social, social-cognitive, emotional, and physiological underpinnings of each subtype of aggression are targeted separately.

Clearly, given the high correlation between the subtypes of aggression (Vitaro & Brendgen, 2005), many aggressive children would benefit from both treatment packages. However, a differentiated approach to the treatment of the subtypes of childhood aggression may make sense not only for those aggressive children who display primarily one subtype of aggressive behavior but also for those children who display both subtypes as well. The idea is that careful targeting of the mechanisms driving each subtype of aggression may enhance the efficacy of our intervention efforts with all aggressive children.

Currently, intervention programs for aggressive children have not progressed to the point of overtly distinguishing between reactive and proactive aggression and explicitly targeting one or the other subtype of aggression. However, over the past several decades, programs for aggressive children have increasingly focused on reducing children's tendency to aggress when provoked, as well as the anger that drives this behavior. In the following section, we will first provide a framework for categorizing these intervention approaches and then review their history and development.

CURRENT INTERVENTION PROGRAMS FOR YOUNG CHILDREN'S ANGER

Sukhodolsky, Kassinove, and Gorman (2004) describe three approaches that interventionists take when working to reduce children's levels of anger and aggression: skill development, problem solving, and affective education. Essentially, these three approaches map onto the targets of behavior, social cognition, and emotion in interventions for young children.

The skill development, or behavioral, approach uses modeling, coaching, and role-playing to teach children social skills and prosocial behaviors. The idea here is that children become angry and aggressive when they lack the skills to make friends and get along well with other children. It is believed that providing children with these skills will lead naturally to decreases in anger and aggressive behaviors. Many years ago, Ladd and Mize (1983) translated these principles into a model of social skills training with three basic objectives: improving skill understanding, promoting skill performance, and encouraging maintenance and generalization of skills. Early intervention programs for peer-rejected and aggressive children focused solely on the development of social skills and prosocial behavior as a means of curbing anger and aggression (e.g., Bierman, 1986; Bierman, Miller, & Stabb, 1987). Although these efforts provided a promising first step, it soon became clear that children who experience serious problems with anger and aggression would benefit from a more comprehensive treatment approach (Bierman & Powers, 2009).

The next component to be included in programs targeting children's anger and aggression was termed problem solving. This approach followed the SIP model, and programs addressed the cognitive biases and distortions that characterize peer-rejected and aggressive children (Crick & Dodge, 1994). Problem-solving interventions were often based on the work of Spivack and Shure (Shure, 1994; Spivak, Platt, & Shure, 1976) and emphasized step-by-step processing of social situations. Children were instructed to stop and consider all aspects of a problem before acting. They progressed through a series of questions, such as "What is the problem?" and "What would happen if I did that?" Instructors helped children to brainstorm solutions to problems and evaluate possible responses. Children finished by implementing an appropriate response and evaluating its effectiveness. These interventions emphasized breaking down automatic and instantaneous social-cognitive processes into gradual and deliberate steps. Children were directed through each step separately and systematically to master social cue perception and interpretation, generation of nonaggressive responses, and improved consequential thinking skills. By allowing children to practice SIP in this step-by-step manner, problem-solving interventions targeted cognitive deficits that result in anger and aggressive behavior. Importantly, these programs did not replace a focus on behaviors with a focus on social cognitions. Rather, they encompassed the teaching of behavioral skills within the broader SIP framework, as theorists began to understand the social-cognitive processes that precede and drive both aggressive and prosocial behaviors in young children.

Much more recently, intervention efforts for children's anger and aggression have begun to include a focus on what Sukhodolsky, Kassinove, and Gorman (2004) refer to as affective education. This component includes the identification and understanding of emotions in the self and others, as well as skills related to the effective regulation of emotion. Again, these more recent programs do not typically neglect the behavioral and social-cognitive skills that are essential to decreasing levels of aggression in young children. They do, however, include a focus on emotion knowledge and management as additional critical skills for young children struggling with aggressive behaviors.

Sukhodolsky and colleagues (2004) conducted a meta-analysis of intervention programs for anger in children and adolescents in which they evaluated findings from 40 empirical studies. Their results revealed an overall effect size of .67 across these studies. However, effect sizes varied somewhat across programs using only skill development (behavioral focus; Cohen's d = .79), only problem solving (social-cognitive focus; Cohen's d = .67), only affective education (emotion focus; Cohen's d = .36), or a combination (Cohen's d = .74). Interestingly, when findings were broken down by type of outcome measure (physical aggression, anger experience, self-control, problem solving, and social skills), results suggested that programs designed to target one domain often actually had a greater effect on another area of functioning. For example, programs targeting problem solving alone were shown to impact children's experience of anger even more than their problem-solving abilities.

In the following sections, we will briefly describe three intervention programs for aggressive children that combine skill development, problem solving, and affective education, as well as the empirical support for each program. These descriptions will highlight the current state of the science in the development of intervention programs for anger and aggression in young children.

Second Step

The Second Step program (Grossman et al., 1997) includes an explicit focus on problem-solving techniques, in that it targets children's ability to proceed through each SIP step adaptively. Much like the Spivack and Shure model, this intervention asks children to (a) identify the problem, (b) generate solutions, (c) evaluate their possible solutions, (d) select and enact a solution, and (e) evaluate the outcome of the interaction. Lessons provide opportunities for children to practice each SIP step.

In addition, Second Step incorporates affective education by teaching children to identify feelings in themselves and others, take the perspectives of others, and respond empathically to others' emotion. The program focuses on emotion understanding and empathy by discussing verbal and visual cues that might suggest certain emotions and then uses stories, discussion, and role-play exercises to help children develop these skills.

Beyond emotion understanding, the Second Step program also includes an emphasis on emotion regulation that focuses on recognizing and reducing angry feelings. First, it teaches children strategies to recognize physiological changes in their bodies that are associated with angry arousal. Children also identify triggers, like teasing, that often make them angry. Then, children use positive self-talk and other stress reduction techniques to stay in control of their emotions. Discussion and rehearsal of these steps is thought to improve children's ability to regulate emotions, thus reducing angry outbursts leading to reactive aggression.

Grossman et al. (1997) evaluated Second Step in an initial trial including 790 second- and third-grade students in 49 classrooms. Trained classroom teachers taught the Second Step curriculum twice per week for 4 to 5 months. Observed physical aggression decreased from pre- to postintervention for students participating in the program but not for their peers in the control condition. Later trials in the United States and in Norway also had positive results. In the United States, teacher reports suggested improved student behavior, improved social reasoning, and, for girls, better cooperation after participation in the intervention. Participants also showed significantly less aggression during observations (Frey, Nolen, Edstrom, & Hirschstein, 2005). In Norway, Second Step participation was related to higher ratings of social competence and lower ratings of externalizing behavior (Holsen, Smith, & Frey, 2008).

Promoting Alternative Thinking Strategies

The Promoting Alternative Thinking Strategies (PATHS; Greenberg & Kusche, 1993) program is the most comprehensive of the three reviewed here. It emphasizes that children's aggression is the result of the dynamic interplay of several constructs, including affect and emotion language, manifest behavior, cognitive processes, and communicative skills. Thus, PATHS takes a multipronged approach to targeting behavioral and emotional difficulties. In particular, it incorporates prosocial skill-building, problem-solving, emotion understanding, and emotion regulation skill-building techniques into a comprehensive package taught by classroom teachers to elementary-school-aged children in weekly lessons throughout the school year. The program includes an explicit focus on the development of prosocial behaviors and social skills, and it includes activities designed to improve communication among peers and build friendships between children. Much like Second Step, PATHS also includes a social-cognitive component that teaches children to "stop and think" when they encounter difficult social situations, and then to progress through SIP-like steps. Next, PATHS lessons target emotion understanding by helping children identify and label emotions in themselves and others. Special tools like an emotions thermometer help children assess and describe the intensity of their feelings. Finally, emotion regulation skills are highlighted in the lessons. Children learn the "turtle technique," which teaches them to go into a "shell," count to 10, take a deep breath, and then express how they're feeling in a calm way. Other featured emotion regulation skills include delaying gratification, controlling impulses, reducing stress, and using self-talk. Finally, the curriculum includes a supplemental unit that emphasizes generalization of skills. Integration with academic classroom lessons, playground time, and other peer-related settings encourages students to extend key concepts for use throughout the day.

Several trials have evaluated the efficacy of the PATHS program both in the United States and abroad. In an early trial, Greenberg, Kusche, Cook, and Quamma (1995) found that children who participated in the PATHS program showed significant improvements in their emotional understanding and expression, social skills, and peer relations relative to their peers in the control group. PATHS was also evaluated as part of the Fast Track Program, a comprehensive intervention targeting aggression as well as social and academic competence. Peer reports and observational data suggested that children who participated in the PATHS curriculum were less aggressive than their counterparts in the control group. In addition, results suggested that program effectiveness was related to the quality of implementation (Conduct Problems Prevention Research Group, 1999). The PATHS program was later evaluated in a Scottish primary school (Kelly, Longbottom, Potts, & Williamson, 2004) and five schools in the United Kingdom (Curtis & Norgate, 2007). Results suggested improvements in behavioral and emotional functioning, including emotion vocabulary, cooperation, empathy, self-control, and peer relations.

The Rochester Resilience Project

Although the Rochester Resilience Project (Wyman et al., 2010) is not as comprehensive as PATHS, of the three programs described, it is the most focused on anger and anger regulation. In this program, school-based mentors teach children a hierarchical set of skills focused on emotion self-monitoring and regulation in 14 weekly lessons for which children are pulled from their regular education classrooms. The lessons emphasize three skills taught through adult-led activities and real-time practice in natural settings. The first skill involves monitoring one's own and others' emotions. Children are taught emotional vocabulary and cues to identifying feelings in the self and other. The next skill concerns emotion regulation; children are taught self-control and tools for reducing the escalation of emotion, such as a "feelings thermometer" to depict emotion intensity and the concept of using "mental muscles" to gain control over emotions. Finally, the third skill helps children to maintain control of their emotions while working through difficulties with peers. Deep breathing, stopping to think, and using an "imaginary umbrella" to protect against hurtful words are taught to improve children's objectivity and emotion regulation during interpersonal conflict.

The efficacy of the Rochester Resilience Project was tested in an initial trial of 226 kindergarten to third-grade children (Wyman et al., 2010). Students were rated by their teachers on social and emotional functioning before and after the intervention, and office disciplinary referrals were collected pre- and postintervention. Children who received the intervention showed improvement in teacher-rated task orientation, behavior control, assertive behavior, and peer social skills compared to their peers in the control group. In addition, children who participated in the intervention had reduced office disciplinary referrals and out-of-school suspensions during the 4-month intervention period.

EXPANDING THE FOCUS ON ANGER IN INTERVENTIONS FOR AGGRESSIVE CHILDREN

Greater Exposure to Angry Feelings

As can be seen from the description of these three programs, there has been a steady increase in the focus on emotion understanding and regulation in intervention programs for aggressive children. To some extent, these programs also target the specific emotion of anger and its regulation. However, in our view, these programs would benefit from a greater focus on exposure to angry feelings within the context of the intervention. Thus, after children have been taught basic skills for recognizing and regulating their angry feelings, situations could be structured within the context of the intervention group that would purposefully elicit angry feelings in children. Adult leaders could then encourage children to practice their developing anger regulation skills, while coaching and supporting as much as is necessary. For example, children could be asked to negotiate the allocation of scarce resources or to play competitive games. If a group of aggressive children must divide up too few snacks, decide who gets to play with a handheld video game first, or handle losing a game, the opportunity to practice anger regulation skills will arise almost without fail.

Exposing children to actual anger-inducing experiences provides them with an opportunity to practice their anger regulation skills online. Role-plays and other forms of simulated practice are important in the initial stages of teaching children skills and techniques for regulating anger. However, we should also challenge children to use their emerging anger regulation skills in the moment in situations where they experience high levels of angry arousal.

Creating interventions that incorporate these types of anger-inducing situations will require substantial innovation, planning, foresight, and courage. And, clearly, opportunities for children to practice anger regulation skills online would need to be accompanied by considerable support, coaching, and scaffolding. We believe, though, that this sort of real-world practice is at the heart of what is missing from current approaches to teaching children how to regulate their anger. And, it may be the key to obtaining faster and longer lasting generalization of anger regulation skills from the treatment setting to home and school environments.

Why, then, have we shied away from exposing children to their strong angry feelings in the context of our intervention programs? One possibility is that the taboo against anger that exists in our society is being perpetuated by the very researchers who study and treat children's aggression. In spite of encouraging children to believe that "all feelings are okay," many of us do not feel comfortable with children's anger, especially if we feel responsible for it. We may even believe that the goal of our intervention programs is to prevent children from ever becoming angry, rather than teaching children adaptive ways of coping with the anger that they all experience. Our goal should be to help children learn effective and constructive ways to manage angry feelings, rather than pursuing the unrealistic goal of banishing angry feelings altogether.

It is also likely that we have avoided giving children full-fledged opportunities to practice their anger regulation skills in our interventions because we (and our institutional review boards) worry about the ethics and pragmatics involved in doing so. When children become angry, they are sometimes going to resort to aggression, no matter how much coaching and scaffolding we provide. How do we keep all of the children in our intervention groups safe under these circumstances? Many of us are already taking efforts to manage naturally occurring anger and aggression within our therapeutic groups. Anyone who has worked with groups of aggressive children has experience in planning for the disagreements and scuffles that inevitably result. Most of us use as much scaffolding, praise, and support as possible, but we also use as many time-outs and as much "safe holding" as necessary. We also make sure that our groups are adequately staffed to allow for individual attention when children require it. Planning for exposure to anger is not really any different from planning for these naturally occurring altercations; in fact, it is in some ways easier, because we can more readily predict when aggressive episodes may occur.

The risks involved in exposing children to anger are obvious. However, in our opinion, the benefits may well justify these risks. Only when children are placed in actual anger-provoking situations are they allowed the opportunity to practice their anger regulation skills, to learn that they can actually control their angry feelings, and to experience the power of feeling angry but not resorting to aggression. These experiences provide much more than a chance to habituate to angry feelings; they provide practice in the challenge of regulating anger. Moreover, in the cognitive-behavioral tradition, these experiences may fundamentally change the meaning of anger for aggressive children. Through successful experiences such as these, aggressive children may learn that anger is something that they can control, not something that controls them. For all of these reasons, we suggest that interventions for aggressive children would do well to include greater exposure to angry feelings.

Assessment of Anger as an Outcome of Interest

Additionally, we believe that researchers should more systematically assess constructs related to children's anger and its regulation when evaluating the efficacy or effectiveness of programs designed to reduce children's aggressive behavior. The constructs most often assessed when evaluating these programs include (a) aggressive behavior, (b) social-cognitive variables such as hostile attributional biases or problem-solving response generation, (c) broad measures of prosocial behavior or social skills, (d) global assessments of externalizing and internalizing psychopathology, or (e) broad measures of social-emotional functioning. Beyond these constructs, we believe that measures of anger and its regulation should be assessed more explicitly. For example, Sukhodolsky, Kassinove, and Gorman (2004) suggest including self-report measures of anger intensity and arousal. Additional self-report measures of self-monitoring for angry feelings may also be important to include, as may teacher-, parent-, or peer-report measures of overt anger expression. These measures would allow us to more carefully assess the impact of our intervention efforts on children's anger and its regulation.

Moreover, it may prove helpful to assess both reactive and proactive subtypes of aggression separately as outcome measures when evaluating interventions for young children's aggression. This assessment approach may bring us closer to an understanding of whether our intervention programs are succeeding when they aim to target children's anger explicitly and whether they are effective at targeting reactive aggression in particular. Of most interest, they may help to reveal whether reductions in children's anger and increases in children's anger regulation skills mediate outcomes for reactive aggression.

CONCLUSION

In conclusion, our field has made significant progress as we have worked to develop more effective intervention programs for young children struggling with aggressive behaviors. A notable development has been an increasing focus on the need to include emotion understanding and regulation as critical targets of these programs. Substantial strides have been made as we work to focus on anger more specifically as an essential emphasis in our work with young aggressive children. However, more work remains to be done. In the last section of this chapter, we have highlighted two important goals for the future: exposure to anger as a critical component of interventions for aggressive children, and assessment of outcomes related to anger when evaluating these programs.

REFERENCES

Arsenio, W. F., Gold, J., & Adams, E. (2004). Adolescents' emotion expectancies regarding aggressive and nonaggressive events: Connections with behavior problems. *Journal of Experimental Child Psychology: Special Emotional Cognition in Children, 89*, 338–355.

Averill, J. R. (1982). *Anger and aggression: An essay on emotion*. New York, NY: Springer-Verlag.

Bierman, K. L. (1986). Process of change during social skills training with preadolescents and its relation to treatment outcome. *Child Development, 52*, 230–240.

Bierman, K. L. (2007). Anger and aggression: A developmental perspective. In T. A. Cavell & K. T. Malcolm (Eds.), *Anger, aggression, and interventions for interpersonal violence* (pp. 215–238). Mahwah, NJ: Lawrence Erlbaum Associates Publishers.

Bierman, K. L., Miller, C. L., & Stabb, S. D. (1987). Improving the social behavior and peer acceptance of rejected boys: Effects of social skill training with instructions and prohibitions. *Journal of Consulting and Clinical Psychology, 55*, 194–200.

Bierman, K. L., & Powers, C. J. (2009). Social skills training to improve peer relations. In K. H. Rubin, W. M. Bukowski, & B. Laursen (Eds.), *Handbook of peer interaction, relationships, and groups* (pp. 603–621). New York, NY: Guilford Press.

Brown, K. S., & Parsons, R. D. (1998). Accurate identification of childhood aggression: A key to successful intervention. *Professional School Counseling, 2*, 135–140.

Conduct Problems Prevention Research Group. (1999). Initial impact of the Fast Track prevention trial for conduct problems: II. Classroom effects. *Journal of Consulting and Clinical Psychology, 67*, 648–657.

Crick, N. R., & Dodge, K. A. (1996). Social information-processing mechanisms on reactive and proactive aggression. *Child Development, 67*, 993–1002.

Crick, N. R., & Dodge, K. A. (1994). A review and reformulation of social information-processing mechanisms in children's social adjustment. *Psychological Bulletin, 115*, 74–101.

Curtis, C., & Norgate, R. (2007). An evaluation of the Promoting Alternative Thinking Strategies curriculum at key stage 1. *Educational Psychology in Practice, 23*, 33–44.

De Castro, B. O., Merk, W., Koops, W., Verrman, J. W., & Bosch, J. D. (2005). Emotions in social information processing and their relations with reactive and proactive aggression in referred aggressive boys. *Journal of Clinical Child and Adolescent Psychology, 34*, 105–116.

Denham, S. A., & Burton, R. (2004). *Social and emotional prevention and intervention programming for preschoolers*. New York, NY: Kluwer Academic/Plenum.

Dodge, K. A. (1991). The structure and function of reactive and proactive aggression. In D. J. Pepler & K. H. Rubin (Eds.), *The development and treatment of childhood aggression* (pp. 201–218). Hillsdale, NJ: Lawrence Erlbaum Associates.

Dodge, K. A., & Coie, J. D. (1987). Social information processing factors in reactive and proactive aggression in children's peer groups. *Journal of Personality and Social Psychology, 53*, 1146–1158.

Dodge, K. A., & Schwartz, D. (1997). Social information processing mechanisms in aggressive behavior. In D. M. Stoff & J. Breiling (Eds.), *Handbook of antisocial behavior* (pp. 171–180). New York, NY: Wiley.

Dodge, K. A., Lochman, J. E., Harnish, J. D., Bates, J. E., & Pettit, G. S. (1997). Reactive and proactive aggression in school children and psychiatrically impaired chronically assaultive youth. *Journal of Abnormal Psychology, 106*, 37–51.

Dodge, K. A., Pettit, G. S., McClaskey, C. L., & Brown, M. (1986). Social competence in children. *Monographs of the Society for Research in Child Development, 51*(3, Serial No. 213).

Fabes, R. A., Eisenberg, N. (1992). Young children's coping with interpersonal anger. *Child Development, 63*, 116–128.

Frey, K. S., Nolen, S. B., Edstrom, L. V., & Hirschstein, M. K. (2005). Effects of a school-based social-emotional competence program: Linking children's goals, attributions, and behavior. *Journal of Applied Developmental Psychology, 26*, 171–200.

Greenberg, M. T., & Kusche, C. A. (1993). *Promoting social and emotional development in deaf children: The PATHS project*. Seattle, WA: University of Washington Press.

Greenberg, M. T., Kusche, C. A., & Speltz, M. (1991). Emotional regulation, self control, and psychopathology: The role of relationships in early childhood. In D. Cicchetti & S. L. Toth (Eds.), *Internalizing and externalizing expressions of dysfunction: Rochester Symposium on Developmental Psychopathology* (Vol. 2, pp. 21–66). Hillsdale, NJ: Lawrence Erlbaum Associates.

Greenberg, M. T., Kusche, C. A., Cook, E. T., & Quamma, J. P. (1995). Promoting emotional competence in school-aged children: The effects of the PATHS curriculum. *Developmental Psychopathology, 7*, 117–136.

Grossman, D. C., Neckerman, H. J., Koepsell, T. D., Liu, P. Y., Asher, K. N., Beland, K., … Rivara, F. P. (1997). Effectiveness of a violence prevention curriculum among children in elementary school: A randomized controlled trial. *Journal of the American Medical Association, 277*, 1605–1611.

Holsen, I., Smith, B. H., & Frey, K. S. (2008). Outcome of the social competence program Second Step in Norwegian elementary schools. *School Psychology International, 29*, 71–88.

Hubbard, J. A. (2001). Emotion expression processes in children's peer interaction: The role of peer rejection, aggression, and gender. *Child Development, 72*, 1426–1438.

Hubbard, J. A., & Dearing, K. F. (2004). Children's understanding and regulation of emotion in the context of their peer relations. In J. B. Kupersmidt & K. A. Dodge (Eds.), *Children's peer relations: From development to intervention* (pp. 81–99). Washington, DC: American Psychological Association Press.

Hubbard, J. A., Dodge, K. A., Cillessen, A. H. N., Coie, J. D., & Schwartz, D. (2001). The dyadic nature of social information processing in boys' reactive and proactive aggression. *Journal of Personality and Social Psychology, 80*, 268–280.

Hubbard, J. A., McAuliffe, M. D., Morrow, M. T., & Romano, L. J. (2010). Reactive and proactive aggression in childhood and adolescence: Precursors, outcomes, processes, experiences, and measurement. *Journal of Personality, 78*, 95–118.

Hubbard, J. A., Parker, E. H., Ramsden, S. R., Flanagan, K. D., Relyea, N., Dearing, K. F., …Hyde, C. T. (2004). The relations between observational, physiological, and self-report measures of children's anger. *Social Development, 13*, 14–39.

Hubbard, J. A., Smithmyer, C. M., Ramsden, S. R., Parker, E. H., Flanagan, K. D., Dearing, K. F.... Simons, R. F. (2002). Observational, physiological, and self-report measures of children's anger: Relations to reactive versus proactive aggression. *Child Development, 73*, 1101–1118.

Izard, C. E. (1993). Four systems of emotion activation: Cognitive and noncognitive processes. *Psychological Review, 100*, 68–90.

Kelly, B., Longbottom, J., Potts, F., & Williamson, J. (2004). Applying emotional intelligence: Exploring the promoting alternative thinking strategies curriculum. *Educational Psychology in Practice, 20*, 221–240.

Kempes, M., Matthys, W., Maassen, G., van Goozen, S., & van Engeland, H. (2006). A parent questionnaire for distinguishing between reactive and proactive aggression in children. *European Child and Adolescent Psychiatry, 15*, 38–45.

Ladd, G. W., & Mize, J. (1983). A cognitive-social learning model of social skill training. *Psychological Review, 90*, 127–157.

Larson, J. (1994). Cognitive-behavioral treatment of anger-induced aggression in the school setting. In M. J. Furlong & D. C. Smith (Eds.), *Anger, hostility, and aggression: Assessment, prevention, and intervention strategies for youth* (pp. 393–440). Brandon, VT: Clinical Psychology.

Lemerise, E. A., & Arsenio, W. F. (2000). An integrated model of emotion processes and cognition in social information processing. *Child Development, 71*, 107–118.

Little, T. D., Brauner, J., Jones, S. M., Nock, M. K., & Hawley, P. H. (2003). Rethinking aggression: A typological examination of the functions of aggression. *Merrill-Palmer Quarterly, 49*, 343–369.

Little, T. D., Jones, S. M., Henrich, C. C., & Hawley, P. H. (2003). Disentangling the "whys" from the "whats" of aggressive behavior. *International Journal of Behavioral Development, 27*, 122–133.

McAdams, C. (2002). Trends in the occurrence of reactive and proactive aggression among children and adolescents: Implications for preparation and practice in child and youth care. *Child and Youth Care Forum, 31*, 89–109.

McAuliffe, M. D., Hubbard, J. A., Rubin, R. M., Morrow, M. T., & Dearing, K. F. (2007). Reactive and proactive aggression: Stability of constructs and relations to correlates. *Journal of Genetic Psychology, 167*, 365–382.

Nas, C. N., Orobio De Castro, B., & Koops, W. (2005). Social information processing in delinquent adolescents. *Psychology, Crime and Law, 11*, 363–375.

NICHD Early Child Care Research Network. (2004). Trajectories of physical aggression from toddlerhood to middle childhood. *Monographs of the Society for Research in Child Development, 69*(Serial No. 278).

Phillips, N. C., & Lochman, J. E. (2003). Experimentally manipulated change in children's proactive and reactive aggressive behavior. *Aggressive Behavior, 29*, 215–227.

Poulin, F., & Boivin, M. (1999). Proactive and reactive aggression and boys' friendship quality in mainstream classrooms. *Journal of Emotional and Behavioral Disorders, 7*, 168–177.

Price, J. M., & Dodge, K. A. (1989). Reactive and proactive aggression in childhood: Relations to peer status and social context dimensions. *Journal of Abnormal Child Psychology, 17*, 455–471.

Raine, A., Dodge, K., Loeber, R., Gatzke-Kopp, L., Lynam, D., Reynolds, C., ... Liu, J. (2006). The reactive-proactive aggression questionnaire: Differential correlates of reactive and proactive aggression in adolescent boys. *Aggressive Behavior, 32*, 159–171.

Salmivalli, C., & Nieminen, E. (2002). Proactive and reactive aggression among school bullies, victims, and bully-victims. *Aggressive Behavior, 28*, 30–44.

Scarpa, A., & Raine, A. (1997). Psychophysiology of anger and violent behavior. *Psychiatric Clinics of North America, 20*, 375–394.

Schippell, P. L., Vasey, M. W., Cravens-Brown, L. M., & Bretvald, R. A. (2003). Suppressed attention to rejection, ridicule, and failure cues: A unique correlate of reactive but not proactive aggression in youth. *Journal of Clinical Child and Adolescent Psychology, 32*, 40–55.

Schwartz, D., Dodge, K. A., Coie, J. D., Hubbard, J. A., Cillessen, A. H. N., Lemerise, E. A., & Bateman, H. (1998). Social cognitive and behavioral correlates of aggression and victimization in boys' play groups. *Journal of Abnormal Child Psychology, 26*, 431–440.

Shure, M. (1994). *I Can Problem Solve (ICPS): An interpersonal cognitive problem-solving program for children*. Champaign, IL: Research Press.

Smithmyer, C. M., Hubbard, J. A., & Simons, R. F. (2000). Proactive and reactive aggression in delinquent adolescents: Relations to aggression outcome expectancies. *Journal of Clinical Child Psychology, 29*, 86–93.

Snyder, J., Schrepferman, L., Brooker, M., & Stoolmiller, M. (2007). The roles of anger, conflict with parents and peers, and social reinforcement in the early development of physical aggression. In T. A. Cavell & K. T. Malcolm (Eds.), *Anger, aggression, and interventions for interpersonal violence* (pp. 215–238). Mahwah, NJ: Lawrence Erlbaum Associates Publishers.

Spivak, G., Platt, J. J., & Shure, M. B. (1976). *The problem solving approach to adjustment*. San Francisco, CA: Jossey-Bass.

Sukhodolsky, D. G., Kassinove, H., & Gorman, B. S. (2004). Cognitive-behavioral therapy for anger in children and adolescents: A meta-analysis. *Aggression and Violent Behavior, 9*, 247–269.

Vitaro, F., & Brendgen, M. (2005). Proactive and reactive aggression: A developmental perspective. In R. E. Tremblay, W. M. Hartup, & J. Archer (Eds.), *Developmental origins of aggression* (pp. 178–201). New York, NY: Guilford.

Vitaro, F., Brendgen, M., & Tremblay, R. E. (2002). Reactively and proactively aggressive children: Antecedent and subsequent characteristics. *Journal of Child Psychology and Psychiatry and Allied Disciplines, 43*, 495–506.

Waschbusch, D. A., Willoughby, M. T., & Pelham, W. E. (1998). Criterion validity and the utility of reactive and proactive aggression: Comparisons to attention deficit hyperactivity disorder, oppositional defiant disorder, conduct disorder, and other measures of functioning. *Journal of Clinical Child Psychology, 27*, 396–405.

Weinshenker, N. J., & Siegel, A. (2002). Bimodal classification of aggression: Affective defense and predatory attack. *Aggression and Violent Behavior, 7*, 237–250.

Wyman, P. A., Cross, W., Brown, C. H., Yu, Q., Tu, X., & Eberly, S. (2010). Intervention to strengthen emotional self-regulation in children with emerging mental health problems: Proximal impact on school behavior. *Journal of Abnormal Child Psychology, 38*, 707–720.

12

Gender-Inclusive and Gender-Informed Treatment of Anger

EPHREM FERNANDEZ AND KATHLEEN MALLEY-MORRISON ■

In the quest for an anger treatment approach that is gender inclusive and gender informed, this chapter poses three questions. First, how do males and females compare with respect to anger? Second, how do males and females compare in their attitude and response to psychotherapy? At the confluence of these two streams of research arises the third question: How do answers to the first two questions feed into anger treatments that can meet the shared and particular needs of males and females?

The research relevant to these questions is spread out across different areas of psychology and spans a period of approximately three decades. Attention is directed to more recent empirical studies appearing in this century and meta-analytic and narrative reviews that cumulate the literature available at different points in time. Preceding the three central issues posed in this chapter is a brief clarification of terminology. Toward the end of the chapter are two case studies illustrating anger and its treatment in a male and a female.

TERMINOLOGY

The term *gender* is increasingly distinguished from other terms such as *sex*, *gender identity*, and *gender role* (Lee, 2005). Whereas sex is a biological category, gender is more of a personal construct (Lorber & Farrell, 1991; Rothenberg, 2010). Thus, gender identity is one's perception of self on a continuum of masculinity–femininity. Gender role is a social construct referring to the extent to which one's work and other activities fit with the sociocultural norms for males versus females. In most of the literature reviewed here, the terms *gender* and *sex* are used interchangeably. When citing other authors, we retain their particular choice of terms unless there is reason to correct any potential confusion.

Another set of terms often used interchangeably encompasses *anger*, *hostility*, *aggression*, and *violence*. These have been elaborated upon in Chapter 1 of this volume. As indicated, anger is typically viewed as an emotion, though it can also take the form of a mood (as in irritability/irascibility) and a temperament (as in hostility). In all its forms, anger is essentially an unpleasant feeling. Inherent in it are (a) a cognitive appraisal of wrongdoing and (b) a motivation to counter or redress that wrongdoing in ways that may range from retaliation to resistance. Aggression is behavior intended to hurt or inflict injury/damage; it can be physical or verbal/psychological. Violence is reserved for behavior that, as intended, results in physical injury or damage. As emphasized in Chapter 1, anger need not lead to aggression or violence, and the latter two behaviors need not entail anger. However, the three often co-occur. This chapter is primarily concerned with anger, but it also taps into relevant research on aggression and violence where the anger is implicit.

The term *gender inclusive* is adopted from the work of Hamel and Nicholls (2007) and numerous authors within that volume. It stems from the idea that anger and related problems of aggression and violence are not exclusive to either males or females. To the extent that these phenomena occur in females as well as males, both groups are candidates for appropriate treatment. However, this does not suggest a generic treatment of anger, but one that is gender informed—by research on (a) how males and females differ in anger and (b) how they differ in their approach and response to treatment. We now turn to these two questions in succession.

ARE THERE GENDER DIFFERENCES IN ANGER?

The prevailing opinion on this issue has been succinctly stated by Kring (2000) in her landmark review: "Conventional wisdom suggests that anger is a 'male' emotion: women don't get angry, and if they do, they certainly don't show it" (p. 211). Research on stereotypes tells us that most people surveyed believe that men and women do not differ in the *experience* of anger (Johnson & Shulman, 1988; Smith et al., 1989) and that women *express* less anger than men (Birnbaum & Croll, 1984; Fabes & Martin, 1991). These stereotypes surface even among preschoolers when they are asked to make attributions about emotionally ambiguous vignettes (Parmley & Cunningham, 2008).

Some writers in the feminist tradition approach this question from the perspective of the whole emotional spectrum as it differs between women and men. Shields (2002) remarks: "Emotion is identified as feminine, but anger, a prototypical emotion, is identified as masculine" (p. 11). Calling this the "gendered response view of emotion," Ross and Van Willigen (1996) elaborate:

> Women respond with depression; men with anger. Gendered response predicts that men have higher levels of anger than women because men are socialized for competitive and combative roles that allow and even encourage the outward expression of anger. In contrast, women, especially mothers, are socialized for nurturing, caring, and supportive roles that discourage anger, so they turn their frustrations and hostilities inward, which increases depression but decreases anger (p. 574).

Calling upon clinical wisdom, Sharkin (1993) recognizes there may be some truth to the idea of suppressed anger in women and uninhibited anger in men. However, he hastens to point out that these may reflect extreme ends of functioning peculiar to the particular population of men and women who seek professional help. Such a dichotomy may not be representative of anger in society at large. Reviewing empirical studies in the wider arena, he maintains, "If anything is to be concluded at this point, it is that few significant gender differences with anger seem to exist" (p. 388).

Given the widespread notion of anger suppression in women, Bartz, Blume, and Rose (1996) hypothesized that controlling for social desirability confounds would wipe out the gender differences in reported anger. They administered the State Trait Anger Expression Inventory (STAXI; Spielberger, 1988) and the Marlowe-Crowne Social Desirability Scale (MCSDS; Crowne & Marlowe, 1960) to a sample of more than 500 college students in introductory psychology classes. Regression analyses showed that gender and its interaction with social desirability and negative affect accounted for *less than 1%* of the variance in STAXI scores for anger. Moreover, in both males and females, the STAXI scores (with the expected exception of the anger control subscale) were negatively related to social desirability bias; the negative correlation was highest between anger-out and social desirability bias, $r = -.44$. So, although anger was minimally different between males and females, its outward expression was dampened by impression management—regardless of gender. In a more recent study of students, Carlozzi et al. (2010) had 53 students from eighth and ninth grades complete the STAXI. No significant gender differences emerged on any of the anger subscales.

Turning to clinical subjects, Fernandez and Scott (2009) administered the STAXI to chemically dependent inpatients prior to anger management. STAXI scores showed no gender differences on any of the six subscales except for anger-in. Women patients had significantly higher internalized anger, as depicted in Figure 12.1. Additional details emerged from the anger that patients self-monitored between treatment sessions. Averaged across individuals, the frequency of anger was significantly higher in women (3.15 episodes per week) than men (0.92 per week) and the duration of anger was substantially longer in women (296.46 minutes per week) than men (107.69 minutes per week), but the average peak intensity of anger was higher in men (5.12) than women (4.22) (see Figure 12.1). Taken together, this suggests that in men, the anger tends to occur as outbursts: intense but relatively brief and occasional. In women, on the other hand, possibly because of greater inhibition, anger is less intense but more prolonged and frequent. By examining these and other parameters of anger activity as in the Anger Parameters Scale (Fernandez, Vargas, & Garza, 2010; Garza, Fernandez, & Vargas, 2011), a new level of detail can be incorporated in the search for gender or individual differences in anger.

In summary, Kring's conclusion that "gender differences are far outnumbered by gender similarities in anger" (2000, p. 224) is upheld if assessment is directed at the experience of anger as a whole. However, as psychometric developments allow us to deconstruct the concept of anger into multiple parameters of anger activity, we may become more adept at detecting some subtle and interesting individual or group differences in anger.

THE EXPRESSION OF ANGER

Beyond the frequency, duration, and intensity parameters, one way in which anger can be further deconstructed is in terms of expression styles. Here the question is

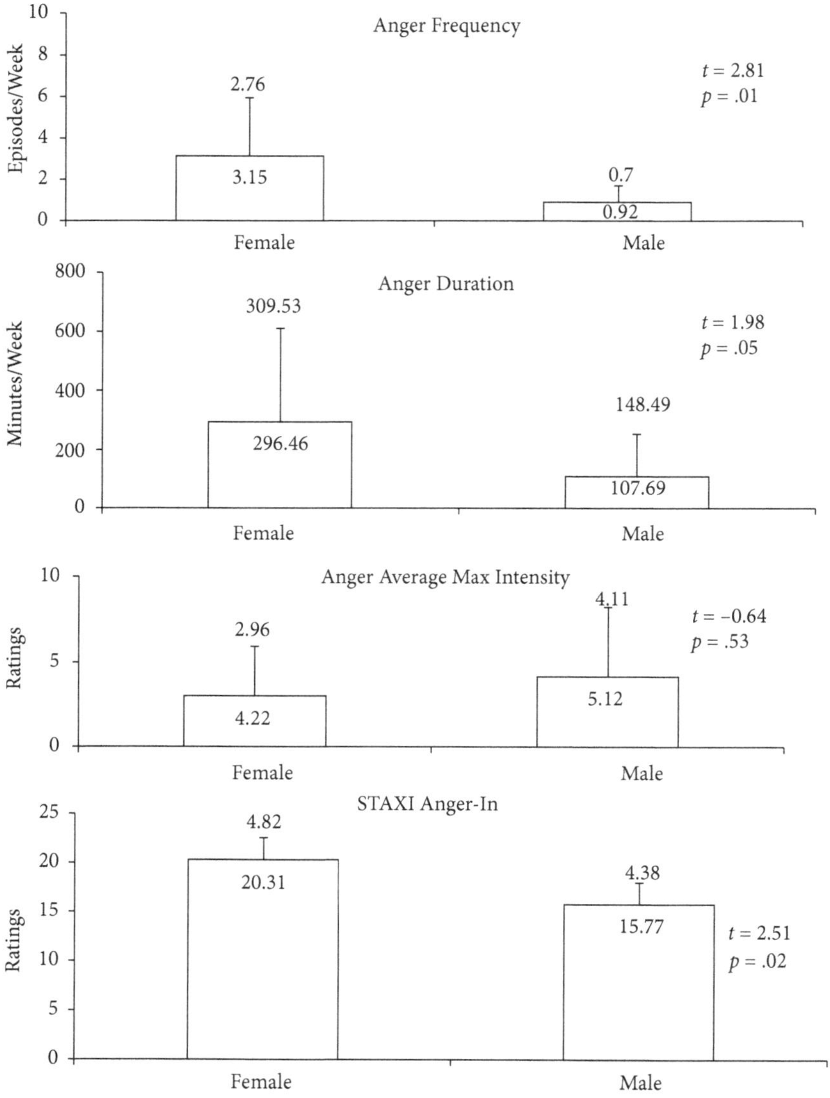

Figure 12.1 Self-monitored anger and STAXI anger-in, by gender. Based on Fernandez and Scott (2009).

not one of how often, how long, or how much anger, but rather "How is the anger expressed?"

The question of gender differences in anger expression has often evoked a dichotomous answer: Men express whereas women suppress anger. For instance, it has been argued that women suppress anger because society is patriarchal (Lerner, 1977) and because it is inconsistent with their nurturant role as mother and wife (Friday, 1977). In contrast, "Men are, quite simply, taught to be emotionally inexpressive, except for the emotion of anger and rage. Men tend to transform all negative or painful emotions into anger again and again" (Long, 1987, p. 309).

Again, the STAXI is a source of some relevant data on this matter. In this instrument, anger expression is basically distinguished into anger-in versus anger-out, the former referring to suppressing anger within oneself, the latter referring to expressing anger to others. Bartz et al. (1996) reported minimal gender differences in STAXI anger expression scores for college students. An examination of norms for the STAXI-2 (Spielberger, 1999) reveals significant gender differences in the means for several *individual* items pertaining to anger-in and anger-out. However, when norms are examined for the subscales, males and females tend to be minimally different.

In a classic survey of anger, Averill (1983) reported that in college students and community residents, there was no significant gender difference in frequency or intensity of anger, though women were four times more likely to cry when angry. Thomas (2003) has further observed that women are usually more inclined than men to talk about their anger either with the instigator or with a confidante.

In an experimental study, Kring and Gordon (1998) found no gender differences in reported anger or other emotional responses to a film clip, though women displayed more negative facial expressions and men had higher skin conductance reactivity. Thomas (2004) found that both American and French women were inclined to somatize their anger in the form of headache, dizziness, and dyspepsia. This may also be connected to Freud's view that suppressed anger is converted into depression, which, as it turns out, is more common in women than men (Cox, Van Velsor, & Hulgus, 2004).

Quantitative integration of results across studies raises hopes for a more reliable answer to this present question. However, early attempts at synthesizing research on male–female differences in aggression and anger were restricted to North American samples, drew heavily from laboratory experiments, and used select classes of dependent measures. Therefore, Archer (2004) conducted a meta-analysis of sex differences in aggression and anger as measured by observation, peer report, and self-report data from real-world settings such as schools, colleges, mental health settings, and the community at large; included were studies from North America as well as other countries. Results were expressed in terms of effect size, positive values indicating that males scored higher than females, and negative effect sizes indicating the reverse.

Archer (2004) found that for direct physical aggression, the mean weighted effect size was .39 on self-report measures, .53 on observations, .40 on teacher reports, and .84 on peer reports. These values were notably less for verbal aggression, where effect size was .30 for self-report, .14 for observations, .24 for teacher reports, and .51 for peer reports.

Analysis of indirect aggression as indexed by the Buss-Durkee Hostility Inventory (BDHI; A. H. Buss & Durkee, 1957) yielded effect sizes in the female direction: −.74 on observations, −.19 on peer ratings, −.13 on teacher ratings, and −.16 on "displaced aggression." In other words, BDHI items that tap into such behaviors as gossiping and social ostracism were endorsed to a greater extent by women than men. With regard to anger that was measured by self-report, the effect size was negligible at −.003.

The overall picture from the Archer (2004) meta-analysis of almost 200 studies is captured in Figure 12.2. As can be seen, males exceed females in direct physical aggression (average effect size across all dependent measures = .53) and less so

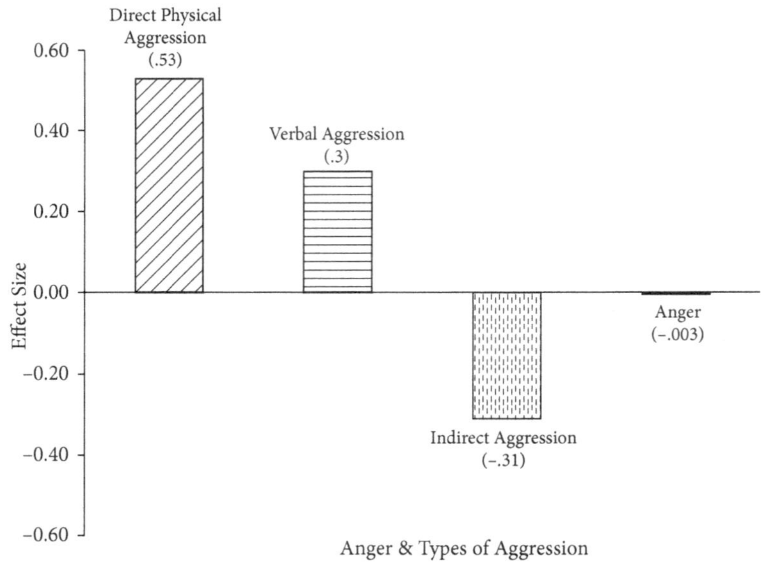

Figure 12.2 Gender-difference effect sizes for anger and types of aggression. Positive effect size indicates males > females; negative effect size indicates females > males. Based on meta-analysis by Archer (2004).

in verbal aggression (average effect size across all dependent measures = -.31). On indirect aggression, females exceeded males (average effect size across all dependent measures = −.31). This contrasts with the near absence of any difference in anger between males and females (average effect size = −.003).

Collectively, the meta-analytic findings reinforce the idea that anger is an emotion open to considerable modulation before it is expressed in the form of aggression. The same provocation that leads to identical levels of anger in four individuals may be accompanied by physical aggression in one, verbal aggression in another, indirect aggression in a third, and no aggression whatsoever in the fourth. It is not the amount of anger but its expression that most differentiates males and females. Unfortunately, as noted by Archer (2004), the indirect aggression/anger scale on the BDHI confounds behaviors related to anger externalization and behaviors related to anger displacement. As elaborated in Chapter 1 of this volume,, it is possible to disentangle these into separate scales called "locus" and "direction" of anger, in addition to incorporating four other important dimensions of anger expression. This could allow an even greater degree of detail in the specification of gender or individual differences in the manifestation of anger.

In their summary of other reviews, Fischer and Evers (2010) concluded that physical aggression is higher in men and verbal aggression slightly higher in men. While not altogether incorrect, this overlooks the sex of the opponent. As pointed out by Archer (2004), "Although there is a consistent difference in the male direction for same-sex opponents, there is nearly always a difference in the female direction for opposite-sex opponents" (p. 297). With the common practice of sexual segregation early in childhood, most male aggression at this early stage is toward other males. Adulthood is when the cross-gender aggression becomes more apparent, as shown in the next section.

INTIMATE RELATIONSHIPS AND ANGER

As explained in Chapter 1, it is a mistake to equate violence (or, for that matter, aggression) with anger or vice versa. Though correlated, one can occur without the other. Armed robbery may be motivated by material greed, vandalism by a sense of thrill, and rape by sheer lust (Fernandez, 2008). However, it is a safer assumption to say that violence between intimate partners is likely to be an offshoot of anger rather than of greed, amusement, or hedonic urge. Therefore, our examination of gender differences in anger is next extended to this particular kind of relationship.

The question "Who is the perpetrator?" in intimate partner violence (IPV) has been a matter of controversy (Kurz, 1993; Straus, 1993). The National Violence Against Women Survey (Tjaden & Thoennes, 2000) reported 41% of female as compared to 19% of male respondents suffering physical injury in the preceding year. However, National Family Violence Surveys (Straus, 1993) reported that 25% of men and 25% of women admitted to engaging in unilateral acts of violence; furthermore, both partners had physically assaulted each other in the preceding year. In a recent and extensive book devoted to domestic violence, Hamel (2007) observed, "Other large surveys, longitudinal studies, and research on dating populations reveal high levels of mutual violence, some well above 50%, and initiated at roughly equal rates by both genders" (p. 8). Increasingly, there is a call for studying and treating not only the so-called male batterers but also partner-abusive women (Graham-Kevan, 2007, 2009; Leisring, 2011).

Where there is a gender difference in IPV is in the means of delivering violence. In men, this usually involves the use of fists to beat up their partners (e.g., Straus & Gelles, 1990). In women, IPV is more likely to be meted out with the aid of weapons and other implements and in a more surreptitious manner (e.g., Cook, 1997).

More important (from a clinical perspective) are gender differences in the aftermath of IPV. Women are the ones who sustain a greater number and severity of physical injuries in these relationships (Johnston & Campbell, 1993). Moreover, women report feeling more fear of injury (e.g., Morse 1995). The aftermath encompasses psychological distress, too. As reviewed by Hamel (2007), "In the majority of studies conducted on the effects of physical abuse, females report higher levels of anxiety, fear, depression, posttraumatic stress, health problems, substance abuse, and lost wages due to days missed on the job than males" (p. 10).

It should be pointed out that research on anger in close relationships has focused on heterosexual couples. Though hardly confined to heterosexual couples, anger, aggression, and violence have only recently become the subject of enquiry in lesbians and gay men. The family is a complex mosaic of other relationships with their own unique patterns of anger, aggression, and violence (Malley-Morrison, 2004). In fact, of all the types of family violence, that between/among siblings is the most prevalent (Caffaro & Con-Caffaro, 1998; Finkelhor, Ormrod, Turner, & Hamby, 2005). There has been much attention to parental abuse of children and (more recently) elder abuse (Malley-Morrison, Nolido, & Chawla, 2006). However, the research that has been accumulating on these relationships is not always explicitly linked to anger and therefore is best left as an interesting arena for further investigation but outside the bounds of this article.

SETTINGS: WORK AND HOME

The foregoing findings echo the conclusion reached by Kring (2000): "Gender differences are far outnumbered by gender similarities in anger" (p. 224). We take up her call for a progression from the global question of anger differences between men and women to the question of the context and elicitors of anger in men versus women.

One context where both gender and anger have a presence is the work environment. Given that annoyances average about 10 per day for individuals in the work environment and anger is experienced by 25% of individuals in the workplace (Bensimon, 1997), this is the one context where gender differences in anger invite some scrutiny. Yet, a perusal of 257 undergraduate students' narratives about workplace anger revealed that women and men were not dissimilar in the number or type of issues that provoked their anger, for example, anger over coworkers' performance, work performance of supervisors, relationships with coworkers or supervisors, interacting with subordinates, or dealing with the public or other factors such as pay scales, promotion opportunities, and administrative policies (Gianakos, 2002). Furthermore, no gender difference was found in the ways of coping with anger. Control-related and escape/avoidance-related responses were used by both males and females in expressing anger in organizational work settings.

As Domagalski and Steelman (2007) remark, could organizational norms supersede gender norms for anger? In their study, no significant main effect of gender was found at work: Males and females were equally likely to exercise anger control in the presence of subordinates, to exhibit anger in the presence of subordinates, and to show anger in the presence of their supervisor than in the presence of their subordinate. However, there was a significant interaction between gender and status within the organizational hierarchy, with males of low status being more likely than females of the same status to outwardly express anger in the presence of supervisors.

Fischer and Evers (2011) studied a sample of Dutch men and women who had been in a steady relationship for at least 1 year (on average 3 years). These were classified into traditional (if the man had more hours of paid work) versus egalitarian (if the woman had equal or more hours of paid work). Putting aside the irregularities in such an operational definition, it was found that women in traditional relationships did perceive themselves as having (on average about 29%) less "relational power" than their male partners and they were significantly more inclined to suppress anger than women in egalitarian relationships. However, regardless of relationship type, women were more indirect in their anger expression. There was a main effect of gender on overall anger, with women reporting more anger than men. More often than not, men blamed women for the start of conflict and claimed credit for the resolution of conflict. In general, egalitarian relationships showed fewer gender differences in anger.

LIFE SPAN AND CROSS-CULTURAL CONTEXTS

The meta-analysis by Archer (2004) made the interesting observation of an early age of onset of sex differences in anger/aggression. These differences become apparent as early as 2 years old when males are evidently more aggressive than females. According to Eron, Gentry, and Schlegel (1994), this male tendency to aggressiveness is already in place by 8 years old. If attributed to testosterone, then it can only be prenatal testosterone. As Archer (2004) points out, aggression does not peak when testosterone peaks at puberty in males. Throughout elementary school and high school, males are more overtly angry/aggressive than females (Cox, Stabb, & Hulgus, 2000).

Archer's (2004) meta-analysis revealed that sex differences in physical aggression reached a maximum between 18 and 30 years old, and therefore cannot be due to testosterone that peaks during puberty. Higher levels of indirect aggression in females than males were reflected in peer reports, increased with age, and peaked between 11 and 17 years of age. The declining aggression with age (especially in males) could be due to the corresponding loss of physical strength (Archer, 2004).

The gender difference in indirect expression of anger seems to persist developmentally and cross-culturally. For example, in a sample of high school adolescents in the United States, indirect anger, as measured by the Aggression Questionnaire (A. H. Buss & Warren, 2000) and exemplified by nonconfrontational behaviors like giving someone "the silent treatment," was higher in females than in males, whereas males were higher in direct methods of physical or verbal displays of anger. This was corroborated by ratings from same-sex peers (Fives, Kong, Fuller, & Di Giuseppe, 2011). Indirect forms of aggression (such as ostracism and gossiping) have been found to be much more prevalent in female than male members of the Aka, a hunter-gatherer tribe of Central Africa.

In another cross-cultural study, Ramírez, Fujihara, and Van Goozen (2001) had university students from Japan, the Netherlands, and Spain read vignettes about anger. They found that gender differences in anger arousal or disposition were negligible, with the exception of the Dutch sample, in which males had higher levels of anger than females.

It pays to revisit the meta-analysis by Archer (2004) because of its integration of data from almost 200 studies of people from over a dozen nations around the world. Findings pointed to a male bias in physical aggression, ranging from 0.27 in New Zealand to 1.16 in Israel, the largest effect sizes appearing in children, teenagers, and young adults. Furthermore, it was found that the general pattern shown in Figure 12.1 (males exceeding females in direct physical aggression and less so in verbal aggression, and females exceeding males in indirect aggression) was ecologically generalizable. This pattern held across all 13 nations for self-report, 9 nations for observations, and 5 nations for peer reports. Also, effect sizes were in the male direction but near zero for school samples and in the female direction for community samples.

ELICITORS OF ANGER

Ekman and Friesen (1975) have suggested five main antecedents of anger: frustration, threat, insult, witnessing someone else being violated, and being the recipient of another's anger. Many of these same elicitors have been disclosed by participants in our research projects, psychological events (e.g., insult and deception) far outweighing physical assault as triggers of anger.

Again, "It is within the context of interpersonal relationships where gender differences in anger are most often found" (Kring, 2000, p. 222). For example, in men, anger is more likely to be directed at male strangers, whereas women's anger is more often directed at male partners in a relationship (Allen & Haccoun, 1976; Blier & Blier-Wilson, 1989). This may be one reason why female anger tends to be less publicly visible than male anger.

Within these relationships, Fehr and Baldwin (1996) found that betrayal of trust was the prime anger elicitor regardless of gender, but women were more angered than men when betrayed, rebuffed, neglected, or undeservedly criticized by them. According to D. M. Buss (1989), women were angered more than men by condescending remarks, inconsiderate neglect, rejection, alcohol abuse, and emotional constriction. Men, on the other hand, reported more anger at women's moodiness and self-absorption. Strachan and Dutton (1992) observed that an audiotape of conflict related to sexual jealousy aroused more anger in women than in men.

Recently, Thomas (2004) postulated that we can more effectively uncover the contextual and eliciting conditions of anger by using interviews rather than questionnaires. She has found that such a phenomenological approach yields richer detail than allowed by forced-choice answers or numerically rated items on a questionnaire. Comparison of two phenomenological investigations of anger in males and females reveals rather similar themes underlying anger. One of these themes is the moral element in anger. Denham (2002) found that women judged wrongdoers with reference to moral standards and then evaluated the moral implications of their response to the wrongdoing. In the same way, Thomas (2003) found that in men, anger and the response to it was governed by appraisals of right versus wrong. This, of course, is implicit in the very definition of anger; all anger implies some breach of standards, so no gender differences are expected in this regard. Where thematic variations may reside are in the specifics of morality or value systems. Unfortunately, most views on this matter are still speculative and in need of systematic research.

LESSONS FROM GENDER DIFFERENCES IN PSYCHOTHERAPY

Now that gender differences have been localized to particular parameters of anger activity and particular styles of anger expression, and within particular contexts, we are one step closer to the question of how to treat anger in men versus women. However, an intermediate question needs to be addressed: Are there gender differences in psychotherapy? Two key questions emerge here. First, are men and women suited to different types of therapy? Second, are men and women best matched with a therapist of their own gender? Additionally, are there important gender differences in readiness/motivation for treatment and outcome of treatment that may warrant special consideration when designing anger treatments for men and women? These are the questions to which we now turn our attention.

Type of Therapy

One broad distinction in psychotherapy is between that which is relatively interpretive in nature and that which is predominantly supportive in orientation.

Ogrodniczuk, Piper, Joyce, and McCallum (2001) randomly assigned a sample of 89 patients to interpretive or supportive psychotherapy conditions. The dependent measures related to depression, anxiety, and general distress. It was found that male clients had better outcomes when receiving interpretive therapy, whereas female clients had better outcomes in supportive therapy. This was taken as suggesting that male clients may profit from cognitive problem solving, whereas female clients may benefit from listening and reflection of feeling

In their review of literature on gender-driven preferences for type of therapy, Park and Hatchett (2006) concluded that men are more inclined to directive techniques that emphasize behavioral action and cognition; women, by contrast, tend to prefer experiential counseling that accesses emotional content and promotes catharsis. Furthermore, they cite research that points to a slightly greater male preference for the workshop or psychoeducational format as compared to talk therapy, for which there is a greater female preference. When presented with videos of multimodal therapy versus emotion-focused therapy, males and females did not differ in their preferences. However, as the authors acknowledge, one possible explanation for this is the failure of the experimental manipulation in which subjects were reportedly bored by the hour-long video presentations of each type of therapy; besides, the videos selected may not have been the most appropriate exemplars of each therapeutic orientation.

Also akin to the aforementioned therapeutic styles is the distinction between nondirective techniques versus those that entail more direct confrontation. Nadelson, Notman, and McCarthy (2005) deem the confrontive methods as employed in 12-step programs for alcoholics to be more suited to men than to women. At least for that population, separate rehabilitation programs are now available for substance-dependent women.

Gender of Therapist

In the mental health arena, much deliberation goes into optimizing the fit between provider and patient. One key variable on which therapist and client are often matched is gender. This has ramifications for therapeutic alliance, which may also be referred to as rapport and related to transference.

In their article on gender and psychotherapy, Nadelson et al. (2005) air some popular sentiments about therapy for women: "Many support the view that women should be treated by women in order to avoid being misunderstood or treated from a male-oriented perspective" (p. 414). Would there be a similar misalignment of perspectives when male clients are treated by women therapists? The authors go on to say, "Women often seek women's groups because in groups of men or even in mixed groups they feel powerless, intimidated, and uncomfortable about speaking up" (p. 416). Actually, this is not supported by records of (mixed) group therapies such as the encounter group sessions led by Carl Rogers. The authors add, "The popular belief is that women patients do better in therapy with women therapists because women therapists are more relational, empathic, and less likely to disempower women patients" (p. 417). However, on further examination, they concede that there is little if any evidence to support this. If anything, recent research has revealed that female clients of female therapists have greater difficulty with disclosure than female clients of male therapists or male clients of female therapists (Pattee & Farber, 2008).

In the specific instance of abuse, a victim of the opposite sex is, understandably, more likely to select a same-sex therapist than one of the opposite sex. As Nadelson et al. (2005) point out, females who have been sexually abused are less likely to seek a male therapist than a female therapist. This rule does not apply exclusively to females or males or to abuse in its sexual form: Would the preference for a female therapist remain immutable in cases of female or male victims of female abuse (be it physical or psychological abuse)? Transference, as formulated in psychoanalysis, can be directed at males or females. The more irreconcilable the victim and offender, the more the client's anger or disaffection is expected to generalize to the whole demographic group of the offender; the more the therapist resembles the offender, the more likely the client will experience transference of those feelings from offender to therapist.

Kulish (1989) learned from interviews that the majority of psychoanalysts gave weight to the gender of the therapist as an influencing factor in transference. Recently, Kalb (2002) indicated that classical Freudian psychoanalysis acknowledged but understated the importance of therapist gender in transference. Gender is one of the real and salient characteristics of the analyst that enters into therapy, creating a transferential response that is itself gendered. The impact of concrete aspects of gender on transference, however, fades as therapy progresses.

Transference is viewed as a catalyst for insight in psychodynamic therapy, but it may occasionally prove overwhelming to the ego for such a transferential relationship to be maintained. Much depends on the client's changing needs for support versus challenge in therapy. If the client is ready to work through the conflict with the offender or those of the offender's gender, then what began as therapy from a therapist of the same sex may transition into therapy provided by a therapist of the opposite sex, as in a case example by Nadelson et al. (2005). In mixed-group therapy, both male and female facilitators are often present to accommodate the gender-specific predilections of clients and to create a milieu where cross-gender relationship issues can be addressed.

Another way of handling gender-related transference is outlined by Gestalt therapist Amendt-Lyon (2008). She acknowledges that sometimes a female client prefers a female therapist to work on mother–daughter issues, and other times the same client may prefer a male therapist to work on father–daughter issues. She concedes that as a woman, there are limits to the degree to which she can realistically portray a father. Yet, a good Gestalt therapist endeavors to take on both polarities as well as other points in between:

> Sometimes I inhabit the role of someone's mother and sometimes that of the father.... For instance, I may have been in the role of the patient's father, strict and achievement-oriented (while the patient was a "mama's boy") for a while; suddenly, I may shift to the soft, caring mother who looks upon her child with adoring eyes (while the patient becomes an "adolescent" who wants to escape Mom's affection); next I am experienced as being very much like the patient's grandmother (while the patient is her charming "cavalier"); then I am seen as an interesting, potential sex partner for a few months (while erotic energy charged our relational field and I could "tolerate" this without becoming

> unsure of myself); and finally, as an older woman who happens to be the patient's psychotherapist (at termination) (pp. 111–112).

It is this protean style of the therapist that may vitiate the impact of therapist gender on therapeutic outcome (at least in gestalt therapy). Amendt-Lyon (2008) cites research of Schigl (1999, 2006), which found no gender-based differences in outcome in a sample of more than 400 former patients of Gestalt therapists in Austria. One should therefore be mindful that what clients prefer is not necessarily what helps them most. A meta-analysis by Bowman, Floyd, Scogin, and McKendree-Smith (2001) revealed that although there was a more favorable outcome in therapy provided by females as opposed to males, the effect sizes were too small as to be clinically significant. In therapy, there may be a preference for same-gender dyads as opposed to cross-gender dyads. Of course, that preference might be accommodated where feasible, to minimize discord and to uphold the norms of customer service, though its substantive contribution to outcome is evidently weak.

Readiness and Motivation for Therapy

It is a stable finding that far more women than men seek out therapy (e.g., Ang, Lim, Tan, & Yau, 2004; Komiya, Good, & Sherrod, 2000; Scher, 1990). As Park and Hatchett (2006) have argued, this cannot be explained away in terms of the higher prevalence of disorders (such as depression) in women, for there are other disorders (e.g., substance dependence) that are more prevalent in men. Yet, two thirds of the clients at university counseling clinics are female. Park and Hatchett (2006) view this largely in terms of a gender difference in attitude to therapy as it is portrayed. In their own experimental study, Park and Hatchett (2006) found that females and those with higher scores on the femininity scale (of the Bem Sex Role Inventory; Bem, 1981) were, as predicted, more receptive than males to seeking mental health care.

Once commenced, therapy also persists longer in female than male clients (Korobkin, Herron, & Ramirez, 1998). In a study by Cottone, Drucker, and Javier (2002), a sample of 163 clients with depressive or anxiety disorders received treatment from clinical psychology doctoral students. Findings indicated that client gender, therapist gender, and therapist/client gender matching did not differentially alter psychological symptoms. However, there was a gender difference in attrition. About 15% more female than male clients advanced beyond the intake phase, and 35% more female than male clients completed the 3-month program of therapy. The findings need to be qualified by methodological limitations such as the unbalanced design (more than three times more females than males) and the failure to randomly assign clients to therapists on the basis of gender or other factors.

Therapeutic Outcome

In the earlier-mentioned study of chemically dependent inpatients, Fernandez and Scott (2009) found that gender differences (on anger-in, anger frequency, anger duration, and anger intensity) were apparent prior to anger treatment but diminished over the course of four sessions of anger management. Basically, women and men were both responsive to this program of anger regulation.

Equally important is the issue of gender differences in durability of treatment outcome. In one study of PTSD patients, women reportedly had more durable treatment gains from exposure therapy (Felmingham & Bryant, 2012). Whether this generalizes to anger treatment outcome is a question that calls for further research comparing different treatment modalities.

Owen, Wong, and Rodolfa (2009) studied 93 male and 229 female clients treated by 31 psychotherapists for a range of emotional problems (including relationship difficulties). Data were analyzed by multilevel modeling in which the client was treated as "nested" within the psychotherapist. As expected from a long line of previous research, there was no difference in outcome as a function of client gender, nor was there a difference in outcome as a function of therapist gender.

GENDER-INFORMED TREATMENT OF ANGER

Given the foregoing findings, there are aspects of anger treatment that are broadly applicable to both men and women and other aspects that are better tailored according to gender. Following is a point-by-point summary of these suggestions:

1. Both males and females experience anger sometimes to the point of aggression and violence. Therefore, both groups are appropriate candidates for inclusion in treatment.
2. The expression of anger differs according to gender, with men generally being more direct and women generally being more indirect. This may tie in to the observation that confrontive techniques of psychotherapy are less preferred by women than men. In such cases, anger treatment need not be delivered with the bluntness or brutal honesty that was almost made legendary in the style of Fritz Perls.
3. The eliciting conditions of anger tend to differ a little according to gender, with women more often aggrieved by issues in personal relationships and men more inclined to be provoked by strangers. This, in itself, is not grounds for different techniques. Anger remains an interpersonal emotion for the most part, and treatment needs to address this element, be it with reference to strangers or to intimate partners.
4. In general, informational aspects of therapy are more appealing to men, whereas experiential aspects are more appealing to women. Therefore, anger management workshops may be well received by men, whereas for women anger psychotherapy may be better received than a mere educational workshop.
5. Because there is a pattern of women being more verbal and men more action oriented in their expression of anger, the former are more drawn to verbal psychotherapy, whereas the latter are more drawn to behavior modification. Specific behavioral techniques of anger regulation (e.g., response prevention and stimulus control) may be more appropriate for

men, and women undergoing anger management may seek a greater amount of verbal disclosure and dialogue about anger.

6. Of the verbal psychotherapies, those that are interpretive find greater favor among men, whereas supportive orientations are more favored by women. This difference can be accommodated during the process of reappraising anger: Whereas the strict rational-emotive approach of Ellis may suffice for men, Beck's approach of cognitive coping may be more meaningful for women. In the former approach, dysfunctional anger is often viewed as the product of catastrophizing, entitlement, or personalizing errors that warrant correction; as part of the latter, anger is also attributed to overgeneralizations, but instead of didactic correction, they are framed within the broader context of coping with certain realities.
7. The affective or emotion-focused therapies tend to be preferred by women rather than men. Thus, certain types of art therapy (e.g., painting) are welcomed by women, though dramatic role-playing as in the Gestalt empty-chair technique has, in our experience, been applicable irrespective of gender.
8. Regardless of the aforementioned nuances, the treatment of anger (not unlike other emotional disorders such as depression and anxiety) is facilitated by certain conditions laid down by Carl Rogers: empathy, congruence, and unconditional positive regard. In and of themselves, these are not sufficient for treatment success, but without them, the efficacy of any therapy is compromised.
9. Matching of therapist and client in terms of gender is not crucial in psychotherapy. As in the treatment of other emotional difficulties, a gender-competent therapist for anger problems is one who can build rapport with either a male or a female client. In gender-mixed group therapy, however, it is often a matter of balance in representation that a male and female cotherapist are often present.
10. With regard to the process of therapy, the evidence points to less receptiveness in males than females in the initiation of therapy, and greater attrition in males than females by the completion of therapy. This means that special effort is needed to promote retention of male clients with dysfunctional anger. This may be even more important in mixed groups where a gender balance allows for appropriate role-playing of relationship-related anger scenarios.
11. With regard to treatment outcome, the bulk of evidence indicates minimal gender difference. So, if men and women can endure anger treatment programs, they are both likely to benefit to a comparable degree.
12. Given the gender differences in anger and psychotherapy, it seems a risk to invest in merely one school of therapy. After a few decades of differentiation, the field of psychotherapy is undergoing a transformation toward integration. For anger regulation, too, integrative therapy has its exemplars, such as cognitive relaxation (Deffenbacher, McNamara, Stark, & Sabadell, 1990) and cognitive-behavioral-affective therapy (CBAT; Fernandez, 2010). It is through such an array of techniques that are theoretically based and technically compatible that the different needs of clients can be better accommodated.

A Case Anecdote of Anger and Its Treatment In a Man

When Dr. R read the letter from the neighborhood school, he yelled, "Damn that school if my daughter is not good enough for it" as he crumpled the letter and flung it to the floor. "That's the last time I make any contributions to them," he said, even as his wife urged patience. The next morning, he drove to the school and demanded a meeting with the principal. During that meeting, his voice rose and his hands gestured with anger as he accused the school of exploiting the community and remarked, "Don't we measure up to your standards? Who do you think you are?" The conversation became more adversarial as the principal called in an assistant to sit in on the meeting. At that point, Dr. R remarked that he was leaving and that the school was no better than "an old unwanted warehouse that ought to be burned to the ground along with the lot of you." This was taken as a threat and the school security, which was on standby, was called in. They immediately took Dr. R in for further questioning. After some escalation of the conflict, Dr. R's anger subsided into remorse as he recanted his statement. He explained that he had been sleep deprived from long hours of medical practice and that he did not mean to threaten anyone, though he felt "cheated" that his daughter was refused admission.

At the metropolitan hospital where he worked, Dr. R was generally liked by his patients, though he had had a few heated exchanges with case managers. On one of these occasions, he was known to have yelled, "My patients will keep coming, but if you keep this up, you won't have a job." On another occasion, he referred to a group of medical malpractice attorneys as "scum who deserved to be exterminated or sent to a concentration camp." Because of the fallout from such remarks, one of his associates recommended stress management. Dr. R availed himself of this option.

In the course of consulting a professional psychologist, Dr. R soon acknowledged that his anger was getting him into trouble at work and in the community, though not at home. Retrospective accounts over the preceding year pointed to a pattern of anger that was low in frequency and relatively short in duration, but high in intensity, quick in latency, and moderate in threshold. In other words, though his anger episodes were occasional and brief, he was reacting quickly, and very strongly, sometimes only due to (what most people would regard as) minor provocation. Stylistically, his anger was externalized, verbal with a hint of physical threat, reflected rather than deflected, and relatively uncontrolled, but typically accompanied by remorse and amenable to restoration. This boded well for cognitive-behavioral therapy.

After psychoeducation about anger and its effects on health and functioning, Dr. R readily signed a contingency contract to do his best to minimize his anger intensity and anger immediacy (inverse of latency). He seemed motivated though hurried in his plan to gain control over his anger. He quickly learned to anticipate and prepare for familiar triggers of his anger, especially in his daily routine; for these he was trained in response prevention (in particular moderation of voice, facial expressions, and hand gestures) plus stimulus control (avoiding extreme situations in which anger would be inevitable).

In the intervention phase that followed, Dr. R was trained to counter anger-related arousal by relaxing on cue; this entailed diaphragmatic breathing, progressive muscle relaxation, and autogenic relaxation at the earliest signals of anger. He was also taken through an elaborate process of reappraisal in which he would pose questions to himself such as "Was the wrongdoing intentional?", "What was the real damage done?", and "What would be the outcome of an anger outburst?" Furthermore, he was introduced to conflict resolution and problem solving. This emphasized communication skills that promoted negotiation instead of entitlement, assertiveness rather than intimidation, and movement toward compromise wherever possible. Techniques of thought stopping and distraction were also suggested in case a quick-interrupt mechanism was more practicable in the short run.

In the final postvention phase, Dr. R was familiarized with outlets for the safe expression of residual anger. These ranged from written disclosure to expressive art. He was not particularly drawn to these techniques, though he asked if baseball and playing percussion would be appropriate substitutes. The answer, as he was advised, was affirmative, especially in case of any anger that lingered after his attempts at intervention.

These techniques were presented to Dr. R in a skills-training format over eight sessions. By the end of the treatment program, the client's self-monitored data showed a marked decline in intensity and inverse latency (quickness) of anger, as well as a drop in frequency. At 1-month and 3-month follow-ups, the client evidenced maintenance of these treatment gains. He also reported being relatively free of anger-related problems at work and in other settings; this was confirmed by collateral reports from his wife.

A Case Anecdote of Anger and Its Treatment in a Woman

Mrs. S tried to maintain a semblance of professional interaction with her new colleague, though she harbored growing resentment toward him. After weeks of giving him instructions that sounded like orders, criticizing details of his work, and watching him "like a hawk," she was also hindering his efforts to improve anything in the office on the grounds that "he did not understand the history of the organization." She could not bring herself to interact with him but began to complain in private to her superior and to coworkers. Soon, "work became a headache" that continued till she got home; there, she would remain irritable with her husband. When the latter paid little attention, she would get frustrated to the point of giving him the "silent treatment," often abdicating her usual household responsibilities and neglecting any incoming mail such as bills to be paid. Motivated by the growing discord, she referred herself for counseling.

The female counselor soon determined that Mrs. S's anger was primarily attributable to her problems at work. The anger was found to be relatively low in intensity but long in duration, as if Mrs. S were holding it in like a long-standing grudge. In terms of style of anger expression, Mrs. S was deflecting this anger from work onto her spouse at home. Never physically aggressive, she would resort to sarcastic and curt comments. Rather than retaliating, she was more inclined to be "resistant" toward her husband. Toward her colleague at work, she never had an angry outburst but was covertly aggressive to ensure he would not be hired beyond the probationary period. She had gone so far as to circulate anonymous complaints about him to other administrators. Although she asserted that this was necessary, it seemed to trouble her sense of morality somewhat.

Mrs. S was admitted to an anger treatment group that began with psychoeducation. The counselor explained the health consequences of anger, including somatization into physical symptoms such as headaches, which Mrs. S complained about. Though Mrs. S argued that most people did not regard her as an angry person, she acknowledged having concealed a lot of her anger. She signed a contingency contract to reduce her suppressed anger, especially to "get over" her grudges by expressing grievances more constructively. As part of response prevention, she learned to refrain from indirect channels of anger at work and "dumping" of anger at home. As part of stimulus control, she also identified and learned to avoid one situation that inevitably drove her to annoyance—attending (nonmandatory) Friday lunches with her new colleague who had a penchant for talking about antique cars.

In a subsequent phase of intervention, Mrs. S acquired the skill of countering anger-related arousal by relaxing on cue; this entailed diaphragmatic breathing, progressive muscle relaxation, and autogenic relaxation at the inception of anger. She also learned the elaborate process of reappraisal, which was designed to dispute anger-related cognitions by such questions as "Was the wrongdoing intentional?". "What was the real damage done?", and "What would be the outcome of an anger outburst?" A further component consisted of communication skills for problem solving and conflict resolution. These placed a premium on direct interaction rather than subversive acts, well-meaning feedback rather than a façade of approval, and movement toward compromise wherever possible. Thought stopping and distraction were also included as potentially quick-interrupt mechanisms against anger.

Finally, in the postvention phase, Mrs. S was introduced to outlets for the safe expression of any residual anger. These included a variety of mediums from written disclosure to expressive art. Mrs. S showed much enthusiasm for this as a usable approach in her home environment. She built on her talent for visual art by painting whenever there was pent-up anger. She found the Gestalt empty-chair technique helpful in rehearsing how to address others with whom she was angry. Finally, she mentioned a preference for weekly individual counseling that would give her the chance to talk in confidence with a professional instead of "dumping on her husband" or indulging in poorly regulated chat sessions at work.

By the end of the group treatment program, Mrs. S's self-monitored data revealed a substantial decline in duration of anger, as well as a drop in anger quickness (inverse of latency). These treatment gains were maintained at 1-month and 3-month follow-ups. Along with her self-reported reduction in anger, Mrs. S reported a reduction in the frequency and duration of her headaches. Her improved physical and emotional health in this regard was confirmed by collateral feedback from her husband.

CONCLUSION

The previous case studies illustrate how to isolate particular points of dysfunctional anger in people. By examining the five parameters (frequency, duration, intensity, latency, and threshold), it is further possible to generate a profile of the person. In the case of the male client, that profile approximates the *Diagnostic and Statistical Manual of Mental Disorders* (DSM) criteria for intermittent explosive disorder. In the case of the female client, the profile may be aptly described as passive aggressive personality disorder. These certainly do not typify either males or females, and they do not constitute the main categories of anger dysfunction, but they do serve as examples of the unique configurations that can emerge in the context of idiographic investigation.

Throughout this chapter, there has been a search for gender differences in the experience and expression of anger and the attitude and response to psychotherapy. However, the evidence does not permit us to make inferences about any individual client on the basis of gender ipso facto. It would be a grave mistake to infer direct or indirect anger, physical or nonphysical expression of anger, passive aggressive or explosive anger, or receptiveness and response to treatment purely on the basis of whether the client is male or female. Any associations that have emerged here are merely probabilistic rather than definitive. There is enormous room for individual differences, which may even exceed any differences along the lines of gender or other sociodemographic categories for that matter.

ACKNOWLEDGMENTS

Thanks to Professor Penny Leisring of Quinnipiac University for comments on an earlier draft of this manuscript.

REFERENCES

Allen, J. G., & Haccoun, D. M. (1976). Sex differenced in emotionality: A multidimensional approach. *Human Relations, 29*, 711–722.

Amendt-Lyon, N. (2008). Gender differences in Gestalt therapy. *Gestalt Review 12*, 106–121.

Ang, R. P., Lim, K. M., Tan, A., & Yau, T. Y. (2004). Effects of gender and sex role orientation on help-seeking attitudes. *Current Psychology: A Journal for Diverse Perspectives on Diverse Psychological Issues, 23*, 203–214.

Archer, J. (2004). Sex differences in aggression in real-world settings: A meta-analytic review. *Review of General Psychology, 8*, 291–322.

Averill, J. R. (1983). Studies on anger and aggression: Implications for theories of emotion. *American Psychologist, 38*, 1145–1160.

Bartz, A. E., Blume, N. E., & Rose, J. (1996). Gender differences in self-report measures of anger: The role of social desirability and negative affect. *Journal of Social Behavior and Personality, 11*(5), 241–253.

Bem, S. L. (1981). Gender schema theory: A cognitive account of sex typing. *Psychological Review, 88*, 354–364.

Bensimon, H. F. (1997). What to do about anger in the workplace. *Training and Development, September, 51*, 28–32.

Birnbaum, D. W., & Croll, W. L. (1984). The etiology of children's stereotypes about sex differences in emotionality. *Sex Roles, 10*, 677–691.

Blier, M. J., & Blier-Wilson, L. A. (1989). Gender differences in self-rated emotional expressiveness. *Sex Roles, 21*, 287–295.

Bowman, D., Floyd, M., Scogin, F., & McKendree-Smith, N. (2001). Psychotherapy length of stay and outcome: A meta-analysis of the effect of therapist sex. *Psychotherapy: Theory, Research, Practice, Training, 38*, 142–148.

Buss, A. H., & Durkee, A. (1957). An inventory for assessing different kinds of hostility. *Journal of Consulting Psychology, 21*, 343–349.

Buss, A. H., & Warren, W. L. (2000). *Manual: Aggression questionnaire*. Los Angeles, CA: Western Psychological Services.

Buss, D. M. (1989). Conflict between the sexes: Strategic interference and the evocation of anger and upset. *Journal of Personality and Social Psychology, 5*, 735–747.

Caffaro, J., & Conn-Caffaro, A. (1998). *Sibling abuse trauma: Assessment and intervention strategies for children, families and adults*. Binghamton, NY: Haworth Maltreatment & Trauma Press.

Carlozzi, B. L., Winterowd, C., Harrist, R. S., Thomason, N., Bratkovich, K., & Worth, S. (2010). Spirituality, anger, and stress in early adolescents. *Journal of Religious Health, 49*, 445–459.

Cook, P. (1997). *Abused men: The hidden side of domestic violence*. Westport, CT: Praeger.

Cottone, J. G., Drucker, P., & Javier, R. A. (2002). Gender differences in psychotherapy dyads: Changes in psychological symptoms and responsiveness to treatment during 3 months of therapy. *Psychotherapy: Theory/Research/Practice/Training, 39*(4), 297–308.

Cox, D. L., Stabb, S. D., & Hulgus, J. F. (2000). Anger and depression in girls and boys: A study of gender differences. *Psychology of Women Quarterly, 24*, 110–112.

Cox, D. L., Van Velsor, P., & Hulgus, J. F. (2004). Who me, angry? Patterns of diversion in women. *Health Care for Women International, 25*(9), 872–893. doi:10.1080/07399330490493412

Crowne, D. P., & Marlowe, D. (1960). A new scale of social desirability independent of psychopathology. *Journal of Consulting Psychology, 24*, 349–354.

Deffenbacher, J. L., McNamara, K., Stark, R. S., & Sabadell, P. M. (1990). A combination of cognitive, relaxation, and behavioral coping skills in the reduction of general anger. *Journal of College Student Development, 31*, 351–358.

Denham, G. (2002). The essence of women's moral perspectives in anger expression situations. *Journal of Psychiatric and Mental Health Nursing, 9*, 391–397.

Domagalski, T. A., & Steelman, L. A. (2007). The impact of gender and organizational status on workplace anger expression. *Management Communication Quarterly, 20*(3), 297–315.

Ekman, P., & Friesen, W. V. (1975). *Unmasking the face*. Englewood Cliffs, NJ: Prentice-Hall.

Eron, L. D., Gentry, J. H., & Schlegel, P. (Eds.). (1994). *Reason to hope: A psychosocial perspective on violence and youth*. Washington, DC: American Psychological Association.

Fabes, R. A., & Martin, C. L. (1991). Gender and age stereotypes of emotionality. *Personality and Social Psychology Bulletin, 17*, 532–540.

Fehr, B., & Baldwin, M. (1996). Prototype and script analyses of laypeople's knowledge of anger. In G. J. O. Fletcher & J. Fitness (Eds.), *Knowledge structures in close relationships: A social psychological approach* (pp. 219–245). Mahwah, NJ: Lawrence Erlbaum.

Felmingham, K. L., & Bryant, R. A. (2012). Gender differences in the maintenance in response to cognitive behavior therapy for posttraumatic stress disorder. *Journal of Consulting and Clinical Psychology, 80*, 196–200.

Fernandez, E. (2008). The angry personality: A representation on six dimensions of anger expression. In G. J. Boyle, D. Matthews, & D. Saklofske (Eds.), *International handbook of personality theory and testing: Vol. 2: Personality measurement and assessment* (pp. 402–419). London, England: Sage Publications.

Fernandez, E. (2010). Toward an integrative psychotherapy for maladaptive anger. In M. Potegal, G. Stemmler, & C. Spielberger (Eds.), *The international handbook of anger: Constituent and concomitant biological, psychological, and social processes* (pp. 499–514). New York, NY: Springer.

Fernandez, E., & Scott, S. (2009). Anger treatment in chemically-dependent inpatients: Evaluation of phase effects and gender. *Behavioural and Cognitive Psychotherapy, 37,* 431–447.

Fernandez, E., Vargas, R., & Garza, C. (May, 2010). *Five parameters for mapping the angry person: Results from a community sample.* Presented at the Association for Psychological Science 22nd Annual Convention, Boston, MA.

Finkelhor, D., Ormrod, R., Turner, H., & Hamby, S. (2005). The victimization of children and youth: A comprehensive national survey. *Child Maltreatment, 10*(1), 5–25.

Fischer, A. H., & Evers, C. (2010). Anger in the context of gender. In M. Potegal, G. Stemmler, & C. Spielberger (Eds.), *The international handbook of anger: Constituent and concomitant biological, psychological, and social processes* (pp. 349–360). New York, NY: Springer.

Fischer, A. H., & Evers, C. (2011). The social costs and benefits of anger as a function of gender and relationship context. *Sex Roles, 65,* 23–34.

Fives, C. J., Kong, G., Fuller, J. R., & DiGiuseppe, R. (2011). Anger, aggression, and irrational beliefs in adolescents. *Cognitive Therapy and Research, 35,* 199–208.

Friday, N. (1977). *My mother/my self.* New York, NY: Delacorte.

Garza, C., Fernandez, E., & Vargas, R. (May, 2011). *The five parameters of anger: A configural analysis.* Presented at the Association for Psychological Science 23rd Annual Convention, Washington, DC.

Gianakos, I. (2002). Issues of anger in the workplace: Do gender and gender role matter? *Career Development Quarterly, 51*(2), 155–171.

Graham-Kevan, N. (2007). Distorting intimate violence findings: Playing with numbers. *European Journal of Criminal Policy Research, 13,* 233–234.

Graham-Kevan, N. (2009). The psychology of women's partner violence: Characteristics and cautions. *Journal of Aggression, Maltreatment and Trauma, 18,* 587–603.

Hamel, J. (2007). Domestic violence: A gender-inclusive conception. In J. Hamel & T. L. Nicholls (Eds.), *Family interventions in domestic violence: A handbook of gender-inclusive theory and treatment* (pp. 3–26). New York, NY: Springer Publishing.

Hamel, J., & Nicholls, T. L. (Eds.). (2007). *Family interventions in domestic violence: A handbook of gender-inclusive theory and treatment.* New York, NY: Springer Publishing.

Johnson, J. T., & Shulman, G. A. (1988). More alike than meets the eye: Perceived gender differences in subjective experience and in its display. *Sex Roles, 19,* 67–79.

Johnston, J., & Campbell, L. (1993). A clinical typology of interpersonal violence in disputed-custody cases. *American Journal of Orthopsychiatry, 63*(2), 190–199.

Kalb, M. B. (2002). Does sex matter? The confluence of gender and transference in analytic space. *Psychoanalytic Psychology, 19*(1), 118–143.

Komiya, N., Good, G. E., & Sherrod, N. B. (2000). Emotional openness as a predictor of college students' attitudes toward seeking psychological help. *Journal of Counseling Psychology, 47*(1), 138–143.

Korobkin, S. B., Herron, W. G., & Ramirez, S. M. (1998). Severity of symptoms of depression and anxiety as predictors of duration of psychotherapy. *Psychological Reports, 82*, 427–433.

Kring, A. M. (2000). Gender and anger. In A. H. Fischer (Ed.), *Gender and emotion: Social psychological perspectives* (pp. 211–231). Cambridge, England: Cambridge University Press.

Kring, A. M., & Gordon, A. H. (1998). Sex differences in emotion: Expression, experience, and physiology. *Journal of Personality and Social Psychology, 74*, 686–703.

Kulish, N. M. (1989). Gender and transference: Conversations with female analysts. *Psychoanalytic Psychology, 6*(1), 59–71.

Kurz, D. (1993). Social science perspectives on wife abuse: Current debates and future directions. In D. Kurz (Ed.), *Violence against women: The bloody footprints* (pp. 252–269).Thousand Oaks, CA: Sage Publications. Retrieved from http://search.proquest.com/docview/618388877?accountid=7122

Lee, J. (Ed.). (2005). *Gender roles*. New York, NY: Nova Biomedical Books.

Leisring, P.A. (2011). Top 10 reasons why women's perpetration of intimate partner violence is an important area of enquiry. *Partner Abuse, 2*, 452–467.

Lerner, H. (1977). The taboos against female anger. *Menninger Perspective, 8*, 4–11.

Long, D. (1987). Working with men who batter. In M. Scher, M. Stevens, G. Good, & G. A. Eichenfield (Eds.), *Handbook of counseling and psychotherapy with men* (pp. 305–320). Newbury Park, CA: Sage.

Lorber, J., & Farrell, S. A. (Eds.). (1991). *The social construction of gender.* Newbury Park, CA: Sage Publications.

Malley-Morrison, K. (2004). Introduction. In K. Malley-Morrison (Ed.), *International perspectives on family violence and abuse: A cognitive-ecological approach* (pp. 3–13). Mahwah, NJ: Lawrence Erlbaum Associates Publishers.

Malley-Morrison, K., Nolido, N. E., & Chawla, S. (2006). International perspectives on elder abuse: Five case studies. *Educational Gerontology, 32*(1), 1–11.

Morse, B. (1995). Beyond the Conflict Tactics Scale: Assessing gender differences in partner violence. *Violence and Victims, 10*(4), 251–269.

Nadelson, C. C., Notman, M. T., & McCarthy, M. K. (2005). Gender issues in psychotherapy. In G. O. Gabbard, J. S. Beck, & J. Holmes (Eds.), *Oxford textbook of psychotherapy* (pp. 411–420). New York, NY: Oxford University Press.

Ogrodniczuk, J. S., Piper, W. E., Joyce, A. S., & McCallum, M. (2001). Effect of patient gender on outcome in two forms of short-term individual psychotherapy. *Journal of Psychotherapy Practice and Research, 10*(2), 69–78.

Owen, J., Wong, Y. J., & Rodolfa, E. (2009). Empirical search for psychotherapists' gender competence in psychotherapy. *Psychotherapy Theory, Research, Practice, Training, 46*(4), 448–458.

Park, H. L., & Hatchett, G. T. (2006). Do sex, sex role orientation, and exposure to gender-congruent therapy models influence receptivity to psychotherapy? *Journal of College Student Psychotherapy, 20*(3), 3–17.

Parmley, M., & Cunningham, J. G. (2008). Children's gender-emotion stereotypes in the relationship of anger to sadness and fear. *Sex Roles, 58*, 358–370.

Pattee, D., & Farber, B. A. (2008). Patients' experiences of self-disclosure in psychotherapy: The effects of gender and gender role identification. *Psychotherapy Research, 18*(3), 306–315.

Ramírez, J. M., Fujihara, T., & Van Goozen, S. (2001). Cultural and gender differences in anger and aggression. *The Journal of Social Psychology, 141*, 119–121.

Ross, C. E., & Van Willigen, M. (1996). Gender, parenthood, and anger. *Journal of Marriage and the Family, 58*, 572–584.

Rothenberg, P. S. (2010). *Race, class, and gender in the United States: An integrated study.* New York, NY: Worth Publishers.

Scher, M. (1990). Effect of gender role incongruities on men's experience as clients in psychotherapy. *Psychotherapy: Theory, Research, Practice, Training, 27*, 322–326.

Schigl, B. (1999). Wirkung und Wirkfaktoren von Gestalttherapie aus katamnestischer Sicht der KlientInnen Ausgewählte Ergebnisse einer evaluativen Untersuchung. *Neue Entwicklungen in der integrativen Gestalttherapie: Wiener Beiträge zum Theorie-Praxis-Bezug*, 222. Retrieved from http://www.mitglied.lycos.de/gestalt-therapie/Studie.pdf

Schigl, B. (2006). Doing gender by doing therapy, Überlegungen zu einer gendersensiblen Gestalttherapie mit frauenspezifischem focus. *Gestalttherapie Zeitschrift für Gestaltperspektiven, 2*, 97–107.

Sharkin, B. S. (1993). Anger and gender: Theory, research, and implications. *Journal of Counseling and Development, 71*, 386–389.

Shields, A. (2002). *Speaking from the heart: Gender and the social meaning of emotion.* New York, NY: Cambridge University Press.

Smith, K. C., Ulch, S. E., Cameron, J. E., Cumberland, J. A., Musgrave, M. A., & Tremblay, N. (1989). Gender-related effects in the perception of anger expression. *Sex Roles, 20*, 487–499.

Spielberger, C. D. (1988). *State-Trait Anger Expression Inventory.* Orlando, FL: Psychological Assessment Resources.

Spielberger, C. D. (1999). *Professional manual for the State-Trait Anger Expression Inventory-2 (STAXI-2).* Odessa, FL: Psychological Assessment Resources.

Strachan, C. E., & Dutton, D. G. (1992). The role of power and gender in anger responses to sexual jealousy. *Journal of Applied Social Psychology, 22*, 1721–1740.

Straus, M. (1993). Physical assaults by wives: A major social problem. In R. Gelles & D. Loseky (Eds.), *Current controversies on family violence* (pp. 67–87). Newbury Park, CA: Sage.

Straus, M., & Gelles, R. (1990). *Physical violence in American families.* New Brunswick, NJ: Transaction Publishers.

Thomas, S. P. (2003). Men's anger: A phenomenological exploration of its meaning in a middle-class sample of American men. *Psychology of Men and Masculinity, 4*, 163–175.

Tjaden, P., & Thoennes, N. (2000). *Extent, nature, and consequences of intimate partner violence: Findings from the National Violence Against Women Survey.* NCJ 181867. Washington, DC: U.S. Department of Justice.

13

Culture-Sensitive Regulation of Anger

A. ANTONIO GONZÁLEZ-PRENDES

The impact of culture on interpretations of mental health cannot be underestimated and is best summarized in a statement by the former Surgeon General of the United States, Dr. David Satcher, who stated that "what it means to be mentally healthy is subject to many different interpretations that are rooted in value judgments that may vary across cultures" (U.S. Department of Health and Human Services [USDHHS], 1999, p. 5). Definitions of culture commonly refer to the heritage of a people characterized by shared beliefs, values, meanings, and symbolic representations, which are transmitted from generation to generation and manifested in traditions, behaviors, and standard practices (Ashford, LeCroy, & Lortie, 2006; Cormier, Nurius, & Osborn, 2009; Robbins, Chaterjee, & Canda, 2006; Zastrow & Kirst-Ashman, 2007). At the same time, practitioners working with culturally diverse populations need to adopt a broad perspective that considers other dimensions of culture, beyond race and ethnicity, which influence the process of adaptation such as gender, language and other forms of expression (e.g., music, writing, food), religion, socioeconomic status, elements of discrimination and oppression, geography, and politics (McGoldrick, Giordano, & Garcia-Preto, 2005). Cultural differences may exist not only among individuals from various countries or nationalities but also among racial/ethnic groups that reside within the same society. Therefore, practitioners should be alert to individual cultural adaptations, brought on by the process of acculturation, among persons of the same cultural heritage.

Culture-sensitive therapeutic approaches should account for how clients' problems are affected by sociocultural variables that influence how they experience their environment. Such environment may provide or limit access to empowering resources necessary for the implementation of healthy, prosocial solutions. Also to be accounted for are how sociocultural norms regulate the way one responds to life events. Sue and Sue (as cited in Ivey, D'Andrea, & Ivey, 2012) suggest that the culturally competent practitioner is one who:

- is aware of his or her assumptions about human behavior and appreciates his or her own culture while recognizing its possible inherent biases about human behavior and mental health;

- appreciates the client's cultural background and understands its impact on the client's style of emotional expression, world- and self-views, and help-seeking practices; and
- tailors interventions to be congruent with the client's culture.

Therefore, drawing conclusions about a client's beliefs and behaviors without evaluating those beliefs and behaviors against the framework of the client's culture runs the risk of pathologizing a behavior that may be quite accepted and adaptive within the client's culture. For instance, consider that in some cultures the behavior of "holding eye contact" is seen as a sign of straightforwardness and honesty. In those cultures the *lack* of eye contact may be interpreted as a sign of avoidance, dishonesty, deception, or shame. However, not all cultures place the same meaning on eye contact. In some other cultures (e.g., Zapotec Indians and other indigenous groups in Mexico), such blatant and direct eye contact is seen as a sign of disrespect, particularly when it is among strangers or with someone who is considered a superior (e.g., a mental health practitioner). Lack of such cultural awareness could create a level of cultural dissonance between the client and therapist that undermines the process of therapy. This was the case of a 23-year-old Chinese American, female college student who sought help for feelings of depression through her university's counseling center. She attributed her depression to her parents' asking her to pursue a particular career path in which she had no interest. At a point in the counseling process, the counselor encouraged the woman to adopt a more assertive stance toward her parents. However, she came from a traditional Chinese family, with a hierarchical structure in which assertively confronting her parents was anathema to the family's culture. Therefore, the prospect of confronting her parents raised her anxiety and exacerbated her situation. Moreover, she believed that it would be disrespectful to challenge the counselor (whom she saw as an authority figure) on his suggestion of assertiveness. To escape her mounting anxiety, the client eventually withdrew from therapy. The counselor believed that assertiveness was a suitable intervention to help the client confront her parents. However, within the framework of the client's Chinese cultural background, the assertive confrontation of her parents was seen as disrespectful and disruptive of family harmony. Thus, the value of maintaining harmony within the family trumped the value of assertiveness. This form of cultural dissonance, rooted in the lack of cultural competency on the part of mental health practitioners, has been suggested as one of the factors that contribute to the underutilization of mental health services and high treatment dropout by ethnic minorities in the United States (Griner & Smith, 2006; Ponterotto, 1987; Rios-Elliot et al., 2005).

In 2001, *Mental Health: Culture, Race and Ethnicity, A Supplement to Mental Health: A Report of the Surgeon General* (USDHHS, 2001) called for increased research focusing on racial and ethnic minorities to develop increased cultural competency and establish evidence-based treatments for such populations. However, as Hays (2006) points out, even though the past 15 years have seen an increase in books that address cultural issues, this publicity has not translated into research that focuses exclusively on minority groups. Whaley and Davis (2006) also emphasized the need for culturally adapted interventions of empirically supported mental health treatments to address the needs of ethnic/racial minority populations. A meta-analysis of 76 studies by Griner and Smith (2006) evaluated outcomes associated with culturally adapted mental health interventions and reported an overall positive effect of such interventions. Interventions adapted to participants of the same cultural group were four times more effective than interventions provided to groups consisting of mixed participants. The researchers suggested that cultural adaptations of mental health interventions are more efficacious when they are tailored to specific cultural groups. Furthermore, Griner and Smith (2006) concluded that even multicultural adaptations of interventions (i.e., designed to be sensitive to various cultural groups) are still more efficacious than those with no cultural adaptations.

ANGER AND CULTURE

A culture-sensitive approach to effective anger regulation must consider the intricate relationship between anger and culture and how cultural norms and display rules shape culturally approved expressions of anger. For instance, Mauss, Butler, Roberts, and Chu (2010) compared Asian American and Euro-American college women with regard to the value that each group places on emotional control and their responses to anger provocation. The authors reported that Asian American women experienced less anger and displayed less intense forms of anger expression than the Euro-American women. The authors further indicated that differences in emotional experience and expression were partially mediated by the relative value each group placed on emotional control, thus suggesting the potential influence of cultural background on the experience and expression of anger.

Matsumoto, Hee Yoo, and Chung (2010) assert that expressions of anger can be found across cultures, albeit with some culture-specific modifications and variability. Along similar lines, Olatunji, Lohr, and Bushman (2007) suggest that across cultures anger has an evolutionary role that serves as an adaptive response to a perceived threat. Similarly, Kövecses (2000, 2010) argues that the conceptualization of anger has universal aspects that cut across cultures (e.g., the metaphor of anger as a heated, pressurized container residing within the human body) as well as culture-specific elements (e.g., the prototypical model for venting anger). It has been suggested that established cultural rules along two key dimensions, *collectivism–individualism* and *masculinity–femininity*, have a regulating effect on how individuals adjust and respond emotionally to situations, as well as on their subjective perceptions of well-being, happiness, and distress (Fernández-Berrocal, Salovey, Vera, Extremera, & Ramos, 2008; Okazaki & Tanaka-Matsumi, 2006). Consequently, it would seem that emotional expression within a particular culture would be mediated by whether the culture places a greater value on a collective orientation of interdependence and social harmony or whether it places a greater value on an individualistic orientation of independence and self-determination. When it comes to anger, some authors have suggested that cultural norms and display rules, universal and culture specific, influence the expression of anger and underscore the appropriateness of such anger expression (Adam, Shirako, & Maddux, 2010; Konwar & Ram, 2004; Matsumoto et al., 2010). Similarly, it has been suggested that one of the universal aspects in the conceptualization of anger across cultures is the notion that anger is generally seen as a divisive and disruptive element, with the potential to cause social disorganization, chaos, and intragroup aggression (Matsumoto et al., 2010; Potegal & Novaco, 2010). Potegal and Novaco (2010) further assert that this perspective is more pronounced in collectivist societies that place a greater value on maintaining internal equilibrium and social harmony rather than in societies with a more individualistic and egalitarian perspective. Therefore, when it comes to the open and direct expression of anger or other negative emotions, collectivist societies would be less likely to approve the overt and amplified expression of such negative emotions (i.e., anger) than individualistic societies. As Hatch and Forgays (2001) suggest, the process of learning emotional regulation begins early in life. This was illustrated in a study by Keller and Otto (2009) comparing cultural socialization of emotional regulation during infancy in two contrasting communities. The Nso group, a rural farming community of northwest Cameroon (a collectivistic society), was compared to Western urban families from northern Germany (an individualistic society). Differences in early-life socialization strategies showed that the Nso group taught children early in life to control emotions with special emphasis on the suppression of negative emotions, whereas the German group emphasized the expression of emotions, particularly the maintenance of positive emotionality.

Nonetheless, practitioners should avoid making sweeping generalizations based on the collectivistic–individualistic dimension and in the process risk overlooking intraculture variability. That is, culture-sensitive mental health practitioners must guard against overlooking the differences (e.g., socioeconomic, religious, educational, political, etc.) that may exist among members of the same racial/ethnic/cultural group and how such differences may impact upon emotional regulation in general and anger regulation in particular. Therefore, rather than making broad and sometimes mistaken assumptions about the influence of culture on a particular individual, practitioners need to be cognizant of the level of acculturation and adaptation exhibited by the individual client. This may indicate how closely the individual identifies with the beliefs and values or adheres to the traditions and customs of the original culture. This point is particularly relevant when working with immigrants or first- or second-generation individuals who live within a larger dominant culture that is not their original one. For this purpose, Berry's model of acculturation (Berry, 2003; Sam & Berry, 2010) provides a framework for evaluating a person's level of acculturation. The model identifies four acculturation strategies: integration, assimilation, separation/segregation, and marginalization. It also identifies two dimensions that underscore the level of identification and engagement that individuals have with their original and adopted cultures: (a) *cultural maintenance,* which looks at the degree to which individuals identify with or maintain their heritage culture; and (b) *cultural engagement,* which looks at the degree to which individuals are engaged with and participate in the daily life of the larger culture. For example, according to Sam and Berry (2010), assimilation is the acculturation strategy that individuals use when they do not wish to maintain identity with their original culture and, instead, seek to fully participate in the host culture. The main point here is that although it is important to appreciate the general contextual framework of the client's culture, it is equally important to appreciate the uniqueness of each individual who seeks mental health treatment. Practitioners should strive to understand the person's level of acculturation as well as the psychological changes and adaptation associated with the particular acculturation strategy.

It has also been suggested that the experience and expression of anger within a given cultural group may be mediated by emotional control values and gender role socialization that dictate the culture-appropriate behaviors for emotional experience and expression for men and women (Cox, Van Velsor, & Hulgus, 2004; Fischer & Evers, 2010; Hatch & Forgays, 2001; Mauss et al., 2010; Tanaka-Matsumi, 1995). Yet, across cultures the direct and overt expression of anger tends to be more accepted in men than in women (Kövecses, 2000; Stearns, 1994). For instance, it has been suggested that in American society women are socialized to see the direct expression of anger as a possible threat to relationships and one that may result in social rejection (Hatch & Forgays, 2001). Consequently, such anger is often left in silence or diverted to either indirect forms of anger expression or other pathologies (Cox, Stabb, & Bruckner, 1999; Cox et al., 2004; Cox & St. Clair, 2005; Hatch & Forgays, 2001; Munhall, 1993; Sharkin, 1993; S. P. Thomas, 1989).

The need to maintain an appreciation for the uniqueness of the client was illustrated in a discussion of a single case study on the treatment of anger in an African American woman (González-Prendes & Thomas, 2009). In this case the authors suggested that, if treatment of anger in African American women is to be successful, practitioners must address the contextual nature of anger, including culture-based expectations of strength that may contribute to increased stress and anger. For instance, some authors (Beaubeouf-Lafontant, 2007; Harris 1995; Martin, 2002; S. A. Thomas & González-Prendes, 2009; Thompkins, 2004) have argued that for African American women, historical and culture-bound expectations of strength often create unrealistic expectations and demands to help others while ignoring their own distress. González-Prendes and Thomas (2009) suggested that this may create a double bind for the woman: On the one hand she may experience anger and resentment related to the lack of control over her own life and the lack of attention to her own needs, and on the other hand she may feel that expressing anger and dissatisfaction is nothing more than complaining, and therefore a sign of weakness. The authors further suggested that an important aspect of treatment was to help the woman rewrite the script of these messages to construct a more balanced and realistic view of herself, nurture the historical and cultural tradition of strength in a more self-empowering manner, and develop a healthier and more functional sense of personal responsibility for her anger.

Multiculturalism in Psychotherapy

Multicultural therapy has been described as a "metatheoretical approach to helping...composed of an array of therapeutic strategies and techniques that assist mental health professionals in working more effectively, respectfully, and ethically with persons from diverse groups and backgrounds" (Ivey et al., 2012, p. 497). Hays (2008) suggests that multicultural therapy is not a form of therapy per se, but rather a reconceptualization and adaptation of other therapies to make them more responsive to the cultural contexts of clients.

In a discussion of culturally responsive cognitive-behavioral therapy (CBT), Hays (2009) provides 10 suggestions to help integrate cultural considerations into CBT: (a) assess the client's needs for culturally respectful behavior; (b) identify cultural strengths and supports, including the role of religion or spirituality and other forms of internal and environmental supports; (c) clarify and separate the internal (e.g., cognitive) from the environmental influences on the problem with particular attention to cultural factors; (d) address environmentally based problems by increasing individual strengths and supports and building culturally congruent skills that will help the client interact more effectively with the social environment; (e) validate self-reported experiences of oppression; (f) emphasize collaboration over confrontation as this will enhance a sense of client–therapist alignment and client empowerment, particularly among minority clients; (g) avoid seeming insensitive to cultural beliefs and behaviors (the therapist may want to question the "helpfulness" or utility of a thought rather than its validity); (h) avoid challenging core cultural beliefs; (i) develop culturally congruent helpful self-statements based on the client's culturally related strengths and supports; and (j) formulate homework assignments that align with the client's culture and that include the client's input.

Culture-Sensitive Assessment of the Problem

A culture-sensitive regulation of anger should begin with the therapist conducting a thorough, wide-ranging, and comprehensive assessment of the client's sociocultural environment (Okazaki & Tanaka-Matsumi, 2006). This should include an evaluation of the various systems and influences that impact the client's life (e.g., family; socioeconomic status; educational/work skills; legal issues; health, including physical illnesses and disabilities; cultural/racial identity; religion/spirituality; gender; age; and cognitive development) as well the specifics of the presenting problem. A comprehensive assessment could help to identify areas of conflict that may be contributing to the client's anger (e.g., experiences of racism, ethnocentrism, homophobia, disempowerment conditions, and helplessness) as well as sources of strength (e.g., family support, ethnic identity, etc.) and cultural significance (e.g., spirituality). Two models that lend themselves to this type of assessment are identified by their acronyms: the RESPECTFUL model by Ivey et al. (2012) and the ADDRESSING model by Hays (2008). The RESPECTFUL model includes 10 factors that affect the way clients construct meaning from their life events: (R) religion and spirituality; (E) economic class; (S) sexual identity; (P) psychological maturity; (E) ethnic/racial identity; (C) chronological challenges; (T) traumatic experiences and threats to one's well-being; (F) family history and identity; (U) unique physical characteristics; and (L) location of residence and language. Hays's ADDRESSING model recognizes the influences of (A) age and generational factors; (DD) disabilities: developmental and acquired in later life; (R) religion and spirituality; (E) ethnic and racial identity; (S) socioeconomic status; (S) sexual orientation; (I) indigenous heritage; (N) national origin; and (G) gender. These approaches allow for a systematic exploration and evaluation of critical areas of cultural meaning to the client and a conceptualization of the problem that is attentive to the client's sociocultural background. For instance, the assessment of the client's identification with and adherence to religious or spiritual practices can provide valuable information as to preferred ways of coping and responding to life's events, including the role of anger expression. For example, in a description of culturally sensitive care of a Muslim patient (Lawrence & Rozmus, 2001), the authors indicated that, for Muslims, a major illness is considered God's will and therefore the expression of anger at the illness would be deemed as inappropriate.

Culture-Sensitive Regulation of Anger

Although the research in the area of culture-sensitive regulation of anger is scant at best, some authors have suggested that a multimodal approach that integrates diverse therapeutic strategies may be an effective option when working with culturally diverse populations (Fernandez, 2010; Hancock & Siu, 2009). But, how do we begin to conceptualize and develop effective and culturally sensitive approaches to regulate anger? As a starting point, we can look at Kövecses's (2000, 2010) discussion of universal aspects in the conceptualization of anger. Kövecses investigated how anger is conceptualized across four different cultures and languages: English, Hungarian, Chinese, and Japanese. The author suggested that there are commonalities among the various culturally based conceptual models. In the four models anger is seen as a force that follows a pattern that progresses through several stages. Commonalities among the stages include the following:

- The presence of a cause or triggering effect
- Awareness of the existence of anger (i.e., anger arousal)
- Attempt at controlling the expression of anger
- Loss of control over the expression of anger
- Expression in the form of retribution

Kövecses's (2000, 2010) conceptualization model not only provides a framework to assess anger by exploring triggers, level of arousal, and expressions of anger but also could serve to identify possible points of intervention. These may include strategies to identify triggers and implement steps to prevent the escalation of anger; interventions to lessen the intensity of anger arousal such as time-out, thought stopping, relaxation, mindfulness, or cognitive reframing; or finding creative and culture-congruent ways to help express anger effectively and prosocially through verbal communication, musical expression, or creative writing.

Another option in the development of effective and culturally sensitive approaches to regulate anger is to consider developing cultural adaptations to mainstream therapies. For instance, traditional CBT approaches have been deemed to be appropriate and efficacious with culturally diverse populations (see Hays & Iwamasa, 2006). Some of the reasons given for this are the emphasis that CBT places on empowerment, its collaborative nature that lets the client define the problem and the desired goals of therapy, the need to tailor interventions to the needs of the person, the ongoing process of case formulation throughout therapy that elicits and respects the client's views on the progress of therapy, and a nonjudgmental approach and appreciation for the strengths and uniqueness of the individual (Hays, 2009). At the same time, the CBT practitioner must recognize that CBT, like most mainstream psychotherapies, is rooted in Eurocentric perspectives of individualism, self-determination, intrapsychic phenomena, and rationality (Abudabbeh & Hays, 2006; Kelly, 2006). The risk here for the uninformed practitioner is that he or she may overlook or discount elements of oppression in the client's life, the importance of spirituality, and prevalent attitudes of interdependence and social harmony that are characteristics of some cultures.

Multicomponent Treatment

The more diverse the clients are, the more likely their needs can be met in a multicomponent treatment. This idea is consistent with using an integrative psychotherapy approach to work with diverse populations. As compared to singular monolithic treatments, multicomponent treatments integrate cognitive, behavioral, affective, experiential, insight, and art-based strategies, among others, to work with culturally diverse clients (Elligan, 2000; Fernandez, 2010; González-Prendes & Thomas, 2009; Hays, 2009). One example of a multicomponent approach to treatment was described by Elligan (2000) in what he called rap therapy. In this single case study Elligan (2000) incorporated the use of rap/hip hop music and creative writing into a CBT and social learning theory model to form a culturally sensitive approach to psychotherapy to regulate anger and reduce aggression with a young African American male. Following the initial assessment, which included an evaluation of the influence of rap music in the young man's life and building the therapeutic alliance, rap music and creative writing were used as a means of facilitating cognitive reframing and allowing the client to emotionally process issues in his life that fueled his anger and that otherwise had not been addressed (e.g., the death of his father, who had been murdered). Elligan (2000) used behavioral strategies such as modeling, role-playing, and positive reinforcement to encourage writing and facilitate the transition from writing to action. As Elligan points out, this transition is evident in a decreased and eventual extinction of angry outbursts and the implementation of prosocial behaviors to effectively regulate the anger. For instance, initially the young man was encouraged to use rap or poetry to write about the death of his father and the adverse impact that his anger expression had on his mother. The young man then transitioned to speaking about these issues with his mother and the therapist. Finally, he began to identify and put in place alternative strategies that were consistent with his writing to handle his aggressive impulses and reduce anger outbursts in the classroom with teachers and students. Throughout the process the therapist modeled and reinforced the desired behaviors.

Another novel therapy that integrates techniques for anger treatment in diverse populations is Fernandez's (2010) cognitive-behavioral-affective therapy (CBAT). This is a sequential integration of cognitive, behavioral, and affective strategies at the various stages of the treatment process: prevention, intervention, and postvention. During the prevention phase, the client receives education on various aspects of anger and engages in a behavioral contract with the goal of minimizing maladaptive anger. A contingency point system is used to reward the client's progress toward the goal. Other strategies used during this phase include self-monitoring, behavioral rehearsal (e.g., role-playing anger-triggering events), response prevention (e.g., a more functional response than the usual maladaptive one), and stimulus control. The intervention phase may include thought-stopping strategies, reappraisal of the assumed intentionality on the part of the offender, distraction, autogenic relaxation, and situational imagery. In the postvention stage, a number of affective and art/creative strategies may help the client address persistent, residual anger. At this phase the empty-chair technique may help the client to safely experience and express residual unexpressed anger. Drawing from diverse traditions in psychotherapy, Fernandez (2010) also suggests using creative strategies such as writing (e.g., writing a letter about unresolved anger), painting, music, and sculpting, suggesting that "art offers a universally applicable medium for the expression of anger" (p. 509).

González-Prendes and Thomas (2009) presented a single case study that describes a three-phase culture-sensitive multimodal therapy to treat anger in an African American woman. The treatment was delivered in a three-stage process that incorporated many of the client's identified strengths (e.g., aptitude for music, poetry, spirituality, racial/cultural identity) with psychoeducation about various aspects of anger, cognitive strategies (challenging and reframing dysfunctional beliefs), behavioral strategies (self-monitoring, relaxation, assertiveness and conflict resolution skills, role-play, experiential activities, imaginal exposure), and mindfulness/meditation. The initial assessment of the client included an ecological person-in-environment approach that identified important sociocultural factors that gave special meaning to the client's action. Culture-influenced messages about the responsibilities of being "a strong Black woman" that were deemed to contribute to her experience of anger and stress prior to treatment were addressed, nurtured, and reframed in a more empowering manner. At the end of treatment the client had experienced significant anger reduction and felt more empowered to regulate her anger and express her feelings in a more effective and healthier direction.

Case Vignette

Charles, a 33-year-old, single, African American male, was mandated to attend anger treatment following a scuffle with a work supervisor who was thought to have made a racist remark. The supervisor pressed charges and Charles was charged with assault and sentenced to probation for 2 years and ordered to attend anger management. He remained at his job pending successful completion of anger management therapy. Charles had had similar anger outbursts at work where he was either verbally or physically aggressive.

Coming to treatment. At first, Charles came to treatment with a serious and guarded demeanor. Though not manifestly angry or hostile, he did not hide the fact that he would rather not be there. He clearly stated that he did not have a problem with anger, and that the only time he would get angry was when he was provoked by other people. When asked to elaborate on that point, he stated that the only thing that would make him angry was when others went out of their way to "disrespect" him. He further indicated that he believed that the only reason he was in his current predicament was because the supervisor was a White man. Charles then proceeded to elaborate on what he saw as the unfairness and injustices experienced by Black men in American society. He was convinced that if the altercation had occurred between two Black men or two White men, the outcome would have been different and it would have never ended up in court. Charles's initial perspective on the problem was important because it provided a contextual framework of the sociocultural environment of the client where the intersection of race (Black) and gender (male) were key factors to understand Charles's reality. A conscious effort was made to convey to Charles an understanding of the challenges faced by a Black man within the larger American society, particularly a man with Charles's background: incarceration, poor education, and underdeveloped work skills. Moreover, he grew up without a father in a low-socioeconomic environment that provided few opportunities for advancement, and one where toughness and aggressiveness were valued and rewarded with some level of respect.

Assessment. Besides an evaluation of the presenting problem, a comprehensive assessment was conducted to identify key influences in Charles's life, as well as the reciprocal interaction that Charles had with various systems. The aim was to identify potential sources of strength and conflict to be addressed in therapy. A brief summary is presented below:

***Family*:** Charles had strong relationships with his mother and his 4-year-old daughter (strengths). He spent time with his daughter, took her to the park, and went for ice cream. He indicated that his daughter was his source of motivation and that he wanted to be the type of father for her that his father was not for him (strength). His father abandoned Charles at age 7, and this was a source of anger and resentment in his life (conflict). He had a good relationship with his half-brother. He was not married but maintained a friendly relationship with the mother of his daughter.

***Education/work skills*:** Charles dropped out of school in the 11th grade. He liked to read and write and listen to music (strengths).

Employment/work skills: Charles performed mostly manual labor and had no formal work skills training (conflict). He had worked at his present place of employment for 3 years. By all accounts he was a responsible worker who did not miss time from work (strength). However, he was at risk of losing his job due to anger outbursts of verbal and physical aggression (conflict).

Health including illnesses and disabilities: Charles was in good health (strength). He enjoyed playing sports and other physical activities.

***Cultural/racial identity*:** Charles strongly identified with African American life and history, particularly with the struggles of the civil rights movement (strengths).

***Religious/spirituality*:** Charles was not a religious person. However, he saw himself as a spiritual individual (strength).

***Legal*:** Charles served 5 years in prison from ages 20 to 25 for possession and distribution of illegal substances. While in prison he improved his reading and writing skills. During his teen years he smoked marijuana, but now he did not use any illicit drugs and drank beer occasionally. He was on probation for 2 years following the physical altercation with his supervisor (conflict).

Socioeconomic (conflict)*:* Charles grew up poor in the inner city of a large urban community where violence and illegal drug activity were common. Getting respect from others was coveted, and being "disrespected" was a trigger for violence and required retaliation. He learned early in life that an angry and aggressive demeanor was rewarded with "respect" from others. The family supported itself on low-paying jobs and government assistance. He was keenly aware of the lack of opportunities for advancement, and experiences of racism and discrimination fueled his anger.

***Cognitive development*:** Charles was intelligent and insightful (strengths).

***Gender*:** Charles was an African American male with a prison record. He believed that he was stereotyped and the target of discrimination because of his race and gender (conflict).

***Age*:** No significant concerns.

Treatment. The treatment approach selected in this case was CBT, which has been found to work effectively in reducing anger (Beck & Fernandez, 1998; Deffenbacher, Dahlen, Lynch, Morris, & Gowensmith, 2000; Reilly & Shopshire, 2000). The anger treatment for Charles was a multimodal, culturally adapted CBT approach with three stages similar to those outlined in Meichenbaum's stress inoculation training approach (1985, 1996). Each stage had specific general objectives that provided a framework for the work to be done in each stage. In the *first stage* the overall objectives of therapy for Charles were:

- building a collaborative alliance with the client and identifying his strengths;
- gathering detailed information about the presenting problem and formulating a case conceptualization that not only included cognitive and behavioral elements but also framed the problem against the client's sociocultural background;
- educating the client about the problem and enhancing the level of motivation to address the problem.

In the *second stage* the overall focus of treatment was to introduce Charles to specific skills that were congruent with his sociocultural background and that would help to regulate anger effectively. This included:

- recognizing the early onset of and derailing anger episodes; and
- using cognitive strategies to reframe anger-inducing thoughts and applying behavioral strategies to monitor anger and rehearse socially appropriate responses to potentially problematic situations.

The *third stage* of treatment focused on:

- applying and generalizing therapeutic gains to the client's life outside therapy;
- reinforcing successes and troubleshooting problems in regulating anger; and
- anticipating and planning how to address possible future roadblocks.

The first stage. If therapy with Charles were to succeed, it would be necessary to establish a sound collaborative alliance. This proved to be a challenge. Influenced by his social environment, Charles held the belief about the world as a hostile, dangerous, and unforgiving place; he viewed people as untrustworthy and unreliable. Consequently, he had adopted rules of conduct that encouraged the use of anger and aggression to deal with problems. Although Charles admitted that at times he acted angrily and aggressively, he rationalized these behaviors as the outcome of being picked on by a larger society that denied him opportunities based on his race and social location, and by superiors who in his view had prejudices against him due to his race and prison record. A culture-sensitive outlook of the presenting problem compels the practitioner to consider the issue within the sociocultural context of the client. Therefore, when Charles's anger was framed against the realities of his sociocultural/political environment (i.e., African American male with a prison record, growing up without a father in the inner city of a large urban community with significant violence and drug-related activity, with poor education, even poorer opportunities for advancement, and experiences of racism and discrimination), it was not difficult to understand his experience of anger. Some authors suggest that the perception of injustice or moral violation is an important factor in the experience and expression of anger (Kassinove & Sukhodolsky, 1995; Potegal & Novaco, 2010; Wranik & Scherer, 2010). Furthermore, Potegal and Novaco (2010) point out historical events (e.g., the feminist movement, Abraham Lincoln's stand against slavery and slave owners) where the experience of anger based on the appraisal of real injustices led to action aimed at correcting the perceived problem. One could argue that a number of other social-political movements (e.g., civil rights, gay and lesbian rights, etc.) grew out of the similar accurate perception of maltreatment and oppression perpetrated on a group of people and inspired corrective political and social action. When appropriate, it is important for practitioners to formulate and clearly convey to the client an understanding of the anger against the framework of his or her sociopolitical environment. However, such an understanding does not necessarily imply an approval of the client's self-defeating and maladaptive behavior. In such cases the challenge is to help the client implement effective prosocial action to correct the injustice or unfair treatment. During the initial stage of therapy, Charles's generalizations about the world and people were not challenged so as to not risk alienating him and engendering defensiveness on his part. Instead, it was decided to adopt a more empathic approach and directly convey to Charles a clear understanding of the difficulties that he was facing in his life. DiGiuseppe (1995) has suggested that in order to navigate this delicate initial phase and establish a collaborative alliance with the angry client, it may be necessary to "acknowledge and validate their frustration and disappointment at the hands of the 'enemy'" (p. 136). Thus, a conscious effort was made to convey to Charles an understanding of the challenges faced by an African American man within the context of the larger American society. Rather than focusing on the maladaptive aspects of his anger, the conversation focused on normalizing aspects of his experience of anger. For instance, the point was made to Charles that it would be common to experience anger in the face of unjust or unfair treatment such as may be reflected in experiences of racism or other forms of discrimination. At that point, Charles began to react differently. His guarded and hostile demeanor appeared to soften and later on in therapy he indicated that for the first time he had felt that someone in authority (i.e., the therapist in this case) understood his position.

Another reason for not initially challenging Charles's experience and expression of anger was that for him, anger had been functional. In his social environment it was important for a man to command respect, and one way to command such respect was by maintaining an angry/aggressive demeanor. From that perspective anger had served him well. Furthermore, he believed that most of his anger-fueled acts of aggression were provoked by being the recipient of others' "disrespectful" behavior toward him. Given the importance of the value of "respect" in Charles's sociocultural milieu, a conscious effort was made during this initial phase of treatment to convey respect to Charles. This was done by directly eliciting Charles's input and explicitly appreciating and valuing such input, and by asking for his permission before introducing or presenting him with new information or suggestions. This process strengthened the therapeutic relationship and empowered Charles by inviting him to be an equal partner in the therapeutic process.

During that initial stage a number of strengths were identified that would eventually be used to advance the process of therapy. Charles was an intelligent and insightful individual who despite a lack of formal education enjoyed reading and writing, two skills he had significantly improved while in prison. He also connected with African American history and the civil rights movement. At the same time, a strong aspect of his character revolved around the relationship with his daughter and his desire to be a good father to her. It was this latter point that would serve as a source to motivate Charles to examine his behavior and to consider possible alternatives that would be in his and his daughter's best interest. Consequently, Charles's problem was framed not as an "anger problem," but rather as a problem with the way he expressed anger. From this perspective, Charles was able to engage in a "pros and cons" evaluation of the behaviors by which he expressed anger. This exercise allowed him to connect with the consequences of his behavior. Charles acknowledged that expressing his anger through aggression could eventually result in his return to prison, resulting in his daughter growing up without her father the same way that he had grown up without his father. Therefore, being available to be a father to his daughter became the motivating factor during the early days of therapy. This compelled Charles to consider learning to regulate his anger in more effective ways that would facilitate attaining his objectives without the use of aggression. Now that Charles was more agreeable to consider working on healthier alternative ways of anger expression, the decision was made, eliciting Charles's permission, to introduce a discussion on the thought–emotion–behavior connection. Using a psychoeducational model, Charles began to focus on how his thoughts affected his emotional and behavioral responses. He agreed to read about this topic, and to facilitate this process, educational materials were introduced in session.

This first phase of therapy generally may last between two and four sessions. In Charles's case, by the end of the fourth session it was felt that there was (a) a collaborative relationship in place, (b) a conceptualization of the case that recognized the thought–emotion–behavior link framed against Charles's sociocultural background, (c) an initial acceptance by Charles that expressing anger through aggression was problematic, and (3) increased motivation to learn alternative ways of expression.

The second stage. The second stage of treatment focused on skills acquisition and rehearsal. The process here took on two tasks. The first task was to help Charles develop skills to address bouts of anger and reduce the probability of acting out aggressively. This included (a) helping Charles to increase awareness of anger triggers and warning signs (i.e., cognitive, behavioral, affective, physiological, and situational); (b) implementing self-monitoring strategies to record the frequency, intensity, and duration of his anger episodes as well as the "where," "when," and "with whom" of his anger; and (c) learning to derail anger episodes before they reached "full steam" (i.e., taking *time-out* by walking away from or avoiding situations that were likely to trigger anger, using *thought-stopping*, *distraction*, *relaxation*, and *mindfulness/meditation* techniques). These strategies were congruent with Charles's sociocultural background. For instance, although Charles did not see himself as a religious person, he did see himself as a spiritual individual who was rather open to using meditation and diaphragmatic breathing for relaxation and to induce a sense of spiritual well-being. His predilection for writing was integrated in therapy. However, Charles did not particularly care for structured logs to monitor his anger; instead, he preferred to process his experiences through free-form writing. He was encouraged to use Ellis's A-B-C paradigm (Ellis & Tafrate, 1997), identifying the activating event, beliefs, and emotional/behavioral consequences associated with specific events, as a framework for his writing. Another self-monitoring strategy relied on Charles's alertness to physical sensations. Here we used an exercise that we called "where do you feel your anger?" The aim was to help Charles to identify in his body the physical signs that warned him of potential anger escalation (e.g., clenching of the jaw, balling of the fist, muscle tightness, etc.). Upon noticing these warning signs, Charles would implement some of the strategies that he had learned and rehearsed in therapy to derail bouts of anger (i.e., time-out, thought stopping, relaxation, etc.). Although these strategies were not considered ultimate solutions to Charles's anger problems, they were valuable tools in helping him avoid the escalation of anger episodes.

The second task of this stage focused on Charles identifying and reframing key cognitions that loaded his anger reactions. Because Charles did not respond well to traditional structured CBT tools to facilitate cognitive and behavioral change (e.g., workbooks, logs, thought records, behavior monitoring schedules, etc.), we adopted a less structured approach that made use of his interest in writing and reading. It was decided that those strengths combined with his interest for Black history and the civil rights struggles of African Americans in the United States would provide the means by which he could begin to reassess and reframe his old perspectives and behaviors and develop healthier cognitive and behavioral alternatives. For instance, on one occasion, he came to therapy experiencing a heightened state of anger and frustration toward his employer due to perceived unjust treatment. This was the type of situation that often had triggered an aggressive response from Charles. However, on that day the focus of that session became, "How would Dr. Martin Luther King have handled the situation in a nonviolent manner?" After he discussed possible alternatives, he was asked what he would need to tell himself to facilitate a reduction of anger and frustration and implement nonaggressive solutions. However, a clinician working with angry clients must recognize that anger could very well be a response to *real* injustice, unfairness, or maltreatment. At that point the challenge is not to get rid of anger, but to help the client reduce the internal level of tension and arousal so that the anger may be channeled into the implementation of prosocial behaviors that may facilitate a resolution of the problem.

Client *empowerment* should be a hallmark of any culture-sensitive therapy, particularly when working with historically oppressed populations. To maintain a theme of empowerment throughout therapy, Charles's input was elicited at all stages of treatment and particularly in the development of homework assignments. He was simply asked, "What do you think would be helpful for you to do during the coming week to reinforce what we talked about here today?" He often considered what Dr. Martin Luther King or some other African American historical figure would have thought or done about a particular issue. This would prompt Charles to read and write about this topic and in the process trigger alternative perspectives and behaviors to his traditional angry and aggressive responses. Other themes that underscored his tendency to anger quickly were addressed using similar strategies. Some of these themes included the tendency to personalize events and see himself as intentionally targeted for maltreatment by others. When Charles had difficulty identifying the thoughts that preceded anger episodes, imaginal exposure exercises were done in session to help him recall and reframe such beliefs. Those occasions also provided opportunities for Charles to use the Upsetness Scale to practice regulating his anger and to identify other nonanger responses to upsetting events

(González-Prendes, 2007). This tool is an adaptation of the anger meter (Reilly, Clark, Shopshire, Lewis, & Sorensen, 1994) and consists of a 10-point subjective scale with increasing levels of upsetness intensity where 1 (lowest level) indicates "mild disappointment" and 10 (highest level) indicates "enraged." The deliberate use of the term *upsetness* instead of *anger* was intended to reinforce the notion of a wider range of emotional responses to upsetting circumstances.

By the end of the second stage, Charles had developed an increased awareness of how his thoughts influenced his emotions and behaviors. Role-play and reverse role-play were used to rehearse behaviors. By this point, Charles had attended 15 weekly sessions, and although he had made significant progress in regulating his anger, he recognized that he was dealing with long-standing beliefs and personality traits that would continue to fuel residual anger and present challenges in his life. Consequently, he agreed to participate in six additional sessions, with the first three sessions meeting every other week and the last three taking place once per month.

The third stage. The third stage of treatment was conceptualized as a maintenance stage with the recognition that some residual anger is likely to surface and that the client may benefit from a less intensive approach to anger regulation therapy. The focus of this stage is primarily to reinforce the successful application of previously learned techniques for anger regulation and to troubleshoot difficulties and setbacks. Writing became the main conduit for Charles to process and work through specific events in his life and express feelings such as positive emotions that he experienced toward his daughter, or to process residual anger that he had toward his father. A continuous challenge was to encourage Charles to translate his writing into healthy action. For instance, writing about his feelings for his daughter or the anger toward his father was one thing, but a more elegant solution was deemed to be not only writing but also verbalizing such feelings in an appropriate fashion.

At the end of the six agreed upon visits, there was mutual agreement to terminate therapy. However, Charles recognized that he would need to continue the work that he had started in therapy. Nevertheless, he felt more confident to do so because he had some tangible tools that he could use for that purpose. Charles had even begun to consider options to improve his life situation (e.g., further his education) beyond just learning to regulate his anger in healthier and more effective ways.

CONCLUSION

Culture-sensitive regulation of anger must be able to attend to salient aspects of the client's culture as well as to the uniqueness of the individual and recognize the role that cultural norms and display rules play in the expression of emotions in general and anger in particular. To overlook this is to risk making stereotypical generalizations about groups of people and thus ignore the uniqueness of the person. This chapter underscored key elements of a general treatment framework to develop and implement culture-sensitive approaches to regulate anger. The point of caution here is that one size does not fit all. As such, clinicians are well advised to consider a multimodal approach when working with culturally diverse clients. Therefore, this framework should be considered as a structure that needs to be completed with assessment and treatment strategies that are sensitive to the particular cultural characteristics and needs of the client. Elements of this framework are (a) conducting a comprehensive, culture-sensitive assessment that identifies individual strengths, the impact of the individual's sociocultural background on the client's schemas and self- and worldviews, culturally sanctioned norms and behaviors that the person uses to respond to the challenges in his or her life, and preferred practices to solve problems and seek help; (b) building a collaborative therapeutic alliance and empowering the client by conveying respect and actively including the client's input in all phases of therapy; (c) using a strength-based approach that creatively integrates the client's personal and cultural strengths to facilitate the process of therapy; and (d) implementing a multimodal approach that makes use of cognitive, behavioral, affective, experiential, and art-based strategies that are congruent with the client's culture.

Nonetheless, it remains that there is a dearth of empirical research on this topic. Thus, the challenge for practitioners and researchers remains the need to develop empirical studies to establish the efficacy of culture-sensitive anger regulation therapies that are specific to culturally diverse populations.

REFERENCES

Abudabbeh, N., & Hays, P. A. (2006). Cognitive-behavioral therapy with people of Arab heritage. In P. A. Hays & G. Y. Iwamasa (Eds.), *Culturally responsive cognitive-behavioral therapy: Assessment, practice, and supervision* (pp. 141–160). Washington, DC: American Psychological Association.

Adam, H., Shirako, A., & Maddux, W. W. (2010). Cultural variances in the interpersonal; effects of anger in negotiations. *Psychological Sciences, 21*(6), 882–889.

Ashford, J. B., LeCroy, C. W., & Lortie, K. L. (2006). *Human behavior in the social environment: A multidimensional perspective* (3rd ed.). Belmont, CA: Thomson/Brooks-Cole.

Beaubeouf-Lafontant, T. (2007). "You have to show strength": An exploration of gender, race and depression. *Gender and Society, 21*, 28–51.

Beck, R., & Fernandez, E. (1998). Cognitive behavioral therapy in the treatment of anger: A meta-analysis. *Cognitive Therapy and Research, 22*, 63–74.

Berry, J. W. (2003). Conceptual approaches to acculturation. In K. Chun, P. Balls-Organista, & G. Marin (Eds.), *Acculturation: Advances in theory, measurement and applied research* (pp. 17–37). Washington, DC: American Psychological Association.

Cormier, S. C., Nurius, P. S., & Osborn, C. J. (2009). *Interviewing and change strategies for helpers: Fundamental skills and cognitive-behavioral interventions* (6th ed.). Belmont, CA: Brooks/Cole.

Cox, D. L., Stabb, S. D., & Bruckner, K. H. (1999). *Women's anger: Clinical and developmental perspectives*. Philadelphia, PA: Brunner-Mazel.

Cox, D. L., & St. Clair, S. (2005). A new perspective on women's anger: Therapy through the lens of anger diversion. *Women and Therapy, 28*, 77–90.

Cox, D. L., Van Velsor, P., & Hulgus, J. F. (2004). Who me, angry? Patterns of angry diversion in women. *Health Care for Women International, 25*, 872–893.

Deffenbacher, J. L., Dahlen, E. R., Lynch, R. S., Morris, C. D., & Gowensmith, W. N. (2000). An application of Beck's cognitive therapy to general anger reduction. *Cognitive Therapy and Research, 24*, 689–697.

DiGiuseppe, R. (1995). Developing the therapeutic alliance with angry clients. In H. Kassinove (Ed.), *Anger disorders: Definition, diagnosis, and treatment* (pp. 131–149). Washington, DC: Taylor & Francis.

Elligan, D. (2000). Rap therapy: A culturally sensitive approach to psychotherapy with young African American men. *Journal of African American Studies, 5*(3), 27–36.

Ellis, A., & Tafrate, R. C. (1997). *How to control your anger before it controls you.* Secaucus, NJ: Birch Lane Press.

Fernandez, E. (2010). Toward an integrative psychotherapy for maladaptive anger. In M. Potegal, G. Stemmler, & C. Spielberger (Eds.), *International handbook of anger: Constituent and concomitant biological, psychological, and social problems* (pp. 499–513). New York, NY: Springer.

Fernández-Berrocal, P., Salovey, P., Vera, A., Extremera, N., & Ramos, N. (2008). Cultural influences on the relation of perceived emotional intelligence and depression. *Presses Universitaires de Grenoble, 18*(1), 91–107.

Fischer, A. H., & Evers, C. (2010). Anger in the context of gender. In M. Potegal, G. Stemmler, & C. Spielberger (Eds.), *International handbook of anger: Constituent and concomitant biological, psychological, and social problems* (pp. 349–360). New York, NY: Springer.

González-Prendes, A. A. (2007). Cognitive-behavioral treatment of men and anger: Three single case studies. *Cognitive and Behavioral Practice, 14*, 185–197.

González-Prendes, A. A., & Thomas, S. A. (2009). Culturally sensitive treatment of anger in African American women: A case study. *Clinical Case Studies, 8*, 383–402.

Griner, D., & Smith, T. B. (2006). Culturally adapted mental health interventions: A meta-analytic review. *Psychotherapy: Theory, Research, Practice, Training, 43*(4), 513–548.

Hancock, T. U., & Siu, K. (2009). A culturally sensitive intervention with domestically violent Latino immigrant men. *Journal of Family Violence, 24*, 123–132

Harris, T. (1995). The disease called strength: Some observations on the compensating construction of Black female character. *Literature and Medicine, 14*, 109–126.

Hatch, H., & Forgays, D. K. (2001). A comparison of older adolescents and adult females' responses to anger-provoking situations. *Adolescence, 38*, 557–570.

Hays, P. A. (2006). Introduction: Developing culturally responsive cognitive-behavioral therapies. In P. A. Hays & G. Y. Iwamasa (Eds.), *Culturally responsive cognitive-behavioral therapy: Assessment practice, and supervision* (pp. 3–19). Washington, DC: American Psychological Association.

Hays, P. A. (2008). *Addressing cultural complexities in practice: Assessment, diagnosis, and therapy* (2nd ed.). Washington, DC: American Psychological Association.

Hays, P. A. (2009). Integrating evidence-based practice, cognitive-behavioral therapy, and multicultural therapy: Ten steps for culturally competent practice. *Professional Psychology: Research and Practice, 40*(4), 354–360.

Hays, P. A., & Iwamasa, G. Y. (2006). *Culturally responsive cognitive-behavioral therapy: Assessment, practice, and supervision.* Washington, DC: American Psychological Association.

Ivey, A. E., D'Andrea, M. J., & Ivey, M. B. (2012). *Theories of counseling and psychotherapy: A multicultural perspective* (7th ed.). Thousand Oaks, CA: Sage.

Kassinove, H., & Sukhodolsky, D. G. (1995). Anger disorders: Basic science and practice issues. In H. Kassinove (Ed.), *Anger disorders: Definition, diagnosis, and treatment* (pp. 1–26). Washington, DC: Taylor & Francis.

Keller, H., & Otto, H. (2009). The cultural socialization of emotion regulations during infancy. *Journal of Cross-Cultural Psychology, 40*(6), 996–1011.

Kelly, S. (2006). Cognitive-behavioral therapy with African Americans. In P. A. Hays & G. Y. Iwamasa (Eds.), *Culturally responsive cognitive-behavioral therapy: Assessment, practice, and supervision* (pp. 47–72). Washington, DC: American Psychological Association.

Konwar, N., & Ram, U. (2004). Cultural differences in anger. *Psychological Studies, 49*(2–3), 193–195.

Kövecses, Z. (2000). The concept of anger: Universal or culture specific? *Psychopathology, 33*, 159–170.

Kövecses, Z. (2010). Cross-cultural experience of anger. In M. Potegal, G. Stemmler, & C. Spielberger (Eds.), *International handbook of anger: Constituent and concomitant biological, psychological, and social problems* (pp. 157–174). New York, NY: Springer.

Lawrence, P., & Rozmus, C. (2001). Culturally sensitive care of the Muslim patient. *Journal of Transcultural Nursing, 12*(3), 228–233.

Martin, M. (2002). *Saving our last nerve: Mental health tactics for the Black woman.* Roscoe, IL: Hilton Publishing.

Matsumoto, D., Hee Yoo, S., & Chung, J. (2010). The expression of anger across culture. In M. Potegal, G. Stemmler, & C. Spielberger (Eds.), *International handbook of anger: Constituent and concomitant biological, psychological, and social problems* (pp. 125–137). New York, NY: Springer.

Mauss, I. B., Butler, E. A., Roberts, N. A., & Chu, A. (2010). Emotion control values and responding to anger provocation in Asian-American and Euro-American individuals. *Cognition and Emotion, 24*(6), 1026–1043.

McGoldrick, M., Giordano, J., & Garcia-Preto, N. (2005). Overview: Ethnicity and family therapy. In M. McGoldrick, J. Giordano, & N. Garcia-Preto (Eds.), *Ethnicity and family therapy* (pp. 1–40). New York, NY: Guilford Press.

Meichenbaum, D. H. (1985). *Stress inoculation training.* New York, NY: Pergamon.

Meichenbaum, D. H. (1996). *Mixed anxiety and depression: A cognitive-behavioral therapy approach.* New York, NY: Newbridge Communication.

Munhall, P. (1993). Women's anger and its meaning: A phenomenological perspective. *Health Care for Women International, 14*, 481–491.

Okazaki, S., & Tanaka-Matsumi, J. (2006). Cultural considerations in cognitive-behavioral assessment. In P. A. Hays & G. Y. Iwamasa (Eds.), *Culturally responsive cognitive-behavioral therapy: Assessment, practice, and supervision* (pp. 247–266). Washington, DC: American Psychological Association.

Olatunji, B. O., Lohr, J. M., & Bushman, B. J. (2007). The pseudopsychology of venting in the treatment of anger: Implications and alternatives for mental health practice. In T. A. Cavell & K. T. Malcolm (Eds.), *Anger, aggression, and interventions for interpersonal violence* (pp. 119–141). Mahwah, NJ: Lawrence Erlbaum Associates.

Ponterotto, J. G. (1987). Counseling Mexican Americans: A multimodal approach. *Journal of Counseling and Development, 65*, 308–312.

Potegal, M., & Novaco, R. W. (2010). A brief history of anger. In M. Potegal, G. Stemmler, & C. Spielberger (Eds.), *International handbook of anger: Constituent and concomitant biological, psychological, and social problems* (pp. 9–24). New York, NY: Springer.

Reilly, P. M., Clark, H. W., Shopshire, M. S., Lewis, E. W., & Sorensen, D. J. (1994). Anger management and temper control: Critical components of posttraumatic stress disorder and substance abuse treatment. *Journal of Psychoactive Drugs, 26*, 401–407.

Reilly, P. M., & Shopshire, M. S. (2000). Anger management group treatment for cocaine dependence: Preliminary outcomes. *American Journal of Drug and Alcohol Abuse, 26*, 161–177.

Rios-Elliot, B., Aguilar-Gaxiola, S., Cabassa, L., Caetano, R., Comas-Díaz, L., Flores, Y., … Ugarte, C. (2005). *Critical disparities in Latino mental health: Transforming research into action*. Washington, DC: National Council of La Raza.

Robbins, S. P., Charterjee, P., & Canda, E. R. (2006). *Contemporary human behavior theory: A critical perspective for social work* (2nd ed.). Boston, MA: Allyn and Bacon.

Sam, D. L., & Berry, J. W. (2010). Acculturation: When individuals and groups of different cultural backgrounds meet. *Perspectives on Psychological Science, 5*, 472–481.

Sharkin, B. S. (1993). Anger and gender: Theory, research, and implications. *Journal of Counseling and Development, 71*, 366–379.

Stearns, P. N. (1994). *American cool: Constructing a twentieth-century emotional style*. New York, NY: New York University Press.

Tanaka-Matsumi, J. (1995). Cross-cultural perspectives on anger. In H. Kassinove (Ed.), *Anger disorders: Definition, diagnosis, and treatment* (pp. 81–90). Washington, DC: Taylor & Francis.

Thomas, S. A., & González-Prendes, A. A. (2009). Powerlessness, anger and stress in African American women: Implications for physical and emotional health. *Health Care for Women International, 30*, 93–113.

Thomas, S. P. (1989). Gender differences in anger expression: Health implications. *Research in Nursing and Health, 12*, 389–398.

Thompkins, T. (2004). *The real lives of strong Black women: Transcending myths, reclaiming joy*. Evanston, IL: Agate Publishing.

U.S. Department of Health and Human Services. (1999). *Mental health: A report of the Surgeon General*. Rockville, MD: U.S. Department of Health and Human Services, Substance Abuse and Mental Health Services Administration, Center for Mental Health Services, National Institutes of Health, National Institute of Mental Health.

U.S. Department of Health and Human Services. (2001). *Mental health: Culture, race, and ethnicity—A supplement to mental health: A report of the Surgeon General*. Rockville, MD: U.S. Department of Health and Human Services, Substance Abuse and Mental Health Services Administration, Center for Mental Health Services, National Institutes of Health, National Institute of Mental Health.

Whaley, A. L., & Davis, K. E. (2006). Cultural competence and evidence-based practice in mental health services: A complementary perspective. *American Psychologist, 62*, 563–574.

Wranik, T., & Scherer, K. R. (2010). Why do I get angry? A componential appraisal approach. In M. Potegal, G. Stemmler, & C. Spielberger (Eds.), *International handbook of anger: Constituent and concomitant biological, psychological, and social problems* (pp. 243–266). New York, NY: Springer.

Zastrow, C. H., & Kirst-Ashman, K. K. (2007). *Understanding human behavior and the social environment* (7th ed.). Belmont, CA: Thomson/Brooks-Cole.

14

Treatment of Anger in Different Populations

Common and Unique Factors

EPHREM FERNANDEZ ■

A glance through the preceding chapters reveals that treatments for anger in different populations do have common features as well as unique properties. In this concluding chapter, the commonalities are presented with reference to examples from the foregoing material. This is followed by an outline of specific factors that are more appropriate for the particular clinical or demographic group being treated. Certain contraindications of anger treatment are also identified. The end product is a core set of techniques that can be incorporated into an integrative approach to anger regulation. Supplementing this approach are specialized strategies meant for certain populations or settings of interest. All citations herein are of chapters within this volume unless otherwise stated.

COMMON TECHNIQUES

Psychoeducation

Embedded in every anger treatment approach described in this volume is some basic information about anger. In their treatment of anger in clients with substance abuse and mental health problems, Shopshire and Reilly (Chapter 5) use a manual and participant workbook in which many myths about anger are dispelled. Forbes, McHugh, and Chemtob (Chapter 4) inform combat veterans about the place of anger in posttraumatic stress disorder (PTSD). Novaco and Whittington (Chapter 7) make psychoeducation an important part of the preparatory phase of anger treatment. Not only is time spent on the obvious question "What is anger, in relation to aggression and violence?" but also psychoeducation sheds light on the many short- and long-term adverse effects of dysfunctional anger. This is not just informational but also has the added benefit of weaving in a rationale for anger treatment.

Self-Monitoring

The observation and recording of one's own behavior or activity is known as self-monitoring. When clients present for anger management, it is typically because of some history of anger-related incidents at home, at work, while in transit, or in some other environment. What the clinician cannot witness firsthand can nevertheless be accessed from the client's diaries or logs of anger describing where and when it occurred. This is newly referred to as Ecological Momentary Assessment (Stone & Shiffman, 1994; Rizvi, Steffel, & Carson-Wong, Chapter 8). Regardless of the type of treatment or the population of interest, ecologically relevant and timely monitoring is a valuable supplement to the questionnaires that are often completed retrospectively in controlled settings (Novaco & Whittington; Lochman et al., Chapter 10). Along these lines, paper-and-pencil methods of graphing anger have been used to measure various parameters such as frequency, duration, and intensity of anger (Fernandez & Malley-Morrison, Chapter 12). The anger thermometer (Shopshire & Reilly; Hubbard & Swift, Chapter 11; Lochman et al.) allows self-monitoring with reference to a visual metaphor of anger. With the advent of portable information technology, anger activity can be measured with even greater efficiency (e.g., Bishop, Ngau, & Pek, 2008; Elkins, Moore, McNulty, Kivisto, & Handsel, 2013). More than being just a source of data, self-monitoring also produces reactivity. In other words, under the mere act of measurement, the measured variable begins to drift in the desired direction. The improvement is not of the order of treatment gains (Fernandez & Beck, 2001), but it can set in motion therapeutic progress.

Functional Analysis

Closely tied to self-monitoring and well steeped in the tradition of learning theory is functional analysis. This is the analysis of patterns that relate the behavior of interest to different categories of controlling factors. Also known as SORCK analysis, the stimulus (S), organismic variables (O), response (R), consequence (C), and contingencies (K) are linked together. The powerful treatment implications of functional analysis of anger are recognized by Willner, Jahoda, and Larkin (Chapter 6) and also implied in the "chain analysis" of dialectical behavior therapy (DBT; Rizvi et al.). Some version of functional analysis is implicit in most chapters (e.g., Day & Vess, Chapter 9; Lochman et al.; González-Prendes, Chapter 13) where maladaptive anger is linked to proximal or distal triggers and consequences. This may be further expanded into a broader framework where anger dysfunction is connected to predisposing, precipitating, correlating, consequential, exacerbating, and perpetuating factors (Fernandez & Kerns, 2012; Fernandez & Wasan, 2010).

Evoking Emotion

It is difficult to treat emotional distress without evoking it to some degree—at least within the safety of the therapeutic setting. Not surprisingly, there is a consensus across chapters that anger treatment entails evoking anger (imaginally or in vivo) and preferably along a graduated hierarchy of exposure (see Deffenbacher, Chapter 2;

Pascual-Leone & Paivio, Chapter 3; Forbes et al.; Willner et al.; Novaco & Whittington). Lochman et al. induce anger in teenagers by having group members taunt one another in a controlled and supervised setting, so that the recipients of this provocation find occasion to implement coping techniques. Only young children seem to have been spared anger simulation exercises, though Hubbard and Swift are quick to point out that such an omission is ill-conceived and not in the interest of the client.

Relaxation

To the extent that anger is associated with a surge in autonomic arousal and cortical activation, relaxation is an appropriate remedy. There is no chapter in this volume that does not utilize some form of relaxation. The standard is a combination of progressive muscle relaxation and diaphragmatic breathing (as in Forbes et al.), though hot showers may work for some clients (Rizvi et al.) and massage might appeal to others. In any case, physical relaxation is best coupled with mental relaxation, which can be achieved through guided imagery (Deffenbacher; Novaco & Whittington) and mindfulness meditation (Day & Vess). The overall effect of such relaxation (as well documented in the psychophysiology literature) is to increase activity of the parasympathetic nervous system rather than the sympathetic nervous system. In this way, relaxation and anger are dynamically connected in what Wolpe (1954) termed reciprocal inhibition. Deffenbacher's research on treatment of angry drivers reveals relaxation to have more support than any of the other anger reduction techniques.

Response Prevention

When anger is evoked as part of self-regulation training, the expectation is not that the angered individual will resort to his or her habitual maladaptive responses but that he or she will adopt a competing response. The technique of response prevention, as used in obsessive-compulsive disorders, attempts this in the form of a behavior that is incompatible with the maladaptive habit. Thus, Deffenbacher instructs and trains angry drivers to keep their hands at 10 and 2 o'clock on the steering wheel so that they are less inclined to deliver obscene gestures with their fingers. Training individuals to mute facial expressions and hand gestures is a similar self-restraining procedure incorporated within cognitive-behavioral-affective therapy (CBAT; Fernandez, Chapter 1). A more extreme alternative is what is called "opposite action" as used in DBT (Rizvi et al.) where the client engages in a behavior such as a "hug" that conveys the very opposite of anger.

Experiential Techniques

If emotion is evoked within the therapeutic setting, so must it be experienced. This is the norm across chapters in this volume. Granting the client license to experience anger respects first-person subjectivity that is at the root of phenomenological psychology. Moreover, it puts the person in touch with the subjective feeling and not just cognitions and behaviors. Such enhanced awareness is generally a key to greater control. Pascual-Leone and Paivio go further to assert that it takes emotion to change emotion, and Forbes et al. concur that it is not possible to treat trauma without some re-experiencing of the trauma. As part of emotion-focused therapy, the Gestalt chair can serve as a forum for imaginal dialogues that reactivate memories of perceived wrongdoers. In the same vein, Lochman et al. recommend journaling as a medium for self-expression of anger. Drama therapy is also entertained as an option (Novaco & Whittington). González-Prendes cites research in which music is successfully used as a medium for a young man's transition from maladaptive anger to a prosocial lifestyle. The experiential school of therapy encompasses many techniques that are not to be confused with the notion of unbridled catharsis, a subject to be addressed later in this chapter.

Problem Solving

Accurate analysis and constructive action are the hallmarks of problem solving. As per Mynors-Wallis (2005), this can be broken down into about six steps: (a) defining the problem, (b) brainstorming for options, (c) analyzing pros versus cons for each option, (d) selecting the best option, (e) implementing the best option, and (f) reviewing the outcome. Problem solving is also an iterative process of returning through the same cycle to progressively arrive at a more acceptable solution. Although framed as part of cognitive-behavioral therapy (Turk & Fernandez, 1991), elements of problem solving have found application in the treatment of every population described in this volume. For teenagers, Lochman et al. use a five-step process; for young children, Hubbard and Swift point out that problem solving can break the string of automatic thoughts and impulsive behaviors. Across cultural boundaries, too, evaluation of pros and cons is an important step in generating healthy alternatives to angry behavior (González-Prendes). Problem solving has even been successfully adapted for the intellectually disabled (Willner et al.) and those with psychoses (Novaco & Whittington). Basically, it provides a decision-making tool in which the client is actively involved.

Therapeutic Alliance

No matter how much they come recommended, anger techniques are effective only when delivered in a spirit of alliance between therapist and client. This kind of bonding has been given various labels ranging from rapport to transference. It is an underlying feature of every approach to anger treatment. For example, Fernandez and Malley-Morrison examine transference when the client and therapist are of the opposite sex. Day and Vess stress therapeutic engagement with forensic clients and the need to repair occasional ruptures in this alliance. A key to the therapeutic alliance is empathy (Pascual-Leone & Paivio) and supportiveness (Novaco & Whittington), though, as González-Prendes cautions, this does not require tolerance of self-defeating behavior. Without authenticity on the part of the therapist, the alliance is likely to be diminished. To put it in Rogerian terms, empathy, unconditional positive regard, *and congruence* are needed for rapport and therapeutic progress (Rogers, 1954).

Reappraisal

As conceptualized in the opening chapter, inherent in anger is a perception or appraisal of wrongdoing. A corollary is that anger can be reduced by reappraisal, which entails re-evaluating or challenging the client's attributions or interpretations about the provoking event/behavior. This is exemplified in every chapter of this volume, particularly in the work of Deffenbacher, where "anger-engendering cognitions" are countered with cognitions that are more adaptive. This disputation is carried out by recourse to logic and evidence. Thus, the procedure called "check the facts" as used in DBT (Rizvi et al.) is essentially an empirical approach to disputing cognitions. Given that angry individuals may make erroneous assumptions of the intentionality of actions, Lochman et al. caution school children against attributing unfounded blameworthy motives to others. Day and Vess stress the need to delve deeper into the implicit theories or whole belief systems underlying anger and dysfunctional behavior in offenders. Such fundamental schemata about self and world may be the driving forces of cognitive distortions that angry individuals are prone to.

It should be pointed out that occasions do arise when cognitive errors are absent, the anger is quite justifiable, and the client suffers. Rather than flogging the client's cognitive appraisals ad infinitum, coping statements are apt, as in A. T. Beck (1999). Specifically, cognitions that help the client recognize wrongdoing or injustice for what it is and survive or transcend it may be better received than cognitions that seem to be outright contradictions of the client's reality. Coping statements such as "As bad as it is, I can make it through" are utilized in Deffenbacher's work on angry drivers as well as Lochman's Coping Power curriculum. Cognitive coping with anger is also featured in the Profile of Anger Coping Skills (Willner, Brace & Phillips, 2005).

Social Skills Training

As noted in the opening chapter, anger is a relational emotion. Therefore, reducing anger is not just a matter of self-regulation but also dependent on the way one interacts with others. This calls for social skills, which are referred to throughout this volume, though with different labels. Thus, Hubbard and Swift train young children to begin by identifying emotion from facial cues and physiological sensations (as in the Second Step program). These children are then coached in prosocial behavior. Other interpersonal skills include calmly verbalizing one's feelings of anger and asserting one's needs in a firm but nonaggressive way (Novaco & Whittington; Rizvi et al.). As can be seen, social skills training invariably requires two important procedures: proper social modeling plus ample rehearsal. Deffenbacher adds the important qualifier that as the skills are acquired by the client, the coaching by the clinician has to be faded out.

Shaping

In the endeavor to change behavior, the lure or pressure toward producing instant results is not something that the seasoned clinician falls for. Rather, the target behavior is reached by successive approximations or the principle known as shaping.

This is implicit in all treatments featured in this volume. For example, Lochman et al. introduce short-term goals before aiming for long-term goals; within their case study, emphasis is placed on "small steps" in changing anger-related maladaptive behavior. Furthermore, in the Coping Power group, selective reinforcement is used to slowly extinguish disruptive behavior and gradually strengthen prosocial behaviors. As illustrated in the case of a substance-dependent patient (Shopshire & Reilly), anger does not switch from the maladaptive to the adaptive instantly but at a slow and steady pace punctuated with occasional relapse. The treatment plan for violent offenders is similarly susceptible to setbacks best overcome by patient and consistent shaping (Day & Vess).

Insight

Though insight has traditionally been identified with psychodynamic therapies, it is also a feature of other verbal psychotherapies. Unlike the psychoeducational component of anger treatments, which is essentially didactic in style, the therapeutic dialogue that transpires is often one of collaborative discovery, to use the terminology of A. T. Beck (1976). This is the style of cognitive therapy as delivered to angry drivers, too (Deffenbacher). It allows more room for the emergence of insight on the part of the client. This is illustrated in the extended dialogue between therapist and client in the chapter by Pascual-Leone and Paivio. The collaborative approach to insight is particularly suited to clients with intrapsychic conflicts (as illustrated in a case narrative by Wootton, 2009) or clients who are resistant to directives (as illustrated in the case study by Day and Vess).

UNIQUE/TAILORED TECHNIQUES

Gender

Regardless of the school of therapy or the clinical population being served, anger treatment is necessarily gender inclusive. This is because anger occurs in both men and women, albeit with some notable differences in the way it is expressed (Fernandez & Malley-Morrison). Some core techniques like self-monitoring, functional analysis, and relaxation remain broadly applicable. However, in evoking emotion and reappraising it, special effort must be made to reflect themes that are germane to the person's gender. Furthermore, the treatment of anger must be sensitive to the empirically demonstrated gender differences in help seeking and completion of therapy. Finally, as reported in the same chapter, preferences for types of therapy differ as a function of gender. On average, men are more receptive to behavior modification and informational aspects of therapy; women tend to have a greater penchant for verbal psychotherapy and emotionally expressive techniques. Confrontive techniques are eschewed by women more so than men. This does not dictate a rigid assignment of different techniques to men versus women. Rather, it places a premium on therapist versatility in tailoring techniques to the themes and preferences of men and women.

Culture

Like gender, culture is an inescapable aspect of clients in therapy, and in multicultural societies, the ideal is multicultural therapy. However, as González-Prendes asserts, multicultural therapy is not a brand of therapy but an adaptation of existing therapies to make them culture sensitive. The difference is not so much one of method as one of content. For example, reappraisal remains highly applicable, under the proviso that it addresses culturally relevant themes of anger. The issues or situations that characteristically trigger anger in immigrant groups are disenfranchisement, unemployment, poverty, limited access to social services, communication barriers, and cultural isolation; these are likely to be quite different from issues that preoccupy members of the host community. The author further stresses that psychotherapy wedded to values of autonomy and rationality may not sit well with certain ethnic groups that are not keen on individualism or not sold on rationality. After all, what is rational is a matter of cultural relativism. Therefore, comprehensive assessment of the client's cultural identification is needed. Once the cultural frame of reference is set, the core techniques common to anger treatments can be adapted for use in the particular individual.

Developmental Milestones

Where the individual is in terms of life span development may require adjustments to anger treatment methods (Fernandez, 2003a, 2003b). Young children will benefit less from cognitive therapy than from behavioral techniques for dealing with goal frustration, which is often the primary reason for their anger. Thus, Hubbard and Swift use creative analogies suited to the relatively concrete thinking in elementary school children: a "feelings thermometer" to rate anger, an "imaginary umbrella" to shield one against hurtful words, a "turtle shell" to recede into while counting to 10, and "mental muscles" to control emotions. By comparison, adolescents at a higher level of cognitive development are more likely to rise to the challenge of logical and empirical reasoning that are part and parcel of cognitive therapy. Social maturation is also more advanced at this stage, so that role modeling may involve not only parents but also peers. The relevance of the latter is highlighted in the Coping Power program of Lochman et al. Here, attention is paid to the risk of affiliation with rejected adolescents, how to resist or circumvent peer pressure, and how to select appropriate peers.

Cognitive Deficits

In the intellectually disabled population, cognitive deficits (in verbal production and comprehension, memory, and executive function) may pose obstacles to the kind of reappraisal that invokes logic and empirical evaluation. As Willner et al. point out, this is where instructions have to be kept simple and delivered slowly, with adequate memory aids; text may be supplanted with pictorial representations. Similarly, in dealing with psychiatric patients with profound cognitive deficits in addition to emotional disturbance, there is a special need for clear and cogent communications by clinical staff (Novaco & Whittington).

Motivational Deficits

Some clinical populations are especially limited in readiness or commitment to anger treatment. This concern often arises in considering those who are court mandated to receive treatment. Therefore, treatment should be preceded and guided by what is called motivational interviewing (Miller & Rollnick, 2013), especially for those in the correctional system (Day & Vess) and for those who are involuntarily committed to psychiatric hospitals (Novaco & Whittington). In the sociodemographic arena, many ethnic minority members are ambivalent if not distrusting of anger treatment (González-Prendes), and men are less inclined to seek or complete therapy for anger (Fernandez & Malley-Morrison). One established technique for securing commitment in therapy is the behavioral contingency contract, which has been used in drug and alcohol rehabilitation. Now a feature of CBAT for anger (Fernandez, 2010; Fernandez & Scott, 2009), the contingency contract is particularly appropriate for individuals with motivational deficits.

Collateral Involvement

In those with significant cognitive or motivational deficits, self-monitoring may not be dependable. In such cases, the help of staff or caregivers can be enlisted. Some treatments include family members too, and therefore require collateral input anyway. For example, in the Coping Power program of Lochman, parents are enlisted to implement treatment of the child at home and parents are themselves the target of parenting skills training. Dysfunctional anger in intimate relationships (Fernandez & Malley-Morrison) can benefit from conjoined therapy and assessment, assuming of course that this arrangement is mutually acceptable to both parties concerned.

The Inpatient Milieu

Psychiatric hospitals and prisons present a unique set of hurdles for anger management. This pertains largely to the coercive and aversive atmosphere that often prevails in such environments. Novaco and Whittington refer to the noise, enforced treatment, and methods of restraint in some psychiatric hospitals. Day and Vess allude to the highly regimented prison environment with its own perils of internal strife and abuse. In these settings, any therapeutic progress would be eroded without some containment of the routine and familiar sources of frustration. This invokes the principle of stimulus control as used in behavior modification (Fernandez, 2010). An extension of stimulus control would be to ensure that upon discharge or release, the patient or the inmate does not return to environments and living arrangements with their own frustrations that set off a relapse to dysfunctional anger.

Different Themes

Reappraisal is directed at certain themes in the cognitive life of each population. For example, Day and Vess refer to the network of beliefs in violent offenders; this includes the supposition that their goals are blocked by others, that violence is normal, and that what happens is uncontrollable. Each population holds a different network of appraisals variously referred to as schema, outlook, attitude, or mindset. This influences the very way in which information is processed. Therefore, cognitive therapy faces the task of not merely changing isolated appraisals but also restructuring any underlying schema that may be unique to the population of interest.

CONTRAINDICATIONS

Catharsis in its obsolete sense of the unbridled expression of anger may have some support in psychodynamic theory, but it has been largely abandoned even within the emotion-focused therapies for anger (Pascual-Leone & Paivio). Rizvi et al. point out that breaking, throwing, punching, and similar reactions to anger often lead to escalation of conflict and more anger. Moreover, because of the attendant increase in arousal, such actions may not be conducive to anger reduction. When engaging in destructive or threatening behaviors, the individual is more likely to be reactivating angry cognitions than defusing them. In contrast to the primal sort of catharsis, more sublime methods of anger expression are often permitted. These include emotional writing (e.g., Pennebaker & Chung, 2007) and visual art (e.g., Liebman, 2007). Such options are best reserved for a postvention phase, when residual anger lingers due to the limited success of prevention and intervention techniques (Fernandez, 2010).

There is also limited enthusiasm for the equally obsolete view that anger can be extinguished by merely paying little or no attention to it. Research has shown that attention to tantrums does reinforce the display of anger in these circumstances (e.g., Onodera 2011), in the same way that solicitude reinforces a variety of illness behaviors. This is particularly the case if the behavior is motivated by secondary gain such as a concession or submission from others. However, when anger is not driven by such factors, to be indifferent to or dismissive of it will only likely aggravate it, as clinical judgment informs us.

When anger expression is secondary to another emotion such as fear (Novaco) or shame (Pascual-Leone & Paivio), then it is the primary emotion that warrants the most attention. This does not diminish the utility of anger regulation skills, which can indeed render "symptom relief." However, until the underlying primary emotion is recognized and treated, the anger is likely to persist or recur.

Given the distinctions made between anger and aggression/violence, people who are aggressive or violent but without grievance should not be referred for anger management as they often are. Therefore, the chapters by Hubbard and Swift and Lochman et al. distinguish between proactive aggression, which is instrumental in nature, and reactive aggression, which is affective in nature and typically attributable to anger.

INTEGRATIVE THERAPY FOR ANGER

As in other areas of psychotherapy application (see Castonguay, Newman, Borkovec, Holtforth, & Maramba, 2005), there is a continuing shift away from standalone techniques of anger regulation toward a plurality of techniques. This received an impetus with the dawn of cognitive-behavioral therapy (CBT). As applied to anger, CBT usually encompasses two key ingredients: reappraisal and relaxation.

With a further boost from the integrative movement in psychotherapy, anger treatment has become even more inclusive of what were previously categorized as divergent schools of therapy. Of special note is the inclusion of experiential techniques alongside cognitive and behavioral counterparts, as in CBAT (Fernandez, 2010; Fernandez & Scott, 2009). In this new formulation, techniques are not merely thrown into a package for ad hoc use by the client, nor are they presented as a menu or smorgasbord. Instead, each technique is selected and then carefully sequenced. Because anger is a process with three discernible phases (onset, progression, and offset), it warrants treatment in three different phases: prevention of anger onset, intervention upon escalating anger, and postvention of residual anger. Within each of these phases are select techniques that also unfold in a contingent fashion. The result is a more comprehensive but programmatic approach to the regulation of anger.

CONCLUSION

With the identification of several common factors across different schools of anger treatment, it is now possible to position these too within an integrative program for anger regulation. Many of these (e.g., psychoeducation, reappraisal, relaxation, and expressive techniques) are already cornerstones of CBAT, whereas others (e.g., therapeutic alliance, insight, and shaping) are the stylistic features that function as undercurrents in the program. What remains to be done is to emphasize additional "core" techniques (e.g., social skills training and problem solving) within this sequence. Finally, emergent perspectives such as acceptance, forgiveness, and mindfulness are already being applied to dysfunctional anger. It is expected that in time, these too will be sequenced to make an even more integrative yet programmatic treatment for anger, one that remains gender inclusive, culture sensitive, and adaptable to the unique needs of the individual.

REFERENCES

Beck, A. T. (1976). *Cognitive therapy and emotional disorders*. New York, NY: International Universities Press.

Beck, A. T. (1999). *Prisoners of hate: The cognitive basis of anger, hostility, and violence*. New York, NY: Harper Collins.

Bishop, G. D., Ngau, F., & Pek, J. (2008). Domain-specific assessment of anger expression and ambulatory blood pressure. *Personality and Individual Differences*, *44*, 1726–1737.

Castonguay, L. G., Newman, M. G., Borkovec, T. D., Holtforth, M. G., & Maramba, G. G. (2005). *Cognitive-behavioral assimilative integration*. New York, NY: Oxford University Press.

Elkins, S. R., Moore, T. M., McNulty, J. K., Kivisto, A. J., & Handsel, V. A. (2013). Electronic diary assessment of the temporal association between proximal anger and intimate partner violence perpetration. *Psychology of Violence*, 3, 100–113.

Fernandez, E. (2003a). Anger regulation in adolescence. In T. Gullotta & M. Bloom (Eds.), *Encyclopedia of primary prevention and health promotion* (pp. 195–199). New York, NY: Kluwer Academic/Plenum Publishers.

Fernandez, E. (2003b). Anger regulation in childhood. In T. Gullotta & M. Bloom (Eds.), *Encyclopedia of primary prevention and health promotion* (pp. 190–195). New York, NY: Kluwer Academic/Plenum Publishers.

Fernandez, E. (2010). Toward an integrative psychotherapy for maladaptive anger. In M. Potegal, G. Stemmler, & C. Spielberger (Eds.), *The international handbook of anger: Constituent and concomitant biological, psychological, and social processes* (pp. 499–514). New York, NY: Springer.

Fernandez, E., & Beck, R. (2001). Cognitive-behavioral self-intervention versus self-monitoring of anger: Effects on anger frequency, duration, and intensity. *Behavioural and Cognitive Psychotherapy, 29*, 345–356.

Fernandez, E., & Kerns, R. D. (2012). Pain and affective disorders: Looking beyond the "chicken and egg" conundrum. In M. A. Giamberardino & T. Jensen (Eds.), *Pain comorbidities: Understanding and treating the complex patient* (pp. 279–296). Seattle, WA: International Association for the Study of Pain (IASP) Press.

Fernandez, E., & Scott, S. (2009). Anger treatment in chemically-dependent inpatients: Evaluation of phase effects and gender. *Behavioural and Cognitive Psychotherapy, 37*, 431–447.

Fernandez, E., & Wasan, A. (2010). The anger of pain sufferers: Attributions to agents and appraisals of wrongdoing. In M. Potegal, G. Stemmler, & C. Spielberger (Eds.), *The international handbook of anger: Constituent and concomitant biological, psychological, and social processes* (pp. 449–464). New York, NY: Springer.

Liebmann, M. (2007). *Art therapy and anger.* London: Jessica Kingsley Publishers.

Miller, W. R., & Rollnick, S. (2013). *Motivational interviewing: Helping people change* (3rd ed.). New York, NY: Guilford Press.

Mynors-Wallis, L. (2005). *Problem-solving treatment—A practical manual.* Oxford, England: Oxford University Press.

Onodera, K. (2011). Effect of non-contingent reinforcers provided by classmates on tantrums of a child in a regular elementary school classroom. *Japanese Journal of Special Education, 49*(4), 387–394.

Pennebaker, J. W., & Chung, C. K. (2007). Expressive writing, emotional upheavals, and health In H.S. Friedman & R.Cohen Silver (Eds.), *Foundations of health psychology* (pp. 263–284). New York, NY: Oxford University Press.

Rogers, C. R. (1954). *Psychotherapy and personality change.* Chicago, IL: University of Chicago Press.

Stone, A. A., & Shiffman, S. (1994). Ecological momentary assessment (EMA) in behavioral medicine. *Annals of Behavioral Medicine, 16*(3), 199–202.

Turk, D. C., & Fernandez, E. (1991). Pain and cancer: A cognitive-behavioral perspective. In M. Watson (Ed.), *Cancer patient care: Psychosocial treatment methods* (pp. 15–44). Cambridge, England: Cambridge University Press.

Willner, P., Brace, N., & Phillips, J. (2005). Assessment of anger coping skills in individuals with intellectual disabilities. *Journal of Intellectual Disability Research, 49*, 329–339.

Wolpe, J. (1954). Reciprocal inhibition as the main basis of psychotherapeutic effects. *Archives of Neurology and Psychiatry, 72*, 205–226.

Wootton, J. (2009). Anger and pain. In: J. C. Ballantyne, J. P. Rathmell, and S. M. Fishman, (Eds.), *Bonica's Management of Pain* (4th ed., pp. 1208–1220). Philadelphia: Lippincott, Williams &Wilkins.

AUTHOR INDEX

SUBJECT INDEX